BEHAVIORAL ASSESSMENT

New Directions in Clinical Psychology

Behavioral Assessment

New Directions in Clinical Psychology

Edited by

JOHN D. CONE, Ph.D.
Associate Professor, Department of Psychology,
West Virginia University

and

ROBERT P. HAWKINS, Ph.D.
Professor, Department of Psychology,
West Virginia University

BRUNNER/MAZEL, Publishers • New York

Second Printing

Copyright © 1977 by John D. Cone and Robert P. Hawkins

Published by
BRUNNER/MAZEL, INC.
19 Union Square, New York, N.Y. 10003

Library of Congress Cataloging in Publication Data

Main entry under title:
Behavioral Assessment.

Bibliography: p.
Includes indexes.
1. Personality assessment.   2. Behaviorism.   I. Cone, John D., 1942-
II. Hawkins, Robert P., 1931-   [DNLM: 1. Behavior therapy. 2. Projective technics. 3. Personality assessment. WM145 B419]
BF698.4.B43   155.2'8   77-23502
ISBN 0-87630-147-2

CONTRIBUTORS

HUGH V. ANGLE, Ph.D.
: Assistant Professor, Department of Psychiatry, Duke University Medical Center, Durham, North Carolina

ANSLEY BACON, Ph.D.
: Graduate Assistant, Department of Educational Psychology, West Virginia University, Morgantown, West Virginia

DAVID H. BARLOW, Ph.D.
: Professor of Psychiatry and Psychology, Section of Psychiatry and Human Behavior, Brown University, Providence, Rhode Island

ALAN S. BELLACK, Ph.D.
: Associate Professor, Department of Psychology, University of Pittsburgh, Pittsburgh, Pennsylvania

EVERETT H. ELLINWOOD, M.D.
: Professor, Department of Psychiatry, Duke University Medical Center, Durham, North Carolina

MARILYN T. ERICKSON, Ph.D.
: Professor of Psychology, Psychology Department, Virginia Commonwealth University, Richmond, Virginia

JAMES H. GEER, Ph.D.
: Professor and Chairman, Psychology Department, State University of New York at Stony Brook

MARVIN R. GOLDFRIED, Ph.D.
: Professor of Psychology, Psychology Department, State University of New York at Stony Brook

LINDA RUDIN HAY, M.A.
Clinical Psychology Intern, Department of Psychiatry and Human Behavior, Brown University and Butler Hospital, Providence, Rhode Island

WILLIAM M. HAY, M.A.
Clinical Psychology Intern, Department of Psychiatry and Human Behavior, Brown University and Butler Hospital, Providence, Rhode Island

MICHEL HERSEN, Ph.D.
Professor of Clinical Psychiatry, Department of Psychiatry, Western Psychiatric Institute and Clinic, University of Pittsburgh School of Medicine, Pittsburgh, Pennsylvania

RICHARD R. JONES, Ph.D.
Research Scientist, Evaluation Research Group, Inc., Eugene, Oregon

PETER J. LANG, Ph.D.
Professor, Department of Psychology, University of Wisconsin, Madison, Wisconsin

MARSHA M. LINEHAN, Ph.D.
Assistant Professor, Department of Psychology, The Catholic University of America, Washington, D. C.

SAMUEL A. LIVINGSTON, Ph.D.
Associate Program Research Scientist, Center for Occupational and Professional Assessment, Educational Testing Service, Princeton, New Jersey

MICHAEL J. MAHONEY, Ph.D.
Associate Professor, Department of Psychology, Pennsylvania State University, University Park, Pennsylvania

RICHARD M. McFALL, Ph.D.
Professor, Department of Psychology, University of Wisconsin, Madison, Wisconsin

ROSEMERY O. NELSON, Ph.D.

Associate Professor of Psychology, Psychology Department, University of North Carolina, Greensboro, North Carolina

RICHARD T. WALLS, Ph.D.

Professor, Educational Psychology and Rehabilitation Research and Training Center, West Virginia University, Morgantown, West Virginia

THOMAS J. WERNER, M.A.

Graduate Assistant, Educational Psychology and Rehabilitation Research and Training Center, West Virginia University, Morgantown, West Virginia

OWEN R. WHITE, Ph.D.

Coordinator of Planning, Development and Evaluation, Experimental Education Unit, University of Washington, Seattle, Washington

BETH E. WILDMAN, M.A.

Psychology Department, Virginia Treatment Center for Children, Richmond, Virginia

THOMAS ZANE, M.A.

Graduate Assistant, Educational Psychology and Rehabilitation Research and Training Center, West Virginia University, Morgantown, West Virginia

PREFACE

This book is the outgrowth of the West Virginia conference on behavioral assessment held in Morgantown, in October of 1975. That conference was held because of the recurring observation by many prominent psychologists and educators that behavioral alternatives to traditional modes of assessment were appearing in increasing numbers and that many seemed to lack an adequate conceptual and methodological base. The conference served to bring together scholars with a variety of interests in behavioral assessment for the purpose of achieving a better definition of the field. During the two-and-one-half days of meetings, lively discussion was held about nearly every imaginable aspect of assessment, behavioral and otherwise.

The chapters that follow represent distillations of much of this discussion, elaborations of the major presentations given at the conference, and some invited papers that were not presented. The resulting book provides a state-of-the-art reflection of the conceptual and methodological foundations of behavioral assessment, and points the way for developments over the next several years. The emphasis throughout is more on conceptual-methodological issues than on practical, how-to-do-it suggestions, though certainly many practical examples are also included. It is our feeling that still more effort needs to be focused on providing a firm foundation for the field. Such a foundation might help reduce needless duplication and identify needed research and development.

The book should serve as a useful supplemental text in courses on assessment at the graduate and upper-division undergraduate levels and as a guide to the clinical practitioner. Courses in psychology, education, educational psychology, and human development that teach behavior modification will also find the book valuable, and the extensive bibliography should assure the book's usefulness as a reference source as well.

In editing the book we have tried to provide a context for it in our introduction and last chapter and to bridge the separate chapters with appropriate editorial comments. In addition, cohesiveness has been en-hanced by reference of many of the authors to the chapters of others. In retrospect we may have gone a bit overboard in our efforts to "fit" the various papers into a cohesive whole, the result of which was occasional badgering of an author to generate "just one more rewrite." To those who stuck with us to the end, we offer our heartfelt thanks for your patience and sustained good humor. To those whose good humor may have been diminished by our zeal or clumsiness, we offer apologies. To the reader we offer a book we hope you will enjoy. We know you will learn from it.

Finally, our thanks must be given to Laura S. Rice and Susan Barrows who did so much to help in the production of the book, and to Ray Koppelman and Roger F. Maley for supporting the conference that made it all possible.

J. D. C.
R. P. H.

Morgantown, W. V.
May, 1977

CONTENTS

INTRODUCTION

The behavioral revolution in intervention procedures in clinical psychology is well-established and continuing to flourish. Not so far along in its development is the related field of behavioral assessment, though it, too, is beginning to see a rapid upsurge in activity, as evidenced by the number of recent symposia, books, and articles on the subject. As Goldfried notes in Chapter 1 of this volume, we appear to be at a point in the development of behavioral assessment where the demand for procedures outstrips their availability, and, he adds, "As a result, we are faced with the danger that poorly conceived assessment procedures may begin to fill the existing vacuum, and may establish themselves as 'behavioral measures.' "

The realization of this danger is probable in a context where insufficient attention has yet been given to the conceptual and methodological underpinnings of behavioral assessment procedures. How-to-do-it handbooks have appeared before there have been careful treatments of methodological issues, creating a situation providing the rationale for the present book. In what follows, we have attempted to focus on the conceptualization and methodology of behavioral assessment, and to show where its distinct conceptualization dictates a methodology that is correspondingly distinct. That is, new ways of conceiving of behavior require altered modes of measuring it, and may require modifications in procedures and criteria used to establish the quality of these measuring devices as well.

The field of behavioral assessment has many parallels with that of traditional evaluation in clinical psychology. The contrasts between these approaches are described briefly in this Introduction and more fully by Goldfried in Chapter 1. It suffices here merely to note that while all clinical psychologists assess behavior, not all do so behaviorally. The major differences are in what they look at and in what they do with what they see. The methods used are of the same general types, but the specific methods and the individualization of method to the specific clinical problem differ greatly.

To place the present book, and, indeed, the field in some perspective, it may help to think of assessment in clinical psychology, generally, as involving a number of stages. Others have offered models for conceptualizing the process (cf. Mash & Terdal, 1976; Sundberg & Tyler, 1962), but for the purposes of the present book we have arbitrarily chosen to view clinical assessment as involving five phases. These phases are not precisely discrete; they often overlap. In addition, recycling to early phases sometimes occurs during later phases, when new information comes to light. Taken together, the phases form what might be called "the behavioral assessment funnel," for they begin with a maximally broad band assessment (Cronbach, 1970), narrow rapidly to focus on those areas delineated during the broad band phase, and then maintain a narrow focus through the phases involving continuous monitoring and follow-up. The assessment purposes served during these various phases differ (Hawkins, 1976a). The five phases are as follows:

1) *Screening and general disposition.* In this phase the general type of problem and areas of difficulty are determined. Disposition is considered, and decisions are made as to the nature of additional, more precise assessment. The methods used here are generally very broad band, and often of low fidelity (Cronbach, 1970), such as interviews or wide-ranging problem checklists. Frequently no quantification is involved. This phase and the following one are often ignored or treated only briefly in the assessment literature. Indeed, little objective evidence is available on the processes involved in determining intervention targets (Hawkins, 1975). Much is said about how to measure the severity of a problem, but little is said about how that problem is to be selected as crucial. It is not at all clear, for example, that two different assessors given the same information about a client would select the same problem areas for further investigation and possible intervention.

2) *Definition of problem.* This phase includes two functions: a) measurement and b) hypothesis formation. The clinician is likely to shift back and forth between the functions a few times during the phase. Measurement may be oriented toward classification of the problem for administrative records, as when a client is classified with labels from the *Diagnostic and Statistical Manual II* (American Psychiatric Association, 1968); it may

be oriented toward determining what general type of intervention is needed (e.g., to change the client, the client's environment, or both); it may be oriented toward placement of the client in an appropriate treatment program; or it may be oriented toward some other general decision. Hypotheses may be generated as to what behavioral excesses and deficits might play a key role in creating the major problem or problems in the case, whether the behavioral deficits are learning or motivation problems (Mager & Pipe, 1970), what behavioral resources the client has, what environmental factors may contribute to the problem, and what environmental factors may be employed in ameliorating the problem. The hypotheses entertained in this phase will be determined by the clinician's theoretical assumptions regarding adjustment and regarding problems of the type being assessed, as well as by data from the case.

This phase may be viewed as the middle of the assessment funnel's upper portion. An analogy in education would be the administration of a standardized reading achievement test, which can be used for determining which grade to place a child in, or even which reading group, but not what specific skills the child needs to learn next.

3) *Pinpointing and design of intervention.* The third phase requires that the clinician select specific behaviors or environmental events as targets for change. A very narrow band, high fidelity (Cronbach, 1970) assessment is needed. Thus, this phase may be seen as the narrowest point in the cup of the assessment funnel. The pinpointing aspect of the assessment need not be formal; indeed, the best pinpointing often is informal. Again, an analogy in education would be going beyond formal achievement tests, which specify age and grade equivalents, to more specific assessment of the subskills involved in reading and math. The use of informal reading inventories (e.g., Potter & Rae, 1973) and "diagnostic teaching" generally serves a narrow band, pinpointing purpose. Several of the behavior checklists presented by Walls, Werner, Bacon, and Zane in Chapter 4 of this book serve a pinpointing function, particularly the more "prescriptive" ones.

Phase three involves making tentative plans as to what intervention(s) to employ, assessing the feasibility of those plans, revising the plans, and perhaps again assessing their feasibility. The clinician is making predictions as to the effects of various interventions, and a number of predictive assessments may be useful. Examples would be assessing the relative promise of a number of reinforcers (e.g., Bersoff & Moyer, 1976), assessing client "motivation" for behavior change (Cautela & Upper, 1975), and assessing specific client or environmental resources that are likely to be employed. The phase ends with the clinician's obtaining baseline or pre-intervention data.

4) *Monitoring of progress.* At this point the clinician implements the intervention while continuing to use the assessment method selected for the baseline data. A relatively continuous measurement of client progress is needed, and the measurement must usually be fairly economical, especially if it is done on a daily basis. Thus, the self-monitoring methods to be described by Rosemery Nelson in Chapter 8 and Michael Mahoney in Chapter 9 are of considerable value. It is important that the measurement method be quite relevant to the objectives of the intervention and sensitive to the intervention's effects; consequently, it should be criterion referenced and of high fidelity. An analogy in education would be the progress assessment described by Resnick, Wang and Kaplan (1973) and the continuous daily measurement described by White in Chapter 14.

It is at this portion of the assessment process that the contributions of applied behavior analysis are most obvious. The precise definition and measurement of relatively small bits of behavior (compared to what most tests measure) are excellent methods for obtaining data sensitive to an intervention. In addition, of course, applied behavior analysts are likely to verify that the effects obtained are, indeed, due to the intervention, by obtaining an adequate baseline before intervening and by scientific verification procedures such as reversal or multiple baseline designs (Hersen & Barlow, 1976).

Because the same monitoring measures are usually taken repeatedly over time, and because they cover a fairly narrow range of behaviors and environmental events, this phase of the process may be viewed as the "neck" of the behavioral assessment funnel.

5) *Follow-up.* It is appropriate that the "neck" of the assessment funnel be long, because responsible assessment should usually involve some kind of follow-up after intervention is terminated. The measures obtained will appropriately be somewhat narrow in focus still, just as during the intervention. In fact, the follow-up measures will usually include those used during the previous phase. Exceptions to this can be found, as when the treatment takes place in a residential setting, where some of the eventual changes in behavior may not even be possible, or at least the opportunities for them are grossly different from those in the client's subsequent environment. In that case, and no doubt in others, assessment in follow-up may be much broader than during the major intervention, in violation of the funnel metaphor. Some of the social validity measures suggested by Wolf (1976) are necessarily of this nature.

A complete behavioral treatment of assessment would examine the stimuli controlling assessor activities at each point in the phases outlined above. A major source of these controlling stimuli would derive from the daily behavior of the client in relevant situations. Interestingly, only a few points in the five phases have been subjected to much study by behavioral assessment researchers (Hawkins, 1975; Mash & Terdal, 1974, 1976); both traditional and behavioral descriptions of assessment generally ignore much of the sequence. For example, Pervin (1970) describes assessment simply as the "systematic observation of behavior under specified conditions and in relation to specific stimuli" (p. 71). Note the similarity of this "traditional" definition to a more recent "behavioral" one by Kazdin (1975), who identifies two components of assessment "usually used by behavior modifiers: 1) assessment of the behavior itself and 2) assessment of the events which precede and follow the behavior. In short, assessment focuses on the behavior of the client as well as environmental events" (p. 18). O'Leary and Wilson (1975) define behavioral assessment as "an attempt to identify the environmental and self-imposed variables which are *currently* maintaining an individual's maladaptive thoughts, feelings, and behaviors" (p. 18).

BEHAVIORAL VERSUS TRADITIONAL ASSESSMENT

The emphasis on current environmental variables identifies the essentially *ahistoric quality* of behavioral assessment and is consistent with a similar focus in the intervention procedures usually associated with it. The behavioral assessor does not deny the importance of historical factors—indeed, the client's learning history is viewed as quite important—but the value of attempting to uncover the historical causes of an individual's current problems is generally minimized. Though even behavioral assessors find some historical information of value as a sort of baseline on the frequency of important events, the essentially ahistorical focus is one of the characteristics that differentiates behavioral from traditional forms of assessment. Other conceptual philosophic differences have been noted frequently (Goldfried & Kent, 1972; Goldfried & Sprafkin, 1974; Kazdin, 1975; Mash & Terdal, 1976; Mischel, 1968; 1973).

Goldfried and his colleagues (Goldfried & Kent, 1972; Goldfried & Sprafkin, 1974) have nicely contrasted the assumptions underlying the two forms of assessment and they need not be reiterated here. The major point of departure appears to be in the nature of the causes of the client's present behavior. Traditional, trait-oriented assessors are likely to view these causes as essentially intrapsychic. That is, observable behaviors are viewed as *products* of something more fundamental and not observable, a trait or personality structure located within the individual. Further, the trait or personality structure itself is seen as the relatively enduring product of early childhood experiences. For behavioral assessors, the causes of behavior are likely to be looked for in current and observable biological, physical, and social stimuli.

The implications of these assumptions for clinical assessment are considerable. First, for the traditionalist, observable behavior is a sign of an underlying cause and is of only trivial significance in its own right. A variety of responses might serve as satisfactory indicators of the cause. Second, since the causes are enduring products of early experiences, their behavioral manifestations should be consistent over time. Third, the underlying causes are thought to produce generalized forms of responding. That is, a trait manifests itself in various ways and across a variety of different situations.

One might, of course, differentiate within what we are loosely calling the "traditional" approach to assessment. Some trait theorists assume more than nominal existence of their constructs (e.g., Allport, 1937), while some view them as merely convenient summaries of behavioral consistencies (e.g., Guilford, 1959). "Additive-non-additive," "interactive," "static-dynamic" are other dimensions upon which the assumptions of trait theorists differ. However, the differences within traditional views of assessment appear much smaller than the differences between them and behavioral orientations.

RESPONSE-SPECIFICITY IN BEHAVIORAL ASSESSMENT

In addition to its essentially ahistorical character, another important feature of behavioral assessment is its emphasis on the *specificity of responding*. Since the causes of that behavior are to be found in contemporary environmental events which may be relatively impermanent, behavioral consistency across time and setting is not necessarily expected nor required. Moreover, to the extent that subtle environmental differences produce finely differentiated response repertoires, it is not expected that correlated clusters of responses or response classes will be identified either. As McFall notes in Chapter 5 with respect to assertive behavior, responses tend "to be very situation specific, with little evidence of within-subject consistency or of inter-item correlation." Indeed, it is differential responding across situations that enables the assessor to determine the variables controlling the behavior, as Nelson, Rudin-Hay, and Hay (in press) have noted.

The anarchistic quality of this state of affairs has not been fully appreciated by most of us writing in the area of behavioral assessment. We still speak of "constructs" (cf. Goldfried, Chapter 1 of this volume; Jones Reid & Patterson, 1975), "capabilities" (cf. Goldfried, Chapter 1), "anxiety," "fear," "long-term reliability" (cf. Bellack & Hersen, Chapter 3 in this volume), as though there were an order out there somewhere pulling things together. To date, however, a definition for that order has proved elusive, causing some to lament that "the cardinal weakness of behavior modification (is) that we are constantly coping with pathology in detail" and that we need a "theory of pathological behavior that explains how responses are organized, automatically signalling targets for intervention which command many behavioral units" (Lang, Chapter 6 in this volume).

Reflecting the specificity of responding, it has become commonplace in behavioral assessment to speak of three response systems (Lang, 1968, 1971) or responding in three major content areas (Cone, 1975). These systems or areas have been described as the verbal-cognitive, motoric, and physiological. Lang (1971) has reviewed the correspondence between behaviors characterizing emotion and concluded that the three systems operate independently. There is also a great deal of independence of behaviors within, as well as between, systems. Despite this independence of responses one still hears reference to "triple response mode assessment," *as though there were a single behavior, trait, or construct manifesting itself in three different ways.* Indeed, much of the literature dealing with the convergence of behavior in two or more systems seems based upon trait notions of underlying constructs such as fear, anxiety, assertiveness, or depression that manifest themselves in distinct but related ways. If there are relationships it seems they will have to be predicted and organized along lines other than those dictated by currently available theoretical positions. It may be that a period of atheoretical, unprejudiced, inductive empiricism may be necessary to the discovery of new relationships that will produce more satisfactory theory in the area. In any event, the reader is alerted to the repeated mention of three-response system assessment in the chapters that follow.

The systems are, unfortunately, not defined precisely. The verbal-cognitive system is the least straightforward of the three. The content of this system appears to be internal feelings, thoughts, and affect revealed by the client primarily through the subjective use of self-report methodology (see Bellack & Hersen's chapter for a distinction between subjective and objective uses of self-report). Thus, when the client reports *feeling* tired or *thinking* s/he hears a train whistle, cognitive content or behavior in the verbal-cognitive response system is being tapped. Such "cognitions" currently are not susceptible to independent verification. Hence, they must be taken as *ipso facto* valid, at least for the present. Some (e.g., Jones in Chapter 13) exclude these events from the realm of behavioral assessment altogether.

Reports of cognitive (internal) activity must be distinguished from those of overtly observable, independently verifiable events. A client reporting that s/he sweats profusely when speaking before strange audiences is reporting behavior with a physiological content. The statement can be corroborated. It is clearly different from saying "I *feel* I sweat profusely when speaking before strange audiences."

The problems associated with the essential unverifiability of self-reports of subjective experience have led some to argue that they be lumped together with verbal behavior generally, and the entire class be viewed as behavior in the motor domain, system, or content area. Thus, we are left with two systems, not three, and can search for relationships within and between these. That is, statements of feelings, thoughts, etc., are motoric acts, just as wringing one's hands or jumping rope, or stating that "I go to the store three times a week." Perhaps the truth or falsity of verbal statements is less important to the behavioral assessor than an analysis of the events controlling their occurrence and their relationship to other forms of responding.

The motoric and physiologic content areas or systems are not well defined either. Obviously the former is the latter to an extent, the distinction being primarily between activities of the striate musculature that are usually observable without instrumentation and activities of muscles and glands that are autonomically innervated.

THE DIRECT-INDIRECT DIMENSION OF ASSESSMENT

It has been argued (Cone, 1975) that, regardless of the type of response being assessed or the content area in which it falls, there are a limited number of clearly identifiable methods used by traditional and behavioral assessors alike. These may be organized along a continuum of directness representing the degree to which they involve observations of the behavior of clinical interest in the environments of clinical interest, or surrogates of either the behavior or the environment. Thus, interviews and self-reports are classified as indirect in that the clinically relevant behavior and environment are not observed by the clinician directly, but are described to him/her by the client. That is, the client reports to the clinician about a behavior that has occurred at a distant time and place. S/he says, "My interaction with my husband/wife is much more pleasant now," and the clinician responds as though the quality of that interaction has actually improved. Of course, the clinician will also respond to other aspects of client behavior involved in the report, but those data are usually of secondary importance to the quality of the marital interaction. The assessor would like to observe the interaction firsthand, but for practical reasons usually does not, being satisfied with indirect evidence that it has really improved.

While interviews and self-reports anchor the indirect end of the methods continuum, observation by the clinician of the clinically relevant behavior itself in the context of its natural environment anchors the direct end. Behavior checklists, self-monitoring, and assessment in analogue situations fall somewhere between these extremes. The directness-indirectness continuum parallels the bandwidth-fidelity dimension suggested by Shannon's information theory for the study of electronic communications (Shannon & Weaver, 1949) and applied to personality and abilities assessment by Cronbach (1970, pp. 180-182). Interviews and self-reports tend to be rather broad band, low fidelity methods, whereas direct observation in the natural environment tends to be narrow band and correspondingly higher in fidelity.

It should be noted that the directness continuum described here is different from its more traditional use in clinical assessment (cf. Janis, Mahl, Kagan & Holt, 1969; Mischel, 1972; Scott & Johnson, 1972). Customarily, the distinction has paralleled the objective-projective measurement one, with objective, self-report measures being viewed as direct (but not necessarily valid) indicants of subjective states and projective devices being disguised or indirect ones. Interestingly, this more traditional use of the terms direct and indirect appears focused primarily upon responding in the cognitive content area. It reflects differential confidence in the ability and willingness of the client to describe his/her own true inner state. Thus, if the cognitive content is too difficult for the client to admit directly, s/he may reveal it indirectly through responses to ambiguous stimuli. We would suggest that, though the use of self-report is about as direct a reflection of cognitive content as is currently available, it is still theoretically indirect in that the thought, feeling, or affect reported was not observed by the assessor him/herself at the time of its occurrence. The directness-indirectness distinction being proposed here is not universally accepted, as later chapters in this volume will show.

Nonetheless, it seems fruitful to view the methods used by both traditional and behavioral assessors in this way and to organize them along the continuum.

There appear to be five major methods used in assessment, regardless of one's orientation: a) the oral verbal reports obtained in interviews; b) written self-reports obtained on questionnaires; c) retrospective ratings by others; d) self-monitoring; and e) direct observation. These and certain subcategories can be ordered on the direct-indirect continuum, according to how close the stimulus conditions are to the stimulus conditions of the relevant natural environment, how close the response is to the actual target behavior (or how reliably the event observed represents the target behavior, when products of the behavior are measured), and how temporally proximal the measurement is to the behavior's occurrence. Thus, a client's verbal representation of past events, presented in the clinician's office, is a very indirect form of assessment; observation of a client emitting the target in an analogue situation is intermediate in directness; while measurement of the target behavior in the natural environment is maximally direct. Obviously, the kinds of generalizability that can be reasonably assumed from more direct measures tend to be greater.

We have attempted to organize the methods described in the book along the directness continuum, starting with methods that are less direct (though usually broader band) and moving toward more direct (usually narrower band) ones. Thus, after the introductory section, Part II involves discussions of interviews, written self-reports, and behavior checklists, a type of rating by others. Part III includes examples of the use of several different assessment methods, primarily ratings by others (McFall) and direct observation by the assessor (Lang; Geer). The chapters in this section focus on methods typically used in analogue settings (controlled environments) for the assessment of social skills and physiological responding. Part IV presents the most direct of the five methods mentioned above, self-monitoring (observation of and by one's self), and observations by the assessor, both conducted in the natural environment.

The final section (Part V) deals in depth with a variety of issues confronting behavioral assessors, many of which will have been alluded to in previous chapters. The reader might find it useful to consider the following questions while reading the chapters of this book:

1) Against what criteria should performance on behavioral measures be assessed?

2) What types of norms, if any, would be useful? For what indi-
vidual-client assessment purpose would they allow a device to be
useful (Hawkins, 1976a)?

3) What are the differences between norm-referenced and criterion-
referenced measures, and which do behavioral assessors use? For
what purposes might one of these be more useful than the
other?

4) Is there an idiographic-nomothetic distinction to be made in
behavioral assessment?

5) Is there any place for the use of traditional measures in behavioral assessment?

6) Which traditional psychometric procedures, if any, should be
used in developing or evaluating the adequacy of behavioral
measures?

7) Should relationships between responses in the three major systems really be expected, and, if so, why?

8) How prevalent are vestiges of "trait" thinking in the writings
of behavioral assessors, and do references to "personality," "constructs," "capabilities," "physiological behavior as indicative of
. . .," and "total scale scores" reflect such vestiges?

9) What are the ethical issues in behavioral assessment?

10) How much emphasis should be given the assessment of environmental events occurring prior to and following behavior?

11) Should the assessment of environmental factors and events be
formally coordinated with assessment of the behavior of interest
in some type of interactive measuring device?

12) Should more uniform procedures be used by behavioral assessors?
What would be gained and/or lost?

13) How should behavioral assessment be taught?

14) Would behavioral assessment benefit from the development of
theory? If so, what form should such a theory take?

15) What are the parallels between assessment in clinical and educational contexts?

16) What emphasis should be placed on rate measures?

A word of caution should be interjected concerning the comprehensive-
ness of the book's coverage of behavioral assessment. As stated earlier, a
complete treatment of the subject would need to deal with assessor

activity in each of the five phases of the assessment process. This book, reflecting the current status of the field, is not a complete treatment. Questions of how one decides what to measure, how the data are combined to make predictions, and how these predictions result in assignment to particular intervention strategies are dealt with minimally. Further, the book does not address general uses of ratings by others, though it has an excellent chapter specifically on the use of behavior checklists, and McFall's chapter describes an approach to constructing a problem solving skill assessment device that is quite similar to suggestions made by Campbell, Dunette, Arvey and Hellervik (1973) regarding behaviorally based rating scales.

The book constitutes a reflection of the newly-emerged field of behavioral assessment, a conception of this field, and an attempt to suggest future directions. It is not a how-to-do-it handbook, yet it can serve to introduce the clinical practitioner to many useful measurement devices. In addition, it should put the practitioner, researcher, academician, theoretician, and student in touch with the issues, approaches, and methods that currently concern outstanding behaviorists addressing the problem of assessment.

Part I

INTRODUCTION TO
BEHAVIORAL ASSESSMENT

Editors' Comments

In the following chapter Goldfried describes how the behavioral view of assessment differs from the traditional view. He shows the levels of inference used by the behavioral assessor and compares these with the inferences made by those using traditional methods. He points out that behavioral assessors do not view the subject as having a "personality" and proposes the concept of "learned capabilities" as a useful alternative. He argues persuasively for the importance of content validity in behavioral assessment and points out several examples where it has apparently been ignored. He offers procedures for establishing content validity in development of behavioral assessment procedures, including content validity of both *stimuli* and *responses*. A careful reading of this chapter should help any behavioral clinician interested in designing assessment procedures or in judging the adequacy of an existing procedure.

Many behavioral assessors, particularly those of an operant or behavior analytic persuasion, will take issue with one or another of Goldfried's positions. For example, it might be argued that a concept such as "learned capabilities" is still a hypothetical construct and thus an insufficient improvement over "personality." "Response probabilities" might be offered as a preferred concept, and clinical issues might be viewed as the measurement and prediction of human response probabilities and their related environmental determinants (a definition that would also apply to educational, vocational, and other assessment as well, except that the responses and environments of interest would differ). Some will take issue with Goldfried's grouping of cognitive factors among the organismic variables,

1

and others may object to even the acceptance of cognitive factors as variables to be assessed (e.g., Jones, Chapter 13). But this kind of controversy is healthy. It shows that behavioral assessors are not all from the same mold, as some nonbehaviorists depict them. And such controversy will clarify the issues in such a way that a view of assessment will evolve which is maximally consistent with an empirical approach.

In this chapter Goldfried very concisely presents several unresolved issues that are of profound importance, and certainly this chapter should provoke some very worthwhile research. He concludes with a brief discussion of an ethical issue raised in the design of behavioral assessment devices.

1

BEHAVIORAL ASSESSMENT IN PERSPECTIVE

MARVIN R. GOLDFRIED

The field of personality assessment is forever changing. One of the clearest barometers of its progress over the years is the ever-changing title of the journal specifically devoted to assessment. This journal was initially founded in 1936, at which time it was entitled *Rorschach Research Exchange*. In 1947, as various other projective techniques were included within the clinician's standard test battery, the expanded scope of personality assessment was reflected by the change in title to *Rorschach Research Exchange and Journal of Projective Techniques*. The name was again changed in 1950 to *Journal of Projective Techniques*, indicating the relatively less dominant role played by the Rorschach in clinical assessment. The search for greater objectivity led many clinicians and researchers toward non-projective assessment procedures, such as the MMPI, and in 1963 the title was changed to *Journal of Projective Techniques and Personality Assessment*. Over the years, the disappointing research findings on the validity of projective techniques caused the projective movement to wane in popularity, and in 1971 this was reflected in the journal's change to its present title, *Journal of Personality Assessment*. Whether a new title will be forthcoming is not immediately clear. What is clear, however, is that the field is making room for the very definite trend toward behavioral assessment.

Preparation of this paper was facilitated in part by Grant MH24327 from the National Institute of Mental Health. Portions of this paper were adapted from Goldfried, M. R., Behavioral assessment, *in* I. B. Weiner (Ed.), *Clinical Methods in Psychology*, New York: Wiley-Interscience, 1976; and Goldfried, M. R. and Linehan, M., Basic issues in behavioral assessment, *in* A. R. Cimincro, K. S. Calhoun, and H. E. Adams (Eds.) *Handbook of Behavioral Assessment*, New York: Wiley-Interscience, 1977.

3

The interest in behavioral assessment is an obvious by-product of the growing popularity of behavior therapy techniques. For reasons that will become increasingly apparent throughout this chapter, most of the traditionally available personality assessment methods are of little use to the behaviorally oriented clinician. As a result, a different paradigm for assessment has been developed.

The field of behavioral assessment appears to be at a point where the need for measures currently outstrips the available procedures. As a result, we are faced with the danger that poorly conceived assessment procedures may begin to fill the existing vacuum, and may establish themselves as "behavioral measures." There is a striking similarity here to the status of psychological assessment in the 1940's, where a hospitable *Zeitgeist* resulted in the proliferation of numerous projective techniques. Rabin (1968) has described this trend as follows:

> The sudden freedom from the shackles of the psychometric tradition that was experienced by some psychologists led to rather spurious trends in the field of projective techniques. Since projection and projective techniques were so broadly defined, any type of situation that was conducive to the elicitation of individual differences and "uniqueness" or idiosyncracy in response could be nominated to membership in the new assessment armamentarium. Many issues of journals published "still another projective technique," mainly on the basis of novel stimuli of different modalities and some differentiation between normals and some psychopathological classifications. Little attention was paid to the theoretical underpinnings of these new methods or to the conceptualization of the response patterns within some theoretical framework of personality theory. Many of them were mere suggestions, prematurely published, and lacking in sufficient data of a validating nature (p. 15).

History has an unfortunate way of repeating itself. Although there admittedly have been numerous conceptual and methodological advances over the past 30 years, behavioral assessment is not immune to many of the pitfalls that have been experienced in the past. Once any measure appears in the literature, it becomes capable of developing its own momentum. If a behavioral assessment procedure is clearly specified and easily administered, researchers and clinicians are likely to use it. At that point, it becomes a "frequently used" behavioral assessment procedure, thereby justifying its use by assessors in the future. It then only requires a factor analysis—and perhaps a short form—to provide it with a completely independent life of its own.

If this analysis is a bit exaggerated—and I am not certain that it is—
it is only to make a point: There are certain basic issues in current
attempts to develop and validate behavioral assessment measures that need
to be attended to in order to insure that the field will progress in a
methodologically sophisticated and clinically useful manner. Many of
the other chapters in this book focus directly on such issues, which will
be considered broadly here.

Exactly what is this "new" approach to assessment and how is it different from what has traditionally been used? Which specific methods
qualify as behavioral assessment procedures and which do not? How is
behavioral assessment related to behavior therapy? And where does the
field of behavioral assessment have to go in the future in order to firmly
establish itself within the general scope of clinical psychology? The
remainder of this chapter will attempt to address itself to these questions.

ON THE DISTINCTION BETWEEN BEHAVIORAL AND
TRADITIONAL ASSESSMENT

Although there are numerous differences between the behavioral and
traditional approaches to personality assessment, most of these differences are closely tied to the underlying theoretical assumptions that each
approach adheres to in attempting to understand human functioning.
Obviously, it is an oversimplification to categorize under one heading
the wide variety of nonbehavioral personality theories that are in existence. Despite their diversity, however, most nonbehavioral theories share
a common assumption in that they conceive of personality as consisting
of certain relatively stable and interrelated motives, characteristics, and
dynamics that underlie and are responsible for the person's overt actions.
In order to fully understand why an individual behaves in a particular
way, then, one needs to obtain a comprehensive understanding of the
underlying dynamics. From this vantage point, to simply observe and
tally overt behavior in various life situations is inadequate, in that the
essence of personality is deeper and more inferential than what may be
directly observed. Instead, the assessment frequently focuses on the structural or dynamic components assumed to make up personality structure.
This may be done by means of paper-and-pencil questionnaires, or by
projective tests that presumably enhance the tendency of individuals
to manifest underlying personality characteristics.

When behavior therapists and behavioral assessors talk about "personality," they do so in a very different way from personality theorists.

As Goldfried and Kent (1972) have observed, "Personality may be construed as an intervening variable that is defined according to the likelihood of an individual manifesting certain behavioral tendencies in the variety of situations that comprise his day-to-day living" (p. 412). What this means is that "personality" is more or less a shorthand term for summarizing the sum total of an individual in his or her social environment. An individual does not *have* a personality, but rather the concept "personality" is an abstraction that one may make after observing a person interacting in a comprehensive sampling of situations. Similarly, an individual cannot undergo "personality change," but only behavior change; once behavior has changed, however, the individual's personality may be conceptualized differently.

From within a behavioral framework, it is perhaps most useful to view an individual's personality as one would any other set of learned capabilities (cf. Wallace, 1966). A secretary may show varying degrees of competence, depending upon his or her ability to carry out various tasks, such as typing, shorthand, answering the phone, making appointments, and whatever else may exist within the particular "role" of secretary. A psychologist's capability is determined by his/her effectiveness in the sum total of those activities in which he/she is required to function. Similarly, a human being's interpersonal capabilities can be described in reference to those various skills associated with functioning in various life situations. Stated in this way, however, the concept "personality" has little practical utility for behavioral assessment, in that it would be a nearly impossible task to obtain systematic samples of all day-to-day situations. In actual practice, behavioral assessment has instead focused on behavior patterns associated with a given class of performance capabilities, such as social skills or fearfulness.

These different conceptions of personality associated with traditional and behavioral viewpoints have important implications for test construction. From within the more traditional framework, the nature of the situation in which the individual is functioning is of less interest in the assessment than are underlying motives, dynamics, or structural components. From within a behavioral orientation, the capability conception of personality carries with it the implication that relevant and carefully sampled situations need to be reflected in one's personality measure. Thus, the *content validity* of the test becomes particularly crucial, as one must obtain a representative sample of those situations in which a particular behavior of interest is likely to manifest itself. When the APA *Standards for Educational and Psychological Tests* (1974) speaks of content validity as a requirement for proficiency tests but not tests of personality, it is clearly referring to more traditional conceptions of personality.*

The basic difference between traditional and behavioral assessment procedures is best reflected in a distinction originally made by Goodenough in 1949, when she drew the comparison between a *sign* and *sample* approach to the interpretation of tests. When test responses are viewed as a sample, one assumes that they parallel the way in which a person is likely to behave in a non-test situation. Thus, if a person responds assertively on a test, one may assume that this or similar assertive behaviors also occur in other situations as well. When test responses are viewed as signs, an inference is made that the performance is an indirect or symbolic manifestation of some other characteristic. An example would be a predominance of Vista responses on the Rorschach, where the individual reports that the things seen appear as if they were at a distance. In interpreting such a response, one does not typically conclude that the individual is in great need of optometric care, but rather that such responses presumably indicate the person's ability for self-evaluation and insight. For the most part, traditional assessment has employed a sign as opposed to sample approach to test interpretation. In the case of behavioral assessment, only the sample approach makes sense.

Goldfried and Kent (1972) have drawn a direct comparison between traditional and behavioral orientations toward assessment, with the focus specifically on the assumptions associated with each of the two approaches. This comparison is depicted graphically in Figure 1. What this figure basically attempts to illustrate are the implicit assumptions associated with drawing conclusions from one's assessment procedures, as well as the assumptions involved in validating the accuracy of this conclusion. The arrows pointing upward reflect those inferences or lines of inductive reasoning from one's testing, while the arrows pointing downward depict the implicit assumptions entailed when one deduces how a person is likely to behave in the non-test situation.

The different assumptions associated with the assessment and prediction process are arranged graphically in Figure 1 according to the degree to which inferences depart from what is directly observable. At the most basic level, there exists what is referred to in the figure as *method* assumptions. When an individual responds to a test in a given way, one hope-

---

* Some of the similarities between behavioral assessment and criterion-referenced tests are outlined by Livingston in Chapter 12.

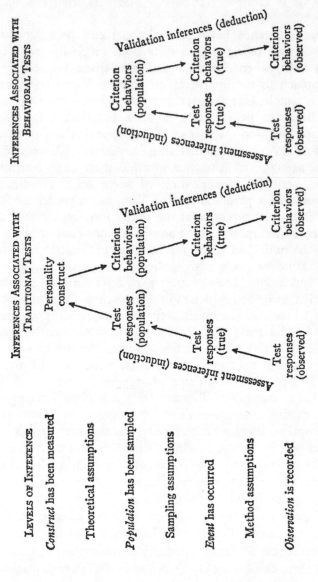

FIG. 1. Levels of inference in traditional and behavioral tests. (From Goldfried & Kent, 1972, p. 416).

fully has obtained a "true" response, minimally affected by unwanted sources of error, such as unreliability of scoring or the reactivity of the measurement process itself. Similarly, in selecting certain criterion behaviors to be used in confirming the accuracy of one's deductions, it is assumed that the method associated with establishing the criterion (e.g. judges' ratings) reflects the "true" state of affairs, in the sense of being minimally influenced by method variance.

Following the assumption that the observation is an accurate reflection of some event, one then makes an inference as to the extent to which this event is (or these events are) an accurate *sample* of some larger population of events. In making an inference from the test, there exists the implicit assumption that the test response is part of a hypothetical population of many such responses, which conceivably could be elicited if the test were increased in length. In a similar vein, in deciding which specific behavior will comprise the criterion during the validation process, one typically selects criterion behaviors from a larger pool of behaviors that are assumed to reflect the characteristic or behavior pattern one is interested in assessing.

The third level depicted in the figure—which is involved only in the case of traditional tests—is associated with inferring a given *personality construct* from a population of test responses. This entails assumptions of a theoretical nature. Thus, after one assumes that the test responses elicited on the test are a good sampling of the potential of possible test responses, the task then involves interpreting what these test responses reflect about the individual's personality. Once certain personality characteristics have been induced from the testing, this personality description is then used to deduce how these characteristics or traits are likely to manifest themselves in non-test settings.

This schematic comparison of traditional and behavioral test behaviors is admittedly abstract. Hopefully, a concrete example will serve to illustrate the similarities and differences. Assume, for example, that one wishes to assess the extent to which a male is capable of openly expressing his feelings with members of the opposite sex. In using a *traditional test of personality*, the method assumptions refer to the belief that the test scores—such as Form Dominance on the Rorschach or Social Introversion on the MMPI—are only minimally affected by artifacts associated with the measurement and scoring process itself. At the next level of inference, one must assume that the testing procedure has accurately sampled from the population of potential responses presumably indicative of the personality characteristic associated with emotional expressiveness. At the final level of inference, some interpretation needs to be made regarding the precise nature of the personality characteristic or construct that has been manifested by the test responses themselves. In inducing personality constructs associated with emotional expressiveness in heterosexual situations, one's assumptions can be based on a relatively formalized theory of personality. An interpretation of the TAT, for example, may draw on Murray's (1938) theory of personality and infer emotional expressiveness on the basis of how certain needs (e.g., nurturance and succor) are reflected in the subject's stories. The theoretical assumptions can also be less formal and more intuitive in nature, as is the case when one infers emotional reactivity on the Rorschach based on the extent to which form is dominant or subordinate when color responses are reported by the subject. Finally, a strictly empirical approach to interpretation may be used, as in the case of the MMPI Social Introversion scale.

The particular construct believed to be related to emotional expressiveness is likely to vary from theory to theory. Once the construct is integrated within a broader theoretical framework, variations may exist regarding exactly what deductions are made about how emotional expressiveness manifests itself in real-life situations. Given the deduction of a population of criterion behaviors, one must then sample the particular behaviors that will define the criterion (e.g., expression of positive feelings toward a loved one), and then decide on the specific method by which these criterion behaviors may be observed (e.g., direct observation, ratings of acquaintances).

This description of the way in which traditional tests are used in making predictions is, in fact, oversimplified. It is rare that a single type of test response would be used to infer a personality construct. The more typical practice is to use several types of test and non-test responses as they manifest themselves within a battery of tests in order to induce a personality construct. Additional inferences surrounding the implications of a given personality construct are also likely to draw on the assessor's implicit theory and clinical experiences.

In attempting to assess emotional expressiveness in heterosexual situations by means of a *behavioral test,* the procedure would consist of providing the subject with the opportunity to respond to a sample of heterosexual situations where emotional expressiveness is called for. The precise way in which these interactions are simulated (e.g. paper-and-pencil, role-playing, contrived situations, naturalistic observation) carries with it certain method assumptions, whereby one assumes that the person's "true" response is uncontaminated by the methodology. The second level of inference involves sampling assumptions, in the sense that one must be satisfied that the interactions one has measured reflect a representative sampling of the population of possible interactions of an emotionally expressive nature. In referring to Figure 1, it becomes apparent that theoretical inferences are typically not made in behavioral assessment, in that predictions of non-test behavior are made directly from the criterion behaviors sampled. In our example, then, the emotional expressiveness sampled provides a sufficient basis for making various predictions or deductions as to how the individual is likely to behave in real-life heterosexual situations.*

The basic point that is being made in comparing traditional and behavioral tests is not necessarily that behavioral assessment procedures have been found to be superior. Although indirect evidence does exist regarding the potentially greater predictive accuracy of behavioral tests (cf. Goldfried & Kent, 1972), no direct comparative prediction studies have been carried out as yet. What *is* being suggested is that the assumptions underlying behavioral assessment are fewer and more clearly delineated, and therefore more readily accessible to empirical confirmation or disconfirmation. When the predictive efficiency of a test is less accurate than one might desire, one or more of the underlying assumptions associated with the prediction process are likely to be at fault. Not only does a behavioral measure involve fewer assumptions, but whatever assumptions do exist can more readily be tested empirically, and any necessary modifications be made toward the goal of enhancing its predictive ability.

THE IMPORTANCE OF CONTENT VALIDITY

As noted earlier, when the objective of assessment is to provide an estimate of the individual's capabilities or performance across a range of situations, representative sampling of the situations in the domain of interest is essential. In Figure 1, this is reflected in the inference level where it is assumed that one's test responses have adequately sampled from the population of criterion behaviors.

---

* It should be acknowledged that the capabilities conception inherent in behavioral assessment *does* imply the formulation of some sort of unobserved construct. However, the constructs employed—such as assertiveness—are not related to any abstract theoretical formulation. Rather, they are closely tied to observable behaviors, have clear behavioral referents within appropriate situational contexts, and serve mainly to summarize the class of criterion behaviors sampled. In this sense, such inferences might be most appropriately construed as "intervening variables" (MacCorquodale & Meehl, 1948). This point is discussed in further detail elsewhere (Goldfried & Linehan, 1977).

In their discussion of the behavioral-analytic approach to assessing competence, Goldfried and D'Zurilla (1969) have outlined a procedure for sampling criterion behaviors, thereby establishing the content validity of the measure. The initial step consists of a *situational analysis*, involving a sampling of typical situations in which a given behavior of interest (e.g., aggressive behavior, heterosexual interaction) is likely to occur. The next phase consists of a *response enumeration*, which entails a sampling of typical responses to each of the situations generated during the situational analysis. Both this phase and the previous one may be carried out by means of direct observations and reports from individuals who have occasion to observe the behaviors within a naturalistic setting, as well as by self-observations by those for whom the assessment is specifically designed. In the final phase of the criterion analysis, a *response evaluation* is conducted to judge each response with regard to capability level. These judgments are carried out by significant others in the environment who typically label behavior patterns as being effective or maladaptive. Thus, each situation may have associated with it an array of different responses, which can be grouped functionally according to their judged capability level. This three-stage criterion analysis may then be used to select the items in one's measuring instrument, and also to provide empirically-derived criteria for scoring.

Goldsmith and McFall (1975), in an analysis of interpersonal competency among male psychiatric patients, followed the behavioral-analytic model and intensively interviewed patients to obtain a sample of problematic interpersonal situations. The interview protocols were condensed to a list of 55 common problem situations covering several general situational classes (e.g., dating, making friends, having job interviews, relating to authorities, etc.). Responses were then generated and evaluated for effectiveness by hospital staff. The resulting Interpersonal Situation Inventory and Interpersonal Behavior Role-Playing Test were used to evaluate a skill-training program. Pre-post change scores on both procedures discriminated between the treated and assessment-only groups.

Freedman (1974) similarly used the behavioral-analytic model to collect and key items for assessing delinquent behavior among adolescent boys. Her data reveal that the responses in role-played situations significantly differentiated among three groups of adolescent boys who were independently found to vary according to level of interpersonal competency.

Within the area of assertion, MacDonald (1974) used the behavioral-analytic model to collect and key items for her College Women's

Assertion Sample. McFall and Lillesand (1971), in the development of their Conflict Resolution Inventory, also used an empirical sampling technique to obtain situations involving unreasonable requests that college students had difficulty in refusing.

Although many other behaviorally oriented measures appear to sample a wide variety of situations, it is important to note that the *appearance* of validity, so-called face validity, is *not* evidence of content validity. For example, although items in the Fear Survey Schedule-II (Geer, 1965) were generated empirically, most other forms of the schedule have no such empirical base. Although all forms of this test have face validity, only Geer's has demonstrated content validity. Cautela and Kastenbaum's (1967) Reinforcement Survey Schedule also suffers from sampling problems, and thus lacks content validity; it seems to be based largely on the intuitive decisions of the authors. By contrast, MacPhillamy and Lewinsohn's (1972) Pleasant Events Schedule includes items that were generated from an actual situational analysis within a college population.

In the area of assertion, where questionnaires are rapidly proliferating, one frequently runs into sampling problems. Until recently, the most frequently used assessment inventory was the Wolpe and Lazarus Assertiveness Questionnaire (Wolpe & Lazarus, 1966) which is a compilation of intuitively generated items. A steady stream of inventories has since appeared in the literature, including the Rathus Assertiveness Scale (Rathus, 1973), the College Self-Expression Scale (Galassi, DeLo, Galassi & Bastein, 1974), the Adult Self Expression Scale (Gay, Hollandsworth & Galassi, in press) and Gambrill and Richey's (1975) Assertive Inventory. For the most part, these inventories were taken from previous questionnaires, supplemented on occasion by unsystematically collected reports from students or clients. This is hardly a procedure for satisfying sampling assumptions.

It is interesting to note that in almost all cases when content validity has been attended to, it has been for a college or institutionalized population. This is perhaps an indication of the difficulty of the process. As noted in a candid remark by Goldsmith and McFall (1975), the construction of their assessment procedures was far more time-consuming than the development of their treatment program. It is unfortunate that we are left with an array of instruments useful for research (and, perhaps, clinical work) with college and institutional populations, but few instruments with sufficient content validity for use with the general population.

Questions of content validity may also be raised with respect to the widely used behavioral avoidance tests. These tests typically involve measuring how close a person can approach a feared object in a laboratory setting. It is questionable whether this situational context adequately represents the domain of situations to which the approach behavior is to be generalized. Bernstein (1973), in a series of studies on behavioral avoidance tests, has demonstrated that approach behavior varies as a function of situational context. In addition, procedures that involve assessing fear of heights by having subjects climb ladders on roofs, or evaluating public speaking anxiety by having subjects give a speech in front of a small group of confederates, may be similarly questioned as to content validity. Although these tests may be useful in the analogue research context, care should be taken in using them to assess perform-ance in a wider performance domain. If it is impossible to administer behavioral avoidance tests in a representative sample of situations in which the feared object might be encountered, a possibility worth ex-ploring might be to arrange "contrived" situations within the laboratory. This might involve the use of imagination, role-playing, or other con-textual aids as part of the behavioral avoidance test.

Related to the issue of content validity is the extent to which certain behavior patterns are sampled over time. Unfortunately, relatively few behavioral assessors have addressed themselves to the question of whether or not the behavior sample is a comprehensive one. Inasmuch as class-room and home observations are often made during brief intervals over a relatively short period of time, the representativeness of such a sample becomes a most serious question. A notable instance in which this is not an issue is the case of the time-sample behavioral checklist developed by Paul for use with psychiatric patients (Mariotto & Paul, 1974; Paul, Tobias & Holly, 1972). Such observations are carried out in the hospital setting, whereby the patient's behaviors are sampled during each of their waking hours for the entire day.

When it is feasible to observe behavior for only brief time periods, the behavioral assessor should seriously consider the possibility of utiliz-ing the observations of individuals typically present in the subject's na-tural environment, such as relatives, teachers, nurses, and other significant individuals. This could be accomplished by use of behavior checklists completed through interview, for example. This obviously represents a trade-off, where one settles for less detailed and possibly less accurate observations, but obtains behavior samples occurring over a longer period of time, and in a wider range of situations. In addition, the reactivity problem becomes minimized. A further discussion of behavior checklists may be found in Chapter 4 by Walls et al.

BEHAVIORAL ASSESSMENT AND BEHAVIOR THERAPY

If one interprets behavior therapy in its broadest sense as the application of principles of psychology in general to problems that manifest themselves within the clinical setting (Goldfried & Davison, 1976), it follows that the number and variety of behavior therapy procedures available to the clinician will be large and forever changing. This is clearly a double-edged sword that provides one with several potentially effective treatment methods, but also with the dilemma of which method to use in any given case.

One of the initial tasks of the behavioral assessor in the clinical setting is to take what the client may have presented as a very general problem, and define it in more concrete and operational terms. Individuals seeking professional help sometimes talk in abstractions, frequently complaining that "things are not right," or "I don't seem to have any direction," or "the joy of life is just not there." In searching for the determinants of such vaguely described feeling states, the task of the behavioral assessor, then, is to find out more precisely what the person may be doing or not doing, thinking or not thinking, and/or what the environment is or is not providing. In this regard, efforts toward the development of computer-assisted behavioral assessment represent an exciting and potentially fruitful beginning (Angle, Hay, Hay & Ellinwood, Chapter 15).

Behavior therapists have frequently been faulted on the grounds of dealing with the symptom and failing to acknowledge the potential operation of "underlying causes." Although every attempt is made to obtain a parsimonious understanding of behavior, this is no way implies that behavioral assessment need be superficial. For example, take the case of a male whose presenting problem is that he and his wife have frequent fights. Although there might be an initial temptation to directly instigate and reinforce cooperative or affectionate behavior between the couple, such a procedure might be clinically naive under certain circumstances. A possible reason why this person frequently argues with his wife may be because he has been drinking to excess, and when he's drunk, he becomes more aggressive. And the reason that he drinks so much may be because he is very anxious. And the reason he is so anxious may be because he finds himself under continual pressure at work. And the reason he is under such pressure may be because he expects too much of himself and others (i.e., unrealistically high standards for self- and other-reinforcement). The question here becomes: What variable should one focus on in order to decrease the fighting behavior? A related question is: Where should one stop in this search for "underlying causes"? From the behavioral orientation, the heuristic employed is that one stops looking when one arrives at the variable that may have caused the behavior originally, but is not longer operating (cf. Goldfried & Davison, 1976). Suppose the man has perfectionistic standards for himself and others. Why is he that way? In all likelihood, he has modeled such standards from significant figures during his early social learning experiences. However, one cannot go back and change past interactions, but instead must work with what exists at present. One would probably want to focus on the unrealistically high standards as they are currently manifesting themselves in covert and overt behavior, with the assumption that the other problematic behaviors in the individual's life are maladaptive consequences of the individual's distorted expectations and attitudes.

In focusing on the types of variables one attends to in a behavioral assessment, the acronym SORC has been employed (Goldfried & Sprafkin, 1976). This indicates the focus on *S*ituational antecedents, *O*rganismic variables, *R*esponse dimensions, and *C*onsequences.

In evaluating the *situational antecedents* of behavior, the behavioral assessor differs most radically from those using a more traditional approach to assessment. For example, focus is placed on obtaining a detailed account of the specific situations that are likely to make an individual anxious. This information is useful not only for assessment purposes, but has clear implications for therapeutic intervention (e.g., hierarchy construction associated with systematic desensitization). In addition to learning more about situations eliciting various forms of emotional responses, some of the situational antecedents that are assessed can function more as discriminative stimuli, in the sense that they serve as cues for the person to behave in different ways. Here the distinction being made is between respondents and operants. In the case of operants, knowledge about the specific nature of the discriminative stimuli can similarly have implications for treatment. For example, with a child showing certain behavior problems, simple knowledge that he or she behaves appropriately in school but is a problem at home requires further clarification, with the assessment focusing on exactly what events happen at home and at school that serve as cues for appropriate and inappropriate behaviors.

Among those *organismic* variables involved in a behavioral assessment, one might include such aspects of an individual's physiological makeup as general energy or activity level, hormonal and chemical imbalance, and any psychoactive drugs present within his/her system, all of which can serve as important determinants of behavior.

Also included among relevant organismic variables are cognitive factors. Except when one is working with young children, mental retardates, or back ward schizophrenics, the failure to attend to mediating cognitive processes can easily lead one to overlook what may be an essential determinant of maladaptive functioning. Based on early learning experiences, individuals develop various "cognitive sets" about the world around them, some of which may be distorted and serve to mediate various maladaptive responses and emotional reactions. Thus, if an individual walks around with the inaccurate expectation that large classes of situations are potentially "dangerous," maladaptive emotional reactions and overt behaviors may be a direct and appropriate reaction to what essentially is a distorted perception. In such instances, the important maintaining variable may be the distortion, and should eventually be the direct target of the therapeutic intervention (Ellis, 1962; Goldfried & Goldfried, 1975; Goldfried, Decenteceo & Weinberg, 1974).

In focusing on *response* variables, we are referring to the actual sampling of various behaviors. The dimensions one focuses on in looking directly at behavioral samples include frequency, strength, duration, and latency of response. In assessing any response category, one frequently makes the distinction between respondents and operants, the former usually referring to some emotional reaction, and the latter to some voluntary behavior. In many cases, this distinction is not at all clear-cut, as in the case of individuals who show some reluctance to go out and find a job. Although they may be truly fearful of seeking employment, the procrastination may also be reinforced by various fringe benefits, such as unemployment checks and the attention and sympathy of others.

The fourth class of variables are the *consequences* of certain behaviors, which are important because of the well-established principle that so much of what we do—whether it be deviant or adaptive—is maintained by its consequences. Even in instances where a given course of action has a mixed payoff, in the sense of having both positive and negative consequences, the fact that the behavior continues to persist is frequently explained by the immediate positive consequences that ensue, as opposed to long-range negative consequences. For example, drug users have obvious pleasurable sensations after their fix, but experience numerous long-term negative consequences because of their involvement in drugs.

In observing the consequences of certain behaviors, it is apparent that there are certain social settings that may inadvertently reinforce behaviors that they also label as maladaptive. As Goffman (1961) and Rosenhan (1973) have vividly described, there are numerous instances where psychiatric hospitals force dependence on patients, but then interpret this dependence as being indicative of their disturbance. In instances where the maladaptive behavior exists by virtue of conflicting incentives in the environment, the more appropriate direction to take therapeutically would be toward environmental, rather than individual, modification.

UNRESOLVED CONCEPTUAL AND RESEARCH ISSUES

In concluding this overview of behavioral assessment, it is appropriate to raise some additional considerations yet to be answered by behaviorally oriented researchers and clinicians. Many of these issues are practically and conceptually complex, and clearly present a challenge to the ingenuity of behavioral assessors.

Comparative Validity of Behavioral and Traditional Assessment

In light of the growing interest in behavioral assessment procedures, it is somewhat surprising to find that virtually no research has been carried out to compare their validity and predictive efficiency with more traditionally oriented methods. When one considers that problems with the validity and reliability of many traditional assessment procedures were, to a large extent, responsible for the rejection of traditional models of human functioning, this lack of comparative research is even more surprising. Although a few isolated studies have tended to support a more behaviorally oriented approach to assessment (Goldfried & Kent, 1972), there are insufficient findings at present to draw any firm conclusions regarding the comparative validity of both orientations. Just as one can view behavior therapy as a broad orientation for approaching the gamut of clinical problems, so can one construe behavioral assessment as providing clinical psychology with a new paradigm for measuring human functioning. As has been demonstrated in the case of various behavior therapy procedures, the acceptance of a behaviorally oriented approach to assessment by clinical psychology in general is not likely to occur until it can be shown that it does a better job than the available techniques.

Standardization of Behavioral Assessment Measures

Behavioral assessment in clinical practice is, to a great extent, based on the conceptual ability and clinical intuitiveness of the particular assessor. Even in the case of research applications of behavioral assessment, one typically finds that assessment procedures focusing on a given target behavior differ from study to study. For example, assessment of assertiveness via role-playing typically varies according to the content of the situation used, the duration of the role-played interaction (i.e., single response vs. extended interaction), as well as the very mode of role-playing itself (e.g., face-to-face vs. interaction with a tape recorder). A question yet to be answered is whether such procedural variations make a difference. In this regard, comparative research on the validity of our assessment procedures is clearly needed (e.g., Galassi & Galassi, in press; Jeger & Goldfried, 1976). Only after such research is done can we hope to develop standardized measures which, in turn, would allow for clear interpretation and generalization of research findings across outcome studies. Further, standardized measures will provide us with comprehensive sets of normative data needed to assess the clinical significance of obtained behavior change.

Difficulty Level of Behavioral Measures in Outcome Research

There is a potentially important, and yet unstudied, interaction inherent in most clinical outcome research—namely the interaction between difficulty level of the task presented to the subject and the potency of the therapeutic intervention employed. This issue can be clearly illustrated in the case of speech anxiety. Situation tests of speech anxiety may vary by virtue of the size and composition of the audience, the preparation period given to the subject, the length and topic of the speech, as well as other variables that can contribute to the potential aversiveness of the situation. That public speaking situations can be differentially anxiety-arousing is apparent to any behavior therapist who has ever constructed a desensitization hierarchy. In any given outcome study, however, the researcher typically decides on a fixed level of aversiveness, and employs this task within pre- and posttesting. The assumption is that, if the therapies differ in their effectiveness, differential change will appear at posttest. However, if the situation test employed is too "difficult," the researcher runs the risk that his therapeutic intervention procedure may not be extensive or powerful enough—at least as it is typically employed within the context of an outcome study—to reflect any differential change. Conversely, if the test is too "easy," then even the less potent interventions may seem to be comparably effective. At present, there are no parametric studies that focus on this most crucial issue.

Absence of Theoretical Framework

In the attempt to establish a different paradigm for understanding and modifying human functioning, behavior therapists have discarded much of personality theory as such, and instead maintained that any given behavior pattern may be more profitably understood within the current environmental context. This orientation is reminiscent of the view Skinner presented some years back (Skinner, 1950), when he questioned the necessity for theories of learning. Thus, rather than employing conceptualizations such as "need for achievement" or "self-actualization," behavior therapists have instead sought to determine the functional relationship involved with any given response. To say that each person's behavior will vary from situation to situation, however, is just as naive as asserting that everything an individual does may be understood in terms of his personality structure. The true state of affairs undoubtedly lies somewhere between these two extremes.

Much has yet to be done in deriving a set of constructs useful in behavioral assessment. Although Mischel (1973) has offered some tentative proposal for the relevant dimensions of human behavior on which we might focus, the methodology described by Bem and Allen (1974) appears potentially more fruitful, in that it attempts to keep theory construction very closely tied to functional relationships observed at an idiographic level. The existence of such a theoretical framework can provide us with important guidelines for deciding on the targets for our assessment procedures.

The Scope of Behavioral Assessment

Just as it is shortsighted to define behavior therapy according to its available pool of techniques, so is it limiting to define behavioral assessment as being equivalent to the currently employed methods. Although one may readily acknowledge that there are certain assessment procedures more likely to be associated with behavioral assessment (e.g., role playing, self-monitoring), behavioral assessors also use procedures employed by clinicians and researchers of other orientations, such as the interview (cf. Chapter 2 by Linehan).

From a comprehensive viewpoint, behavioral assessment might best be conceptualized as involving a sampling of the individual's responses to various aspects of his or her environment. If one accepts this broader vantage point, however, it is easy to point to certain traditional assessment techniques that are consistent with a behavioral orientation. As an example, consider, of all tests, the Rorschach. One particular approach to interpreting the Rorschach involves a scoring procedure based on a sample approach, whereby the inkblots are conceptualized as perceptual-cognitive stimuli and the protocol is scored along the dimension of perceptual differentiation and integration (Goldfried, Stricker & Weiner, 1971). In essence, the behaviorally oriented assessor using the Rorschach for this purpose would be saying to her/himself: "In presenting this set of ambiguous stimuli to the subject, I am attempting to obtain a sample of this person's ability to take something that is vaguely structured and impose a certain cognitive order." Although the objection may be made that the ten Rorschach inkblots represent a somewhat unique sample of stimuli, this does not necessarily make its use "nonbehavioral." In fact, many of our currently available behavioral assessment techniques also suffer from poor content validity. Apart from the conceptual arguments associated with the use of the Rorschach as a perceptual task, the fact of the matter is that research findings with this particular scoring system have been most impressive (Goldfried et al., 1971).

The issue of whether or not certain traditional procedures might be useful for behavioral assessment is even more apparent within the clinical setting. Take the example of a teenage girl who is unwilling to talk about what might be bothering her, but might be willing to offer the clinician a sample of her concerns more indirectly by means of the TAT. The argument that the empirical status of the TAT does not justify such use of the test may also apply to some of the behavioral assessment procedures employed in clinical practice, such as the interview. More often than not, one hears the behavior therapist justifying the use of a certain assessment procedure on the grounds that "it is clinically useful" and that its utility is consistent with the general behavioral orientation. But what if one suggests that the TAT might be employed to shape an otherwise inarticulate client's talk about relevant material by first soliciting less anxiety-producing verbalizations, and then making successive approximations to discussions of target problems? Meichenbaum (1976) has suggested use of TAT-like pictures in the assessment of a client's cognitive behavior in target situations.

In summary, the level of methodological sophistication of many of our clinical assessment procedures clearly indicates a need for greater refinement and research. Although we should be developing new techniques for clinical behavioral assessment, it would be premature to discard assessment techniques simply because they do not fit the conventional stereotype of behavioral assessment.

ETHICAL ISSUES IN BEHAVIORAL ASSESSMENT

A great deal has been written about the ethical problems associated with behavior therapy. While such ethical concerns are probably no different from those inherent in any approach toward therapeutic intervention, behavior therapists have been particularly sensitive to the moral decisions in selecting the goals and methods of therapy. By contrast, few concerns have been raised regarding the ethics of behavioral assessment.

Within the context of outcome research, review committees frequently exist to protect the welfare of the participating subject. Subjects must offer their informed consent, and safeguards typically exist against subjecting individuals to dangerous procedures. An important, and yet frequently unnoticed, ethical concern associated with behavioral assessment in outcome research deals with the specific targets for change. For example, in utilizing role-playing assessment to evaluate the effectiveness of assertion training, the question of what is "appropriately assertive" clearly involves a value judgment. Does one include a scene depicting a man coming home from work, expecting a "nice home-cooked meal," only to find that his wife has been busy all day and has only had time to prepare a TV dinner? Is it appropriate to include an item requiring a subject to ask for a third cup of coffee of a waiter who is too busy to even begin serving individuals at other tables? Or should subjects be encouraged to express their true feelings about a gift they dislike when a friend has gone to great lengths to purchase it for them? Such decisions clearly extend well beyond the present limits of our behavioral assessment technology.

Part II

INDIRECT METHODS

Editors' Comments

Behavioral assessors generally show a preference for methods that require little inference. Thus, this text contains no discussion of tests that are based on various personality theories and hypotheses. Instead, as Goldfried has already pointed out in Chapter 1, behavioral assessors are interested in *sampling* from the areas of the person's behavioral repertoire that seem to be most relevant to the questions being raised.

This does not mean that behavioral assessors always sample *directly*. The direct observation and measurement of behavioral and environmental events in natural environments are the ideal method of assessment, from the viewpoint of many behavioral assessors, but while this might be feasible routinely in a school or institutional environment, it would be far too expensive for use with many populations and problems. In such cases behavioral assessors, like traditional assessors, often rely on the verbal report of persons who have directly observed or subjectively "experienced" the events of interest.

Verbal report is considered an indirect measure when the content of the report is taken as a representation of other events. Thus, in an interview, when a client reports, "I explained the situation calmly to her," this is taken as an approximate representation of actual past events, and is thus an indirect measure of them. However, at the same time as the client is describing these events, s/he may be speaking in a very soft, quiet, controlled manner that the clinician observes and draws conclusions about. This portion of the assessment would be a *direct* method, since the quality of the *verbal behavior itself* is being observed, and the observation takes place *at the time* of its occurrence. Direct methods will be discussed

23

in Parts III and IV of the book. Verbal report is an indirect method when its content is used to represent other events.

A measure will also be indirect to the extent that there is a time lapse between the occurrence of an event and the recording of that occurrence. Thus, Nelson's chapter on self-monitoring does not appear in this section of the book because in self-monitoring the client is to record his/her responses and other events relatively immediately upon their occurrence. The longer the delay between the events and their recording, the closer self-monitoring approaches the more familiar indirect method of verbal report. Therefore, this section on indirect methods includes general interviewing, which requires retrospective spoken report on a very wide range of behavioral and environmental events; self-report scales, which typically use retrospective reports (usually on paper) on only one type of problem; and behavioral checklists, which typically use retrospective reports on very specific performances within a wide range of problem areas, often obtained through interview of someone who knows the client well.

It should be evident, then, that while behavioral assessors do not totally reject verbal report, they share the skepticism of its literal interpretation held by most traditional assessors. However, a behavioral assessor's use of indirect methods will differ most markedly from the nonbehaviorist's in that the former will be much more interested in *current events* than in long past ones, more interested in *overt behavior* than in reported inner feelings and urges, and more likely to construct the assessment around a *task analysis of the skills needed for competence* than around behaviors supposedly indicative of inner disorder. As Mischel (1972) has noted, "research regarding the relative specificity of behavior suggests that sampled predictor behavior should be as similar as possible to the behavior used on the criterion measure." When the similarity is great, the measure is direct; when the similarity is minimal, the measure is indirect. It should be noted that, while most behavioral assessors prefer to maximize this similarity, Staats (1975) has recently provided a learning theory defense of the value of "indirect" assessment methods and some data supporting his interpretation. Undoubtedly the virtues of positioning oneself at various points on the indirect-direct continuum will continue to be argued for some time.

Before describing more specifically what each author has contributed in the following three chapters, perhaps we should point out an omission. Webb, Campbell, Schwartz and Sechrest (1966) have documented the fact that totally unobtrusive measures of behavior can sometimes be made, as when the relative interest in different museum exhibits is measured by the frequency with which floor tiles in front of them must be replaced, or the food consumption in an institution is assessed by weighing food trays before and after a meal. A similar example would be Hayes, Johnson and Cone's (1975) measurement of litter in a prison yard. Most such measurements come under a general class that can be called the *measurement of lasting products* (Hawkins, Axelrod & Hall, 1976). When behavior leaves a lasting environmental effect, the strength of the behavior can be indirectly measured by that effect. This is familiar in education, where teachers may record the accuracy of written answers to arithmetic problems, the stability of a chair made in wood shop, or the creativity of a written story (see Chapter 12 by Livingston and Chapter 14 by White). In more traditional clinical work, lasting products may also provide a useful indirect measure. For example, Schwarz and Hawkins (1970) noted improvement in an adolescent's acne as a result of their modifying self-conscious face-touching behavior. Phillips, Phillips, Fixsen and Wolf (1971) measured delinquents' performance of room cleaning by the visible results it produced. Vargas and Adesso (1976) measured fingernail length to assess effects of three treatments of nailbiting. Similarly, smoking, incontinence, and overeating leave lasting results that can be measured.

In Chapter 2 Marsha Linehan describes the status of interviewing from a behavioral viewpoint. This is one of two chapters in the book dealing with interviews, the second being by Angle, Hay, Hay and Ellinwood (Chapter 15). Linehan, like most behavioral assessors involved in clinical or educational settings, is not ready to throw out the interview as an assessment tool, despite the remarkably limited evidence regarding its validity, and she presents cogent reasons for its retention.

Linehan describes two types of assessment methods involved in interviewing. The most obvious one is the indirect assessment of behavioral and environmental events that occur outside the interview setting. A client reports events from his/her present and past, and the clinician attempts to use that information in assessing the problem, necessarily making the assumption that the client is presenting information sufficient in accuracy and completeness to serve the current assessment purposes. Research on the validity of this assumption is rare, as the chapter will make clear. Because of a predominance of this indirect type of assessment in interviewing, the Linehan chapter appears in the present section on indirect methods.

However, as Linehan points out, one also conducts direct assessment when interviewing. That is, the behavior of the interviewee is directly observed in a social situation that is usually somewhat stressful. Depending on the referral problem and the stimuli presented by the clinician, these observations may provide extremely valuable assessment information. Of course, the typical interview is not designed to maximize this direct assessment function, and clearly the range of stimulus situations available is very limited. One approach to maximizing the assessment of the client's repertoire in specific areas is to set up situations that approximate natural ones the person may face, then to observe systematically the client's performance in these situations. When the client's self-report of what s/he would do in a specified situation is obtained, this can be considered a part of the interview process. If the behavior of clinical interest is actually emitted by the client and observed by the assessor, it will be considered as *direct assessment in controlled environments*, a topic that will be treated in the next section of this text.

It should probably be pointed out that the direct assessment done in interviews includes assessment of nonverbal and para-verbal behaviors. For example, the clinician will make judgments about the person's social sophistication from clothing as well as verbal content. The client's interpersonal skills will be assessed partly on the basis of how s/he moves, sits, and gestures. And many verbal and nonverbal events will provide clues as to the person's values, information that is very important later when the clinician wishes to provide effective praise or censure, or wishes to persuade the client as to the importance of certain changes.

Although there have been a number of publications by behavioral assessors related to interviewing (e.g., Wahler & Cormier, 1970; Holland, 1970), there seems to have been little analysis of how a behavioral approach to conducting interviews might differ from the approach of others. Probably behavioral assessors put less credence in verbal report, on the whole, but there appears to be great variance in this, with some accepting client report at virtual face value and as the only source of information, and others eschewing extensive interviews altogether. In addition, behavioral assessors may be more likely to structure the interview. As far as content is concerned, the behavioral assessor will show more interest in current environment and behavior, rather than long past events, and will focus more on clearly described, overt behavior than on "inner" feelings and urges. But elucidation of differences in interview method between the behavioral and the traditional assessor remains to the future.

Though the interview is doubtless the most universal method for obtaining verbal reports from clients and others, the self-report inventory or scale is also popular.

As Bellack and Hersen note in Chapter 3, the past few years have witnessed a proliferation of scales and inventories designed for use in clinical and research contexts. In the wake of this flurry of activity these authors caution against needless duplication of efforts as they review recent developments in the assessment of fear, anxiety, social skills, and depression.

Bellack and Hersen provide an historical overview of the use of self-report in clinical assessment generally, and mention its less than enthusiastic acceptance by modern behaviorists. They make an interesting distinction between subjective and objective uses of self-reports and point out that problems are not so much the result of the self-report mode *per se* but rather the way in which it is used.

Throughout their chapter Bellack and Hersen refer to the psychometric adequacy of the devices they review. They report the existence of a number of "gaping holes," and emphasize especially the need for "long-term reliability studies for a variety of populations. . . ." Other deficiencies, including the absence of normative data for various populations and the over-reliance upon subject analogues (see McFall's Chapter 5 for a discussion of various types of analogue) are also mentioned. Repeated reference of the interrelatedness of cognitive, motor, and physiological response systems also occurs in their chapter, with some suggestions as to why correspondence between systems has generally been found to be low. (A discussion of additional reasons for this lack of correspondence is included in Chapter 16).

The Bellack and Hersen chapter provides an excellent summary of recent developments in the use of self-report methodology by behavioral assessors and should be of value to anyone considering the benefits such an approach has to offer.

The third chapter in this section, by Walls et al., deals with behavior checklists. A behavior checklist could be generally described as a list of fairly specific, objectively described behaviors whose presence or absence in a learner's repertoire is rated. Often the ratings are simply dichotomous: The person does show the behavior or does not; the person has achieved criterion or has not. At other times the ratings will reflect three or more levels of consistency (frequency) or quality in performance.

The items in a behavior checklist are not trait names or global terms. Thus, a scale asking how "friendly" or how "nervous" the subject is would not be classed as behavior checklist or a behavior rating scale, while one that listed specific "friendly" or "nervous" behaviors, whose frequency was indicated, would be.

It should be evident, then, that a behavior checklist is based on a task analysis. The clinician or educator determines the competent behaviors that make up a particular skill, personal characteristic, or job performance, and these component behaviors—or a sample thereof—are used to compose an assessment device. Currently the determination of component behaviors is almost always done in a rather unsystematic fashion, but researchers are beginning to develop means for validating task analyses (Resnick, Wang & Kaplan, 1973). It should be observed that such validation is quite different from that typifying psychological testing.

The usefulness of behavior checklists for devising individualized educational and therapeutic intervention should be obvious. If one knows what component behaviors are needed to perform a certain task or have a certain impact on others, and if one has a checklist showing how well a particular learner performs each of these behaviors, one already has the beginnings of the person's individual teaching or therapeutic curriculum. If, in addition, the component behaviors are organized so that those which facilitate the acquisition of others are placed earlier in the sequence, one has a learning hierarchy that could constitute a very efficient curriculum (Resnick et al., 1973).

The relationship between general education, training of retarded persons, and clinical therapy begins to become evident in this chapter. It will again be evident in Chapters 12, 14, and 16, in the final section of the book.

The Walls, Werner, Bacon and Zane chapter differentiates between *descriptive* and *prescriptive* checklists, including in the latter those which contain some form of training suggestions for each component skill. It might also be noted that some checklists, such as the Vineland Social Maturity Scale and the Adaptive Behavior Scale, are oriented toward only a very general descriptive function, that of assigning a score to the subject describing his/her general level of functioning. Thus, descriptive checklists alone might be arranged along a continuum, ranging from those which sample only a few skills and provide only an overall summary score, through those which sample skills in several different areas and provide a profile of scores across these areas, to those with a relatively exhaustive assessment of skills. The more exhaustive the list of skills assessed, the more useful the checklist will be in educational or treatment planning.

Most behavior checklists today appear to have shortcomings in the standardization of antecedent stimuli and the specification of response criteria. For example, a checklist may ask whether the child "follows a moving object with his/her eyes" yet fail to indicate the nature of the object, the speed of movement, the distance from the child, how long the tracking must occur, or how consistently the child must track to be rated "pass." All of this, and more, is often left to the examiner's judgment. When the purpose of the assessment is to provide a general developmental score, this lack of standardized administration is important, because it is likely to affect decisions or create biases that are relatively irreversible (e.g., institutionalization, labeling of learner as disabled). When the purpose of the assessment is identification of specific learning requirements, this kind of shortcoming may be less problematic, because during training one is likely to detect errors made in the initial assessment rather quickly.

Walls et al. reviewed over 150 behavior checklists designed for use with a variety of purposes and populations. There are many designed for planning the education and training of retarded persons. There are also checklists for use with alcoholism, vocational training, psychosis, doctor-patient relationships, dental hygiene, and several more.

The authors provide an extensive, useful discussion of reliability and validity issues related to use of checklists for various purposes. Unfortunately, the designers and users of checklists have generally done little to examine the reliability and validity of these instruments for the purposes intended, and this discussion should greatly assist those interested in beginning such research.

Finally, Walls et al. list every checklist, its source, the classes of behavior it purports to measure, the method of administration, the type of rating scale used, and whether validity and reliability data are provided. They also rate the objectivity of the checklist. This chapter should prove of great value to numerous professionals and researchers concerned with adequate assessment and service to various clinical and educational populations.

2

ISSUES IN BEHAVIORAL INTERVIEWING

MARSHA M. LINEHAN

The interview is perhaps the most widely used method of conducting clinical behavioral assessments. Although often supplemented by other procedures, it is generally considered an indispensable part of clinical assessment strategy. In individual therapy, especially with adults, it is often the primary method of assessment. Its use in clinical settings is advocated by many behaviorists, including those who at the same time stress the importance of a rigorous functional analysis in clinical assessment (e.g., Bijou & Peterson, 1971; Goldfried & Pomeranz, 1968; Kanfer Saslow, 1969; Lewinsohn, Biglan & Zeiss, 1976; Mischel, 1968; Peterson, 1968).

Most assessment interviews are carried out with the person seeking or or referred to therapy. The client, however, is not the only interviewee. Concerns about the reliability and validity of self-reports have led many clinicians to interview peers, family members, and other significant persons as important sources of additional information. In the case of child behavioral assessment, interviews with parents and/or teachers are often the primary source of information. In institutional settings frequent interviews with staff members responsible for carrying out a major portion of the therapy are usually necessary to evaluate the progress of therapy, amplify incomplete data gathered via other methods, and clarify hypotheses about the variables controlling client behavior. Thus, in its broadest sense, behavioral interviewing includes interviews not only with the client but also with significant persons in the client's life.

Although the linkage between assessment and therapy is recognized as critical in behavior therapy, the interview is infrequently used as part of the assessment battery in outcome studies on the effectiveness of behavior therapies. When it is included, it is often for purposes of screening (Linehan & Goldfried, 1975), eliciting the cooperation of the subject, or determining potential problems which may be encountered in using other assessment methods (Lewinsohn & Shaffer, 1971). If included as a method of assessment, the primary use of the interview in psychotherapy research studies has been to measure global levels of motor, cognitive and/or emotional functioning and to assess specified behavioral targets (Lichtenstein, 1971). It is rarely used as a method for selecting the target behaviors to be modified in behavior therapy research. An exception is the recent work of Sloane and his colleagues (Sloane, Staples, Cristol, Yorkston & Whipple, 1975; Sloane, Staples, Cristol, Yorkston & Whipple, 1976; Staples, Sloane, Whipple, Cristol & Yorkston, 1976), a group of nonbehavioral therapists conducting behavior therapy research, where the clinical interview was used both as a method of selecting the target behaviors and to conduct pre- and post-assessment. It has undoubtedly been used in the target selection process of many single-subject research designs on behavior therapy although its use in such instances is usually not reported or discussed.

No outcome studies on behavior therapy to date, however, have been found where the interview is used as the sole data base for a behavioral assessment. This is probably due to at least four factors: 1) the emphasis in most behavior therapy research on obtaining samples of the criterion behavior directly; 2) the generally suspect nature of self-report and peer-report data; 3) the almost total lack of research on the reliability and validity of behavioral interviewing; and 4) the absence of standardized behavioral interview procedures. These factors are, of course, of at least equal importance in the *clinical* use of the behavioral interview and must be considered in any discussion of behavioral assessment where interviewing is utilized.

FUNCTIONS AND ADVANTAGES OF THE BEHAVIORAL INTERVIEW IN CLINICAL ASSESSMENT

The primary goal of any clinical assessment procedure is, simply put, to figure out what the client's problem is and how to change it for the better. Generally this involves gathering information and formulating and testing hypotheses about the variables associated with both a behavioral analysis of the maladaptive behaviors that brought the client to the therapist in the first place and the variables associated with the selection and implementation of the treatment (Goldfried & Davison, 1976).

Although the process of conducting clinical behavioral analysis has been outlined in a variety of ways (Bijou & Peterson, 1971; Goldfried & Davison, 1976; Holland, 1970; Kanfer & Saslow, 1969; Mischel, 1968), it typically includes information gathering and hypotheses testing in the following phases: 1) identification of problem behaviors and specification of behavioral objectives (target identification); 2) identification of current and potential controlling variables; 3) identification of client (i.e., person) variables which may interact with the treatments under consideration; 4) identification of environmental variables which may enhance or interfere with the treatments selected; and 5) evaluation of the treatment.

A second and less often mentioned goal of clinical behavioral assessment, at least in the initial phase, is to determine the feasibility of establishing a positive interpersonal relationship with the client. This relationship is often crucial to the success of assessment and subsequent possible therapy. In this sense, the assessment process serves as a sample of the client-clinician interaction pattern and may be useful in predicting future patterns. Thus, the interview can serve as a method for both the client and the clinician to assess whether or not they can form a productive relationship.

A third and, at times, equally important goal of behavioral assessment with the client who does remain in therapy is the utilization of the assessment process itself as part of the therapy program. In light of these goals, the interview has several unique advantages.

Information Gathering

The interview is first and foremost a method of obtaining verbal data about the client's behavior and interactions with his environment. Although this information is the person's verbal construction of the events rather than a necessarily factual report, verbal reports from the client and/or significant others are often the only possible data base on which to carry out a behavioral analysis. This is most obviously the case in the assessment of covert events such as thoughts, plans, and phenomenological experiences; it also applies to past events, to infrequent behaviors such as suicide attempts, to private behaviors such as sexual behavior, and to public behaviors where direct sampling might cause more problems for the client. Sometimes a direct measurement of the behavior is possible but not feasible. Even when other, more direct methods are feasible, the clinician must consider the possible methodological problems involved. For instance, direct observation of the behavior may be too reactive; self-monitoring may change the very behavior patterns the clinician wishes to investigate; and structured role-playing may be too embarrassing for the client or invalid because of demand characteristics that may be operating.

As a method of obtaining self-report data, the interview has several unique advantages over paper-and-pencil and the newer and still experimental interactive computer methods (see Chapter 15). The most important advantage is its flexibility. Depending on the interviewer's behavior, the interview can be used to obtain both general information covering many areas of the client's functioning and detailed information in specific areas. As noted by many others (Mischel, 1968; Peterson, 1968; Storrow, 1967), this flexibility allows the assessor to follow leads in pursuing more detail as well as to broaden the "assessment band" when a particular line of questioning hits a dead end or suggests other areas which may be important. An important benefit of this flexibility comes in those cases where the person is reluctant to provide information about an area, does not think the information is important, or assumes that the therapist would not find the information important. This is precisely the type of information that a person is not likely to disclose in a paper-and-pencil questionnaire. For example, a suicidal client may fail to ask for help directly but may make comments such as "I don't want to keep going."

A second advantage related to the flexibility of the interview is that variations in the client's nonverbal behavior and speech patterns as a function of variations in either the clinician's behavior or the content of the interview are often useful indirect signs of emotional responding. As such they may suggest lines of further inquiry which would not be evident if only written assessment data or inventory scores were available.

A third advantage of the interview over other methods of obtaining self-report data is the interpersonal relationship which can be established. Along with flexibility, this advantage of interviewing has been most heavily emphasized in the literature on assessment interviews. Since the quality of this relationship and its influence on information gathering are influenced to a great extent by therapist and client variables (Cozby, 1973), it is also an important source of method variance and will be discussed later at greater length.

A fourth advantage of the interview, closely related to the type of relationship formed, is the potential for greater confidentiality which an interview offers over paper-and-pencil or computer methods of interviewing. Assuming the interview is not being tape-recorded, a client will often divulge information verbally which he/she would not put in a permanent record. For instance, only the unwise client would put a description of current illegal activities in writing, while one might describe such activities in a confidential interview.

A fifth advantage of interviewing over other self-report strategies is that it allows the interviewer to obtain information from persons who, because of inadequate communication skills, may be unable to provide information in any other way. Persons who have impaired thought processes, are mentally retarded, illiterate, or severely depressed may simply be unable or unwilling to provide information in other ways.

Finally, a sixth advantage of the behavioral interview as a method of obtaining self-report is that it not only allows the clinician to modify his/her questions to fit the person's conceptual system but it also affords an opportunity for modification of the interviewee's verbal descriptions as well. In this regard, Cannell and Kahn's (1968) comments about the research interview are equally relevant to the clinical interview:

> The respondent role is by definition an active, self-conscious one; in most circumstances the respondent can meet his expectations best when he understands them fully. Specifically, he needs to know what constitutes successful completion of the role requirements; he needs to know the concepts or terms of reference by means of which he is being asked to provide data. Without this understanding, data accessible to the respondent are likely nevertheless to remain unreported because interviewer and respondent lack a common frame of reference, a common conceptual language, or common standards of response adequacy and excellence (pp. 536-537).

To the extent that the behaviorist's language and emphasis on precise behavioral and environmental descriptions are quite different from the language of the typical client, this opportunity for feedback and clarification of the assessor's expectations seems especially critical in behavioral interviewing.

Hypotheses Clarification and Testing

As an adjunct to other more direct means of behavioral assessment, the interview is important in amplifying incomplete data and clarifying the meaning of the behavioral events from the client's point of view (cf.

Bem & Allen, 1974). Although hypotheses about the variables controlling a particular behavior pattern may be arrived at by observation and analyses of the preceding and consequent events, and these controlling variables are frequently no more clear to the client than to the clinician, in many cases simple questioning can at least elicit information about the client's construction of the events. This information is frequently invaluable in clarifying what aspects of a given situation the client may be attending to. Similarities between apparently dissimilar events may become apparent and thus generate hypotheses as to the variables controlling the behavior of interest.

This information can also, of course, serve an important role in eliminating hypotheses about what variables currently or potentially will control the target behavior. A good example of this is the case of a woman who both engaged in a high rate of self-cutting behavior and also had frequent episodes of extreme fear that she would not be able to prevent or stop the self-cutting. One of the treatment components was to put her in isolation (where cutting instruments were unavailable) following each instance of self-cutting behavior. The method, which was intended as a punisher and tried for several months, was ineffective in reducing the self-cutting behavior. Much time and pain might have been saved had the clinician simply asked the woman how she viewed the time-out experiences. When finally asked, she reported that it was the only time during the day when she felt relaxed and safe from the threat of imminent self-injury. It thus may have been functioning as a reinforcer rather than an absence-of-reinforcement period. Every clinician can cite many similar cases. The point here is that hypotheses can often be generated, clarified, and/or modified by simply asking the client why he/she behaves in a particular way, why an environmental manipulation is not working, or what changes should be made to affect the target behavior.

Observation of the client's interview behavior can also be used as a method of generating hypotheses about interpersonal behavior in the natural environment. Although the client's behavior in the interview situation may not be completely representative of interpersonal behavior in other situations, it nonetheless is an important source of hypotheses about behavioral deficits and assets. The client's physical appearance and nonverbal behavior, such as posture, movements during the interview, facial expressions, etc., can be important clues in the assessment of persons with social skill problems. Speech patterns, as well as the content of the client's verbal responses, can provide hypotheses about the client's communication skills. Further, joint interviews with the client and other significant persons often can be utilized to generate and test hypotheses about the client's behavior with others. Interviews with the client after a joint interview can be used to test hypotheses about the client's ability to accurately perceive and report what went on during a social interaction.

The Interview as the Initial Stage of Therapy

As mentioned previously, an important function of initial assessment interviews is to begin the process of establishing a therapeutic relationship with the client. The clinician's skill in attending to relationship factors during the initial interview is often an important determinant of the client's willingness to begin the often difficult process of behavior change. Even when the primary method of data gathering consists of more direct methods of assessment, the interview is critical in obtaining the client's cooperation and determining possible problems which might arise with other methods of assessment.

The assessment interview can also be important in helping the client conceptualize problems; this is often therapeutic in and of itself (e.g., Meichenbaum, 1975). Certainly in many cases where the client views himself/herself as "going crazy," "losing control," or "a terrible person" because of his/her problems, a behavioral explanation may bring tremendous relief and consequent behavior change. Often the behavioral analysis and consequent pinpointing of behavioral targets and controlling variables will lead to an increase in the client's expectations regarding the possibility of improvement, a change which is, in itself, therapeutic (Goldstein, 1962). In cases where the referral is initiated by someone other than the potential client, a reinterpretation of the person's behavior as either normal or as a function of easily changed environmental factors is sometimes all that is necessary to solve the problem which caused the referral in the first place.

To briefly summarize, the interview seems uniquely valuable as a behavioral assessment technique. The advantages of the interview can be most clearly seen when the goals of the assessment are 1) the obtaining of self-report data; 2) the generation, clarification and, to some extent, elimination of hypotheses about the client's behavior and possible controlling variables; and 3) the beginning of the therapeutic intervention.

CONTENT OF THE BEHAVIORAL INTERVIEW

Over the past 10 years several formats have been proposed for conducting behavioral assessment in the clinical context. Although similar in terms of their emphasis on the functional analysis of problematic behavior, the formats vary in the amount of information viewed as necessary for a complete behavioral analysis. One of the most influential assessment guides has been that proposed by Kanfer and Saslow (1969). They advocate a comprehensive analysis of past and current behavioral and environmental patterns. A complete behavioral analysis, in their view, consists of the collection of a wide range of descriptive information in the following seven areas: 1) initial analysis of the problem situation; 2) clarification of the problem situation (including an analysis of the internal and external antecedents and consequences); 3) motivational analysis; 4) developmental analysis; 5) analysis of self-control; 6) analysis of social relationships; and 7) analysis of the social-cultural-physical environment. Within each general area they detail several specific areas which should be assessed. Although they state that an analysis is not necessarily incomplete if information is lacking on some of the items, the major thrust of their discussion is that each of the areas is usually of major importance.

In a similar vein, Wolpe (1973) suggests obtaining a fairly large amount of information about current and past functioning of the individual in the areas of early family life, education, employment, sexual functioning and current social relationships. Lazarus (1973, 1976) also stresses a comprehensive analysis of the total functioning of the individual. In some ways these formats are reminiscent of the social work case study approach in that they assume that certain specific areas of human functioning are relevant in the assessment of every client regardless of his/her problem.

One can question whether the clinician needs all this information for every client. It would seem that one of the functions of the behavioral interviewer is to make sequential decisions about what types of information are needed in a particular case. Certainly, the great advantage of the interview over other assessment methods is the flexibility it allows the clinician in making such decisions. If the behavioral interview is approached from an idiographic point of view, then the only information needed is that which would allow a precise statement of the behavioral problems and objectives, the probable controlling variables, and the potential resources and problems in the intervention program. Within the give-and-take of the assessment interview the clinician is thus functioning much like the scientist in search of a viable hypothesis.

From this point of view, the comprehensive assessment formats proposed by Kanfer and Saslow, Wolpe, Lazarus, and others might be best viewed as suggestions as to areas which might be fruitfully searched rather than a list of necessary information. Once a tenable set of hypotheses has been formulated, it would seem reasonable to move from the gathering of broad band descriptive material both to the gathering of more precise data and to a more focused testing of the initial hypotheses. For instance, a client may report frequent anger and aggressive behavior toward his/her children as a problem. After obtaining a description of several episodes and discussing them with the client, the clinician may generate several hypotheses, e.g., the client is deficient in assertive skills; the client has unrealistic beliefs about what can reasonably be expected from his/her children; and/or aggressive behavior is being reinforced by other members of the family.

The clinician may then explore each of these hypotheses by detailed questioning. If one or more of the hypotheses still seem tenable, the clinician then may move to more focused testing, such as role-playing to assess skills, imagined exposure to various situations to assess beliefs and emotional responses, or interviews with other family members to assess contingencies. Almost always it is necessary to utilize other methods of assessment—such as self- and environmental monitoring, or *in vivo* observation—both to assess the characteristics of the problem behavior (e.g., frequency, magnitude, duration, pervasiveness) and to accomplish adequate tests of the hypotheses. This more focused approach is similar to that advocated by Stuart (1970), who criticized Kanfer and Saslow's format as lacking in parsimony. Yates (1975) and Goldfried and Davison (1976) also suggest a more idiographic approach to information sampling.

It should be emphasized that this movement from information gathering to hypotheses testing is a continuing cycle which occurs throughout the assessment process. Since the therapy itself is often the final test of the clinician's hypotheses, it should be clear that both information gathering and hypotheses testing continue throughout treatment. In many instances the clinician will find that, although only a small portion of the descriptive material suggested by Kanfer and Saslow is gathered in the initial assessment interviews, a more complete coverage of the material will have been accomplished by the time the initial problematic behaviors have been changed. This frequently leads to a sequence of therapies, each aimed at an additional problematic behavior which has come to light in the previous therapy.

Ultimately the question of how much information should be obtained in the initial assessment interview is an empirical one. Perhaps the computer-conducted interviews described by Angle, Hay, Hay, and Ellinwood in Chapter 15 will provide a means for researching the question. As of now, no studies have been done on the comparative reliability or validity of the various formats and guidelines thus far proposed.

A related issue involves the question of which problematic behaviors should be explored in detail during the assessment interviews. Although the emphasis in the behavioral literature has been on assessing those behavior patterns associated with the client's goals, one does find hints here and there that perhaps the goal of therapy (and thus assessment) should be more far-reaching. For instance, Kanfer and Saslow (1969) state that inadequate data in some areas "must be noted nevertheless because they often contribute to the better understanding of what the patient needs to learn to become an autonomous person" (p. 437). Although "becoming an autonomous person" may at times be the client's goal, it seems clear that in many cases the client's concerns may be focused on more limited objectives. Indeed, necessary parts of the assessment process itself are the determination of what, in fact, the client's goals are and the translation of more general goals into specified behavioral objectives. In many cases, an analysis of the variables controlling the very decisions clients make about behavioral objectives may be required (Bandura, 1969; Goldfried & Davison, 1976).

The complexity of the assessment and of the determination of goals is well stated by London (1964) in a discussion of some of the limitations of behavior therapies:

> The more complex the problem behavior in question, the less any pure Action Model of psychotherapy seems applicable to its solution. Perhaps the failure of such models ultimately results, not from the inability of the therapist to identify mechanisms of action for the achievement of goals, but from the fact that, for complex issues, he is unable to specify very fruitful goals (p. 132).

London is alerting us that at times a specification of target behaviors in need of change must itself be the focus of a considerable portion of the therapy. Furthermore, since in many cases this very specification is all that is necessary to produce behavioral change, it is questionable whether one should arbitrarily separate the assessment process from the intervention process. (The reactivity of the clinical interview in the determination of client goals will be discussed in more detail later.)

Even when meaningful behavioral objectives can be established easily, one should not conclude that the goals of therapy cannot be expanded and modified as therapy progresses. Indeed, to the extent that the clinician is successful in helping the client achieve his/her initial objectives, the goals of the client frequently do expand. Furthermore, with clients who are initially too disturbed to participate meaningfully in the selection of behavioral objectives, the treatment may enable them to progressively take a greater role in the selection of additional treatment goals (O'Leary & Wilson, 1975). The focus of at least the initial stages of behavioral interviewing, however, should be on the specific problems that brought the client into therapy at that particular time.

This does not mean that the behavior viewed by the client as problematic should necessarily be the primary target behavior. Complex behavior-behavior interactions often necessitate the modification of one behavior in order to change a second. At other times, especially if the client expresses doubt about the possibility of any behavioral change, the clinician may choose a more easily modifiable, but less problematic, behavioral target as the focus of the initial intervention.

A related issue is involved in behavioral interviewing with children and institutionalized persons. The choice of what behaviors to focus on and even whom to interview is directly linked to both the choice of therapeutic goals and decisions about who is, in fact, the primary client. The ethical problems involved in doing behavior therapy with these populations have received increasing attention (e.g., Davison & Stuart, 1975) and are complex and controversial. Clearly, the relationship between assessment and therapy requires that these issues be recognized as integrally related to the assessment process.

A further assessment problem arises when the client's presenting problem involves the inability to obtain some environmental objective. For example, the client might complain of an inability to obtain desired reinforcers, e.g. attention from his wife, or a promotion from his/her boss. At this point the assessor often has to expand the assessment focus to include an analysis of contingencies operating on other persons in the environment. A task analysis is often needed to delineate the skills needed to obtain various consequences. Frequently, however, the assessor has to rely on his/her own knowledge of typical behavioral-environmental interactions.

Even if the assessor maintains a focus on the client's presenting problems, the complexities of analysis can be enormous. This is in part due to the absence of a unified and coherent theoretical framework to guide clinical decisions about targets for assessment (Goldfried & Linehan, 1977). Much of the work on behavioral analysis has focused in one way or another on delineating additional areas that the clinician might assess in the search for controlling variables. Frankel (1975), for instance, has recently suggested that the assessor should search for chains of behaviors and environmental consequences occurring over relatively long periods of time. Similarly, the emerging emphasis on cognitive-behavior modification has led to a corresponding emphasis on assessment of cognitive variables (Meichenbaum, 1976). Unfortunately, little work has been done on analyzing the processes of data combination which might be most useful in the clinical context. As Dickson (1975) notes:

> While the Kanfer and Saslow (1969) format for functional analysis provides the behavior therapist with a systematic procedure for gathering data, it does not allow a scientific approach in interpreting the data collected. Thus, the behavioral assessor still is very much an artist in selecting those behaviors for intervention, in deciding what frequencies define excesses or deficits, and in discriminating whether to intervene within the environment containing the controlling stimuli, or within the organism (p. 365).

METHODOLOGICAL ISSUES

Problems in the reliability and validity of verbal reports have been one of the major reasons for the emphasis on direct sampling of behavioral and environmental events in behavioral assessment. Although behavior therapists frequently assert that verbal reports should be seen as the person's verbal construction of events rather than as an accurate representation of the events (Kanfer & Saslow, 1969), in practice it seems clear that even the behavioral clinician often assumes that the client's verbal reports are, in fact, accurate. Reliance on information obtained in behavioral interviews rests on two related assumptions: that clients are capable of accurately observing and reporting their own behavior, environment, and behavior-environment contingencies; and that they are reporting these events accurately in the interview.

Research bearing on the capability to accurately observe and report one's own behavior can be found in the work done on the reliability of self-monitoring. Research by Lipinski and Nelson (1974) and Nelson, Lipinski and Black (1975) indicates that reliability of simple self-monitoring can be improved to acceptable levels when subjects are aware that their accuracy is being monitored. Reliability may also be kept at acceptable levels by reinforcing accurate self-observation (Bolstead & Johnson, 1972; Fixsen, Phillips & Wolf, 1972; Flowers, 1972; Lipinski, Black, Nelson & Ciminero, 1975; Risley & Hart, 1968). In this case the clinician would need an independent (or at least partially independent) source of information about the client's behavior. The clear implications of this research are that, although behavioral self-observations and reports may vary in their accuracy, an individual is frequently capable of accuracy if sufficiently motivated.

As discussed by Mahoney in Chapter 9, behavioral clinicians often ask their clients to monitor and record environmental events. Unfortunately, little research has been done on the accuracy of such reports. Research on the reliability of observational assessments done within a research context, however, is relevant to whether or not persons are capable of accurately observing and reporting the behavior of others in their environment. As with self-monitoring, the research suggests that, if persons are sufficiently trained and motivated, and if frequent reliability checks are made, they can accurately observe and report environmental events (e.g., Kent, O'Leary, Diament & Dietz, 1974).

Thus, the evidence does suggest that persons are capable of accurate observation and reporting of both their own behavior and that of others. It should be stressed, however, that, in the individual case, the clinician must assess not only the client's self- and environmental observation and reporting *capabilities* but also his/her accuracy in the *performance* of these tasks. There is considerable evidence that persons may not be naturally accurate (Mahoney & Thoresen, 1975). For the most part, accuracy is dependent on considerable training and adequate reinforcement contingencies. These issues are discussed in greater detail by both Nelson (Chapter 8) and Jones (Chapter 13).

Since the behavioral clinician is most often interested in the functional relationships between behavior patterns and behavioral-environmental events, it would seem that research bearing on a person's capability in observing and reporting such relationships is essential. The ability to provide this information would require not only accuracy in self and environmental observation, but also skill in selecting which events are most relevant to attend to and report. There is considerable evidence that persons frequently do not observe behavioral-environmental relationships and instead tend to report that behavior is a function of internal predispositions (Jones, Davis & Gergen, 1961).

Presumably, however, with training the motivated client would be able to accurately observe and report such relationships. Indeed, this is an underlying premise of the increasing number of books on self-directed behavior therapy (e.g., Watson & Tharp, 1972; Stuart, 1977). Sufficient research bearing on this issue has simply not been done.

*Threats to the Reliability and Validity of Verbal
Report Information*

Research on the factors influencing the reliability and validity of verbal reports has for the most part been carried out in the context of the research interview, as opposed to the clinical interview. Cannell and Kahn (1968) have extensively reviewed factors influencing invalidity of verbal reports in research interviews. They have categorized their findings under three major sources of invalidity: accessibility of information; cognitive factors; and motivational factors. Threats to the *accessibility of information* come from various sources. The person may simply forget the relevant information as a result of memory decay over time. Information not seen as salient or important may be forgotten, whereas events considered especially important may be accessible to the person because of aversiveness or potentially threatening content. The original possession or comprehension of the information may be limited. *Cognitive sources of invalidity* refer to such variables as clients' understanding of their role in the interview, and whether or not they adequately comprehend the questions of the interviewer. *Motivational variables* which decrease the accuracy of verbal reports include competing activities, clients' embarrassment at their ignorance, dislike of the content of the interview, and fears of the consequences of accurate reporting.

Factors which increase accuracy include liking of the interviewer, prestige of the research agency, and the person's self-label as a dutiful citizen. The research supporting each of these sources of invalidity is summarized by Cannell and Kahn and will not be described in detail here. (Mischel [1968] and Bellack and Hersen in Chapter 3 also summarize the data on the reliability and validity of self-reports, including those obtained verbally.) The extensive research on social desirability, demand characteristics (Orne, 1969), evaluation apprehension (Rosenthal, 1969), and impression management (e.g., Sherman, Trief & Sprafkin, 1975) also suggests a powerful influence of motivational variables on verbal reports.

Very little research of comparable rigor has been carried out to investigate the influence of these variables in clinical interviewing in general or behavioral interviewing specifically. An analysis of the sources of invalidity in the research interview, however, would seem to indicate that the same factors probably apply in the clinical context. A simple translation of some of the terms makes this comparison obvious. For example, both the prestige or status of the clinician and the client's motivation to be a dutiful client are probably related to accuracy in the clinical interview. Research on motivational and relationship factors in the clinical interview, however, has been primarily in terms of their effects on variables such as verbal productivity and fluency (e.g., Pope & Siegman, 1972; Siegman, 1976), client responsiveness (e.g., Pope, Nudler, Vonkorff & McGhee, 1974), self-disclosure (cf. Cozby, 1973) and other related variables. Accuracy of the verbal responses and self-disclosing statements has generally not been investigated.

It would be a mistake to conclude that, because these sources of invalidity exist, all information obtained in the clinical interview is necessarily invalid. Instead, these findings suggest under what circumstances the information is most likely to be inaccurate and under what circumstances it is likely to be fairly accurate. It seems reasonable to hypothesize that some of the factors conducive to accuracy are operating in the average clinical interview. For instance, it is probable that many clients enter the assessment interview with a strong desire to be a dutiful client. The popular literature would suggest that the cultural definition of a dutiful client includes the full and accurate reporting of relevant information about oneself. In addition, it seems reasonable to believe that, at least in those areas related to problems bringing the client to therapy, much of this information is highly salient and thus likely to be remembered. Even when events are not immediately accessible, the client may often be sufficiently motivated to search his/her memory, look through records or check with other people in an effort to retrieve the information. On the other hand, because of deficient observation or labeling of events when they occurred, even the most conscientious client may not have the necessary information available to report. A skillful interviewer may be able to reduce or eliminate other variables associated with inaccuracy, such as embarrassment and fear of the consequences. Unfortunately, these are empirical hypotheses which have not been subjected to experimental validation.

Hypotheses Testing within the Behavioral Interview

Even if nomothetic research is done to delineate the sources of invalidity in the behavioral interview, the accuracy of information given by any particular client is still an empirical question. Although what the client says about himself and his environment is often important in its own right, it is obviously necessary at times to check the report for accuracy. Several hypotheses must be tested, including the following:

1) Whether or not the client's verbal report is an accurate representation of his/her current construction of the events; i.e., whether the client is speaking honestly.

2) Whether or not the client's current construction of prior events is the same as his/her construction of the events while actually experiencing them. For instance, although a client may interpret and report a situation quite accurately and/or rationally during the interview, it is possible that when the client is actually in the situation his/her interpretations are inaccurate and/or irrational. This is an important consideration only insofar as the cognitive constuction of an event is seen as an important determinant of behavior.

3) Whether or not the client's report of events is an accurate and complete report of the events that did occur.

More often than not, the clinician simply assumes that the clients are honestly reporting their experiences. On occasion, however, this is probably not a safe assumption. For instance, court referred persons, children forced into therapy by their parents, and incarcerated adults given privileges for simply seeing the therapist may have little motivation to cooperate with the interviewer. In the final analysis, there is no way to verify whether the client is deliberately distorting events or not.

Some indirect evidence can be obtained by asking questions in different ways or at different times and checking for consistency. At times it might be possible to remove the external motivation for seeing the clinician and compare the client's verbal reports under both conditions. For instance, the author at one time did therapy with court referred adolescents. Although the clients had to show up for a certain number of sessions to avoid going to jail, they were told that they could bring books, etc. and sit in a lounge by themselves or with friends if they did not want to participate in therapy. The probation officer, of course, was told the client showed up for the session.

The clinician can also vary his/her own interview behavior to test whether or not the client's reports change accordingly. Verbal reinforcement, supportive statements, or confronting statements might influence the client's report. Unfortunately, it is difficult in these cases to know whether one is modifying the accuracy of the client's verbal report of his/her construction of the events, modifying his/her actual construction of the events, or modifying the recall of events.

Several methods might be employed within the interview to test whether or not the client's current construction of an event is the same as the construction of the event at the time it occurred. One way is to role-play the situation with the client and have the client report thoughts either at various points during the role-playing or immediately after. Psychodramatic role-playing techniques seem to be especially useful in helping the client realistically experience the situation. A second method is to have the client imagine the situation and report concurrent thoughts. Both of these methods can also be used to validate the client's report of how he/she actually responds in the situations. Such analogue measures of behavior are discussed by McFall in Chapter 5. At this point, it is sufficient to note that role-playing and imagination techniques can be important parts of the behavioral interview.

Reliability and Validity of Interview Based Behavioral Ratings

To date, no research has been done on the reliability and validity of behavioral analyses based on the interview. An enormous amount of research, however, has been done on the reliability and validity of behavioral ratings based on structured psychiatric interviews. Most of these instruments have been designed as measures of global behavioral functioning of psychiatric inpatients or as measures of specific syndromes of psychopathological behavior. The interview formats currently in use typically require the interviewer to rate the intensity and frequency, or the presence or absence of fairly discrete classes of behavior observed or reported during the interview and do not require inferences as to motivation, underlying dynamics, etc. They are thus most relevant to the first phase of the assessment process (identification of problem behaviors and specification of behavioral objectives).

In general, a remarkable degree of interrater reliability has been demonstrated for most of the instruments currently in use. For instance, excellent interrater reliabilities have been obtained for the Inpatient Multidimensional Psychiatric Scale (Lorr, Klett, McNair & Lasky, 1962; Lorr & Klett, 1966; Mariotto & Paul, 1974), the Minimal Social Behavior Scale (Farina, Arenberg, & Guskin, 1957; Lentz, Paul & Calhoun, 1971), and the Psychiatric Status Schedule (Spitzer, Endicott, Fleiss, Cohen, 1970). Test-retest reliabilities have ranged from good to moderate (e.g., Dinoff, Raymaker & Morris, 1962; Spitzer, et al., 1970).

Concurrent validity of the behavioral ratings ranges from fair to good when compared with other behavioral ratings and observational data. For instance, Lentz, Paul and Calhoun (1971) report correlations between .51 and .54 between the Minimal Social Behavior Scale and staff behavioral ratings. Mariotto and Paul (1974) report substantial concurrent validity for the Inpatient Multidimensional Psychiatric Scale when compared to ward ratings and observed frequency of behavior. Several of the factor scores converged with the actual observed frequencies of the component behaviors. In Chapter 12 Barlow reports moderate to high correlations between ratings of depression, using the Beck Depressive Inventory and the Hamilton Rating Scale, and direct observational data. Few other studies have been done to investigate the concurrent validity of behavioral rating scales compared to direct observational data collected on the same dimensions.

From the point of view of behavioral assessment, there are several problems with all of the above assessment procedures. As comprehensive assessment formats, they all have limited content validity. Each instrument focuses on pathological behavior and neglects measurement of behavioral competencies and assets. This is a serious shortcoming if the instruments are to be used for the development of a treatment plan. In addition, the instruments typically do not lead to specification of target behaviors in enough detail to be useful for the behavior therapist.

As methods of conducting a functional analysis, the formats are severely limited in that there is little emphasis given to assessment of environmental events, situation-specificity, or functional relationships. It is questionable whether any of the formats would allow the behavioral clinician to ascertain in any detail the variables controlling the problematic behavior. They do, however, allow a quantification of the severity of the client's problems in certain specified areas and as such might be valuable in developing treatment priorities.

Reactivity: An Ethical Dilemma

The behavioral interview, more than any other method of behavioral assessment, raises important ethical problems for the behavioral clinician. The problems stem in large part from the reactivity of the method and are apparent most in the influence of the interview process itself on the specification of the client's problems and determination of behavioral objectives. Although, as noted earlier, the function of clinical assessment is to determine what the client's problem behaviors are and how to change them for the better, it is clear that the very process of talking to a clinician influences not only how "better" is defined, but also which behaviors are defined as problematic. The interviewer cannot help but communicate his/her own values regarding which problems are most serious and which behaviors are most in need of change. The very process of detailed questioning and focusing on one area as opposed to another communicates to the client the values of the clinician. Certainly it is naive to believe that the behavioral clinician is somehow immune to this (cf. Thomas, 1973).

Another area of potential influence is in the determination of the variables controlling the problem behavior. Behaviorists have been quick to point out the ethical issues raised by positing the locus of controlling variables in some "inner state" and then proceeding to modify this more generic problem (Bandura, 1969). Less attention, however, has been paid to the ethical issues which may be involved in the identification of the controlling variable as a pattern of behaviors functionally related to the problem behavior rather than as an aspect of the environment. This issue is especially relevant in the area of cognitive-behavior modification where by judicial questioning the clinician can easily lead the client to believe that most of his/her problem behaviors are a function of faulty interpretations of the environment rather than of environmental events themselves. It would seem that this influence would be even more likely to occur when the clinician labels his/her own belief system as "rational" (as opposed to simply different and perhaps more functional). On the other hand, ethical problems can also be involved when the assessor focuses exclusively on environmental determinants of a problematic response. For example, in the case of a depressed spouse, an assessment that focuses on the problematic behaviors of the marital partner can lead to a therapy which will result in the termination of the marriage, an outcome which the client may have chosen not to risk had he/she had the option during the assessment.

Although the reactive effects of the interview cannot be eliminated, they can be reduced. Certainly, the emphasis on clearly and directly communicating one's values to the client is warranted (Davison & Stuart, 1975). What is less often attended to, at least among behavior therapists, is that this direct communication of values requires the clinician to accurately label his/her own values. In light of the fact that much of the influence process may be indirect, subtle, and not eliminated by simply stating one's values openly, accurate self-labeling of one's own values would seem useful also in helping the clinician identify those behavior patterns most likely to bias and influence the client. If nothing else, the clinician must be skilled in identifying these patterns in himself.

RESEARCH ISSUES

The paucity of research on behavioral interviewing is truly amazing, especially when one considers that one of the strongest criticisms leveled at traditional assessment approaches by behaviorists is that they rely on unreliable methods of data collection and intuitive judgments in arriving at diagnostic and treatment decisions.

The behaviorist's emphasis on direct behavioral sampling and empirical testing of diagnostic hypothesis does not seem to be a cogent reason for this absence of research, for the fact remains that many behaviorists advocate the use of both behavioral interviewing and seemingly subjective methods of data combination (e.g., Kanfer & Saslow, 1969; Bijou & Peterson, 1971; Goldfried & Davison, 1976). In clinical practice, as previously noted, the interview is widely used as a behavioral assessment technique. Though one might argue that this is simply because clinical practice has not caught up with clinical research, the advantages of interviewing seem to indicate that it is not a procedure to be lightly tossed out. What is needed at this point is a body of research to evaluate the circumstances under which the advantages of behavioral interviewing outweigh the risk and cost. In addition, research is needed to develop methods of improving the reliability and validity of both information gathering and hypothesis generation within the context of the behavioral interview.

A fair amount of research has been done on the psychometric properties of self-report methods utilizing paper-and-pencil procedures, but little research has been done on the reliability and validity of information collected by clinical interviews. Although the sources of invalidity have been heavily investigated in the context of the research interview (Cannell & Kahn, 1968), bridging research to relate these sources of invalidity to the clinical interview has not been done. It does not seem adequate at this point to simply assume that the same factors are operating, especially in the area of relationship variables and their influences on interview behaviors of clients vs. experimental subjects. What is lacking is a contingency analysis of verbal report, especially in the clinical context, and its relationship to the referents of verbal report.

Even if the accuracy of the information obtained in the interview can be verified for certain levels of relevant parameters, the questions of what type of information and how much should be obtained still remain. As noted previously, the various guides in existence differ in this respect. Research is needed to compare the reliability and validity of clinical decisions based on each of the various formats. Unfortunately this research depends on adequate specification and standardization of the interview guides. Work in this area is still to be done.

Research is also needed to develop behavioral assessment guides matched to specified client populations. Goldstein and Stein (1976) make a persuasive argument for the necessity of gathering data on client characteristics of various subgroups as an aid in deciding on appropriate intervention procedures. This same type of information would be useful in designing verbal assessment strategies. For instance, research on the communication styles, motivational sets, and cognitive expectations of various client subgroups approaching the initial interview might lead to the development of assessment formats, including prescriptive interviewer behavior patterns, matched to particular client populations. Although such research would of necessity be nomothetic, it would, nonetheless, be of use in making probabilistic statements about individual clients.

A final area of research deserving attention is the investigation of the process of clinical decision-making in the behavioral interview. At present, selection of content areas to explore, behavioral target selection, and decisions about whether to modify the behavior directly, modify the natural environment, or some combination of the two are more a matter of art than of science. What is needed is a scientific strategy to guide the assessor in making these decisions. It is doubtful, however, that such a strategy can be developed without a far better understanding of the complexities of behavior-behavior and behavior-environment interactions. As noted by Kanfer and Grimm (1975) in discussing problems in behavioral diagnosis, there is currently an urgent need for research that would identify behavioral patterns which are particularly unacceptable or absolutely required in various social settings. In the absence of this knowledge, target identification is frequently a function of the clinician's values or, at times, skills in interpreting the reinforcement contingencies in the client's multiple social environments.

CONCLUSION

Although interviewing is widely used by behaviorists, little or no empirical research has been done to investigate the reliability and validity of the behavioral interview as an assessment procedure. The advantages of the interview in gathering self-report data and in generating, clarifying, and testing certain hypotheses about client behavior and environmental contingencies suggest its continued use as one of several methods in a comprehensive clinical assessment. In the individual case, the interview can be effective as a broad-band assessment method. When used as the first step in a behavioral analysis, the interview focuses the clinician's attention on relevant aspects of the client's behavior and environment. Problems in the accuracy and precision of verbal report data, however, necessitate the addition of other methods (e.g., self-monitoring, naturalistic observation) of obtaining adequate information and verifying hypotheses about controlling variables.

Most attention is paid to the use of the interview as an initial assessment procedure. It can, however, be a valuable adjunct to other methods throughout both the assessment and the intervention process. Its use as a method of determining the salient aspects of the client's own behavior and environment as well as his/her cognitive interpretations of these events would suggest that other methods of assessment may be seriously impeded or needlessly complicated when the interview is not utilized.

Research is urgently needed both to standardize and compare various interview formats and to investigate the process of clinical decision-making in the behavioral assessment interview. Until this research is done, it is doubtful that the utility of the behavioral interview will be improved. Finally, the ethical problems associated with the reactivity of the interview are in need of further deliberation and discussion.

3

SELF-REPORT INVENTORIES IN BEHAVIORAL ASSESSMENT

ALAN S. BELLACK and MICHEL HERSEN

INTRODUCTION

Almost all approaches to psychological-behavioral assessment have periodically fallen in and out of favor. However, no strategy or procedure has had such a long and checkered history as the self-report (i.e., the direct, written or verbal, voluntary presentation by the subject). At varying times and for varying groups, the self-report has run the gamut from being the sole source of data to being almost totally devalued. It has always been recognized that the subject is a ready source of information about himself. The reliability and validity of information garnered by direct subject report have, however, invariably been controversial. Self-reports based on introspection were viewed by nineteenth-century structuralists (e.g., E. B. Titchener) and functionalists (e.g., William James) as the primary vehicle for understanding psychological functioning (Chaplin & Krawiec, 1960). John B. Watson, on the other hand, rejected introspection as a technique for scientific investigation and considered the self-report to be an inexact technique, to be used only for expediency (Chaplin & Krawiec, 1960).

The primary source of data collected by early psychoanalysts was self-report based on retrospection and free association. These reports were presumed to be reliable (i.e., replicable), but were viewed as invalid in the sense that they were (symbolic) distortions of actual function and experience. Nevertheless, by appropriate translation (i.e., interpretation) the assessor (psychoanalyst) could make effective use of the material. The projective testing movement was similarly based on the premise

52

that the subject would provide reliable data, but *could not* overtly report on or explain his actual experience. The projective test item (e.g., Rorschach or TAT card) was to be a neutral stimulus upon which the subject would "project" his unconscious drives, conflicts, etc. It should be noted that, for quite different reasons, both dynamic-analytic theory and modern behavioral approaches share the view that the overt content of self-reports does not provide an accurate picture of behavior or its determinants.

A quite different viewpoint flourished in the period from 1930 to 1960, promulgated by the group that might loosely be categorized as "trait theorists." Common to this orientation was a belief in the existence of broad, enduring personality structures or traits. An individual's trait pattern could be assessed by identifying his thoughts, attitudes, and feelings in any of a variety of situations. The most convenient way to gather these data was presumed to be standardized, paper-and-pencil instruments (personality inventories, scales, or questionnaires). Hundreds of such devices were constructed to assess specific traits, clusters of traits, or the total personality. A tacit assumption of this approach was that the testee could and would provide reliable and valid responses to test items. In the more sophisticated devices the possibility of some distortion was acknowledged. Therefore, psychometric controls for such factors as response styles, social desirability, and dissimulation were incorporated. However, the basic veracity and external validity of self-report responses were characteristically unquestioned. Faith in the utility of self-report was shared by the humanistic-phenomenological orientation. Allport, Maslow, and Rogers each emphasized assessment of the "self-system" and cognitive activity (thoughts, feelings, desires) that were available to awareness. As the focus of assessment was subjective experience, the use of self-reports (either in interview or inventory) was a necessary, as well as desired, approach.

Despite differences in the way in which self-report information is used, the theoretical orientations discussed thus far have placed great reliance on such data. In contrast, behavior modifiers have maintained a highly critical attitude about self-reports. Where self-report techniques have been incorporated, data have been viewed (à la Watson) with skepticism; these techniques are considered to be a poor alternative to more objective assessment. A number of factors have resulted in this orientation. Self-report data are subjective and reflect invisible (often hypothetical) processes, in contrast to the objective, overt data valued by behavior modifiers. This concern is interrelated with questions raised about external or criterion validity of self-report data. There is ample evidence to indicate that responses to traditional self-report devices are not highly correlated with overt behavior (see Mischel [1968] for a thorough, cogent discussion of the reliability and validity of traditional self-report assessment techniques). Campbell and Fiske (1959) pointed out that personality inventories characteristically correlate better with other inventories (regardless of the presumed focus of the inventory) than with external criteria (e.g., overt behavior).

The subjectivity of self-report responses in conjunction with low external validity of traditional inventories resulted in what may have been a premature rejection of self-report by many behavior modifiers. Recent emphasis on cognitive processes (Kanfer & Goldstein, 1975; Thoresen & Mahoney, 1974) has by necessity placed increased reliance on self-reports. It is also becoming more apparent that the three major response modalities (motoric, physiological, cognitive) function somewhat independently and that the motoric does not necessarily supersede the others (Hersen, 1973; Lang, 1971). In subsequent sections of this paper we will: 1) discuss general issues in the use of self-report responses; 2) provide some examples of self-report assessment; and 3) offer a schema for the use of self-reports.

Traditional conceptions of behavior have presumed that individuals made holistic (e.g., total organismic) responses to specific situations and that responses across situations were similar as a function of individual consistency (e.g., personality). Self-report inventories have almost invariably been developed in accord with this view and have subsequently been "invalidated" (e.g., Mischel, 1968) because they do not predict specific responses. Lack of demonstrated validity is not surprising, given the premise upon which the techniques are based and the uses to which they have been put. The situational specificity of behavior has been well documented (see Mischel, 1968). Attempts at finding cross-situational consistency with self-reports or any other means are unlikely to yield positive results. Of more relevance to behavior modification are recent findings that the direction and form of behavioral responses are not necessarily uniform *within* situations. The three primary response components (physiological, motoric, cognitive) do not act in concert in all individuals or within individuals across different situations (Borkovec, Weerts, & Bernstein, 1977; Hersen, 1973; Lang, 1971; Twentyman & McFall, 1975).

The definition and identification of response states (e.g., fear, depression, assertiveness) are confounded by the particular responses examined. For example, one subject might approach a snake, yet experience fearful cognitions and autonomic nervous system arousal, while a second subject avoids the snake, has fearful cognitions, but no autonomic nervous system arousal. Considering each response on a simple occurrence-nonoccurrence basis, there are eight possible combinations of the three responses. Given both situation and response specificity, it is not surprising that asking overall self-report questions (e.g., Are you afraid of snakes?) has not generated much meaningful information.

Self-report inventories *can* (potentially) be useful for two functions. The first is to gather data about motoric responses, physiological activity, and cognitions. Relevant questions include: How many hours per day do you work or sleep? Do your palms sweat or do you have shallowness of breath? Do you have suicidal or self-critical thoughts? These data are objective in that (given adequate definition), with the exception of the cognitions, they can be independently verified. The second function is to gather data about the individual's subjective experience or evaluation of the three primary response components. Relevant questions here include: Do you get enough sleep? Do you feel tense or anxious? Are you depressed or sad? The answers to the second set of questions are not necessarily related to actual experience (i.e., the answers to the first set of questions). They are a function of a number of subjective factors, including expectations, values, and cognitive sets. Historically, the two types of self-report data have been confused. Most inventories have asked *subjective* questions in an attempt to secure *objective* data about behavior. While the lack of correspondence between such self-report data and actual behavior has been recognized, the onus has been incorrectly placed on the self-report response modality rather than on the specific assessment procedures that have been used.

There are several factors other than the source of data (i.e., written or verbal report by the subject) that could lead to a lack of correspondence between report and criterion. The importance of the form of questions asked has already been mentioned. The wording of the test items is subject to interpretation by the testee (Cronbach, 1960). Terms such as anxious, depressed, afraid, assertive, and shy are all relative. The degree of distress sufficient to qualify as depression, as well as the response elements that are considered to be depression rather than anger or anxiety, will vary from subject to subject. The less specific and concrete the wording, the greater the probability of idiosyncratic translation of what the question is asking or what the response choices infer. The so-called "Barnum Effect," the acceptance of broad, nondescript personality descriptions, reflects the latitude of interpretation possible

(Dmitruk, Collins & Clinger, 1973; Ulrich, Stachnik & Stainton, 1963).

Verbal qualifications of degree or frequency (i.e., Likert-type scaling) are helpful in placing a restraint on responses, but still allow considerable margin for subjectivity. Simpson (1944), as reported by Cronbach (1960), found that 25% of students ascribed the term "usually" only to events occurring at least 90% of the time, 50% applied the term to events occurring between 70% and 90% of the time, and another 25% applied it to events occurring less than 70% of the time. Similar variability was found for other common frequency terms, including "often," "sometimes," "seldom," and "rarely."

Questions must be written with explicitly defined terms and with discrete, objective (e.g., quantitative) response choices if accurate responses are to be secured. The following questions will all secure different information: Do you go out on dates often? How often do you go out on dates? How many dates have you had in the past month? Furthermore, the definition of the term "date" is variable enough (e.g., Curran & Gilbert, in press) that the last question is not necessarily equivalent to: How many prearranged social interactions have you had in the past month in which you invited out (or were invited out by) a woman (or man)?

Appropriate structuring of questions is a necessary, but not sufficient, condition for securing externally valid data. The information requested must be available to the subject. That is, the subject must have originally observed his behavior and be able to recall it accurately in response to the question. Whether or not either accurate observation or accurate recall occurs on a regular basis is conjectural. Observation, information storage, and recall are all subject to distortion. There is ample evidence to suggest that even ongoing self-monitoring (SM) yields unreliable and inaccurate data (Kazdin, 1974c; Lipinski & Nelson, 1974). Given that SM is typically presumed to provide more accurate information than recollection, the accuracy of self-report inventory responses must be suspect. In discussing accuracy of observation and recall, distinctions should be made among the kinds of information requested. Quantitative reports (especially of high frequency behaviors), such as reports of the number of cigarettes smoked or the amount of food eaten, are not likely to be highly accurate. Nonquantitative statements (e.g., "I panic whenever I see a dog running loose," or "I have suicidal thoughts") and reports of low or zero frequency responses (e.g., "I have never had sexual intercourse," or "I cry two or three times a week") are much more likely to be accurate.

A final issue in regard to the use of self-reports for securing externally valid data pertains to the use of test responses for idiographic, as opposed to nomothetic, purposes. It is entirely possible that answers to individual questions are valid while summative scores and grouped data do not correlate significantly with external criteria. Overall scores are statistical abstractions that presumably represent general trends and tendencies. *Regardless of the terminology selected, the use of an overall score to predict or summarize typical behavior is a trait conception.* As discussed previously, the use of trait descriptive scores should not be expected to predict (relate to) specific response patterns in specific situations. It is usually more appropriate to examine the responses to specific questions individually or in clusters. For example, the clinical uses of the Fear Survey Schedule (Borkovec et al., 1977) and Reinforcement Survey Schedule (Bellack & Schwartz, 1976) involve identification and examination of individual fear and reinforcement patterns respectively, rather than overall fearfulness and reinforcibility scores.

This recommendation is a direct contradiction to a substantial body of test construction literature, in which individual questions are entirely subservient to full scale scores. The MMPI is the most representative example of this (criterion keying) approach. It is predicated on the notion that individuals with similar overall scores (or patterns) will behave similarly, regardless of the responses to individual questions (Anastasi, 1961). However, the MMPI is more effective for predicting traditional diagnostic labels than specific behaviors. It is unlikely that any attempt at prediction by matching (or rating) overall scores will be effective unless the test items are sufficiently specific to preclude interpretation and are closely related to the criterion. For example, consider two subjects with high scores on the Social Avoidance and Distress Scale (Watson & Friend, 1969), a self-report test of interpersonal anxiety. Subject A has adequate social skills but has a conditioned anxiety response to social situations. Subject B also has a conditioned anxiety response, but in addition has a social skill deficit. Scores for both subjects might well correlate with their scores on other paper-and-pencil social anxiety inventories. If, however, the criteria were a set of overt behavioral measures rated from videotapes of a role-playing test, such as the Social Behavior Situations (Twentyman & McFall, 1975), the results for the two subjects would be quite different (Hersen & Bellack, 1977).

In our discussion thus far, we have emphasized *external validity.* Our focus has been on the relationship between self-reports and objective, external criteria. In that context, a self-report is valid or invalid based on the degree to which reports correspond with actual responses. When the target of assessment is the subjective experience of the actual subject, self-report responses are *ipso facto* valid (except in those instances where intentional distortion occurs). Eble (1961) pointed out that all reliable tests are valid, as they are measures of themselves (i.e., the subject's response to test items). The test user must determine whether the test is valid for his criterion of interest. A subject reporting distress (e.g., anxiety, fear, depression, etc.) can be presumed to be *experiencing* distress regardless of his actual motoric, autonomic, and cognitive responses. It should be noted that while subjective responses involve cognitions, they are discrete from the cognitions associated with most target behaviors. Dollard and Miller (1950) argued that cognitions can be both responses to and stimuli for other cognitions. Self-critical, suicidal, and ruminative thoughts are just as subject to interpretation, evaluation, and affective reactions as are motoric and physiologic responses.

The *validity* of the subjective response must be distinguished from its *utility* (i.e., what the tester can do with the data). Test items can be constructed so as to increase utility by attending to many of the same issues discussed above in relation to increasing validity. Generally, the greater the specificity of the questions (e.g., When and where do you feel depressed?) and the greater the extent of quantification (e.g., On a scale of 1-7, how fearful are you?), the more meaning and generality the response is likely to have.

SELF-ASSESSMENT OF FEAR (THE FEAR SURVEY SCHEDULE)

Of all aspects of behavioral dysfunction, fear has probably been the most widely studied by behavior modifiers. It is one of the most common forms of psychological distress, and has been highly amenable to behavioral analysis and treatment. Fear is usually conceptualized as an aversive emotional state which occurs in conjunction with some specific stimulus class (e.g., snakes, airplanes, crowds). While there are presumed to be motoric and physiological components to the fear response, the subjective experience of fear is central to the response. Self-report, therefore, is a major approach to assessment.

Although methods for obtaining self-reports of fear were employed prior to the formal development of fear survey schedules (e.g., Akutagawa, 1956; Dixon, de Monchaux & Sandler, 1957; Walk, 1956), following Lang and Lazovik's (1963) paper in which the first reference was made to a fear survey schedule (FSS-I), greater concern with the psychometric properties of such self-assessment schedules appeared. The FSS-I was developed along the lines suggested by Akutagawa (1956) and included a list of 50 common fears that were presented in a seven-point Likert scale format. Shortly after the publication of this scale, the FSS-II (Geer, 1965) and the FSS-III (Wolpe & Lang, 1964) were constructed. Even though many items in these two scales are similar, a primary difference between the two schedules is that the FSS-II is an empirically-derived instrument while the FSS-III has its origins in the clinic.

Over the last 10 years many other fear survey schedules have been developed. Some of these involve extensions of preexisting schedules (e.g., Gulas, McClanahan & Poetter, 1975; Manosevitz & Lanyon, 1965), others involve factor analytic studies of an initially unpublished schedule developed by Lang (e.g., Lawlis, 1971; Rubin, Lawlis, Tasto & Namenek, 1969), and still others involve compilations of previous schedules with overlapping items omitted (e.g., Braun & Reynolds, 1969).

Numerous studies concerned with aspects of the self-assessment of fear have been conducted (see Hersen [1973], for a comprehensive review), with the following issues considered: 1) sex differences in responding; 2) population differences (college and inpatient); 3) reliability (test-retest and internal consistency); 4) relationship of fear survey schedules to other personality inventories; 5) relationship of fear survey schedules to other indices of fear (i.e., motoric, physiological); and 6) the factorial structure of the fear survey schedule. Despite the fact that several years have elapsed since Hersen's (1973) initial review of the field, the major points raised in his paper are still germaine as the "state of the art" has not changed radically. In that initial review the following conclusions were reached:

> The need for long-term reliability studies for different population samples tapping a variety of age groups is indicated. Needless duplication of measurement is apparent, and the validation of shortened schedules based on factorial analyses is warranted. Conflicting evidence is presented as to the predictive validity of fear schedules when overt indices of fear are used as criteria. The fear construct is examined in terms of its tripartite structure (verbal, motor, physiological), and questions are raised as to which of the components is to be utilized as the criterion measure (Hersen, 1973, p. 241).

Inasmuch as the issues of reliability, population differences, and factorial validation are rather straightforward, we will focus our attention here on the criterion question. Certainly, the clinical and philosophical implications as to how the verbal report is to be treated are of considerable significance. Specifically, we will be concerned with the relationship of self-reports of fear to overt motoric indices (e.g., approach and avoidance tasks) and physiological measurement. What are some of the factors influencing the subject's verbal report of fear? In that sense, are there important differences in the self-assessment of fear in analogue research, in the single case experimental research context, and in the consulting room practice situation? Finally, in consideration of the aforementioned, what status should we accord to a self-report of intense fear? In our attempt to respond to these questions, we will examine in some detail a few representative investigations.

A low relationship between the self-assessment of fear and actual behavior in a behavioral avoidance test situation was documented by Lang (1968). During the course of selecting college subjects for studies in systematic desensitization, those reporting maximally intense fear of snakes on a three-point scale were further evaluated with respect to more stringent criteria (i.e., questions concerning avoidance of crossing open fields and going camping, physiological responses such as sweating and increased heart rate when confronted with a snake) in an individual interview. For every 100 subjects who rated themselves as intensely snake fearful, only about 20 met these more stringent interview determined criteria (this finding lends support to the notion presented in the Introduction to this Chapter, that greater specificity of questions may result in increased validity of self-reports). Finally, after identifying a relatively homogeneous group of subjects who met these additional criteria, the experimenter exposed them to the behavioral avoidance test procedure requiring their approach to a harmless snake. A —.26 correlation was found between overt behavior and ratings of snake fear on the FSS.

Cooke (1966) obtained a .35 correlation between a response of "very much afraid of laboratory rats" on an FSS and a look-touch-and-hold step of an actual approach task for a group of female undergraduates. The correlation obtained between the approach task and the total score on this FSS was even lower ($r=.04$). Lanyon and Manosevitz (1966) divided subjects afraid of spiders into mild-, moderate-, and intense-fear categories, but found no significant differences on the basis of their behavior in an approach task. Geer (1965) conducted a number of validation studies for the FSS-III by contrasting the overt behavior of high-, medium-, and low-fear college subjects on behavioral approach tasks. In one study, male and female subjects were required to approach a small female German shepherd dog. Although latency and distance measures discriminated among the high-, medium-, and low-fear female subjects, these measures failed to differentiate the male subjects. Indeed, *all* of the males touched the dog. In addition to these studies, low correlations between verbal and motoric measures of fear have been reported by Schroeder and Craine (1971).

In accounting for the apparent verbal-motor discrepancy in the aforementioned studies (particularly Geer's [1965] male subjects), one is tempted to invoke the likely effects of social desirability as an explanatory factor. For example, in our society it is definitely not a socially desirable response for college males to show fear of an apparently tame, albeit large, dog. However, in two studies (Farley & Mealiea, 1971; Geer, 1965), correlations between social desirability scales and fear survey schedules for both male and female college subjects have not exceeded .268. Even though this correlation was statistically significant, the total FSS variance accounted for by the social desirability variable is minimal.

Naturally, results based on the use of yet another self-report instrument (a social desirability scale) are, of course, subject to the same limitations found in all self-report data. These obvious limitations, however, have been overcome by Bernstein and his colleagues (Bernstein, 1973, 1974; Bernstein & Nietzel, 1973, 1974; Bernstein & Paul, 1971; Miller & Bernstein, 1972), who have systematically evaluated the effects of contextual variables (e.g., experimental demand conditions, repeated approach in the avoidance task), with respect to actual approach behavior in high-fearful subjects. In one study (Bernstein & Nietzel, 1974), the results clearly indicated that allowing the subject only one trial in a behavioral avoidance test may not be fully adequate for assessment purposes, particularly as approach behavior *was* significantly greater in a second trial.

The effects of trials and experimental demand characteristics were recently examined by Bernstein (1974). Five groups of 15 snake-fearful female college subjects were exposed to a behavioral avoidance test situation involving a live but harmless four-foot King snake. Four of the groups first received low demand instructions followed by high demand instructions. Conversely, the fifth group received high demand instructions followed by low demand instructions. The results indicated that, "subjects in the demand-increase groups showed significant increases in approach at the second behavior avoidance test, while subjects in the demand-decrease group showed significant reduction in approach" (Bernstein, 1974, p. 896). With this study exemplifying some of the complicating issues, the seemingly simple relationship between a self-report of fear and a motoric index of fear cannot be taken for granted without further consideration of the contextual covariates. Thus, when reexamined in this light, many of the relatively low correlations found between self-report and other indices of fear can be better understood. It is quite possible that if such covariates were included in the statistical analyses, the resulting correlations between self-report and motor behavior might be higher.

An additional consideration that merits further attention when examining the relationship of self-reports and motoric indices of fear is the relevance of the fear being measured for a particular individual or group of individuals. For example, although the recent release of the motion picture *Jaws* has attuned us all to the dangers of sharks attendant with swimming in the ocean, for those of us who live inland (e.g., Pittsburgh) and do not frequent the coastline for our vacations, a fear of sharks is obviously less relevant. Similarly, despite the fact that snake-fearful subjects used in analogue studies may indeed acknowledge their fears when filling our fear survey schedules, for the majority of these subjects (many of whom may have never seen a live snake), the relevance of this fear is not great (unless, of course, they live in a snake-infested area). (See Borkovec, Stone, O'Brien & Kaloupek, 1974; Cooper, Furst & Bridger, 1969, for interesting discussion of the selection of relevant targets for study in analogue research.) Therefore, we would expect the relationship between verbal and motor indices of fear to be greater when the fear under study has increased significance for the subject or subject population. Let us consider some studies in light of the above.

Walk (1956) correlated self-reports of airborne trainees with actual performance in a parachute jump from a high tower. When comparing those trainees who passed and failed the course in parachute jumping, the data indicated that low-fear ratings were related to: 1) achieving correct jumping techniques earlier in training; and 2) success in passing the course. Geer (1966a) divided college subjects into high- and low-fear of public speaking groups and required his subjects to speak extemporaneously for several minutes. The results showed that the two groups were differentiated on a number of formal speech characteristics. High-fear subjects spoke more slowly, evidenced more speech disruptions, and exhibited lengthier silences than their low-fear counterparts. In a subsequent study, Geer (1966b) divided low- and high-fear spider subjects (female) into separate groups and found that for the experimentals who viewed a slide depicting a spider, the highs evidenced greater GSR responding than the lows. On the other hand, Fazio (1969), in a related study, found that self-assessment of spider fear on an FSS by female college subjects accounted for only 25% of the performance variance on a behavioral avoidance test procedure.

Another factor contributing to the degree of correlation between verbal and motor indices of fear is the population (i.e., "normal" versus "clinical") being studied in analogue research. For example, differences in correlation magnitude between "normals" and "schizophrenics" have been examined in two studies (Begelman & Hersen, 1973; Cowden, Reynolds, & Ford, 1961). Cowden et al. (1961) administered a fear questionnaire to 158 chronic schizophrenics and 78 tuberculosis patients. Of these patients, 31 of the schizophrenics and 12 of the tuberculosis patients indicated fear of snakes. These subjects were then exposed to a live Black snake in a behavioral avoidance test situation scored on a 17-point scale. In this situation only four of the 31 schizophrenics displayed any fear, whereas 10 of the 12 tuberculosis patients refused to either approach or touch the snake. The —.54 correlation obtained between self-report and approach behavior for the schizophrenics was interpreted as reflecting the "affect-thought 'split' in schizophrenia." Begelman and Hersen (1973) replicated part of the Cowden et al. (1961) study but, in addition, required both schizophrenics and normals to fill out a second fear estimate of snakes. The results in this study indicated that schizophrenics revised their fear ratings consistent with their approach performance in the behavioral test (pre-FSS-Approach Task, $r=.06$; Approach Task-post-FSS, $r=.40$). By contrast, normal subjects evidenced consistency from pre- to post-FSS ratings (pre-FSS-Approach Task, $r=.73$; Approach Task-post-FSS, $r=.72$). Begelman and Hersen (1973) challenge the Cowden et al. interpretation of an affect-thought split by arguing, "that the verbal performance is a criterion of a different psychological variable. It is a criterion of a S's belief that he has a fearful attitude. Whether he does will be clarified for him, as well as others, in light of how he behaves motorically" (p. 179). Thus, the verbal report here is definitely not eschewed but is viewed as representing a unique form of information. In any event, both the Cowden et al. (1961) and Begelman and Hersen (1973) studies point toward greater concordance between verbal and motor response systems in normals than in schizophrenics. Further work is obviously needed with respect to such possible discrepancies in other clinical groupings.

A final issue contributing to the criterial status of a verbal report of fear relates to the nature of the assessment situation (i.e., assessment in a clinical setting, assessment for a clinical-research project, or assessment for an analogue study). There is no doubt that the status of the verbal report of a clinically phobic patient who consents to experimental behavioral treatment in an Isaac Marks-type study (e.g., Boulougouris, Marks, & Marset, 1971; Marks, Boulougouris, & Marset, 1971) is not the same as the undergraduate subject (perhaps mildly snake fearful) who partakes in academic research (i.e., the analogue study). Hersen (1973) previously noted that "a distinction should be made with respect to assessment and modification of fear in experimental and clinical contexts. In contrast to the analogue situation, patients' reports of subjective experiences in a clinical setting are more likely to be accorded criterial status. This is certainly the case in the imaginal variety of systematic desensitization. Verbalizations of discomfort from distressed patients cannot be discounted either for clinical, ethical, or moral reasons" (p. 255).

Although the above would appear to be a given, there are few data comparing the relationship of the three response systems (cognitive, motoric, physiological) in populations seeking treatment for their fears with this relationship in less pathological populations who are selected (i.e., college students) for analogue treatment investigations. However, there is one carefully conducted clinical study by Leitenberg, Agras, Butz and Wincze (1971) in which the three response systems were monitored concurrently in five of nine patients being treated experimentally for their phobias. The relationships among self-report ratings, motor behaviors, and heart rate measures were complicated. Motoric indices of fear in the five patients decreased during treatment. Concurrent decreases in self-reports of anxiety-fear were obtained in four of the five patients. Moreover, it should be noted that decreases in anxiety-fear ratings were obtained irrespective of changes (no change, decrease, or increase) in the physiological measure (heart rate). If the results of this study are representative of degrees of relationships between verbal and motoric indices and verbal and physiological indices of fear in a clinical population, then, as in the case of the analogue subject, it would appear that many factors are probably contributing to the magnitude of the correlation. The covariates contributing to or limiting these relationships warrant careful study. Further commentary on the interrelationships of the three response systems will appear in the Conclusions section.

SELF-ASSESSMENT OF ANXIETY

Anxiety has been one of the most pervasive of psychological constructs, stimulating extensive amounts of clinical, theoretical, and empirical interest. Paradoxically, there is little agreement about how it should be defined (i.e., what exactly it is). There is some consensus, however, that anxiety is an aversive affective state involving anticipation of danger. As such, it has frequently been considered to be indistinguishable from fear (e.g., Borkovec et al., in press). However, most theorists distinguish the two constructs on one or two bases. First, fear is presumed to have a definite referent (e.g., fear of dogs, snakes, or airplane travel) while anxiety is considered to involve a nonspecific, diffuse threat or dread. The second factor involves the course of action stimulated by the aversive emotion: Fear is associated with flight or avoidance, while anxiety, having no explicit referent, has no specific motor element (e.g., there is nothing specific to avoid).

Despite a number of specific areas of disagreement, theorists holding the non-specific threat conception of anxiety almost invariably agree that it is an emotional reaction whose primary manifestation is phenomenological distress which may (or may not) be accompanied by (or stimulated by) physiological arousal. Motor responses (e.g., fidgeting, postural rigidity, speech disturbances) and performance disruptions are considered to be secondary manifestations. It follows that if the subjective experience of distress is central to anxiety, then self-reports are necessarily the primary assessment vehicle. Spielberger (1972) states that "in essence, if an individual reports that he feels anxious (frightened or apprehensive), this introspective report defines an anxiety state" (p. 30). This definitional restriction to the subjective state implies that motor responses (and autonomic nervous system arousal) are not legitimate criteria for the validation of anxiety assessment devices. (This does not mean that there could not be motoric and autonomic correlates of anxiety or that the construct would be useful in the absence of such correlates.)

Anxiety scales and inventories can be placed in one of three major categories, reflecting different aspects or types of anxiety: 1) measures of trait anxiety; 2) measures of state anxiety; or 3) measures of situation-specific anxiety (e.g., test anxiety, speech anxiety). *Trait anxiety* refers to a general and stable disposition to *become* anxious (Spielberger, 1972). Individuals with high trait anxiety are presumed to become anxious easily and intensely to a wide range of stimuli. Trait anxiety inventories such as the Manifest Anxiety Scale (Taylor, 1953) and State-Trait Anxiety Inventory, Trait form (Spielberger, Gorsuch & Lushene, 1970) ask subjects how they typically feel and/or how they typically respond in a variety of situations. Degree of anxiety is reflected by an overall score.

The characteristic validity studies have examined correlations between trait anxiety scales (which are generally high), and compared susceptibility to stress of individuals scoring high and low on these scales. The latter form of study has involved evaluation of performance on motor and cognitive tasks (high stress should interfere with performance), and self-report of distress under laboratory stress and nonstress conditions (e.g., "ego-involving" instructions, threat of electric shock). Summarizing research on trait anxiety instruments, Sarason (1960) and Spielberger (1972) draw two similar conclusions: 1) These instruments essentially measure fear of failure and concern about one's adequacy; and 2) even for individuals with high "trait anxiety," the arousal of anxiety is primarily a function of the particular stressor or situation.

Endler and his associates (Endler, Hunt & Rosenstein, 1962; Endler & Okada, 1975) have responded to the situational specificity of anxiety responses by developing a multidimensional test of trait anxiety—the S-R Inventory of General Trait Anxiousness. The S-R Inventory assesses anxiety in four general types of situations: 1) interpersonal; 2) physical danger; 3) ambiguous or novel situations; and 4) routine, innocuous situations. Each situation is rated on the degree to which it is typically accompanied by each of nine response modalities (e.g., perspire, feel tense). While adequate validation has not yet been accomplished, this format appears to be more promising than the general, unidimensional scale approach.

State anxiety is conceptualized as a transitory anxiety response which is situationally determined and can vary from moment to moment (Endler & Okada, 1975; Spielberger, 1972). While high trait anxious individuals are expected to have a high threshold for state anxiety, assessment of the two forms of anxiety is independent. Numerous state anxiety scales have been developed, the most popular of which are the State-Trait Anxiety Inventory, State form (Spielberger, Gorsuch & Lushene, 1970) and the Affect Adjective Check List, Today form (Zuckerman, 1960). These instruments parallel the associated trait scales, but ask subjects how they feel right at the moment or how they felt at some immediately preceding point, rather than how they generally feel. The various versions characteristically correlate highly with one another, and scores are generally higher during (externally defined) stress situations than during neutral situations. As discussed above in relation to fear scales, the possibility of bias due to expectancy and demand characteristics in this type of validation study tempers conclusions that can be drawn. However, the psychometric adequacy of these devices suggests that when bias is controlled or unlikely (as in clinical application), they should provide satisfactory data.

The third general approach to anxiety assessment has been the development of *situation-specific* devices. Examples include the Test Anxiety Questionnaire (Mandler & Sarason, 1952) for examination anxiety, and the Fear of Negative Evaluation Scale and Social Avoidance and Distress Scale (Watson & Friend, 1969) for interpersonal anxiety. This situational approach to anxiety assessment borders on what is frequently considered to be fear assessment (i.e., a specific focus and a relatively specific course of action). As such, discussion pertaining to fear inventories is directly relevant to the evaluation of these devices. Hersen and Bellack (1977) reviewed the profusion of self-report scales that have been constructed to assess interpersonal anxiety. They reported that most of these devices are correlated with one another and are negatively correlated with self-reports of dating frequency (e.g., social activity). These scales also reflect anxiety reduction after the application of a variey of behavioral treatments, including systematic desensitization and social skills training. However, they do not consistently correlate with either physiological arousal in role-played interpersonal interactions or with any of a variety of behavioral components of interpersonal skill. Hersen and Bellack (in press) also reported that most of these scales were constructed for particular studies on the basis of face validity. Insufficient attention has been paid to psychometric considerations and reliabilities are often inadequate.

The relationship (or lack thereof) of anxiety scale scores to physiological arousal warrants further comment here. There have been a vast number of attempts to uncover a relationship between these two response modalities with no consistent findings (Borkovec et al., in press; Sarason, 1960). The results of most of these studies can be accounted for on the basis of methodological flaws. One notable error has been the measurement of single, non-individualized autonomic channels (e.g., measurement of skin resistance or heart rate alone for all subjects). Both individual response stereotypy and the complexity of the autonomic response process make it unlikely that such a universal and unipolar approach will reveal a general, meaningful relationship. Lack of correspondence between self-report and physiological measures in a study employing this approach might reflect the recording of inappropriate processes rather than the absence of associated physiological activity.

However, it might well be that no uniform and consistent relationship exists between the physiological and cognitive channels. The assumption that there is a relationship is based on the theoretical basis of the emotion construct, not on explicit data. Lang (1971) questions this assumption, stating, ". . . it is possible and even usual to generate emotional cognitions without autonomic arousal, aggressive behavior without a hostile motive, or the autonomic and avoidant behavior of fear without insight (proper labeling)" (p. 108). Any significant intermodality correspondence might be a situation-specific or subject-specific phenomenon, rather than a fundamental, necessary aspect of behavior.

SELF-ASSESSMENT OF SOCIAL SKILL (ASSERTIVENESS)

One of the most significant contributions of behavior modification has been the recognition of behavioral deficits as a major contributor to behavioral dysfunction. One of the primary areas of deficit involves social skills. Hersen and Bellack (in press) define social skill as the ability to express positive and negative feelings in interpersonal situations without loss of social reinforcement. Social skill involves the coordinated delivery of both verbal and nonverbal response components, and is demonstrated in a variety of interpersonal contexts. The most widely investigated of those contexts are assertion and heterosexual (dating) skills.

Social skills or assertiveness training has become a major focus of interest over the past several years (see Hersen, Eisler & Miller, 1973). As research and clinical application in this area have proliferated, interest in and the need for effective assessment devices have grown. Patient reports of low ability and discomfort in situations requiring assertion have been a primary source of data. Hersen and Bellack (in press), reviewing the assessment literature for social skills, describe 10 self-report scales that have been developed since 1966. Representative examples of inventories applicable for college populations include the College Self-Expression Scale (Galassi, DeLo, Galassi & Bastien, 1974), the Conflict Resolution Inventory (McFall & Lillesand, 1971), and the Rathus Assertiveness Schedule (Rathus, 1973). The Interpersonal Situation Inventory (Goldsmith & McFall, 1975) and the Wolpe-Lazarus Assertiveness Scale (Wolpe & Lazarus, 1966) have been developed for use with psychiatric populations (the Wolpe-Lazarus Scale has also been used with college populations).

Most of these scales were developed with at least moderate attention to psychometric requirements. Reliabilities are characteristically satisfactory. At this point, the area and scales are relatively new. Therefore, in many instances validity data have not been collected. This problem is compounded by the fact that most of the scales have been developed for specific research projects and have not been widely used. However, such data that have been collected are quite promising. In contrast to the data for fear and anxiety, there *does* appear to be a notable relationship between scores on these inventories and motor responses. Eisler, Miller and Hersen (1973) and Eisler, Hersen, Miller and Blanchard (1975) found that psychiatric patients rated high and low on behavioral components of assertion differed significantly on the Wolpe-Lazarus scale. McFall and Lillesand (1971) found significant correlations between scores on the Conflict Resolution Inventory and ratings of performance on a behavioral task. Rathus (1973) reported similar findings for the Rathus Assertiveness Schedule.

While these data are at variance with results for other types of self-reports, they are not entirely surprising. Assertiveness inventories (for the most part) require subjects to indicate whether or not (or the degree to which) they would be likely to engage in relatively specific behaviors. Examples of these questions include: "Do you ignore it when someone pushes in front of you in line?" (College Self-expression Scale); "When the food served at a restaurant is not done to my satisfaction, I complain about it to the waiter or waitress" (Rathus Assertiveness Schedule); "If after leaving a shop you notice that you have been given the wrong change, do you go back and point out the mistake?" (Wolpe-Lazarus Assertiveness Scale).

In contrast, the State-Trait Anxiety Scale (Spielberger et al., 1970) asks subjects to report the degree to which they usually (or at the moment for State version) experience a variety of *feelings*. Subjects respond to items including: "I feel calm," "I feel upset," "I am jittery." Questions on both types of inventories reflect the subjects' *beliefs* about their experience. However, assertive inventories secure beliefs about *behaviors* in specified *situations*. As discussed earlier, for two reasons responses to this type of question should be more closely related to what the subject actually does than responses to general questions about how he feels: 1) the questions refer more directly to the criterion (e.g., behavior); and 2) questions are relatively specific and therefore should be less distorted by general attitudes and beliefs.

In evaluating the current status of self-report scales for assertiveness, Hersen and Bellack (1977) raise a number of issues. 1) The scales result in overall assertiveness scores. Behavioral data (e.g., Eisler, Hersen, Miller & Blanchard, 1975) suggest that "assertiveness" consists of a number of component behaviors that are relatively independent and that assertive skill varies across situations. It would, therefore, be desirable to secure subscale or factor scores on self-report devices reflecting relevant behavioral and situational parameters. (These scores would be useful for preliminary screening purposes and in research rather than for idiographic, clinical assessment. They are convenient summaries, and do not represent trait or construct measures.) 2) Scale reliabilities evaluated thus far have been essentially short-term. Long-term reliability should be determined. 3) The relationship between self-report and motor responses described above pertains to overall scale scores and behavioral ratings of overall assertiveness. The relationship between self-report and motor responses should be increased if more specific data are collected. The relationship between factor scores (as discussed in point 1 above), component behaviors and specific situations should be examined. 4) Normative data for both males and females should be collected and sex differences, if any, analyzed. 5) The emphasis, to this point, has been predominantly on "hostile" or negative assertion. Considerably more attention should be devoted to assessment of positive or "commendatory" assertion. Separate scoring and development of norms for the two facets of behavior appear warranted. 6) Finally, the relationship between an individual's subjective evaluation or feelings about his skill level and the response to treatment should be explored. That is, subjective report might relate to treatment outcome regardless of its relationship to motoric and physiological components of skill.

SELF-ASSESSMENT OF DEPRESSION

Since depression is one of the most ubiquitous complaints presented to mental health practitioners, it is of particular importance that behaviorists have a good grasp of both the major manifestations and the more subtle nuances of the disorder. In a recent review (Pacoe, Himmelhoch, Hersen & Guyett, 1975), differentiation among the classifications of depression (e.g., unipolar, bipolar, neurotic-psychotic, endogenous-exogenous) has been documented. However, despite the within-classification differences, depression as a behavioral disorder is characterized by dysphoric mood, frequently accompanied by motoric changes (e.g., psychomotor retardation) and physiological concomitants (e.g., sleep loss, weight loss, loss of sexual drive, loss of appetite). All of these manifestations of depression can be assessed using the client's or patient's self-report.

As numerous self-assessment inventories have been developed for evaluating levels of depression in clients and patients, in this section we will very briefly review four instruments (Beck Depression Inventory, Lubin's Depression Adjective Check Lists, Zung Self-Rating Depression Scale, and Lewinsohn's Pleasant Events Schedule), the first three of which have been used extensively in treatment outcome research. These schedules will be examined in light of some basic psychometric properties. Inasmuch as the Pleasant Events Schedule (Lewinsohn & Graf, 1973; Lewinsohn & Libet, 1972; MacPhillamy & Lewinsohn, 1974) was developed specifically during the course of behavioral research on depression, we will focus our discussion on this instrument. Suggestions for further refinement and validation of this schedule will be offered. As in the study of fear, particular concern will be directed toward the relationship of self-reports of depression and actual behavioral measurement of depressive features (i.e., the relationship of motor activity, smiling, and talking in depressed patients to self-reports of depression—see Williams, Barlow & Agras [1972]). The possibility of evaluating motoric activity in *clinically* depressed patients with telemetric recordings (e.g., Foster & Kupfer, 1973) and correlating such findings with self-report data during various phases of either behavioral or biological treatments will be explored.

The Beck Depression Inventory is a 21-item self-report inventory consisting of four alternative statements which are scored on a 0-3 basis for severity. It was originally standardized on a sample of 598 psychiatric in- and outpatients at the Philadelphia General Hospital. Its split-half reliability is .93 (Beck, Ward, Mendelson, Mock & Erbaugh, 1961). In a number of studies the Beck Depression Inventory has been shown to correlate well (.65, .61, .66) with ratings of depression made by independent clinicians (Beck et al., 1961; Metcalfe & Goldman, 1965; Nussbaum, Wittig, Hanlin & Kurland, 1963). In a more recent study, Williams, Barlow and Agras (1972) showed that the Beck Depression Inventory correlates .67 with behavioral measures of depression and .82 with the Hamilton Rating Scale (Hamilton, 1960). In addition, the Beck Depression Inventory discriminates well between anxiety and depression (Beck, 1972).

Lubin (1965) developed 14 lists of adjectives (both positive and negative) that differentiate depressed patients from normal controls. Four of the lists contain 22 positive adjectives while 10 contain negative adjectives. When administered, the patient simply checks whether a particular adjective applies to his/her current mood state. Criterion analyses indicated some differences in responses between depressed females and normal female controls and depressed males and normal male controls. In a subsequent validation study the adjective checklists were shortened and significant differences were obtained among depressed patients, non-depressed patients, and normal controls. In a recent study (Lubin, Hornstra & Love, 1974) sensitivity of the Depression Adjective Check Lists-Form E to mood changes in a psychiatric population was shown. Significant correlations between the Depression Adjective Check Lists and both the MMPI D scale and the Beck Depression Inventory in male and female depressives have been obtained (see Lubin, 1966).

The Zung (1965) Self-Rating Depression Scale is a 20-item inventory; 10 items are worded symptomatically positive while the remaining 10 are worded symptomatically negative. The scale is rated on a 1-4 basis, with higher scores indicating greater degree of depression. In the original study (Zung, 1965), self-ratings of depression correlated highly with clinical evaluations and EEG responses to auditory stimulation during sleep. The Zung correlates .79 with the Hamilton Rating Scale (see Brown & Zung, 1972) and correlates .70, .68 and .13 with the D, Pt, and Ma scales of the MMPI (Zung, Richards & Short, 1965).

The Pleasant Events Schedule was developed on the basis of "the behavioral theory of depression that there is an association between rate of positive reinforcement and intensity of depression" (Lewinsohn & Libet, 1972, p. 295). It was also predicated on the assumption that depressed, as opposed to non-depressed, individuals would engage in fewer pleasurable activities and that low scores on the activity schedule would be correlated with depressive mood. The Pleasant Events Schedule-Form I (Lewinsohn & Libet, 1972) consists of 320 events and activities that the depressed client or patient is asked to rate on a five-point scale of pleasantness. Form II consists of 320 items characteristic of college populations, while items in Form III are more characteristic of a general population (Lewinsohn & Graf, 1973). In a series of validity studies (i.e., construct validity), Lewinsohn and his colleagues have demonstrated that: 1) Responses on the Pleasant Events Schedule correlate positively with mood ratings (Lewinsohn & Libet, 1972); 2) there is a substantial relationship between reported number of pleasant activities engaged in and mood level for depressed subjects, non-depressed psychiatric controls, and normal subjects. Data indicate that depressed subjects report engaging in the fewest number of pleasant activities (Lewinsohn & Graf, 1973); and 3) depressed subjects, as compared to non-depressed subjects and psychiatric controls, scored lower on scales derived from the Pleasant Events Schedule measuring pleasure, activity level, and reinforcer potential of varied activities (MacPhillamy & Lewinsohn, 1974).

The three studies summarized offer evidence for the construct validity of the Pleasant Events Schedule; that is, it correlates with other measures that presumably measure depression. However, the correlations are among self-report inventories and are potentially inflated by method variance (cf., Campbell & Fiske, 1959). An individual who reports being depressed is not likely to admit that he enjoys himself often in a variety of ways. There are no data, at this point, to indicate that responses to the Pleasant Events Schedule actually reflect the respondent's *in vivo* activity level or style.

Naturalistic observation by the clinician-researcher or by significant others in the depressed client's environment is necessary. This kind of study could be accomplished rather easily by rating occurrence or non-occurrence of specific activities checked off on the schedule. A second study of interest would involve correlating number of activities listed with actual behavioral measurement of activity for clinically depressed patients who require hospitalization. Behavioral measurement might consist of unobtrusive observations repeatedly made on a psychiatric ward, as in the Williams, Barlow, and Agras (1972) study. A more sophisticated system of measurement involves telemetric recordings of activity that are then automatically computerized (e.g., Foster & Kupfer, 1973). In the Foster and Kupfer investigation, psychiatric patients were continuously monitored while they wore a wristwatch that contained a "telemetric mobility sensing system" that was extremely sensitive to body movement.

We would also like to underscore the importance of evaluating the Pleasant Activities Schedule with differing kinds of clinically depressed populations (see Pacoe, Himmelhoch, Hersen & Guyett, 1975), in addition to other kinds of diagnostic groupings. This is especially relevant in terms of the identification of those individuals manifesting the so-called "vegetative" signs of depression (i.e., eating, sleeping, and sexual disturbances). Finally, the distinction between self-report of subjective experience (e.g., depressed or dysphoric mood) and self-report of other component responses of depression must be reemphasized. As with anxiety, depression is characterized to a great extent by subjective state. Therefore, correlation of response elements is not the sole criterion to be employed in validating assessment instruments.

CONCLUSIONS

Despite the reservations that behavior modifiers occasionally articulate in press about the utility of relying on verbal reports (e.g., Begelman & Hersen, 1971), our review of the fear, anxiety, social skill, and depression literatures suggests that not only is the status of the verbal report relatively secure at this time, but that the number of self-report inventories currently being developed by behaviorists is rapidly increasing. Indeed, in the assessment of both fear and social skills needless duplication of measurement stands out (see Hersen, 1973; Hersen & Bellack, 1977). One of the major reasons for such duplication of effort is that investigators in different laboratories are developing their own assessment devices for specific projects rather than cross-validating existing schedules that already have some proven reliability or validity. Although we certainly do not aim to stultify the creative talents of our fellow researchers, we would urge them to examine the existing literature in a given area carefully before plunging into the development of yet another self-report inventory.

An overview of the self-assessment literature suggests that there are some "gaping holes" from the psychometric standpoint. The absence of long-term reliability studies for a variety of populations who *do not* receive treatment during the intervening test-retest interval is critical. Consider, for example, Suinn's (1969) five-week test-retest reliability study for the FSS-II where a 10-point decrease in overall fear was noted at the second testing session. There is no doubt that this kind of test-retest instability has major implications for evaluating the efficacy of treatment outcomes both in analogue and clinical-research paradigms. It should be mentioned here that the concept of reliability or stability of test scores over time is intertwined with the stability of behavior over time. Long-term reliability is not relevant when the behavior in question changes over time. However, when considering stable response patterns (e.g., behavioral deficits, untreated fears), it is incumbent upon the researcher to demonstrate that measures are applicable (e.g., not a function of temporary or chance variation).

Another major lack concerns the absence of normative data for clinical, volunteer, and college student populations. Comparisons of normative data obtained among the various populations are also of interest (see Hersen, 1971, for an example). Absence of normative data is most striking in the social skills literature and, in general, such data are least available for clinical populations. It is difficult (or impossible) to identify specific areas of deficit and to plan treatment without reference to norms that specify the typical and/or expected levels of functioning. For example, the appropriate amount of eye contact for any specific interaction is not self-evident, but must be empirically determined. In this regard, norms should reflect effectiveness of response variations, as McFall suggests in Chapter 5, as well as their relative frequency. Behaviorists have been soundly criticized for their penchant to examine theoretical and clinical notions carefully at the analogue level with *subclinical populations* (see Pacoe, Himmelhoch, Hersen & Guyett, 1975). Although data derived from studies with the college volunteer subjects are of academic interest, they frequently are of limited value when the assessor is confronted with the clinical situation in an applied setting. It would appear that if behavioral assessment self-report data are to have greater impact in the clinical world, the focus of research will have to be redirected toward the more disturbed subject. Along these lines, we would also recommend that research in this area be disseminated more widely in both psychological and psychiatric publications rather than restricted to the tightly-knit "behavioral club" journals.

Probably the most fascinating issue in self-assessment concerns the relationship of what an individual says he will do, what he actually does in a given test situation, and how both the self-report and the motor response relate to physiological activity. In reviewing some of the literature there is the temptation to make the blanket statement that: "There was no significant correlation between verbal and motoric or verbal and physiological indices of the behavior in question." However, given all the factors (covariates) that either account for or limit the degree of correlation between two different response systems, the abovementioned conclusion is premature. Not only must the assessor consider the context in which the motoric concomitant of a self-report statement is being validated (e.g., the experimental demand situation), but the classification of the individual being treated (volunteer subject vs. hospitalized patient) and the characteristics of the language of the self-report inventory must be considered. As already noted in the Introduction to this Chapter, correlations between self-reports and motoric behavior appear to be greater in social skill than in fear assessment. An explanation for this difference was offered with respect to the detail provided in the self-report query. For example, the subject might be asked to rate his overall fear of non-poisonous snakes on a 1-6 scale, but he has absolutely no idea of the task he will be required to perform in the laboratory situation (i.e., approaching, looking at, touching, and holding the feared stimulus). It is quite possible that if the subject were asked to rate a full and specific description of the laboratory task subsequently required of him, greater concordance between the verbal rating and his behavioral performance might be obtained. Research along these lines is warranted (Hersen & Barlow, 1976, Chapter 4). Similarly, when factor scores are used rather than total scale scores, greater concordance between verbal and motoric indices should be obtained (Hersen, 1973).

The absence of substantial correlations between self-report and physiological indices should also not be taken as a general critique of self-assessment procedures. When we consider that most studies involving physiological measurement usually evaluate only one of the response modalities (e.g., heart rate), it is not at all surprising that correlations are weak in that there are excellent data showing that individuals have their preferred (genetically determined) mode of physiological reactivity (see Lacey, 1950, 1956, 1962; Lacey & Van Lehn, 1952).

In light of the above, a final point needs to be made about the differential responsiveness of the cognitive, motor, and physiological systems during the course of behavioral treatment. The term "attitudinal lag" has been coined to describe the phenomenon of improved motor functioning prior to obtaining proportional changes in cognitive functioning in the same behavioral treatment paradigm (Hersen, 1973). Thus, once again, there seems to be relatively little concordance between the verbal report and motoric indices. However, considering the fact that the majority of behavioral treatments focus on motoric changes (exceptions, of course, are biofeedback and cognitive restructuring approaches), such differential improvements would not be surprising. Perhaps if each of the response systems were to be treated directly, as suggested by Lang (1971), then "attitudinal lag" might be minimized, thus resulting in greater concordance among the three response systems. Furthermore, attitudes and beliefs can be effectively screened out of analogue treatment procedures by pre-selection of subjects and objectification of treatment. However, the patient's subjective state is omnipresent in actual clinical settings. The clinician must deal with the patient's belief and report that he is depressed or fearful regardless of his actual behavior. The clinical endeavor is vastly facilitated if the clinician has carefully assessed the client's subjective state.

4

BEHAVIOR CHECKLISTS

RICHARD T. WALLS, THOMAS J. WERNER,
ANSLEY BACON and THOMAS ZANE

In 1973, our Rehabilitation Research and Training Center became involved in a cooperative project to train and rehabilitate mentally deficient clients. As an initial part of the planning process, we recognized a need for lists of objectives that could be used to *describe* each client's competencies, to *prescribe* curriculum to remediate deficiencies, and to *evaluate* progress. We were not seeking traditional psychometrics that would give us an intelligence quotient, an achievement in grade level, or a personality pattern. Similarly, we wanted to avoid traditional types of rating scales in which the rater "strongly agrees" or "strongly disagrees" that a given global construct such as "motivation" is present. In our conception a behavior checklist would clearly and unambiguously define behaviors performed to given standards under given conditions. Through such lists we would be able to assess each client's competencies at entry and monitor his/her progress through an individually designed rehabilitation and training plan. Rather than attempt to construct such tools, we reasoned that there must somewhere be a standard corpus of instruments from which to select. This was, however, not the case.

Informants consistently furnished the names of a few widely circulated instruments but almost invariably added one or more that was unknown to us. In an attempt to obtain useful documents and determine the scope

Appreciation is expressed to Ray Foster and Joseph Moriarty for helpful suggestions.

Manuscript preparation was supported in part by the Rehabilitation Services Administration (HEW) through the West Virginia Regional Rehabilitation Research and Training Center (West Virginia University and West Virginia Division of Vocational Rehabilitation).

of checklisting, an ad was placed in the *APA Monitor, Educational Researcher, Psychology Today,* and *Behaviour Research and Therapy.* We did not state our definition of "behavior checklist" in the ad, but reviewed all "checklists" sent and evaluated them according to the criteria described below. The ad requested, ". . . behavior checklists used in tabulating behaviors or skills of the mentally retarded, children, psychiatric, or other populations." In addition a form letter with the same request was sent to 823 state schools and facilities, child or adult psychiatric hospitals, narcotic or alcoholism hospitals, child or adult rehabilitation facilities, and mental retardation facilities.

CHECKLIST CHARACTERISTICS

The return was an assortment of more than 200 variously inclusive or exclusive instruments. The list devisers have fashioned a remarkable variety of behavior item formats with similarly diversified scoring requirements.

To illustrate the range of behavioral and metric character, the *Portage Project Checklist** asks if the client "Stacks five rings on a peg in order," to be scored "yes" or "no." In contrast the *Meeker-Cromwell Evaluation of Behavior Development* requires that, "Is aware that conflicting cultural concepts of right and wrong have relative meanings," be rated from "not at all descriptive" to "descriptive to a very large degree" on a scale from 1 to 5.

Hawkins and Dobes (1977) contend that an adequate response definition should have at least three somewhat overlapping characteristics. It should be *objective* (refer to observable characteristics), *clear* (readable and unambiguous), and *complete* (delineating the boundaries of inclusion and exclusion). Many of the "behavior checklists" reviewed do not meet these criteria. Even the most cursory examination of the thousands of pages of checklists and manuals reveals a broad range in the extent to which the items represent objective, clear, and complete behavior definitions. Further, the range of behavioral character within some checklists is considerable.

We needed some means of summarizing the salient characteristics of the instruments. In the final section of this chapter a list of checklists is provided with some descriptors of the nature of each. One of those attributes noted is how objective ("behavioral") the checklist's defini-

---

* The full references to checklists are given in alphabetical order by the name of the checklist in the last part of this chapter.

tions are. The second and third authors independently rated each checklist from 1 to 5 using the following criteria. Rating 5 means that the checklist clearly specifies: a) observable behaviors; b) standards of performance (rate or accuracy of response); and c) conditions of performance (situation prior to response). Rating 4 indicates that one of the above (a, b, or c) is poorly specified or omitted. Rating 3 indicates that two of the above are poorly specified or omitted. Rating 2 indicates that the behaviors are not observable (poorly defined but potentially specifiable), and the standards and conditions are poorly specified or omitted. Rating 1 indicates that the items are so vague and general that specification would be difficult or impossible, and the standards and conditions are poorly specified or omitted.

Using the two raters' scores for each checklist two interrater agreement (reliability) scores were computed. The reliability was 75.8% when agreement was defined as identical ratings on the 1 to 5 scale. However, for an agreement criterion allowing one point difference in rating, reliability was 100%. In addition, a product moment correlation was calculated to assess the degree to which the two raters agreed. This interrater correlation was .76. The variation of items within specific checklists undoubtedly attenuated this correlation. The mean of these two objectivity ratings is reported for each checklist in the listing at the end of this chapter. In addition, examples of the "least objective" and "most objective" items are provided to illustrate the range of item objectivity. These were obtained by having one of the raters simply scan the checklist items.

Most instruments group behaviors into domains (e.g. eating, social), each with several component or contributing skills. These domains (behavior classes) are enumerated in the list as a further guide to the scope of the checklist. While some checklists are concerned with a single domain—e.g., the *Dental Hygiene Behavior Checklist*—others imply a much broader interest with 10 or more behavior classes—e.g., *The Lakeland Village Adaptive Behavior Grid* with eating, toileting, dressing, health and grooming, communication, mobility and dexterity, vocational and recreational, socialization, orientation, and behavior control. This is to be expected in view of the differing ways in which checklists are constructed and used.

Although a few checklists call for specific counts within given time periods, checklists typically are not used for reporting an accurate count, frequency, or duration of behavior. Rather, the capability of the child, student, client, or patient to emit a particular behavior to a given standard under a given condition is noted from the recorder's recent memory, or from direct observation in a natural or constructed situation. For example, in the *Spraings' Behavior Rating Scale for Elementary School*, the recorder recalls whether the child "Seldom completes assignments in the allotted time." However, for the *Learning Accomplishment Profile (LAP)* an observer may set the occasion for responding by "placing the cardboard . . . in front of the child, one edge touching the piece of blank paper . . ." and then noting the child's response.

The two primary purposes for using behavior checklists appear to be a) *description* and b) *prescription*. When description of an individual's current skill repertoire is the sole aim, any checklist that adequately covers the behaviors of interest may be used. If a client "Walks on balance board with assistance," as indicated on the *North Central Regional Center Skill Evaluation and Assessment*, that action is simply known to exist in his/her repertoire. When it is noted that he/she *cannot* walk "on balance board without assistance," training or remediation may be implied, but the procedures are unspecified.

A prescriptive checklist goes further by enumerating the means for remediating or treating any deficiency identified. To illustrate, the *Prescriptive Behavior Checklist for the Severely Retarded* not only describes whether the child can "Go from backlying to sidelying position" but then prescribes procedures for training the skill, beginning with such items as ". . . turn his head to follow a dangling toy when in the backlying position." This particular checklist, its task analyses, and its implementations appear to be exceptionally valuable tools for working with developmental levels 0 to 6.

Another use of descriptive tools is client or program evaluation. The latter may be considered simply as a collective summary of the former. That is, if the clients are progressing well, the program is considered effective. Documentation of client progress through continuous or periodic assessment is valuable from an institution or program perspective and essential for staff who must monitor and facilitate individual achievement. If a client formerly did not "Compose and print paragraphs using 4-6 simple sentences" on the *Colorado Master Planning Guide for Instructional Objectives*, but now accomplishes the task, progress is apparent.

Behaviors or skills to be registered at two or more points in time require that the rating be reliably stable, provided that no relevant intervention occurred. Unfortunately, sophistication in the use of sound principles of measurement, such as reliability assessment, has not always kept pace with the writing and use of behavior checklists.

Several types of reliability (comparable forms, internal consistency, temporal stability, and interobserver reliability) are considered as they relate to behavior checklist construction and use. One traditional indication of instrument reliability has been the use of *comparable forms* given to the same subjects. Although it would be possible to have alternate measures of constructs such as anxious behavior, it is probably not reasonable to have "comparable forms" for hand washing. Is there more than one independent sample from the item universe? The keynote for behavior checklisting has been the attempt to cover the item universe through relatively complete task analysis. To the extent that this is accomplished, there is no comparable form.

Internal consistency is of value for dimensions or domains whose measurement is reflected by several behaviors. To illustrate, the *Ward Behavior Inventory (WBI)* uses 138 yes-no items to indicate "psychopathology." The authors computed Hoyt analysis of variance as well as Kuder-Richardson Formula 20 as indications of internal consistency. High coefficients might indicate that the behaviors within a domain are internally consistent and that such items as "Keeps giggling in a foolish way" and "Refuses or discards his medicine" are marked similarly for the same client. In the same sense, internal consistency would be of value for a behavior dimension or class such as social skills, when the contributing or component behaviors are not hierarchical in nature. Assume, for example that "Works and plays alone," "Obeys rules," and "Completes tasks" from the *Evaluation Check List: Educable Mentally Retarded* are independent of each other. If one is interested in being able to say that the client has high or low "social skills," these more specific competencies should interrelate (be internally consistent). For example, authors of the *Cain-Levine Social Competency Scale* computed odd-even internal consistency separately for the four classes contained in the scale: self-help, initiative, social skills, and communication.

Often scales that are based on developmental competencies (e.g., *Michigan Behavioral Skills Profile*) are organized in a hierarchical format so that behaviors lower in the list are presumably prerequisite to skills at the higher levels. Thus, if a child shows, say, skill 12, it is generally the case that the child has skills 1 through 11, too, these being prerequisite to 12. For hierarchical arrangements, the contributing behaviors should be internally consistent to the highest level of competence by definition. In fact, if it is not maximally internally consistent, the hierarchy should be reexamined. However, if the checklist simply purports to be a collection of behaviors, and no organizing dimensions or item interrelations are claimed, then internal consistency is meaningless.

Stability is a crucial characteristic for behavior checklists. An observer should score the same performance in the same way as he did two weeks prior. For example, if a rater indicates the client, "Complains about others' unfairness and/or discrimination towards him" on the *Walker Problem Behavior Identification Checklist*, will the rater score the item similarly two weeks or two months hence? While this is not precisely the same as instrument decay, as discussed by Campbell and Stanley (1963), it has conceptual similarity. Because of observer forgetting, new learning, a new setting or other interfering factors, the observer's interpretation of the scoring criterion may have changed. In a sense, such "observer drift" is what lack of stability connotes. While it is not a fatigue or boredom factor (Johnson & Bolstad, 1973), when checklists are marked at intervals of several weeks or months, observers may unintentionally alter the definition under study. However, observer drift through boredom or fatigue may occur if all students in a classroom or patients on a ward are checklisted in a single day.

Several authors (e.g., Johnson & Bolstad, 1973) have suggested a videotaped criterion to serve as an anchor. Observers may thus review the standard referent periodically in an attempt to maintain stability. If such precautions are ineffective in producing high item scoring stability, the "behavior" must be discarded or redefined to promote consistent interpretation.

Stability of the measure is, of course, confounded with stability of the client's or student's behavior. Experimental or therapeutic treatments are provided with the expressed aim of changing behaviors. It is not appropriate to attempt to establish item stability with a given subject at two points in time if any significant program-related activity has occurred in that period. An attempt to establish such stability was reported in an "experimental" manual for the *Minnesota Developmental Programming System*. The same observer recorded behaviors of 37 clients twice within a month. The median stability coefficient for 18 behavior domains was .94. A similar attempt was reported with a product moment $r=.93$ for two evaluations using the *Behavior Maturity Checklist* separated by four to six months. Such statements may provide more information about program inadequacy than checklist adequacy. In sum, when repeated measures of performance are taken, lack of stability may make the data uninterpretable due to confounding with various threats to internal or external validity, as noted by Campbell and Stanley (1963), such as history, physical maturation, testing, instrumentation, statistical regression, and reactive effects of treatments.

The primary reliability concern in applied behavior research has become the extent to which two or more independent observers agree. *Interobserver reliability* has been computed by several methods, depending on the design, data characteristics, method of recording, and investigator predilection. The suitability of these methods for such research has been adequately considered by other writers (Bijou, Peterson & Ault, 1968; Hartmann, 1976; Hull, 1971; Johnson & Bolstad, 1973) and is only briefly outlined here to provide comparison with procedures for sound checklist development and use.

The most popular method of computing interobserver reliability has been percentage agreement. A scanning of the articles reported in the *Journal of Applied Behavior Analysis* during 1974 revealed approximately 25 studies using this procedure. It may be computed in several ways. In event recording the smaller number of counts by one observer for a session may be divided by the larger number counted by the other observer (e.g., Schwarz & Hawkins, 1970). A more conservative, but potentially troublesome, estimate is the number of trials in which the counts agree divided by the total number of trials (agreement plus disagreement trials). This estimate is potentially troublesome because it requires that all trials be measured or controlled. In interval recording, when simple occurrence or nonoccurrence of the behaviors being coded is recorded within short time blocks, proportion of agreement is often calculated by dividing the number of agreement intervals by the sum of agreement plus disagreement intervals. Hawkins and Dotson (1975) present data to document the inadequacy of the most commonly used interobserver agreement score in interval recording and suggest alternative procedures. The same procedure is often used to calculate agreement with a momentary time sampling strategy (recording presence or absence of a behavior during a short period of time at the end of each interval). Several of the checklists reviewed, such as the *Classroom Behavior and Consequence Record*, employ either an interval recording or a momentary time sampling procedure. Effective "occurrence agreement" is computed in a similar manner except that trials scored as nonoccurrence by both observers are excluded from the computation. The only occasions included are those during which one or both observers have coded the target behaviors as having occurred. This index is particularly useful when the behavior is infrequent. The converse rationale and procedure may be used to check nonoccurrence of a frequently emitted behavior (Hartmann, 1976).

What does percentage agreement mean where behavior checklists are concerned? First, consider a single behavior as a score unit. For example, the *Resident Evaluation* form asks the observer to code, "Puts ashes in ash trays," as 1) never, 2) seldom, 3) sometimes, or 4) usually. If raters A and B code the behavior at only one point in time, and they do not agree, it is no more instructive to say there was "zero percent agreement" than simply to note that they did not agree. However, if raters A and B code the behavior at several points in time, the number of times they agreed divided by agreements plus disagreements may be instructive in deciding whether the definition of "Puts ashes in ash tray" is adequate and/or whether observer training has been sufficient. If some behaviors are selected from a total checklist for interobserver agreement analysis, but others are not examined, as in the *MR Status Form* manual, clear rationale must be provided for that selection.

In the information about the specific checklists presented later in this chapter, it is reported how well two trained raters agreed on the extent to which each checklist contains objectively observable and codable behaviors. A more informative index might be provided by checklist developers. This could be accomplished by computing interobserver agreement for each behavior class (e.g., dressing) separately or across all component behaviors in the checklist. The latter procedure would not yield a sum of apples and oranges, but rather would provide the potential checklist user a guide to objectivity, precise definition, and adequacy of general instructions for the instrument.

As an illustration, developers of the *Client Checklist* might report percentage interrater agreement across the 13 component scores in the "Table Behaviors" class for a single or specified number of clients. Further, a percentage agreement might be calculated across the 338 component behaviors of the entire checklist. The observers would code each behavior 1) successful, 2) unsuccessful, or 3) sometimes, as required by the checklist. The quotient of agreements divided by agreements plus disagreements should aid reviewers and users in interpreting general dependability. For example, on the *Program Placement Survey*, interobserver reliability was computed for each class or domain by dividing total possible agreements into actual agreements.

A second method of establishing interobserver reliability is to compute a product moment correlation among multiple raters for the same behavior or, as would be more likely, for score pairs of two raters across the component behaviors of a class or list. When an instrument calls, for example, for ratings from 1 through 4 on an equal-appearing interval scale for each contributing behavior, the product moment index is appropriate. In fact, it is sensitive to variations in rating that are not taken into account with percentage agreement indices.

To illustrate the use of product moment correlation, the *Washington Assessment and Training Scales (WATS)* requires the rater to score each behavior on a scale from 1 to 5 with each point on the scale described for each behavior. Interrater correlations were computed separately for the different classes (eating, .77; toileting, .73; dressing, .86; dexterity, .56; mobility, .62; communication, .88; grooming, .94; socialization, .84; vocational aptitude, .84; domestic competence, .89; community skills, .83; adaptive behavior, .29) as well as for the total list, .90. Similarly, the authors of *The TARC Assessment System* reported interobserver correlations for each skill domain.

In percentage agreement if observer A rates a behavior "2" and observer B scores it "5" it is simply a disagreement, but the product moment index takes into account the magnitude of this disagreement. Hartmann (1976) lists several other advantages of this coefficient. It 1) specifies the proportion of total score variance not due to random error; 2) represents the degree of linear association between the two sets of recordings; 3) allows subsequent prediction of variance for one observer from the other's scores; 4) has a specified degree of confidence; 5) allows testing of differences between coefficients; and 6) indicates the smallest difference between scores that can be interpreted with meaning (standard error of measurement).

When occurrence-nonoccurrence or yes-no is the score rather than numerical or continuous information, a product moment correlation termed *Phi* may be computed. These dichotomous data are entered in a simple 2 by 2 tally matrix with observers on one dimension and yes-no on the other. The coefficient is then easily computed and has the metric advantages noted for a correlation. For example, each item in the *Camelot Behavioral Checklist* is scored "Can do" or "Needs training." Observers A and B might: 1) both agree that the client "Discriminates tastes"; 2) both agree that the client does not "Discriminate(s) sounds"; 3) disagree, with observer A indicating that the client "Discriminates temperature" but B saying that he/she doesn't, and 4) disagree, with observer B indicating that the client "Discriminates textures," but A saying that he/she doesn't. After entering these four rubrics of agreements or disagreements across a class (e.g., sensory development) or across the entire list, the *Phi* index would be a helpful descriptor.

Kappa is also a correlation-related statistic derived by Cohen (1968) specifically to measure interobserver reliability of nominal (dichotomous) data. Proportion of agreements expected by chance is subtracted from the numerator and denominator. Thus, *Kappa* yields the proportion of agreements corrected for chance. Discussion of computation procedures and metric properties is provided by Cohen (1968, as cited in Hartmann, 1976).

Selection of one measure or another of interobserver reliability has been largely a matter of personal choice as related to data constraints and characteristics. Percentage agreement has been the popular choice in applied behavioral research, possibly because of computation ease and roots in the behavioral tradition. Strong consideration should also be given to correlation-related measures and the sound measurement foundation they connote. Unfortunately, the majority of checklist makers have chosen neither. In most cases we find no indication of the extent to which we may expect their list of behaviors to be reliably recorded by separate observers. Further, rationale about whether or not the list should be internally consistent or whether the scoring would be stable over time is rarely reported.

VALIDITY

Validity is seldom a problem when dealing with physical measurements such as length and weight. If the balance is functioning properly, we know it is measuring weight. Behaviors appear to connote these same metric properties. When the behavioral descriptors are sufficient, behaviors are as patently valid as other physical properties of matter. Just as one may find that the ore sample weighs 20 grams, one may determine that the key peck occurred 20 times.

If the claim is made, however, that a collection of behaviors or ratings may be combined to provide evidence of some trait, dimension or behavior class, high validity is the primary concern. We want to know how well the individual's position on the continuum of tallies or sums represents the criterion variable. For cases in which the criterion is reliable and unambiguous, concurrent or predictive *criterion-related validity* takes the form of a simple correlation coefficient.

For example, *A Verbal Problem Checklist for Use in Assessing Family Verbal Behavior* requires scoring of presence and amount of 49 verbal behaviors. Husband and wife ratings of two of the behaviors (overtalk and undertalk) were correlated with actual amount of talking to provide indices of criterion-related validity.

When external criteria are less well defined or are unavailable, *construct validity* is especially useful. Predictions about different individuals' positions on the construct or proposed behavior class are made from the theory. The behaviors proposed to measure the domain are then check-listed to determine accuracy of such prediction. Validity may be determined by differences between groups that should theoretically differ, by test results that show theory predicted changes in individuals or environment, and by intercorrelations of different instruments assumed to measure the same class construct (Cronbach & Meehl, 1955). The series of testings serves then to confirm or disconfirm the proposed relationship. In the latter event, the theory *or* the instrument may be at fault.

As an example, the eating, dressing, dexterity, mobility, communication, and socialization dimensions of the *Washington Assessment and Training Scales (WATS)* yielded substantial correlations with the same classes of the *Progress Assessment Chart.* Communication and socialization from the *WATS* were closely related to Bayley IQ, and Total *WATS* correlated .90 with the *Vineland Scale of Social Maturity.*

In addition to variance due to relevant characteristics of the subjects or clients, there may be some systematic variance because of similar methods of rating or response. Such artifact may lead to an overestimate of construct validity. For a completely satisfactory test of instrument validity, Campbell and Fiske (1959) have proposed a multivariable-multi-method procedure. A matrix of methods and variables is constructed so that each of the variables is assessed via the different methods. Common variance from measuring different variables by the same method can thus be eliminated. If correlations between measurements of the same variable with different methods are moderately high, the methods are said to have *convergent validity. Discriminant validity* may be assumed when correlations among the different methods of measuring the same variable are greater than among the same method across variables or among other variables by any method. For example, users of the *Behavior Inventory* can measure the effects of heroin, as well as the effects of marihuana, on recorded work output as correlated with measures of actual output.

Campbell and Fiske (1959) indicate that convergent validity is a "common denominator" among the types of validity discussed to this juncture. All represent attempts to measure the same behavior class by different methods or in different conditions. While observed rates of emission may be consistent and dependable in a limited observation period or under restricted stimulus control, the lack of dependability of generalization to even very similar stimulus settings is a well-known clinical phenomenon. The child taught in the clinic must often be retrained at home or in school. A given behavior checklist may not embody necessary and sufficient conditions to identify the nature of problems across stimulus settings. Situational specificity, or specificity of the conditions of performance, was one of the criteria considered in rating objectivity of the checklists reviewed.

Content validity is particularly important in construction of behavior checklists. Attempting to record all human behaviors is impractical and probably impossible. Thus, each checklist author makes decisions about the particular types of actions that will be helpful. These behaviors are intended to define the performance domain. The extent to which the behaviors selected for the checklist represent the task universe of that domain is the checklist's content validity. This should not be confused with relatively worthless judgments or appearances of relevance that have in the past been termed "face validity." Content validation connotes careful and thorough definition of the objectives and a representative list of behaviors from the desired performance domain.

As an example, content validation of the *Minnesota Developmental Programming System* was reported by virtue of agreement of two psychologists, a director of residential services, two unit directors, a program director, a chief executive officer, a technical assistance consultant, two social workers, a vocational rehabilitation consultant, and an early childhood education specialist on the following criteria: 1) The 18 domains were sufficient for assessment and program planning; 2) the items were worded appropriately and clearly; 3) the items measured the class of behavior named in each domain; 4) the behaviors in the items were observable and objective; and 5) the items were developmentally sequenced in each domain.

The foregoing discussion is not intended to imply that instruments having unmeasured or less than optimal validity are useless. Different purposes will tolerate different levels of dependability and validity. One may ask, for what purposes is this measure valid in its present state? A broadly inclusive descriptive checklist may have wide band width but not as high fidelity (Cronbach, 1970) as an instrument that measures more restricted skills.

COMMENT

Clinical writing and use of behavior checklists have far outdistanced their scientific development. While many prescriptive and descriptive instruments are ostensibly related to the rich body of sound behavioral research, they often violate the principles of consistency of measurement, dependability, representativeness, and generalizability that have been the foundation of operant methods. Developers of checklists should not allow their possible mistrust of and distaste for statistical measurement to obscure their own intent.

Perhaps the issues may be cast in a generalizability model (Cronbach, Rajaratnam & Gleser, 1963). We want to specify the extent of generalizability of test (checklist) results across behaviors within a class or domain, across stimulus conditions in the same setting, across observers, and across settings. Cone (1975) lists the universes of generalization as scorer, item, time, setting, method, and dimension. He proposes testing a taxonomy of behavioral assessment in which these universes of generalization are crossed with eight methods and three content areas. While only a portion of the cells of this matrix are applicable here, the potential checklist user might select an assessment device with greater confidence if he/ she has some notion of the generalizability of the results.

As the "behaviors" in a checklist stray toward the inferential judgment end of the continuum and away from objectively determined referents, dependability is likely to suffer. However, high reliability may at times be purchased at the expense of validity. O'Leary and Kent (1973) report that they raised reliability of their aggression measure by eliminating intent and contextual cues from their definition, but the new definition was not a suitable concept of aggression.

The widespread development of tools is encouraging, since therapeutic efforts cannot wait for optimal tools. But while progress in development and use of checklists is heartening, caution must be exercised to insure their potential to yield broadly consistent measurement. The accomplishments of behavior analysis and therapy are indeed impressive, but a tremendous quality control problem still exists. Resolution of observer bias, observee reactivity, demand characteristics, response sets, instrument decay, inappropriate use in general, and other threats to dependability and generalizability of checklists will require more than a zealous but naive behaviorism.

A LIST OF CHECKLISTS

The results of our search yielded many checklists, of which 166 are reviewed, with selective descriptive notes. We did not find it profitable to attempt to separate the checklists into target populations (e.g., mentally retarded, psychiatric, students) or descriptions of problems (e.g., deviant behavior, alcohol abuse, developmental disability). Basic skills training, which is the emphasis of most of the checklists, is applicable across most populations and problems. Accordingly, we divided the checklists into the categories discussed earlier in this chapter (Prescriptive, Marginal Prescriptive-Descriptive, and Descriptive).

There are several classifications of instruments *not included*. They are 1) classic developmental assessment (e.g., Gesell Developmental Schedules; Bayley Scales of Infant Development); 2) classroom teacher-student interaction (e.g., Interaction Analysis; The Reciprocal Category System); 3) scales that call for self response (e.g., Wolpe Fear Inventory); 4) those that would be of limited usefulness to facilities other than the one at which they were developed; and 5) those that we did not locate. There are undoubtedly a large number in this last category, and we ask readers to send other behavior checklists to facilitate our ongoing search.

The format for this section is as follows, with Prescriptive Checklists listed first and Descriptive Checklists last:

Title: Name of Checklist (Author)

Source: Address or Reference

Behavior Classes: Domains of Behavior

Method: Direct Observation, Memory or Interview

Reliability or Validity Information Provided: Yes or No*

Mean Rating of Reviewers on Objectivity or Behavioral Character: 1.0 to 5.0

    5.0—Clearly specifies (a) observable behaviors, (b) standards of performance and (c) conditions of performance;

    4.0—(a) (b) or (c) above is poorly specified or omitted;

    3.0—Two of above poorly specified or omitted;

    2.0—Behaviors not observable and standards and conditions poorly specified or omitted;

    1.0—Items so vague and general, specification difficult or impossible.

Rating Scale: Scoring Method

Most Objective Item: Example of Item

Least Objective Item: Example of Item

---

* NO indicates that no reliability or validity information was located by the authors. However, such information may possibly be available.

PRESCRIPTIVE CHECKLISTS

Title: APT Skill Assessment (3rd edition) (Brody et al., 1975)

Source: Pennhurst State School and Hospital, Spring City, Pennsylvania 19475

Behavior Classes: Motor area, communication, self-help, social skills, pre-vocational, behavior problems, special skills for the visually impaired.

Method: Direct observation

Reliability or Validity Information Provided: No

*Mean Rating of Objectivity: 5.0

Rating Scale: Yes/No

Most Objective Item: Bedmaking: when given two sheets, spread, and pillowcases; puts lower sheet on bed, tucking in all sides, top sheet and spread tucked in at bottom so the sides are fairly even and few wrinkles. Puts case on pillow and places at top of bed.

Least Objective Item: When seated in a circle of three to five residents, will participate cooperatively in a group task such as passing a ball.

* * *

Title: Commonwealth Plan for Education and Training of Mentally Retarded Children: COMPET (Pennsylvania Departments of Education and Public Welfare)

Source: Department of Education, Box 911, Harrisburg, Pa. 17105

Behavior Classes: Gross motor, fine motor, visual motor, auditory, tactile/kinesthetic, self-concept, communication, conceptual, math, toileting, and 10 others

Method: Direct observation

Reliability or Validity Information Provided: No

*Mean Rating of Objectivity: 4.0

Rating Scale: Yes/No

Most Objective Item: Counts common combinations of currency up to $100.

Least Objective Item: Respects privacy of others

* * *

Title: Denver Developmental Screening Test (Frankenburg, Dodds)

Source: Ladoca Project and Publishing Foundation, East 51st Avenue and Lincoln Street, Denver, Colorado 80216

Behavior Classes: Personal-social, fine motor-adaptive, language, gross motor

Method: Direct observation

Reliability or Validity Information Provided: Yes

*Mean Rating of Objectivity: 5.0

Rating Scale: Yes/No

---

* 1.0 Least Objective; 5.0 Most Objective.

Most Objective Item: Bounce ball to child who should stand three feet away from tester. Child must catch ball with hands, not arms, two out of three trials.

Least Objective Item: When child is playing with toy, pull it away from him. Pass if he resists.

*   *   *

Title: Guide to Early Developmental Training.

Source: Wabash Center for the Mentally Retarded, Inc., 2000 Greenbush Street, Lafayette, Indiana 47904

Behavior Classes: Balance and posture, perceptual motor, locomotion, body image, cognitive development, language development, eating, and three others.

Method: Direct Observation

Reliability or Validity Information Provided: No

*Mean Rating of Objectivity: 4.0

Rating Scale: Yes/No

Most Objective Item: Catches, once out of three times, a large ball tossed from five feet. Arms now bend at elbows and adapt somewhat to the direction of the ball.

Least Objective Item: Becoming aware that his body has different parts and where they are located on his body.

*   *   *

Title: Mid-Nebraska Mental Retardation Services Competitive Employment and Independent Living Screening Tests and Teaching Manuals (Schalock and Staff)

Source: Mid-Nebraska Mental Retardation Services, Special Education Section, Department of Education, Lincoln, Nebraska 68508.

Behavior Classes: Job-related skills, responsibility towards work, work performance, behavior in the job situation, personal appearance, communication, functional academics, personal maintenance, clothing care and use, home maintenance, food preparation, time management, social behavior, community utilization.

Method: Direct Observation

Reliability or Validity Information Provided: No

*Mean Rating of Objectivity: 4.5

Rating Scale: Yes/No

Most Objective Item: Place ten, ¼-inch bolts next to ten, ¼-inch nuts and instruct "Screw the nut on the bolt." *Demonstrate once*. To pass the target behavior, the client must pick up nine of ten using a pincer grasp *and* assemble nine of ten correctly.

Least Objective: Ask client the following employment-related questions (a) What do you *want* to do? (b) What do you *like* to do? (c) What *can* you do?

---

* 1.0 Least Objective; 5.0 Most Objective.

Client should be able to express one job preference that combines "want," "like," and "can."

* * *

Title: Prescriptive Behavior Checklist for the Severely Retarded (Kulics)

Source: Dorothy P. Kulics, 509 Allen Hall, West Virginia University, Morgantown, West Virginia 26506

Behavior Classes: Eye-hand, self-help, language development.

Method: Direct Observation

Reliability or Validity Information Provided: No

**Mean Rating of Objectivity*: 4.0

Rating Scale: Yes/No

Most Objective Item: The child will pick up the circle and place it in the box upon command "put in."

Least Objective Item: The child will hold the circle.

* * *

Title: Steps to Independence: A Skills Training Series for Children with Special Needs (Baker, Brightman, Heifetz, Murphy)

Source: Research Press, 2412 North Mattis Avenue, Champaign, Illinois 61820

Behavior Classes: Self-help readiness skills, basic motor skills, motor activities, eating, dressing, grooming, housekeeping, behavior problems.

Method: Direct Observation

Reliability or Validity Information Provided: Yes

**Mean Rating of Objectivity*: 5.0

Rating Scale: Yes/No

Most Objective Item: Stands and pulls pants up to waist after you put them over both feet.

Least Objective Item: Cannot zip.

* * *

Title: Systematic Curriculum for Independent Living: SCIL (Hannah, Millhouse, Sauvageot, Compton, Cannon, Herod, Froelich)

Source: Developmental Disabilities Project, Research and Training Center, West Virginia University, Morgantown, West Virginia 26506

Behavior Classes: Math, money, time, measurement, functional reading, speech, telephone, postal, writing

Method: Direct Observation

Reliability or Validity Information Provided: No

**Mean Rating of Objectivity*: 4.5

---

* 1.0 Least Objective; 5.0 Most Objective.

Rating Scale: Yes/No; if no, go to prescriptive lessons

Most Objective Item: Counts in order from 0-100

Least Objective Item: Recognizes numbers 0-100 in series

*   *   *

Title: The Teaching Research Curriculum for Moderately and Severely Handicapped (Fredericks, Riggs, Furey, Grove, Moore, McDonnell, Jordan, Hanson, Baldwin, Wadlow)

Source: Teaching Research Infant and Child Center, Corvallis, Oregon; Charles C Thomas, Publisher, Bannerstone House, 301-327 East Lawrence Avenue, Springfield, Illinois

Behavior Classes: Self-help, motor development, receptive oral language, reading skills, expressive oral language, writing skills, cognitive skills

Method: Direct Observation

Reliability or Validity Information Provided: No

*Mean Rating of Objectivity: 4.0

Rating Scale: Yes/No

Most Objective Item: When adult presents one (of 100) object and asks, "What is this?" child responds with name of object

Least Objective Item: Child answers question independently

*   *   *

MARGINAL PRESCRIPTIVE-DESCRIPTIVE
(*Extensively Sequenced*)

Title: Behavioral Characteristics Progression

Source: VORT Corporation, P.O. Box 11132, Palo Alto, California 94306

Behavior Classes: Hygiene, self-care, perceptual skills, language, motor skills, social, academic, sign language, lip reading and 50 others.

Method: Direct Observation

Reliability or Validity Information Provided: No

*Mean Rating of Objectivity: 4.0

Rating Scale: Yes/No

Most Objective Item: Bobs in and out of water five times, breathing rhythmically

Least Objective Item: Undertakes systematic investigation of unfamiliar room

*   *   *

Title: Camelot Behavioral Checklist (Foster) and Skill Acquisition Program Bibliography (Tucker)

Source: Camelot Behavioral Systems, P.O. Box 607, Parsons, Kansas 67357

---

* 1.0 Least Objective; 5.0 Most Objective.

Behavior Classes: Self-help, physical development, vocational, numerical, communication

Method: Direct Observation or Memory

Reliability or Validity Information Provided: Yes

Mean Rating of Objectivity: 3.0

Rating Scale: Yes/No

Most Objective Item: Can walk up stairs one foot on each step

Least Objective Item: Knows full name

* * *

Title: Colorado Master Planning Guide for Instructional Objectives (DD Master Planning Committee)

Source: Division of Developmental Disabilities, 4150 South Lowell, Denver, Colorado 80236

Behavior Classes: Physical communications, self-management, employment skills

Method: Direct Observation

Reliability or Validity Information Provided: No

Mean Rating of Objectivity: 5.0

Rating Scale: Yes/No

Most Objective Item: Client uses a colon to express time, with 50% accuracy

Least Objective Item: Client uses synonyms when writing to avoid repetitions (i.e., happy, joyful) 10% of the time

* * *

Title: Couple's Daily Rating of Affection (Keller)

Source: Charles Keller, M.D., 42 Lake Avenue, Hilton, New York 14468

Behavior Classes: Affectionate words and actions

Method: Memory

Reliability or Validity Information Provided: No

Mean Rating of Objectivity: 3.5

Rating Scale: Yes/No

Most Objective Item: Drug abuse (one dot for each drink over four in six hours; each reefer over four per week)

Least Objective Item: Guessed at fact or feeling partner didn't mention

* * *

Title: Dental Hygiene Behavior Checklist (Abramson, Wunderlich)

Source: Edward E. Abramson, Department of Psychology, California State University, Chico, California 95926

---

* 1.0 Least Objective; 5.0 Most Objective.

Behavior Classes: Tooth-brushing

Method: Direct Observation

Reliability or Validity Information Provided: No

*Mean Rating of Objectivity: 3.0

Rating Scale: Yes/No

Most Objective Item: Puts cap on paste

Least Objective Item: Doesn't disturb others

*   *   *

Title: Life Skills for the Developmentally Disabled (Vol. III: Manual for Training Clients)

Source: Geneva S. Folsom, The George Washington University, Division of Rehab. Medicine, 2300 I Street, N.W., Washington, D.C. 20037

Behavior Classes: Community, academic, shopping, semi-independent living, work, and socialization

Method: Direct Observation or Memory

Reliability or Validity Information Provided: No

*Mean Rating of Objectivity: 2.0

Rating Scale: Yes/No

Most Objective Item: Orders simple meal at carry out

Least Objective Item: Familiar with different types of offenses

*   *   *

Title: Nebraska Client Progress System (Staff)

Source: Special Education Section, Department of Education, Lincoln, Nebraska 68508

Behavior Classes: Attending, body motor, hand motor, toileting, self-feeding, personal hygiene, dressing, clothes selection, clothes maintenance, and 36 others

Method: Direct Observation

Reliability or Validity Information Provided: Yes

*Mean Rating of Objectivity: 4.0

Rating Scale: Yes/No

Most Objective Item: Names shapes including square, triangle, circle, and star when supervisor points to them and asks name

Least Objective Item: Listens to criticism and works for positive change based upon constructive criticism

*   *   *

Title: Self-Care Skill Level Evaluation Checklist (Staff)

Source: Waukegan Developmental Center, 1201 Dugdale, Waukegan, Illinois 60085

---

* 1.0 Least Objective; 5.0 Most Objective.

Behavior Classes: Toileting, showering, washing, grooming, dressing, mealtime

Method: Direct Observation

Reliability or Validity Information Provided: No

Mean Rating of Objectivity: 4.0

Rating Scale: Manual guidance to self-initiated (1 to 5)

Most Objective Item: Holds toothbrush by handle, bristles up, in one hand

Least Objective Item: Shampoos hair

* * *

Title: West Virginia Assessment and Tracking System (Cone)

Source: John D. Cone, Ph.D., Department of Psychology, West Virginia University, Morgantown, West Virginia 26506

Behavior Classes: Auditory, visual, and tactile responsiveness, gross motor, fine motor, uses toilet, eating, dressing, washing and grooming, receptive language, expressive language, social interaction, reading, writing, using numbers, time, domestic behavior, uses money, vocational, recreation and leisure

Method: Interview informant, direct observation

Reliability or Validity Information Provided: No

Mean Rating of Objectivity: 4.0

Rating Scale: 0 to 3, various

Most Objective Item: When two or more persons are present and only one is speaking, child looks toward the speaker

Least Objective Item: Respects others' property

* * *

DESCRIPTIVE CHECKLISTS

Title: AAMD Adaptive Behavior Scale (1974 revision)

Source: American Association on Mental Deficiency, 5201 Connecticut Avenue, N.W., Washington, D.C. 20015

Behavior Classes: Eating, toilet use, cleanliness, appearance, care of clothing, dressing and undressing, travel, other independent functioning, and 29 others

Method: Memory

Reliability or Validity Information Provided: Yes

Mean Rating of Objectivity: 1.5

Rating Scale: Yes/No

Most Objective Item: Orders complete meals in restaurants

Least Objective Item: Can be reasoned with

* * *

---

* 1.0 Least Objective; 5.0 Most Objective.

Title: Abilities Checklist

Source: Donald L. Miller, Muscatatuck State Hospital and Training Center, Butlerville, Indiana 47223

Behavior Classes: Sensory abilities, motor skills, language development, social development, grooming

Method: Memory

Reliability or Validity Information Provided: No

*Mean Rating of Objectivity: 3.0

Rating Scale: Did by self to unable to complete (1 to 4)

Most Objective Item: Stacks up to 3 blocks

Least Objective Item: Relates experiences

*   *   *

Title: Adam, J. N., Developmental Center Behavioral Checklist (Knapp)

Source: Barbara W. MacCasland, Ph.D., J. N. Adam Developmental Center, Helmuth, New York 14079

Behavior Classes: Appearance, language, attention span, affect, behavior

Method: Direct Observation

Reliability or Validity Information Provided: No

*Mean Rating of Objectivity: 1.0

Rating Scale: Very good/poor (1 to 4)

Most Objective Item: Shirt tucked in

Least Objective Item: Depression

*   *   *

Title: Adaptive Behavior Checklist (Allen, Levine, Alker, Loeffler)

Source: Miami Sunland Training Center, 20000 N.W. 47th Avenue, Miami, Florida 33054

Behavior Classes: Eating, walking, reading, writing, job, social

Method: Memory

Reliability or Validity Information Provided: No

*Mean Rating of Objectivity: 3.0

Rating Scale: Check one that best describes

Most Objective Item: Writes or prints short notes

Least Objective Item: Listens and can be reasoned with verbally and seems to enjoy social conversation

*   *   *

Title: Adaptive Behavior Ratings (Staff)

Source: Michael R. Dillon, Superintendent, Connecticut State Department of Health,

---

* 1.0 Least Objective; 5.0 Most Objective.

Central Connecticut Regional Center, Undercliff Road, Box 853, Meriden, Connecticut 06450

Behavior Classes: Language, eating, social, manual dexterity, toilet, gross feet motor

Method: Memory

Reliability or Validity Information Provided: No

*Mean Rating of Objectivity: 2.0

Rating Scale: Circle most appropriate description

Most Objective Item: Walks assisted by hand

Least Objective Item: Goes to familiar people

* * *

Title: Adaptive Functioning Index No. 2 and No. 3 (Marlett)

Source: The Vocational and Rehabilitation Research Institute, 3304 33 Street, N.W., Calgary 44, Alberta, Canada

Behavior Classes: Personal routines, community awareness, and social maturity in vocational and residential settings

Method: Memory

Reliability or Validity Information Provided: No

*Mean Rating of Objectivity: 2.0

Rating Scale: Yes/No

Most Objective Item: Offers suggestions to the supervisor once he knows the job well

Least Objective Item: Shows interest in learning new things so he can do things on his own

* * *

Title: Adolescent Behavior Checklist

Source: Irving J. Taylor, M.D., Taylor Manor Hospital, Ellicott City, Maryland 21043

Behavior Classes: Adolescent behavior problems

Method: Memory

Reliability or Validity Information Provided: No

*Mean Rating of Objectivity: 2.0

Rating Scale: Yes/No

Most Objective Item: Nail-biting

Least Objective Item: Suicidal thoughts

* * *

---

* 1.0 Least Objective; 5.0 Most Objective.

Title: The Adult Performance Scale

Source: Michael R. Dillon, Superintendent, Connecticut State Department of Health, Central Connecticut Regional Center, Box 853, Meriden, Connecticut 06450

Behavior Classes: Personal social, motor, language, academic, job training, work skills

Method: Memory

Reliability or Validity Information Provided: No

Mean Rating of Objectivity: 2.5

Rating Scale: Above average to No skill (1 to 5)

Most Objective Item: Can tell name, address, and age

Least Objective Item: Has ability to listen and hear

*   *   *

Title: Adult Service Treatment Team Resident Evaluation Form

Source: John Campfield, Syracuse State School, P.O. Box 1035, Syracuse, New York 13201

Behavior Classes: General self-help, eating, dressing, socialization.

Method: Memory

Reliability or Validity Information Provided: No

Mean Rating of Objectivity: 3.5

Rating Scale: Yes/No

Most Objective Item: Walks downstairs safely *one* step per tread alternating feet

Least Objective Item: Is conscious of (but may reject) the generally held social expectation that men and women will engage in different recreational activities

*   *   *

Title: Advanced Self-Help Skills Scale (Staff)

Source: Porterville State Hospital, Porterville, California 93257

Behavior Classes: Daily living

Method: Memory

Reliability or Validity Information Provided: No

Mean Rating of Objectivity: 3.0

Rating Scale: Yes/No

Most Objective Item: Irons and launders independently when need arises

Least Objective Item: Shows awareness of proper etiquette and practices it most of the time

*   *   *

Title: Apple Creek State Institute Checklist (Baer)

Source: Apple Creek State Institute, Apple Creek, Ohio 44606

---

* 1.0 Least Objective; 5.0 Most Objective.

Behavior Classes: Feeding, toileting, dressing, grooming, interaction, physical activity

Method: Direct Observation or Memory

Reliability or Validity Information Provided: No

Mean Rating of Objectivity: 2.0

Rating Scale: Circle appropriate description

Most Objective Item: Pants on from ankles

Least Objective Item: Uncooperative

*   *   *

Title: Aroostook Residential Center Checklist (Staff)

Source: Aroostook Residential Center, P.O. Box 1285, Presque Isle, Maine 04769

Behavior Classes: Behavior problems, social behavior, self-help

Method: Memory

Reliability or Validity Information Provided: No

Mean Rating of Objectivity: 2.0

Rating Scale: Yes/No

Most Objective Item: Cleaning plate at meals

Least Objective Item: Bad sport

*   *   *

Title: BMT Assessment Instrument: Global Evaluation Scale (Watson)

Source: Luke S. Watson, Jr., Behavior Modification Technology Inc., Box 597, Libertyville, Illinois 60048

Behavior Classes: Self-help, motor coordination, undesirable behavior, language, miscellaneous

Method: Memory

Reliability or Validity Information Provided: No

Mean Rating of Objectivity: 3.0

Rating Scale: Check appropriate description

Most Objective Item: Client does drink from a glass or cup

Least Objective Item: Client does not accept affection from parents or guardians

*   *   *

Title: Basic Skills Children from the Ages of 0-5 Years Should Acquire (Allessi, Gutmann)

Source: Mary Free Bed Hospital and Rehabilitation Center, 920 Cherry Street, S.E., Grand Rapids, Michigan 49506

Behavior Classes: Cognitive, affective, motor

---

* 1.0 Least Objective; 5.0 Most Objective.

Method: Direct Observation

Reliability or Validity Information Provided: No

Mean Rating of Objectivity: 4.0

Rating Scale: Yes/No + space for a program to teach the skill

Most Objective Item: The child should be able to verbally identify seven pictures out of eight

Least Objective Item: The child should be able to get a drink

         *   *   *

Title: Behavior and Alertness Index (Mego, Wilson)

Source: Veterans Administration Hospital, Tuscaloosa, Alabama 35401

Behavior Classes: Ambulation, eating, continence, grooming, communication, adjustment

Method: Memory

Reliability or Validity Information Provided: Yes

Mean Rating of Objectivity: 3.0

Rating Scale: Never to most or all of the time (1 to 4)

Most Objective Item: Uses toilet without assistance

Least Objective Item: Flustered under stress

         *   *   *

Title: Behavior Assessment Scale (Kenston, Mueller, Frair)

Source: Alaska Psychiatric Institute, 2900 Providence Avenue, Anchorage, Alaska 99504

Behavior Classes: Independence and social interaction

Method: Direct Observation

Reliability or Validity Information Provided: Yes

Mean Rating of Objectivity: 2.0

Rating Scale: None to most or all of the time (1 to 4)

Most Objective Item: Leaves clothes on during the day

Least Objective Item: Disruptive, inconsiderate of others

         *   *   *

Title: Behavior Check List (Staff)

Source: Nebraska Psychiatric Institute, The University of Nebraska Medical Center, 602 S. 45th Street, Omaha, Nebraska 68106

Behavior Classes: Neurotic, maladaptive behavior

Method: Memory

---

* 1.0 Least Objective; 5.0 Most Objective.

Reliability or Validity Information Provided: No

*Mean Rating of Objectivity: 1.0

Rating Scale: True/False

Most Objective Item: Profane language

Least Objective Item: Doesn't know how to have fun

* * *

Title: Behavior Inventory (Babor)

Source: McLean Hospital, Belmont, Massachusetts 02178

Behavior Classes: Alcohol and drug use

Method: Direct Observation

Reliability or Validity Information Provided: Yes

*Mean Rating of Objectivity: 4.0

Rating Scale: Time sampling (15 sec.)

Most Objective Item: If subjects are filling out forms or are engaged in psychomotor testing, code Tst

Least Objective Item: If subjects are engaged in stationary play which requires a minimum of physical activity (cards, Monopoly) code Sta Ply

* * *

Title: Behavior and Learning Survey (Keller)

Source: Charles Keller, M.D., Hilton Family Medicine, P.C., 42 Lake Avenue, Hilton, New York 14468

Behavior Classes: Anxiety, psychoticism, dominance, learning behaviors

Method: Memory

Reliability or Validity Information Provided: Yes

*Mean Rating of Objectivity: 1.5

Rating Scale: Never to almost always (1 to 5)

Most Objective Item: Hits, pushes

Least Objective Item: Feels unworthy, guilty, blames self

* * *

Title: Behavior Maturity Checklist (Soule)

Source: O'Berry Center, P.O. Box 247, Goldsboro, North Carolina 27530

Behavior Classes: Grooming, eating, toileting, total self care, language, social interaction, total interpersonal

Method: Memory or Interview

Reliability or Validity Information Provided: Yes

---

* 1.0 Least Objective; 5.0 Most Objective.

Mean Rating of Objectivity: 2.5

Rating Scale: Circle best alternative of six that describes skill

Most Objective Item: Cannot drink from cup or glass even held by parent

Least Objective Item: Has no interest in leaving immediate area

* * *

Title: Behavior Problem Checklist (Doke)

Source: Larry A. Doke, Moccasin Bend Psychiatric Hospital and Mental Health Center, Chattanooga, Tennessee 37405

Behavior Classes: Verbal, social, maladaptive

Method: Memory

Reliability or Validity Information Provided: No

Mean Rating of Objectivity: 2.0

Rating Scale: Of no concern to   Of much concern (1 to 3)

Most Objective Item: Swearing, cursing, using profanity, insulting others

Least Objective Item: Immature speech

* * *

Title: Behavior Problem Checklist (Peterson, Quay)

Source: Herbert C. Quay, Ph.D., Director, Program in Applied Social Sciences, University of Miami, Coral Gables, Miami, Florida 33124

Behavior Classes: Conduct-Problem, Personality-Problem, Inadequacy-Immaturity

Method: Direct Observation or Memory

Reliability or Validity Information Provided: Yes

Mean Rating of Objectivity: 1.0

Rating Scale: Not Problem to Problem (0-2)

Most Objective Item: Stays out late at night

Least Objective Item: Impertinence, sauciness

* * *

Title: Behavior Profile Evaluation Booklet (Staff)

Source: Anna State Hospital, Developmental Disabilities Division, Anna, Illinois 26906

Behavior Classes: Personal care, motor coordination, socialization, community orientation, educational development, and two others

Method: Direct Observation and Memory

Reliability or Validity Information Provided: No

Mean Rating of Objectivity: 3.0

Rating Scale: Yes/No

---

* 1.0 Least Objective; 5.0 Most Objective.

Most Objective Item: If shown circle, can copy it
Least Objective Item: Knows the difference between day and night

* * *

Title: Behavior Rating and Nursing Observations (Fineman)

Source: Kenneth R. Fineman, Huntington Intercommunity Hospital, 17692 Beach Boulevard, Huntington Beach, California 92647

Behavior Classes: Physical and verbal aggression, maladaptive verbalizations, response to frustrations

Method: Memory

Reliability or Validity Information Provided: No

*Mean Rating of Objectivity: 1.5

Rating Scale: Recorded 3 times per day

Most Objective Item: Throwing objects

Least Objective Item: Passive-aggressive

* * *

Title: Behavior Rating Scale (Kreger)

Source: Oakdale Center for Developmental Disabilities, Laper, Michigan 48446

Behavior Classes: Social and interactive behaviors

Method: Memory

Reliability or Validity Information Provided: No

*Mean Rating of Objectivity: 1.0

Rating Scale: Never to Almost always (0 to 5)

Most Objective Item: Lies; regular lying when questioned

Least Objective Item: Has feelings of failure

* * *

Title: Behavior Rating Scale (Leibowitz, Chorost)

Source: Gerald Leibowitz, 75 South Middle Neck Road, Great Neck, New York 11021

Behavior Classes: Reaction to medication, general behaviors

Method: Memory

Reliability or Validity Information Provided: No

*Mean Rating of Objectivity: 1.5

Rating Scale: Seldom to Often (1 to 4), Yes/No

---

* 1.0 Least Objective; 5.0 Most Objective.

Most Objective Item: Destroys property
Least Objective Item: Feelings easily hurt

* * *

Title: Behavioral Assessment Scales (Staff)
Source: Great Oaks Center, 12001 Cherry Hill Road, Silver Spring, Maryland 20904
Behavior Classes: Motor development and ambulation, communication, feeding, dressing, interaction, educational, personal hygiene, and 4 others
Method: Memory
Reliability or Validity Information Provided: Yes
*Mean Rating of Objectivty: 3.0
Rating Scale: Circle appropriate description
Most Objective Item: Refuses to state name
Least Objective Item: Accepts changes and encourages others to do likewise

* * *

Title: Behavioral Coding System (Cautela, Upper, expanded by Khalili)
Source: Psychological Development Services, 555 North Scott, Belton, Montana 64012
Behavior Classes: Fear, sex, addictions, eating, thinking, emotional, maladaptive
Method: Memory
Reliability or Validity Information Provided: No
*Mean Rating of Objectivity: 2.0
Rating Scale: Yes/No
Most Objective Item: Walking too slowly
Least Objective Item: Recurring thoughts accompanied by anger

* * *

Title: Behavioral Observations of Learning Development: BOLD (Bartman)
Source: Bill Bartman, Bangor Township Schools, Bangor Township, Michigan 49013
Behavior Classes: Social, motor, listening, speaking, reasoning, reading, manipulative-writing, math
Method: Direct Observation or Memory
Reliability or Validity Information Provided: No
*Mean Rating of Objectivity: 2.0
Rating Scale: Yes/No

---

* 1.0 Least Objective; 5.0 Most Objective.

Most Objective Item: Can sort buttons by color (2 colors, black and white).

Least Objective Item: Conforms to ideas and asks help as needed

* * *

Title: Cain-Levine Social Competency Scale (Cain, Levine, Elzey)

Source: Consulting Psychologists Press, 577 College Avenue, Palo Alto, California 94302

Behavior Classes: Self-help, initiative, social skills, communication

Method: Interview

Reliability or Validity Information Provided: Yes

*Mean Rating of Objectivity: 3.0

Rating Scale: Yes/No

Most Objective Item: Can state first name only

Least Objective Item: Can relate objects to action but unable to connect actions into a story

* * *

Title: Categories for Interaction Analysis (Pena)

Source: D. M. Pena, Wayne State University School of Medicine (Annex), 1400 Chrysler Drive, Detroit, Michigan 48207

Behavior Classes: Doctor-patient relationship

Method: Direct Observation

Reliability or Validity Information Provided: No

*Mean Rating of Objectivity: 2.0

Rating Scale: Interval Recording (2 sec.)

Most Objective Item: Explains facts, rationale. . . . You see the knee joint consists of. . . .

Least Objective Item: Constructive silence to encourage communication

* * *

Title: Catawba Hospital Behavioral Checklists (Staff)

Source: Catawba Hospital, Catawba, Virginia 24071

Behavior Classes: Reorientation, remotivation, basic community preparation, advanced community preparation

Method: Memory

Reliability or Validity Information Provided: No

*Mean Rating of Objectivity: 2.0

Rating Scale: Yes/No and comments

---

* 1.0 Least Objective; 5.0 Most Objective.

Most Objective Item: Can set table and prepare simple meals
Least Objective Item: Knows hometown

*   *   *

Title: Catawba Hospital Screening Guidelines for Admissions Unit (Staff)
Source: Catawba Hospital, Catawba, Virginia 24071
Behavior Classes: Screening for admissions (Health, self-care, social behavior)
Method: Interview
Reliability or Validity Information Provided: No
Mean Rating of Objectivity: 1.0
Rating Scale: Yes/No and comments
Most Objective Item: Ambulatory
Least Objective Item: Gets along well with others

*   *   *

Title: Checklist of Behaviors Used to Rate Each Child Twice Daily (Marburg)
Source: Donald Marburg, Austin State Hospital, 4110 Guadalupe, Austin, Texas 78751
Behavior Classes: Meal behaviors
Method: Direct Observation
Reliability or Validity Information Provided: No
Mean Rating of Objectivity: 2.0
Rating Scale: Yes/No
Most Objective Item: Throws food
Least Objective Item: Hogs food

*   *   *

Title: Checklist for Training Staff in Applied Behavior Analysis (Staff)
Source: Eleanor Roosevelt Developmental Services, Balltown and Consaul Roads, Schenectady, New York 12304
Behavior Classes: Staff training behaviors
Method: Memory
Reliability or Validity Information Provided: No
Mean Rating of Objectivity: 3.5
Rating Scale: Completed partial, completed late, completed
Most Objective Item: Passes quizzes with at least 85% accuracy
Least Objective Item: Does assigned reading

*   *   *

---

* 1.0 Least Objective; 5.0 Most Objective.

Title: Child Behavior Rating Scale (Cassel)

Source: Western Psychological Services, 12031 Willshire Boulevard, Los Angeles, California 90025

Behavior Classes: Self-adjustment, home adjustment, social adjustment

Method: Memory

Reliability or Validity Information Provided: No

*Mean Rating of Objectivity: 1.0

Rating Scale: Yes to No (1 to 6)

Most Objective Item: Often bites nails or sucks thumbs and fingers

Least Objective Item: Often lacks status and feels insecure with friends

* * *

Title: Children's Psychiatric Center Problem List (Leventhal, Stollak)

Source: Theodore Leventhal, Children's Psychiatric Center, Inc., 59 Broad Street, Eatontown, New Jersey 07724

Behavior Classes: Problems of children

Method: Memory

Reliability or Validity Information Provided: Yes

*Mean Rating of Objectivity: 1.0

Rating Scale: Yes/No

Most Objective Item: Moves too slowly

Least Objective Item: He is girl-crazy

* * *

Title: Classification Code for Household Activities (Chapin)

Source: Chapin, F. S., Jr. (Ed.). *Human Activity Patterns in the City*. New York: John Wiley & Sons, 1974

Behavior Classes: Shopping and household business, vocation-oriented activities, religious and cultural activities, visiting, and 4 others

Method: Direct observation or Memory

Reliability or Validity Information Provided: No

*Mean Rating of Objectivity: 2.0

Rating Scale: Yes/No

Most Objective Item: Picking up paychecks when not done on company time

Least Objective Item: Elementary education

* * *

---

* 1.0 Least Objective; 5.0 Most Objective.

Title: Classroom Behavior and Consequence Record (Staff)

Source: Eleanor Roosevelt Developmental Services, Balltown and Consaul Roads, Schenectady, New York 12304

Behavior Classes: Antecedents, behavior, and consequences of student in classroom

Method: Direct Observation

Reliability or Validity Information Provided: No

*Mean Rating of Objectivity: 3.0

Rating Scale: Interval Recording

Most Objective Item: Task oriented: reads, writes, figures, etc.

Least Objective Item: Disruptive: behavior associated with the disruption of the work of others

*   *   *

Title: Client Checklist (Larrabee)

Source: John B. Larrabee, Danbury Regional Center, 400 Main Street, Danbury, Connecticut 06810

Behavior Classes: Sit, crawl, creep, walk, motor skills, eye-hand, self-management, eating, language, social, academic

Method: Direct Observation or Memory

Reliability or Validity Information Provided: No

*Mean Rating of Objectivity: 3.0

Rating Scale: Unsuccessful to successful (1 to 3)

Most Objective Item: Walks downstairs, holding rail, two feet per tread

Least Objective Item: Knows object exists even when out of sight

*   *   *

Title: Comprehensive Evaluation Form

Source: William R. Phelps, West Virginia Rehabilitation Center, Institute, West Virginia 25112

Behavior Classes: Vocational, recreational and general activities, physical productivity, response to supervision, social adjustment and expression, attitude

Method: Memory

Reliability or Validity Information Provided: No

*Mean Rating of Objectivity: 1.0

Rating Scale: Yes/No

Most Objective Item: Can client tell time to nearest hour, half-hour, quarter hour, exactly?

Least Objective Item: Evasive

*   *   *

---

* 1.0 Least Objective; 5.0 Most Objective.

Title: Comprehensive Problem Behavior Survey (Renne, Christian)

Source: Charles M. Renne, The National Asthma Center, 1999 Julian Street, Denver, Colorado 80204

Behavior Classes: Health, household responsibility, social interactions, affect, eating, bedtime routine, school, other

Method: Memory

Reliability or Validity Information Provided: No

Mean Rating of Objectivity: 2.0

Rating Scale: Yes/No

Most Objective Item: Destroyed . . . property, either by being careless or by intentionally breaking, burning, marring, etc.

Least Objective Item: Failed to cooperate with treatment

* * *

Title: Craig Developmental Center Educational Progress Report (Staff)

Source: Craig Developmental Center, Sonyea, New York 14556

Behavior Classes: Personality and social adjustments, self-care, health safety skills, motor, work habits, readiness, communication oral, and 5 others

Method: Memory

Reliability or Validity Information Provided: No

Mean Rating of Objectivity: 2.0

Rating Scale: Written description

Most Objective Item: Laundering

Least Objective Item: Courteous and cooperative.

* * *

Title: Daily Behavior Checklist (Kaplan)

Source: Henry K. Kaplan, Division of Mental Hygiene, Mendota Mental Health Institute, 301 Troy Drive, Madison, Wisconsin 53704

Behavior Classes: Cottage behavior

Method: Direct Observation

Reliability or Validity Information Provided: No

Mean Rating of Objectivity: 2.0

Rating Scale: Yes/No; M T W T F (a.m.-p.m.)

Most Objective Item: Used silverware, not fingers

Least Objective Item: No trouble reported in school

* * *

* 1.0 Least Objective; 5.0 Most Objective.

Title: Development and Trainability Assessment (Bannatyne, Bradtke, Kirkpatrick, Rosenblatt, Strunk)

Source: William J. Kirkpatrick, Jr., BKR Project, Sunland Training Center at Miami, 20000 N.W. 47th Avenue, Miami, Florida 33054

Behavior Classes: Recognition of purpose, spatial relations, form-shape sorting, color sorting, diameter size sorting, texture sorting, and 10 others.

Method: Direct Observation

Reliability or Validity Information Provided: No

Mean Rating of Objectivity: 4.0

Rating Scale: Failure to Spontaneously (0 to 6)

Most Objective Item: Matches and places two differently colored buttons into same color hollows in muffin tins

Least Objective Item: Child plays with others socially

*   *   *

Title: Developmental Checklist (Hart)

Source: Verna Hart, Ed.D., Associate Professor, Early Childhood Education for the Handicapped, University of Pittsburgh, Pittsburgh, Pennsylvania 15213

Behavior Classes: Gross motor, fine motor, perception, conceptual, emotional, social communication, self-help

Method: Direct observation

Reliability or Validity Information Provided: No

Mean Rating of Objectivity: 3.0

Rating Scale: Yes/No

Most Objective Item: Has vocabulary of 600-1000 words

Least Objective Item: Formulates negative judgment

*   *   *

Title: Developmental Check List (Staff)

Source: Central Connecticut Regional Center, Undercliff Road, Box 853, Meriden, Connecticut 06450

Behavior Classes: Self-care, motor development, social maturity and manners, language, personality

Method: Memory

Reliability or Validity Information Provided: No

Mean Rating of Objectivity: 3.0

Rating Scale: Not yet to All the time (1 to 3)

---

* 1.0 Least Objective; 5.0 Most Objective.

Most Objective Item: Can unzip front and side zippers

Least Objective Item: Will not stand up for rights

* * *

Title: Developmental Check List (Hart)

Source: Verna Hart, Deaf-Blind Program, University of Pittsburgh, Pittsburgh, Pennsylvania 15213

Behavior Classes: Gross-motor, fine-motor, perceptual, conceptual, social emotional, communication, self-care

Method: Direct observation

Reliability or Validity Information Provided: No

**Mean Rating of Objectivity*: 3.0

Rating Scale: Yes/No

Most Objective Item: Hops on one foot

Least Objective Item: Distress differentiates into more specific responses of fear, disgust, anger

* * *

Title: Developmental Guidelines

Source: Central Connecticut Regional Center, Undercliff Road, Box 853, Meriden, Connecticut 06450

Behavior Classes: Fine motor, cognitive, linguistic and verbal, self-help, social, gross motor

Method: Direct Observation

Reliability or Validity Information Provided: No

**Mean Rating of Objectivity*: 3.0

Rating Scale: Various coding

Most Objective Item: Puts six blocks on formboard in 150 seconds

Least Objective Item: Interested in painting process, not product

* * *

Title: Developmental Screening Inventory for Feeding Readiness (Staff)

Source: Central Connecticut Regional Center, Undercliff Road, Box 853, Meriden, Connecticut 06450

Behavior Classes: Behaviors from 3 months to 2 years

Method: Direct Observation or Memory

Reliability or Validity Information Provided: No

**Mean Rating of Objectivity*: 3.0

Rating Scale: Yes/No

---

* 1.0 Least Objective; 5.0 Most Objective.

Most Objective Item: Places large peg in hole
Least Objective Item: Alert expression

* * *

Title: Diagnostic Behavior Rating Scale (Stumphauzer, Bishop)
Source: J. S. Stumphauzer, Child/Adolescent Clinic, 1237 North Mission Road, Los Angeles, California 90033
Behavior Classes: Self-care, motor, speech and language, individual, social, other problems
Method: Memory
Reliability or Validity Information Provided: No
Mean Rating of Objectivity: 2.5
Rating Scale: Never to Always (0 to 3)
Most Objective Item: Wets bed
Least Objective Item: Does things quickly without thinking

* * *

Title: Eastmont Training Center Checklist (Staff)
Source: Eastmont Training Center, Little Street, Glendive, Montana 59330
Behavior Classes: Academic readiness, fine motor, language, writing, math, time telling, reading, money-handling, independent living skills, and six others
Method: Direct Observation or Memory
Reliability or Validity Information Provided: No
Mean Rating of Objectivity: 3.0
Rating Scale: Yes/No
Most Objective Item: Can rote count 1-100.
Least Objective Item: Can understand morning, afternoon, evening

* * *

Title: Ebensburg State School and Hospital Checklist (Hartley, Madle, Milne, Fatham)
Source: Donald L. Hartley, Ebensburg State School and Hospital, Ebensburg, Pennsylvania 15931
Behavior Classes: Expressive, receptive, temporal, responsive, attention span, self-concept, mobility, perceptual motor, eating, dressing, and two others
Method: Direct Observation or Memory
Reliability or Validity Information Provided: No
Mean Rating of Objectivity: 3.0
Rating Scale: Yes/No

---

* 1.0 Least Objective; 5.0 Most Objective.

Most Objective Item: Executes a chained activity (stack toy) where reinforcement is delayed for at least 30 seconds

Least Objective Item: Cooperates passively while being bathed or washed

* * *

Title: Evaluation Check List: Educable Mentally Retarded (Staff)

Source: Education Department, Craig State School, Sonyea, New York 14556

Behavior Classes: Health, personal grooming, work, safety, social motor, music, academic, field trip participation

Method: Memory

Reliability or Validity Information Provided: No

*Mean Rating of Objectivity: 2.5

Rating Scale: Lack skill to Adequate (1 to 4)

Most Objective Item: Colors within lines

Least Objective Item: Sympathizes with others

* * *

Title: Evaluation Check List: Trainable Mentally Retarded (Staff)

Source: Education Department, Craig State School, Sonyea, New York 14556

Behavior Classes: Field trip participation, health, grooming, safety, manners, attitude and social development, academic skills

Method: Memory

Reliability or Validity Information Provided: No

*Mean Rating of Objectivity: 2.5

Rating Scale: Unable, limited success, adequate

Most Objective Item: Can apply toothpaste

Least Objective Item: Aware of sequential time concept

* * *

Title: Everett A. Gladman Memorial Hospital Activity Department Progress Report (Staff)

Source: Activity Therapy Department, E. A. Gladman Memorial Hospital, 2633 E. 27th Street, Oakland, California 94601

Behavior Classes: Attendance, participation, social behavior, skills, intellectual behavior, attitude and mood, expressed thoughts, appearance, conversations

Method: Memory

Reliability or Validity Information Provided: No

*Mean Rating of Objectivity: 1.0

Rating Scale: Yes/No

---

* 1.0 Least Objective; 5.0 Most Objective.

Most Objective Item: Speaks slowly, hesitantly
Least Objective Item: Unrealistic ideas

* * *

Title: Fairview Development Scale (Giampiccolo and Boroskin)
Source: Research Department, Fairview State Hospital, 2501 Harbor Boulevard,
Costa Mesa, California 92626
Behavior Classes: Perceptual and motor skills, self-help skills, language, social inter-
action, self-direction
Method: Direct Observation or Memory
Reliability or Validity Information Provided: Yes
Mean Rating of Objectivity: 3.0
Rating Scale: Yes/No
Most Objective Item: Sits erect when supported (at least 15 minutes)
Least Objective Item: Startled by sudden sounds

* * *

Title: Fairview Language Evaluation Scale (Boroskin)
Source: Fairview State Hospital, Research Department, 2501 Harbor Boulevard,
Costa Mesa, California 92626
Behavior Classes: Includes 10 levels of language ability
Method: Memory
Reliability or Validity Information Provided: Yes
Mean Rating of Objectivity: 3.0
Rating Scale: Yes/No
Most Objective Item: Repeats an 8- to 10-word sentence after hearing it *once*
Least Objective Item: Speech is completely understandable to a stranger

* * *

Title: Fairview Problem Behavior Record (Ross)
Source: Research Department, Fairview State Hospital, 2501 Harbor Boulevard,
Costa Mesa, California 92626
Behavior Classes: Aggressive, hyperactive, sexual, covert and inappropriate behaviors
Method: Memory
Reliability or Validity Information Provided: No
Mean Rating of Objectivity: 1.0
Rating Scale: Yes/No

---

* 1.0 Least Objective; 5.0 Most Objective.

Most Objective Item: Bites others

Least Objective Item: Hostile

* * *

Title: Fairview Self-Help Scale (Ross)

Source: Research Department, Fairview State Hospital, 2501 Harbor Boulevard, Costa Mesa, California 92626

Behavior Classes: Motor dexterity, self-help skills, communication skills, social interaction, self-direction

Method: Memory

Reliability or Validity Information Provided: Yes

*Mean Rating of Objectivity: 3.0

Rating Scale: Yes/No

Most Objective Item: Speaks sentences of three or more words

Least Objective Item: Knows meaning of "morning," "noon," and "night"

* * *

Title: Fairview Social Skills Scale (Giampiccolo)

Source: Research Department, Fairview State Hospital, 2501 Harbor Boulevard, Costa Mesa, California 92626

Behavior Classes: Self-help skills, communication, social interaction, occupation, self-direction

Method: Memory

Reliability or Validity Information Provided: Yes

*Mean Rating of Objectivity: 2.5

Rating Scale: Yes/No

Most Objective Item: Can count out 13 cents, 38 cents.

Least Objective Item: Usually sulky

* * *

Title: Feeding Skills Scale (Adapted from the Willowbrook Scale of Social Skills Development)

Source: Manhattan Developmental Center, 75 Morton Street, New York, New York 10014

Behavior Classes: Acceptance of food and finger feeding, use of spoon, fork, knife, liquid intake, table habits and manners

Method: Direct Observation or Memory

Reliability or Validity Information Provided: No

*Mean Rating of Objectivity: 3.0

---

* 1.0 Least Objective; 5.0 Most Objective.

Rating Scale: Accomplishes task to Physiological problem (1 to 3)
Most Objective Item: Spreads material placed on bread (unassisted)
Least Objective Item: Plays with spoon

*   *   *

Title: The Florida State Hospital Patient Behavior Rating Sheet: PBRS (Harris)
Source: Clark S. Harris, Florida State Hospital, Chattahoochee, Florida 32324
Behavior Classes: Ward, verbal and memory, overall impressions
Method: Direct Observation
Reliability or Validity Information Provided: No
**Mean Rating of Objectivity*: 3.0
Rating Scale: Very bad to very good (1 to 5) and other
Most Objective Item: Responds with her name (to a prompt)
Least Objective Item: Appropriate interaction with others

*   *   *

Title: Functional Capacity Evaluation (Reynolds: parts adapted from Morrison
 Center Functional Capacity Evaluation, San Francisco, California)
Source: Jay Reynolds, Occupational Therapy Department, West Virginia Rehabi-
 litation Center, Institute, West Virginia 25112
Behavior Classes: Mobility, work, positioning, strength, reaching
Method: Direct Observation
Reliability or Validity Information Provided: No
**Mean Rating of Objectivity*: 4.0
Rating Scale: Time and comments
Most Objective Item: Assume a one-leg stand for ½ minute on each leg
Least Objective Item: Learn whipstitch for leather lacing

*   *   *

Title: Functional Screening Tool (Paulus)
Source: Central Connecticut Regional Center, Undercliff Road, Box 853, Meriden,
 Connecticut 06450
Behavior Classes: Motor, sleep, speech, play, discipline, toilet training, dressing-
 undressing
Method: Direct Observation
Reliability or Validity Information Provided: No
**Mean Rating of Objectivity*: 3.0
Rating Scale: Cannot perform, fluctuating, successful

---

* 1.0 Least Objective; 5.0 Most Objective.

Most Objective Item: Counts three objects, pointing to each in turn

Least Objective Item: Understands reasoning

*   *   *

Title: Group Home Candidate Check List (Turnbull)

Source: Ann P. Turnbull, Department of Special Education, University of North Carolina, Chapel Hill, North Carolina 27514

Behavior Classes: Arithmetic, social competence, health, safety, vocations

Method: Memory

Reliability or Validity Information Provided: No

*Mean Rating of Objectivity: 2.5

Rating Scale: Yes/No

Most Objective Item: Reads and writes symbols 0-10

Least Objective Item: Understands reasons why slang and vulgar words which have sexual overtones should not be used

*   *   *

Title: Hastings Regional Center Lower Functioning Development Scales (Staff)

Source: Hastings Regional Center, Hastings, Nebraska 68901

Behavior Classes: Sensory, motor, self-help, language, cognitive, social-emotional

Method: Direct Observation

Reliability or Validity Information Provided: No

*Mean Rating of Objectivity: 4.0

Rating Scale: Yes/No

Most Objective Item: Sits erect when placed Indian style for 30 seconds or more

Least Objective Item: Familiar with the bathroom

*   *   *

Title: Heterosocial Skills Behavior Checklist

Source: David H. Barlow, Ph.D., Butler Hospital, 333 Grotto Avenue, Providence, Rhode Island 02906

Behavior Classes: Form of conversation, affect, and voice of male in social interaction with female

Method: Memory

Reliability or Validity Information Provided: Yes

*Mean Rating of Objectivity: 2.0

Rating Scale: Appropriate/inappropriate (30-second intervals).

---

* 1.0 Least Objective; 5.0 Most Objective.

Most Objective Item: Male responds at least once to female's vocalizations

Least Objective Item: No special dramatic effects

* * *

Title: Higginsville State School and Hospital Behavioral Scale (Staff)

Source: Higginsville State School and Hospital, P.O. Box 522, Higginsville, Missouri 64037

Behavior Classes: Self-management, communication, interpersonal relations, environmental structuring, environmental access.

Method: Direct Observation

Reliability or Validity Information Provided: No

*Mean Rating of Objectivity: 4.0

Rating Scale: Yes/No and others

Most Objective Item: Covers mouth with hand or tissue when coughing

Least Objective Item: Takes a leadership role in activities

* * *

Title: Household Activities Performance Evaluation (Phelps)

Source: William R. Phelps, Disabled Homemaker Program, Division of Vocational Rehabilitation, Charleston, West Virginia 25305

Behavior Classes: Household skills of disabled homemakers.

Method: Direct Observation

Reliability or Validity Information Provided: No

*Mean Rating of Objectivity: 3.0

Rating Scale: Needs training to Unassisted (0 to 3)

Most Objective Item: Pour hot water from pan to cup

Least Objective Item: Use can opener

* * *

Title: Howe, W. A. Development Center Behavioral Checklist

Source: R. J. Van Dyke, W. V. Howe Development Center, 7600 W. 183rd Street, Tinley Park, Illinois 60477

Behavior Classes: Perceptual skills, self-help skills, communication skills, employment skills, household skills

Method: Direct Observation or Memory

Reliability or Validity Information Provided: No

*Mean Rating of Objectivity: 3.0

Rating Scale: Yes/No

---

* 1.0 Least Objective; 5.0 Most Objective.

Most Objective Item: Identifies (by pointing) more than 25 nouns

Least Objective Item: Knows others' names

* * *

Title: Individual Evaluation Report-ABC Program (Barrett)

Source: Albert M. Barrett, Director of Psychology, Sunland Center, Gainesville, Florida 32601

Behavior Classes: Self-care, behavior changing, social awareness, mental skills

Method: Direct Observation or Memory

Reliability or Validity Information Provided: No

*Mean Rating of Objectivity: 2.0

Rating Scale: Beginning learning to Almost complete (1 to 3)

Most Objective Item: Can put on shoes and socks

Least Objective Item: Resistant, rebellious, stubborn behavior

* * *

Title: Institute for Child Behavior Diagnostic Check List for Behavior-Disturbed Children (Rimland)

Source: Bernard Rimland, Institute for Child Behavior Research, 4758 Edgeware Road, San Diego, California 92116

Behavior Classes: Medical and early childhood behaviors

Method: Memory or interview

Reliability or Validity Information Provided: Yes

*Mean Rating of Objectivity: 1.0

Rating Scale: Yes/No

Most Objective Item: Has the child used the word "I"?

Least Objective Item: Does the child seem to want to be liked?

* * *

Title: L-M Fergus Falls Behavior Rating Sheet (Farview State Hospital Adaptation)

Source: Farview State Hospital, Waymart, Pennsylvania 18472

Behavior Classes: Work, response to others, psychomotor, speech, toilet

Method: Memory

Reliability or Validity Information Provided: No

*Mean Rating of Objectivity: 2.0

Rating Scale: Yes/No

Most Objective Item: Eats by self using spoon properly

Least Objective Item: Negativistic

* * *

---

* 1.0 Least Objective; 5.0 Most Objective.

Title: The Lakeland Village Adaptive Behavior Grid (Gilbèrt)

Source: Grant O. Gilbert, Lakeland Village, P.O. Box 200, Medical Lake, Washington 99022

Behavior Classes: Eating, toileting, dressing, health and grooming, communication, mobility and dexterity, vocational and recreational, and three others

Method: Direct Observation or Memory

Reliability or Validity Information Provided: No

Mean Rating of Objectivity: 3.5

Rating Scale: Yes/No

Most Objective Item: Follows a straight one-inch wide path for a distance of 10 feet

Least Objective Item: Marks with crayon

*   *   *

Title: Lapeer Adaptive Behavior Profile (Staff)

Source: Oakdale Center for Developmental Disabilities, Lapeer, Michigan 48446

Behavior Classes: Independent functioning, physical development, language development, community, social

Method: Memory

Reliability or Validity Information Provided: No

Mean Rating of Objectivity: 2.0

Rating Scale: Yes to No (1 to 3)

Most Objective Item: Can say few words

Least Objective Item: Cooperative

*   *   *

Title: Learning Accomplishment Profile: LAP (Sanford)

Source: Kaplan School Supply Corporation, 600 Jonestown Road, Winston-Salem, North Carolina 27103

Behavior Classes: Gross motor, fine motor, social, self help, cognitive, language

Method: Direct Observation

Reliability or Validity Information Provided: No

Mean Rating of Objectivity: 4.0

Rating Scale: Yes/No + additional comments

Most Objective Item: Jump from height of 12 inches, landing on toes only

Least Objective Item: Run

*   *   *

Title: Lincoln Behavior Scale (Staff)

Source: Lincoln Developmental Center, 861 South State, Lincoln, Illinois 62656

---

* 1.0 Least Objective; 5.0 Most Objective.

Behavior Classes: Motor coordination, care and use of clothes, dining, personal care, expressive communication (vocalization or sign), social and leisure behavior, housekeeping, preacademic, occupation

Method: Direct Observation

Reliability or Validity Information Provided: No

Mean Rating of Objectivity: 3.0

Rating Scale: Yes/No or with prompts

Most Objective Item: Makes change for amounts up to $1.

Least Objective Item: Stays within limits of available money when ordering (meals)

*   *   *

Title: MR Status Form (Staff)

Source: Hunterdon State School, P.O. Box 5220, Clinton, New Jersey 08809

Behavior Classes: Intellectual functioning, adaptive behavior, understanding, physical impairments

Method: Memory

Reliability or Validity Information Provided: Yes

Mean Rating of Objectivity: 3.0

Rating Scale: Yes/No

Most Objective Item: Bites other residents or employees

Least Objective Item: Does not make any motion to try to express himself or convey needs or desires through gestures

*   *   *

Title: Maladaptive Behavioral Assessment (Kreger)

Source: Ken Kreger, Mental Retardation Services, Genesee County Community Mental Health, Flint, Michigan 48501

Behavior Classes: Violent, antisocial, asocial, withdrawals

Method: Memory

Reliability or Validity Information Provided: No

Mean Rating of Objectivity: 1.0

Rating Scale: How often behavior occurs

Most Objective Item: Removes own clothing

Least Objective Item: Seems to feel persecuted

*   *   *

Title: Maladaptive Behavioral Assessment Scale (Staff)

Source: Muskegon Developmental Center, 1903 Marquette Avenue, Muskegon, Michigan 49442

---

* 1.0 Least Objective; 5.0 Most Objective.

Behavior Classes: Inappropriate social and personal habit behaviors.

Method: Memory

Reliability or Validity Information Provided: No

Mean Rating of Objectivity: 2.5

Rating Scale: Never to Hourly (0 to 7)

Most Objective Item: Talks too close to others' faces.

Least Objective Item: Does not recognize own limitations

*   *   *

Title: Materials Development Center (MDC) Behavior Identification Form (Staff)

Source: Materials Development Center, Department of Rehabilitation and Manpower Services, University of Wisconsin-Stout, Menomonie, Wisconsin 54751

Behavior Classes: Work and work-related behaviors (22 categories)

Method: Memory

Reliability or Validity Information Provided: No

Mean Rating of Objectivity: 3.5

Rating Scale: Various (1 to 3)

Most Objective Item: Missed two days without calling in

Least Objective Item: Ability to cope with work problems (frustration tolerance)

*   *   *

Title: Meeker-Cromwell Evaluation of Behavior Development (Meeker, Cromwell)

Source: Research Applications to Education, P.O. Box 30453, Santa Barbara, California 93105

Behavior Classes: Self-development, intact hedonism, conceptual motivational system, interpersonal functioning, cultural functioning

Method: Memory

Reliability or Validity Information Provided: No

Mean Rating of Objectivity: 1.0

Rating Scale: Not descriptive to descriptive (1 to 5)

Most Objective Item: Whines, cries, regresses to baby actions

Least Objective Item: Is aware that conflicting cultural concepts of right and wrong have relative meanings

*   *   *

Title: Meriden Regional Center Evaluation Check List (Staff)

Source: Central Connecticut Regional Center, Undercliff Road, Box 853, Meriden, Connecticut 06450

---

* 1.0 Least Objective; 5.0 Most Objective.

Behavior Classes: Self-care, visual motor, social maturity, language, personality, academics

Method: Memory

Reliability or Validity Information Provided: No

Mean Rating of Objectivity: 2.0

Rating Scale: Yes/No

Most Objective Item: Can string large beads

Least Objective Item: Has very little energy

* * *

Title: The Metro Overt Behavior Rating Inventory: MOBRI (Harmon)

Source: Judson A. Harmon, Cooperative Educational Service Agency No. 19, 9722 Watertown Plank Road, Milwaukee, Wisconsin 53226

Behavior Classes: Disruptive, fear of failure, achievement orientation, hostility and disobedience, self-esteem, positive social orientation

Method: Memory

Reliability or Validity Information Provided: Yes

Mean Rating of Objectivity: 2.5

Rating Scale: Never witnessed to Once a day (1 to 6)

Most Objective Item: Asks to be excused from recitation tasks

Least Objective Item: Is quick to try out new methods and materials

* * *

Title: Meyer Children's Rehabilitation Institute Early Childhood Education Program Developmental Scales

Source: Meyer Children's Rehabilitation Institute, 444 S. 44th Street, Omaha, Nebraska 68131

Behavior Classes: Expressive language, receptive language, visual motor perceptual, memory and general information, personal/social, and five others

Method: Direct Observation

Reliability or Validity Information Provided: No

Mean Rating of Objectivity: 4.0

Rating Scale: Yes/No

Most Objective Item: Identifies 2 out of 3 pictured actions by pointing

Least Objective Item: Is aware of own hands as part of self by playing with them

* * *

Title: Meyer Children's Rehabilitation Institute School Questionnaire (Staff)

Source: Meyer Children's Rehabilitation Institute, 444 S. 44th Street, Omaha, Nebraska 68131

---

* 1.0 Least Objective; 5.0 Most Objective.

Behavior Classes: Reading, arithmetic, behavior problems
Method: Memory
Reliability or Validity Information Provided: No
Mean Rating of Objectivity: 1.5
Rating Scale: Yes/No
Most Objective Item: Sequencing numbers forward
Least Objective Item: Errors on easy words

* * *

Title: Michigan Behavioral Skills Profile (Staff)
Source: Oakdale Center for Developmental Disabilities, Lapeer, Michigan 48446
Behavior Classes: Socialization, self-care, pre-vocational
Method: Memory
Reliability or Validity Information Provided: No
Mean Rating of Objectivity: 2.5
Rating Scale: One year Goal—Two year goal
Most Objective Item: Feeds self adequately using knife, fork, and spoon appropriately and easily, without help
Least Objective Item: Understands concepts of yesterday, today and tomorrow

* * *

Title: Midway Tutoring Progress Report (Staff)
Source: Pre-Vocational Training Program, Midway Program, Grafton State School, Grafton, North Dakota 58237
Behavior Classes: Math, grooming, domestic, social
Method: Memory
Reliability or Validity Information Provided: No
Mean Rating of Objectivity: 1.5
Rating Scale: Not learned to Learned (1 to 5)
Most Objective Item: Counts to 10
Least Objective Item: Knows the value of independence

* * *

Title: Minnesota Developmental Programming System (Bock, Hawkins, Jeyachandran, Tapper, Weatherman)
Source: Warren H. Bock, Outreach Training Program, 301 Health Service Building, St. Paul, Minnesota 55108

---

* 1.0 Least Objective; 5.0 Most Objective.

Behavior Classes: Gross and fine motor, eating, dressing, toileting, grooming, receptive language, expressive language, and 10 others

Method: Direct Observation or Memory

Reliability or Validity Information Provided: Yes

**Mean Rating of Objectivity*: 4.0

Rating Scale: Yes/No

Most Objective Item: Responds to the instruction: "Look at me," with two seconds of eye contact

Least Objective Item: Acts appropriately in any public situation

* * *

Title: Motivation Check List (Staff)

Source: San Angelo Center, Carlsbad, Texas 76934

Behavior Classes: Interest, awareness, participation, comprehension, knowledge, reading, voice, speech

Method: Memory

Reliability or Validity Information Provided: No

**Mean Rating of Objectivity*: 1.0

Rating Scale: Yes/No

Most Objective Item: Refuses to come to meetings

Least Objective Item: Distracted by "voices"

* * *

Title: N.O.S.I.E.

Source: Gilbert Honigfeld, Research Department, Hillside Hospital, Glen Oaks, New York 11004

Behavior Classes: Hygiene and social behavior

Method: Memory

Reliability or Validity Information Provided: No

**Mean Rating of Objectivity*: 1.0

Rating Scale: Never to Always (0 to 4)

Most Objective Item: Keeps his clothes neat

Least Objective Item: Is quick to fly off the handle

* * *

Title: North Central Regional Center Skill Evaluation and Assessment (Staff)

Source: North Central Regional Center, 73 Rockwell Avenue, Bloomfield, Connecticut 06002

---

* 1.0 Least Objective; 5.0 Most Objective.

Behavior Classes: Personal hygiene, laundry, housecleaning, table behavior, manners, cooking, safety knowledge, transportation, and 12 others

Method: Direct Observation

Reliability or Validity Information Provided: No

*Mean Rating of Objectivity: 3.0

Rating Scale: Yes/No

Most Objective Item: Hangs folded towel on towel rack

Least Objective Item: Has proper employment behavioral qualities

*   *   *

Title: Observable Classroom Behavior

Source: Nebraska Psychiatric Institute, The University of Nebraska Medical Center, 602 S. 45th Street, Omaha, Nebraska 68106

Behavior Classes: Visual-motor, auditory-vocal, behavior in classroom

Method: Memory

Reliability or Validity Information Provided: No

*Mean Rating of Objectivity: 1.5

Rating Scale: Yes/No

Most Objective Item: May not be able to memorize first Communion prayers or hymns

Least Objective Item: Does not understand what he hears

*   *   *

Title: Observation Sheet for Teachers

Source: Central Connecticut Regional Center, Undercliff Road, Box 853, Meriden, Connecticut 06450

Behavior Classes: Gross motor, fine motor, language, personal-social

Method: Direct Observation or Memory

Reliability or Validity Information Provided: No

*Mean Rating of Objectivity: 3.0

Rating Scale: Yes/No, Tries, With help

Most Objective Item: Builds tower of six or seven one-inch cubes

Least Objective Item: Great interest and ability in undressing

*   *   *

Title: Occupational Therapy Behavioral Inventory (Esenther)

Source: Ray Graham Association for the Handicapped, 515 Factory Road, Addison, Illinois 60101

---

* 1.0 Least Objective; 5.0 Most Objective.

Behavior Classes: Locomotion, eating, dressing, personal hygiene, social behavior, travel, communication

Method: Direct Observation and Interview

Reliability or Validity Information Provided: No

Mean Rating of Objectivity: 3.0

Rating Scale: Independent performance to N/A (1 to 5)

Most Objective Item: Get into bed

Least Objective Item: Understand Yes and No

* * *

Title: Operant Counting Scale (Sheinbein, Wiggings)

Source: Marc L. Sheinbein, Department of Psychiatry, Children's Medical Center, 1935 Amelia Street, Dallas, Texas 75235

Behavior Classes: Use of senses, coordination, distractibility, inability to delay, emotional detachment, irritability, and six others

Method: Direct Observation

Reliability or Validity Information Provided: No

Mean Rating of Objectivity: 3.5

Rating Scale: Count number of responses

Most Objective Item: Number of times fails to make eye contact when speaking or spoken to

Least Objective Item: Number of times accepting a loss, failure, change in plans, or not getting own way by not showing strong emotional reaction

* * *

Title: Parent Rating Sheet

Source: William R. Phelps, West Virginia Rehabilitation Center, Institute, West Virginia 25112

Behavior Classes: Impressions of parent during interview

Method: Direct Observation

Reliability or Validity Information Provided: No

Mean Rating of Objectivity: 1.0

Rating Scale: Yes/No

Most Objective Item: Slow speech

Least Objective Item: Martyred

* * *

Title: Parents' Evaluation Check List (Geshuri)

Source: Yosef Geshuri, Mental Health Institute, Box 338, Clarinda, Iowa 51632

---

* 1.0 Least Objective; 5.0 Most Objective.

Behavior Classes: General problem behaviors exhibited around the home

Method: Memory

Reliability or Validity Information Provided: No

*Mean Rating of Objectivity: 2.0

Rating Scale: Yes/No (1 to 4)

Most Objective Item: Breaks things around the house, has very little respect for property

Least Objective Item: Exhibits strange behaviors of some kind

* * *

Title: Parten Scale for Child Observation

Source: Parten (1932); Wintre and Webster (1974)

Behavior Classes: Play activities

Method: Direct Observation

Reliability or Validity Information Provided: No

*Mean Rating of Objectivity: 3.0

Rating Scale: Time sampling

Most Objective Item: Touching the therapist

Least Objective Item: Child apparently is not playing, but occupies himself with watching anything that happens to be of momentary interest

* * *

Title: Pennsylvania Training Model: Individual Assessment Guide (Somerton, Turner)

Source: M. Ellen Somerton, Division of Special Education, Pennsylvania Training Model, 123 Forster Street, Harrisburg, Pennsylvania 17102

Behavior Classes: Auditory, tactile, visual, gross motor, fine motor, feeding-drinking, toileting, dressing, washing and bathing, nasal hygiene, oral hygiene, communication, perceptual cognitive, social interaction

Method: Direct Observation

Reliability or Validity Information Provided: No

*Mean Rating of Objectivity: 4.0

Rating Scale: 0%, 25%, 75%, or 100% correct response

Most Objective Item: Child will turn pages of a book, one at a time.

Least Objective Item: Child listens to imitate

* * *

Title: Perceptual Behavior Check List

Source: Nebraska Psychiatric Institute, The University of Nebraska Medical Center, 602 S. 45th Street, Omaha, Nebraska 68106

---

* 1.0 Least Objective; 5.0 Most Objective.

Behavior Classes: Simple classroom perceptual behavior

Method: Memory

Reliability or Validity Information Provided: No

*Mean Rating of Objectivity: 3.0

Rating Scale: Most, Sometimes, Not usually

Most Objective Item: Can he distinguish squares from rectangles of similar size?

Least Objective Item: Does he concentrate on one thing for a reasonable length of time?

*   *   *

Title: Portage Project Check List (Shearer, Billingsley, Frohman, Hilliard, Johnson, Shearer)

Source: David Shearer, Cooperative Educational Service Agency No. 12, Portage, Wisconsin 53901

Behavior Classes: Cognition, self-help, motor, language, socialization

Method: Direct Observation

Reliability or Validity Information Provided: No

*Mean Rating of Objectivity: 3.0

Rating Scale: Yes/No

Most Objective Item: Grasps rattle

Least Objective Item: Aware of sexual differences

*   *   *

Title: Porterville State Hospital Work Evaluation Form (Staff)

Source: Porterville State Hospital, P.O. Box 2000, Porterville, California 93257

Behavior Classes: Amount of work, quality of work, social adjustment, attitude

Method: Memory

Reliability or Validity Information Provided: No

*Mean Rating of Objectivity: 1.5

Rating Scale: Check appropriate description

Most Objective Item: Patient reports for assignment on time

Least Objective Item: More popular than most

*   *   *

Title: A Primary Grade Retarded-Trainable Children's Referral and Behavior Rating Form (Peterson, Gorski, Kreisman)

Source: Rolf A. Peterson, Department of Psychology, University of Illinois at Chicago Circle, Box 4348, Chicago, Illinois 60680

---

* 1.0 Least Objective; 5.0 Most Objective.

Behavior Classes: Walking stairs, toilet, eating, drinking, language, dressing, socialization

Method: Memory

Reliability or Validity Information Provided: Yes

**Mean Rating of Objectivity*: 3.5*

Rating Scale: Check appropriate description

Most Objective Item: Walks up stairs unassisted one step per tread.

Least Objective Item: Unable to keep self amused with a toy or game of some type
during free play period

* * *

Title: Primary Progress Assessment Chart of Social Development (Gunzburg)

Source: Aux Chandelles, PAC Department, P.O. Box 398, Bristol, Indiana 46507

Behavior Classes: Self-help, communication, socialization, occupation

Method: Memory

Reliability or Validity Information Provided: No

**Mean Rating of Objectivity*: 3.0*

Rating Scale: Yes/No

Most Objective Item: Walks up stairs, both feet together on each step

Least Objective Item: Expression shows awareness

* * *

Title: Problem Classification List (Staff)

Source: Atascadero State Hospital, Drawer A, Atascadero, California 93422

Behavior Classes: Assaultiveness, psychiatric symptoms, interaction problems, sex
problems

Method: Memory

Reliability or Validity Information Provided: Yes

**Mean Rating of Objectivity*: 1.0*

Rating Scale: Yes/No

Most Objective Item: Inability to clothe, feed and toilet himself properly

Least Objective Item: Patient is distrustful; has feelings of having been mistreated,
taken advantage of, tricked or pushed around

* * *

Title: Program Evaluation System (Da Silva, Lapuc)

Source: Paul S. Lapuc, Veterans Administration Hospital, Northampton, Massachusetts 01060

Behavior Classes: Self-care, social, eating, hygiene

---

* 1.0 Least Objective; 5.0 Most Objective.

Method: Direct Observation

Reliability or Validity Information Provided: No

*Mean Rating of Objectivity: 3.0

Rating Scale: No attempt to Independently (1 to 7)

Most Objective Item: Put plate, cup, etc. on cart when finished.

Least Objective Item: Communicated for food

* * *

Title: Program Placement Survey (Staff)

Source: Arizona Training Program at Tucson, 29th Street and Swan Road, Tucson, Arizona 85711

Behavior Classes: Self-help, communicative, social behavior, motor behavior, disruptive behavior

Method: Memory

Reliability or Validity Information Provided: Yes

*Mean Rating of Objectivity: 3.0

Rating Scale: Check appropriate description

Most Objective Item: Bathes only if given physical assistance and instruction

Least Objective Item: Attempts to move body to avoid hazard

* * *

Title: Progress Assessment Sheet—Long Stay Psychiatric Wards (Burnheim)

Source: Ronald B. Burnheim, Bloomfield Hospital, Orange, NSW 2800, United Kingdom

Behavior Classes: Self-help, sleep patterns, mood and affect, habits, communication and thought, cooperation, social participation

Method: Memory

Reliability or Validity Information Provided: No

*Mean Rating of Objectivity: 1.0

Rating Scale: Various (0 to 4)

Most Objective Item: Washes own clothes

Least Objective Item: Realistic sense of place

* * *

Title: Pupil Rating Scale (Myklebust)

Source: Grune and Stratton, Inc., 111 Fifth Avenue, New York, New York 10003

Behavior Classes: Auditory comprehension, spoken language, personal-social behavior, orientation, motor coordination

Method: Memory

---

* 1.0 Least Objective; 5.0 Most Objective.

Reliability or Validity Information Provided: No

*Mean Rating of Objectivity: 1.5

Rating Scale: Yes/No

Most Objective Item: Frequently uses incomplete sentences with grammatical errors

Least Objective Item: Extremely immature level of understanding

*   *   *

Title: Rating Scale for Maladaptive Behaviors

Source: Central Connecticut Regional Center, Undercliff Road, Box 853, Meriden, Connecticut 06450

Behavior Classes: Self-destructive, vomiting, phobias, bolting, mouth, aggressiveness, throwing, screaming

Method: Memory

Reliability or Validity Information Provided: No

*Mean Rating of Objectivity: 3.5

Rating Scale: Circle appropriate description

Most Objective Item: Throwing more than five times an hour

Least Objective Item: Intense hysteria for more than 5 common objects or people

*   *   *

Title: Rating Scale for Primary Depressive Illness (Hamilton)

Source: Hamilton (1967)

Behavior Classes: Depressive behaviors

Method: Interview

Reliability or Validity Information Provided: Yes

*Mean Rating of Objectivity: 2.5

Rating Scale: Absent to Severe (0 to 4)

Most Objective Item: Loss of weight

Least Objective Item: Loss of libido

*   *   *

Title: Rehabilitation Indicators (Staff)

Source: Rehabilitation Indicators Project, Institute of Rehabilitation Medicine, 400 East 34th Street, New York, New York 10016

Behavior Classes: Social/leisure, legal/political, vocational/educational, self-care/activities of daily living, economic, environment

Method: Direct Observation, Memory, or Interview

Reliability or Validity Information Provided: No

---

* 1.0 Least Objective; 5.0 Most Objective.

Mean Rating of Objectivity: 3.0

Rating Scale: Yes/No; also time and frequency on some items

Most Objective Item: Washes pots and pans

Least Objective Item: Understands gestures/facial expression of others

* * *

Title: Repertoire of Current Operant Behavior (Staff)

Source: The SID Project, Service Integration for Deinstitutionalization, Travelers Building, 1108 East Main Street, Richmond, Virginia 23219

Behavior Classes: Adaptive behavior and maladaptive behavior

Method: Memory

Reliability or Validity Information Provided: No

Mean Rating of Objectivity: 3.0

Rating Scale: Not at all to High frequency (0 to 4)

Most Objective Item: Drinks from cup or glass unassisted

Least Objective Item: Engages in goal-directed group activity

* * *

Title: Resident Evaluation (Staff)

Source: San Angelo Center, Carlsbad, Texas 76934

Behavior Classes: Eating, hygiene, dressing, physical health, social maturity, work skills, communication

Method: Memory

Reliability or Validity Information Provided: No

Mean Rating of Objectivity: 3.0

Rating Scale: Absent to Excellent (1 to 5)

Most Objective Item: Places waste in trash can

Least Objective Item: Respects others' property

* * *

Title: Resident Profile (Staff)

Source: Oakdale Center for Developmental Disabilities, Lapeer, Michigan 48446

Behavior Classes: Language skills, hearing and vision, self-help, grooming, coordination, socialization

Method: Memory

Reliability or Validity Information Provided: No

Mean Rating of Objectivity: 2.0

Rating Scale: Yes/No

---

* 1.0 Least Objective; 5.0 Most Objective.

Most Objective Item: Chews and swallows coarsely textured food

Least Objective Item: Understands most speeches and gestures

*   *   *

Title: Residential Developmental Check List (Staff)

Source: Central Connecticut Regional Center, Undercliff Road, Box 853, Meriden, Connecticut 06450

Behavior Classes: Eating, bathing, toileting, dressing, grooming, motor development, social maturity and manner, language, personality, occupation

Method: Direct Observation

Reliability or Validity Information Provided: No

*Mean Rating of Objectivity: 3.0

Rating Scale: Yes/No

Most Objective Item: Draws a square with sharp corners

Least Objective Item: Appears insecure or frightened in many daily activities

*   *   *

Title: Roadmap to Effective Teaching: Comprehensive Coordinated Curriculum for Special Education (Staff)

Source: Monterey County, Office of Education, Special Education Department, P.O. Box 851, Salinas, California 93901

Behavior Classes: Motor development, social-emotional, cognitive skills, communication, self-help, individual expression

Method: Direct Observation

Reliability or Validity Information Provided: No

*Mean Rating of Objectivity: 4.0

Rating Scale: Yes/No

Most Objective Item: Cuts line 6″ long within ½″ of line in 15 seconds

Least Objective Item: Accepts legitimate blame

*   *   *

Title: School Behavior Check List for the Elementary Grades (Staff)

Source: Independent School District No. 279, 317 Second Avenue, N.W., Osseo, Minnesota 55369

Behavior Classes: Classroom behaviors

Method: Memory

Reliability or Validity Information Provided: No

*Mean Rating of Objectivity: 2.5

Rating Scale: Check appropriate description

---

* 1.0 Least Objective; 5.0 Most Objective.

Most Objective Item: Stutters or stammers

Least Objective Item: Perceptually in own world, oblivious to presence of others and basic modes of communication

* * *

Title: Selinsgrove State School and Hospital Resident Rating Scale for Mildly Retarded (Staff)

Source: Selinsgrove State School and Hospital, Selinsgrove, Pennsylvania 17870

Behavior Classes: Dining skills, hygiene and grooming, appearance, academic, community, behavior, vocational

Method: Direct Observation or Memory

Reliability or Validity Information Provided: No

*Mean Rating of Objectivity: 3.0

Rating Scale: Yes/No

Most Objective Item: Prints full name

Least Objective Item: Knows basic facts about contraception

* * *

Title: Selinsgrove State School and Hospital Resident Rating Scale for Severely Retarded (Staff)

Source: Selinsgrove State School and Hospital, Selinsgrove, Pennsylvania 17870

Behavior Classes: Toilet, grooming, feeding, communication, play, general

Method: Direct Observation or Memory

Reliability or Validity Information Provided: No

*Mean Rating of Objectivity: 2.5

Rating Scale: Circle appropriate description

Most Objective Item: Trainer cup unassisted

Least Objective Item: Indicates simple needs

* * *

Title: Social Evaluation of Toddlers (Sternlicht)

Source: Manny Sterlicht, Willowbrook State School, 2760 Victory Boulevard, Staten Island, New York 10314

Behavior Classes: Neatness, cleanliness, eating, personal care and appearance, social maturity, spontaneity, alertness, reaction to peers, and four others

Method: Memory

Reliability or Validity Information Provided: No

*Mean Rating of Objectivity: 1.0

Rating Scale: Check does/doesn't

---

* 1.0 Least Objective; 5.0 Most Objective.

Most Objective Item: Says "excuse me."

Least Objective Item: Aware of danger

* * *

Title: Social and Physical Incapacity Scale and Speech, Self-Help, and Literacy Scale (Kushlick, Blunden, Cox)

Source: Wessex Regional Hospital Board, Winchester, England

Behavior Classes: Continence, ambulance, disruptive behavior, speech, self-help, literacy

Method: Memory

Reliability or Validity Information Provided: Yes

*Mean Rating of Objectivity: 1.0

Rating Scale: Check appropriate description

Most Objective Item: Wetting (days)

Least Objective Item: Reads a little

* * *

Title: Social Skills Categories: An Observational System (Pena, Miller)

Source: Deagelia M. Pena, Wayne State University, School of Medicine (Annex), 1400 Chrysler Freeway, Detroit, Michigan 48207

Behavior Classes: Initiation, question or request for help, giving help, refusing help, group consciousness, response to peer

Method: Direct Observation

Reliability or Validity Information Provided: No

*Mean Rating of Objectivity: 1.0

Rating Scale: Yes/No

Most Objective Item: Asks a question of peer

Least Objective Item: Withdraws for security

* * *

Title: Special Education, Individual Therapy, Occupational Therapy, Family Therapy, Psychodrama, Group Therapy, & Recreational Therapy Rating Forms (Staff)

Source: Central Louisiana State Hospital, Pineville, Louisiana 71360

Behavior Classes: Various behaviors

Method: Memory

Reliability or Validity Information Provided: Yes

*Mean Rating of Objectivity: 3.0

---

* 1.0 Least Objective; 5.0 Most Objective.

Rating Scale: True/False

Most Objective Item: Turns in homework

Least Objective Item: Concentrates for only brief periods, then needs to change tasks

* * *

Title: Spraings' Behavior Rating Scale for Elementary School and Junior and Senior High School (Spraings)

Source: Violet Spraings, Department of Educational Psychology, California State University, Hayward, California 94542

Behavior Classes: Social-emotional, motor, learning, conceptual

Method: Memory

Reliability or Validity Information Provided: No

Mean Rating of Objectivity: 2.0

Rating Scale: No to great degree (0 to 4)

Most Objective Item: Seldom completes assignments in the allotted time

Least Objective Item: Poor knowledge of concepts as revealed in understanding vocabulary

* * *

Title: Springfield Public Schools Behavioral Rating Form (Howell)

Source: John F. Howell, Springfield Public Schools, Springfield, Massachusetts 01103

Behavior Classes: Classroom behaviors

Method: Memory

Reliability or Validity Information Provided: Yes

Mean Rating of Objectivity: 2.0

Rating Scale: Never to Always (1 to 5)

Most Objective Item: Complains about body aches and pains

Least Objective Item: The child is flexible

* * *

Title: Staff-Client Interaction (Staff)

Source: Eleanor Roosevelt Developmental Services, Balltown and Consaul Roads, Schenectady, New York 12304

Behavior Classes: Interaction behaviors

Method: Direct Observation

Reliability or Validity Information Provided: No

Mean Rating of Objectivity: 3.5

---

* 1.0 Least Objective; 5.0 Most Objective.

Rating Scale: Time sampling (10 sec.)

Most Objective Item: Reinforces adaptive behaviors, ignoring or handling impersonally maladaptive behavior

Least Objective Item: Uses rehabilitative or nursing techniques

*   *   *

Title: Status Report (Reynolds)

Source: R. D. Reynolds, Psychology Department, Bryce Hospital, Tuscaloosa, Alabama 35401

Behavior Classes: Dress and grooming, self care, ward activity, socializing activities, psychiatric symptomatology, activity, and two others

Methods: Memory

Reliability or Validity Information Provided: No

Mean Rating of Objectivity: 1.0

Rating Scale: Never to Always (1 to 4)

Most Objective Item: Needs help feeding self

Least Objective Item: Is destructive

*   *   *

Title: Structured Clinical Interview

Source: Springer Publishing Company, Inc., 200 Park Avenue South, New York, New York 10003

Behavior Classes: Verbal report of emotional condition

Method: Direct Observation or Interview

Reliability or Validity Information Provided: No

Mean Rating of Objectivity: 2.0

Rating Scale: Yes/No

Most Objective Item: Bangs fist on table or stamps foot

Least Objective Item: Has attack of panicky fear

*   *   *

Title: Student Behavior Inventory (Prien, Johnson)

Source: Erich P. Prien, Memphis State University, Memphis, Tennessee 38152

Behavior Classes: Classroom behaviors

Method: Memory

Reliability or Validity Information Provided: Yes

Mean Rating of Objectivity: 2.0

Rating Scale: Check appropriate description

---

* 1.0 Least Objective; 5.0 Most Objective.

Most Objective Item: Completes all assignments
Least Objective Item: Low self-concept

* * *

Title: Summer COHI Institute General Curriculum (Staff)
Source: Omaha Public Schools, Omaha, Nebraska 68101
Behavior Classes: Mathematics, work attack skills, language skills, reading skills
Method: Direct observation
Reliability or Validity Information Provided: No
*Mean Rating of Objectivity: 3.0
Rating Scale: Yes/No
Most Objective Item: Can read and write numerals to 399 in order
Least Objective Item: Can determine fact from opinion

* * *

Title: Supplement to Diagnostic Checklist for Behavior-Disturbed Children
Source: Bernard Rimland, Institute for Child Behavior Research, 4758 Edgeware Road, San Diego, California 92116
Behavior Classes: Behavioral and medical information about child and family
Method: Direct Observation or Interview
Reliability or Validity Information Provided: No
*Mean Rating of Objectivity: 1.0
Rating Scale: True to Don't know (1 to 5)
Most Objective Item: Bites wrist or back of hand.
Least Objective Item: Generally irritable

* * *

Title: Synergism for the Seventies—Conference Proceedings
Source: George Bennett, Developmental Disabilities Planning Director, West Virginia Commission on Mental Retardation, State Capitol, Charleston, West Virginia 25305
Behavior Classes: Various adaptive and maladaptive
Method: Memory
Reliability or Validity Information Provided: No
*Mean Rating of Objectivity: 2.5
Rating Scale: Yes/No

---

* 1.0 Least Objective; 5.0 Most Objective.

Most Objective Item: Writes or prints own name
Least Objective Item: Has no idea of the value of money

* * *

Title: The TARC Assessment System (Sailor, Mix)

Source: Wayne Sailor, Personnel Training Program, Kansas Neurological Institute, 3107 W. 21st Street, Topeka, Kansas 66604

Behavior Classes: Self-help, motor, communication, social skills

Method: Direct Observation

Reliability or Validity Information Provided: Yes

**Mean Rating of Objectivity*: 3.0

Rating Scale: Yes/No

Most Objective Item: Colors or marks within lines

Least Objective Item: Usually self-controlled

* * *

Title: T. M. R. Performance Profile for the Severely and Moderately Retarded (DiNola, Kaminsky, Sternfeld)

Source: Educational Performance Associates, 563 Westview Avenue, Ridgefield, New Jersey 07657

Behavior Classes: Social behavior, self-care, communication, basic knowledge, practical skills, body usage

Method: Memory

Reliability or Validity Information Provided: No

**Mean Rating of Objectivity*: 2.0

Rating Scale: Yes/No

Most Objective Item: Rote count 1-12

Least Objective Item: Awareness of puberty

* * *

Title: Target Behavior Checklist

Source: Bernard Rimland, Institute for Child Behavior Research, 4758 Edgeware Road, San Diego, California 92116

Behavior Classes: Self-mutilating behavior, violent behaviors, and basic social behaviors

Method: Direct Observation

Reliability or Validity Information Provided: No

**Mean Rating of Objectivity*: 1.5

---

* 1.0 Least Objective; 5.0 Most Objective.

Rating Scale: Yes/No and number

Most Objective Item: Bites tongue

Least Objective Item: Approachable

*   *   *

Title: Teachers' Evaluation Scale

Source: Central Connecticut Regional Center, Undercliff Road, Box 853, Meriden, Connecticut 06450

Behavior Classes: Social behavior, self-care, communication, basic knowledge, body usage

Method: Memory

Reliability or Validity Information Provided: No

*Mean Rating of Objectivity: 2.0

Rating Scale: Negative to Above the goal (0 to 4)

Most Objective Item: Identifies penny, nickel, dime, and quarter

Least Objective Item: Has a sense of "right and wrong" which guides his behavior in most situations.

*   *   *

Title: Technical Counselor's Evaluation Form

Source: William R. Phelps, West Virginia Rehabilitation Center, Institute, West Virginia 25112

Behavior Classes: Work characteristics, kitchen, sewing, housekeeping, laundry, and personal grooming skills

Method: Memory

Reliability or Validity Information Provided: No

*Mean Rating of Objectivity: 1.0

Rating Scale: Good to Poor (1 to 5)

Most Objective Item: Washing, rinsing, drying kitchen utensils

Least Objective Item: Has learning ability, but personality slows learning process

*   *   *

Title: Test Behavior Checklist

Source: V. B. Raulinaitis, M.D., Veterans Administration Hospital, American Lake, Tacoma, Washington 98493

Behavior Classes: Behaviors emitted during administration of the MMPI and Shipley-Hartford tests

Method: Direct Observation

Reliability or Validity Information Provided: No

---

* 1.0 Least Objective; 5.0 Most Objective.

Mean Rating of Objectivity: 2.0

Rating Scale: Yes/No

Most Objective Item: Asked to be excused before completing tests. Reason given

Least Objective Item: Withdrawn—required constant encouragement for any response made

*   *   *

Title: Track Profile (Staff)

Source: State of Oregon, Mental Health Division, Salem, Oregon 97310

Behavior Classes: Self-care, perceptual-motor, social development, communication, self-direction, deviant behavior

Method: Memory

Reliability or Validity Information Provided: No

Mean Rating of Objectivity: 3.0

Rating Scale: Yes/No

Most Objective Item: Pulls clothes on/off; manipulates sleeves; steps in/out by self

Least Objective Item: Unaware of purpose or need for cleanliness, or unable/unwilling to clean oneself

*   *   *

Title: Training Priority Checklist (Shaw, Cone)

Source: Colin Anderson Center, St. Marys, West Virginia 26170

Behavior Classes: Response to reinforcers, response to simple commands, toilet, eating, grooming and dressing, speech, going places, and three others

Method: Memory

Reliability or Validity Information Provided: No

Mean Rating of Objectivity: 4.5

Rating Scale: Circle appropriate description

Most Objective Item: Prints the words from a first grade vocabulary list when the word is spoken only

Least Objective Item: Partially washes face with constant supervision (assistance)

*   *   *

Title: A Verbal Problem Checklist for Use in Assessing Family Verbal Behavior (Thomas, Walter, O'Flaherty)

Source: *Behavior Therapy*, 1974, 5, 235-246

Behavior Classes: Family verbal behavior

Method: Direct Observation

Reliability or Validity Information Provided: Yes

---

* 1.0 Least Objective; 5.0 Most Objective.

Mean Rating of Objectivity: 3.5

Rating Scale: Not at all to A large amount (1 to 4)

Most Objective Item: An interactant speaks considerably more than his partner or others with whom he is interacting, considering the interaction session as a whole

Least Objective Item: An interactant provides too little information considering that which should or might be provided at that point in the discussion

* * *

Title: Vineland Social Maturity Scale (1965 Edition) (Doll)

Source: American Guidance Services, Inc., Publishers' Building, Circle Pines, Minnesota 55014

Behavior Classes: Self-help, self-direction, occupation, communication, locomotion, socialization

Method: Interview

Reliability or Validity Information Provided: Yes

Mean Rating of Objectivity: 3.0

Rating Scale: + to — (1 to 5)

Most Objective Item: Walks down stairs one step per tread

Least Objective Item: Enjoys books, newspapers, magazines

* * *

Title: Vocational Training Evaluation (Staff)

Source: Central Connecticut Regional Center, Undercliff Road, Box 853, Meriden, Connecticut 06450

Behavior Classes: Work, personal, social, emotional

Method: Memory

Reliability or Validity Information Provided: No

Mean Rating of Objectivity: 1.5

Rating Scale: Various

Most Objective Item: Follows directions

Least Objective Item: Does trainee judge future goals realistically?

* * *

Title: Walker Problem Behavior Identification Checklist (Walker)

Source: Western Psychological Services, 12031 Wilshire Boulevard, Los Angeles, California 90025

Behavior Classes: Acting-out, withdrawal, distractibility, disturbed peer relations, immaturity

---

* 1.0 Least Objective; 5.0 Most Objective.

Method: Memory

Reliability or Validity Information Provided: Yes

•Mean Rating of Objectivity: 1.0

Rating Scale: Yes/No

Most Objective Item: Stutters, stammers, or blocks on saying words

Least Objective Item: Has rapid mood shifts; depressed one moment, manic the next

●   ●   ●

Title: Ward Behavior Inventory: WBI (Burdock, Hardesty)

Source: Springer Publishing Company, Inc., 200 Park Avenue South, New York, New York 10003

Behavior Classes: Psychopathological behavior of the hospitalized patient on the ward

Method: Memory

Reliability or Validity Information Provided: Yes

•Mean Rating of Objectivity: 1.0

Rating Scale: Yes/No

Most Objective Item: Says he wants to die

Least Objective Item: Has attack of panicky fear

●   ●   ●

Title: Washington Assessment and Training Scales: WATS (Staff, Office of Handicapped Children)

Source: Dr. Sandra Belcher, Fircrest School, 15230 - 15th Avenue, N.E., Seattle, Washington 98155

Behavior Classes: Adaptive, eating, toileting, dressing, mobility, communication, grooming, socialization, vocational aptitude, domestic, community

Method: Memory

Reliability or Validity Information Provided: Yes

•Mean Rating of Objectivity: 4.5

Rating Scale: No to Yes (1 to 5)

Most Objective Item: No; fed in prone (lying down) position

Least Objective Item: No; does not understand or have information on his civil rights

---

* 1.0 Least Objective; 5.0 Most Objective.

Part III

DIRECT METHODS IN CONTROLLED ENVIRONMENTS

Editors' Comments

This section introduces methods of measurement that are "direct" in the sense mentioned earlier, and it exemplifies the use of these methods in situations, settings, or environments other than the natural one of primary interest to the client, clinician, or researcher. Thus, the methods discussed herein measure *the* behavior(s) of direct clinical interest. They do not rely on verbal representatives of these behaviors as was true of the "indirect" measures presented in the previous section.

However, unlike the procedures to be discussed in the subsequent section, the observation methods to be described here are not used in the natural environment, but in ones designed, contrived, or controlled by the assessor. That is, assessment takes place in an analogue setting—one that has many features of the natural environment, but is unlike it in important ways also.

The principal reason for observing behavior(s) in analogue settings is to facilitate increased control over the assessment enterprise and thereby enhance the quality of the information derived therefrom. A variety of controlled settings have been used in behavioral assessment, including the clinician's office, laboratory playrooms (Forehand, King, Peed & Yoder, 1975), laboratory bars (Sobell & Sobell, 1973), and laboratory bedrooms (Serber, 1974). In each of these uses, contrived settings have made possible the collection of data less expensively than would have been the case if observations had occurred in the natural environment. Related to the cost advantage is the enhanced probability of the occurrence of the

147

response (Goldfried & Sprafkin, 1974). That is, situations are contrived to facilitate the occurrence of clinically relevant behaviors during the time of observation. Because the situation is standardized, comparisons both between and within clients are enhanced by such procedures. Finally, some types of behavior are difficult to measure accurately in their natural context, often requiring sensitive apparatus for their detection. This is especially true of physiological behavior, which is almost always observed in controlled environments.

As McFall notes in the beginning of Chapter 5, there are at least four different dimensions of analogy commonly used in psychological research: analogues regarding 1) subject, 2) setting, 3) response, and 4) treatment. In behavioral assessment in the clinical context, setting and response analogues are most common, the latter being "indirect" measures by our definition. When both are used simultaneously, a double analogue assessment procedure results; an indirect measure in a contrived setting. For example, if a subject is verbally presented with an imaginary situation and is asked to write how s/he would respond in that situation, both the situation and the response are analogues contrived to facilitate assessment. But if the subject is asked to emit the actual behaivor s/he would emit in such a situation, only a situation analogue has been employed.

McFall includes, among analogue measures, the use of role-playing. The example he employs is like the above: The subject is asked to imagine a situation but emit the actual behavior appropriate to that situation. It may be somewhat confusing to use the term "role-playing" for this, because this term seems to denote, instead, the emission of a set of behaviors typical of a person other than oneself. Thus, a client might be instructed to behave as if s/he were "a flirt," "a tough guy," or "very beautiful." This could be useful in treatment as a prompt, so that desired behavior can be obtained and reinforced, weakened, or used as a discriminative stimulus. Such role-playing might also be useful in assessment, to determine how readily the desired behavior is emitted. But instead of considering role-playing as an analogue measure, we would prefer to consider it simply as the use of a particular instruction, the instruction to "behave as-if." The assessments presented by McFall as role-playing might then be considered as simply situation analogues.

Though some writers (e.g., Goldfried & Sprafkin, 1974) have considered role-playing a behavioral assessment method in its own right, our preference is to view it as a set of instructions to the client to behave "as if" s/he were someone else. As noted elsewhere (Cone, 1975), when behaving "as if," the client still has to be observed and his/her responses systematically recorded. The method used to record the behavior might be a rating by the observer, a behavior checklist, self-monitoring, or direct observation. Moreover, these methods may be used contemporaneously with the role-playing, or retroactively from audio- or videotape permanent records of it. In any case, before conclusions may be drawn concerning differences in the client's behavior in various roles or various situations, the methods for measuring that behavior must be shown to be accurate. The behavioral assessor is not as concerned with the role-playing procedures themselves, but with the data generated from them by whatever methods.

In the behavioral assessment literature the most frequent use of analogue or contrived settings has been to facilitate the observation of social skills and physiological behavior. In the social skills area the methods used for recording these observations have most often been ratings by others, or various types of direct observation as discussed by Wildman and Erickson in Chapter 10. In recording physiological responding the methods used have most often involved direct observation procedures aided by electronic sensing and amplifying devices.

In his chapter, McFall discusses not only the value of analogue assessment procedures but also the importance of validating their predictions about behavior in the natural environment. In this regard, he refers to shortcomings with behavioral avoidance tests, emphasizing that it is not the analogues themselves that have been deficient, but rather the way in which they have been used. The same point was made earlier by Bellack and Hersen in their defense of self-reports.

In a thoughtful, self-critical analysis of the development of his own assessment procedures in the area of social competence, McFall takes the reader through an evolution in methodological sophistication that should serve as an excellent model for the field of behavioral assessment as a whole. His early attempts to measure assertive behavior as though it reflected a general trait of assertion were subsequently abandoned in favor of situation-specific scoring and the concept of equifinality. Using his own research to provide examples, McFall skillfully shows how different approaches to assessment contain varying vestiges of trait thinking. His conceptualizations are more advanced than the field itself, and will serve as important beacons for its future development.

In the second chapter of this section Lang discusses the nature of emotional responding. He relates current conceptions of anxiety and fear to those of past theorists, and presents implications for clinical assessment and treatment. Like Barlow (Chapter 11) and Geer (Chapter 7), Lang discusses interrelationships between verbal, motor, and physiological responses and presents evidence regarding their correspondence.

Lang presents an interesting series of studies involving the effects of imagery instructions on certain physiological components of anxiety. The implications for both theory and therapy should interest the reader.

The chapter by Geer, on the assessment of physiological aspects of sexual behavior, complements Lang's more general one by illustrating the direct assessment of physiological responses in an area of particular importance in clinical practice. Measures of arousal in both males and females are described by Geer, with primary focus on indices of genital blood flow. The advantages of genital measures of sexual arousal over others are discussed, including their all-important response-specificity.

Geer summarizes the relatively recent literature on the use of blood volume measures for differentiating clients with atypical sexual behavior (see also Chapter 11 by Barlow), for monitoring the progress and outcome of intervention programs, and as targets of direct intervention efforts themselves. Geer notes that much of the research on these measures has employed atypical populations, that is, persons whose sexual behavior differs markedly from that of the societal norm. Moreover, many of the samples (e.g., homosexuals in therapy) are not even representative of their larger, atypical populations (e.g., all homosexuals), making extrapolations difficult. The representativeness of pilot and standardization samples is a problem inadequately dealt with in behavioral assessment generally, but it is particularly difficult to overcome in the assessment of sexual responding.

Geer deals with other issues of general interest to behavioral assessors, particularly those of the value of norms, prothetic vs. metathetic continua, and the extent to which verbal reports of sexual arousal and physiological measures of it correlate. Geer summarizes literature showing generally higher correspondence than is usually found between cognitive and physiological response systems (cf. Chapter 11 by Barlow, and Chapter 6 by Lang), and suggests reasons for this finding. Some of the speculation is interestingly reminiscent for the James-Lange-Cannon controversy, and could be phrased for Geer's chapter as the difference between "I am sexually aroused, therefore I must have an erection!" on the one hand, and "I have an erection, therefore I must be aroused!" on the other. The question of whether sexual arousal is best viewed as a continuous variable or as one made up of a variety of discrete responses is one asked by behavioral assessors of other dimensions as well, as McFall's earlier chapter in this section indicated.

Geer also deals with the complicated issue of the effects of a client's cognitive activity on the assessment of physiological responding. Evidence is presented to show that instructions to fantasize reliably increase genital blood volume and that interfering with attention to sexually explicit stimulus material reliably reduces them. The problem of identifying precisely the controlling events for physiological responses is one that extends to behavioral assessment generally, and, indeed, to all of psychology. The next section of the book deals with methods that seek to discover these events via direct observation in the natural environment.

5

ANALOGUE METHODS IN BEHAVIORAL ASSESSMENT: ISSUES AND PROSPECTS

RICHARD M. McFALL

Analogue methods are widely employed by psychologists engaged in clinical research on assessment and treatment. Such methods can be sorted into four general categories. There is the *subject* analogue, which is illustrated by the use of introductory psychology students as subjects in therapy-outcome studies. There is the *treatment* analogue, which is illustrated by the study of brief and highly simplified interventions in an effort to understand the operation of more extensive and complex treatment procedures. There is the *situational* analogue, which is illustrated by the analysis of naturalistic behaviors under controlled laboratory conditions. And there is the *response* analogue, which is illustrated by psychological tests that treat one response (e.g., a "color" response on the Rorschach) as though it were equivalent to an analogous response (e.g., "emotional" behavior). It is not uncommon to find all four types of analogue used within a single study, as when a simplified version of some therapy technique is administered in the laboratory to college student volunteers, whose responses are measured on a paper-and-pencil test.

Analogue methods offer several potential advantages over direct methods. Most important, they sometimes permit increased experimental control, thus enhancing the internal validity of a particular experiment (see Campbell & Stanley, 1963). Many psychological problems are simply too

The author is indebted to Jean Goldsmith, Craig Twentyman, Barbara Freedman, Pete Donahoe, Charlene Muehlenhard, and numerous other colleagues at the University of Wisconsin whose ideas and research efforts have contributed so much to this paper.

complex to study directly—at least initially. Experimental analogues can help to simplify and reduce such problems, thus making it possible to control extraneous influences, isolate and manipulate specific variables, and reliably measure their effects. Analogue methods can also help investigators avoid certain ethical problems. For example, the potentially harmful effects of untested surgical or pharmacological procedures can be studied through the use of subject analogues, in which animals are administered such procedures before they are tried with human subjects. Analogues used in assessment enable us to confront subjects safely with situations that otherwise might have serious negative consequences if they were mishandled in real life, such as when a driving simulator is used to assess a student's skill in handling emergency situations. Finally, analogue methods frequently offer the purely practical advantages of increased convenience, efficiency, or economy, as when laboratory measures are used in lieu of costly or unattainable naturalistic measures.

Analogue methods are not without their drawbacks. They invariably require certain compromises with reality. While they may help generate interpretable solutions to simplified experimental problems, their solutions may or may not have relevance for the "real life" problems that initially prompted the research. Reasoning by analogy necessarily involves making abstractions about certain ways in which two things seem to be similar, while ignoring all of the other ways in which they may be different. It is assumed that the abstracted similarities somehow capture the essence of the phenomenon being studied, and that little of essence is left among the overlooked differences. Whether the solutions generated by analogue methods actually have relevance, or external validity, is a function of the particular analogies chosen (see Campbell & Stanley, 1963).

Scientific analogies are neither intrinsically good nor bad. They are simply heuristic devices designed to help solve problems. Polya (1948) likened them to the scaffolding used in the construction of a building. A well-chosen analogy will provide access to otherwise inaccessible problems and provide fresh perspectives from which to discover novel solutions. A poorly-chosen analogy simply will fail to contribute to the development of externally valid solutions. Analogies are really only *bad* to the extent that they are mistaken for actual solutions themselves, rather than being recognized as merely approximations to solutions, or to the extent that they divert attention from the "real life" problems that they were originally designed to serve.

In recent years, analogue methods have come under attack by some psychologists. Unfortunately, the criticisms often have been misguided. The real fault is not so much in the methods themselves, but in the ways that they have been misused. In large part, these misuses have resulted from the unsound theoretical foundations upon which the experimental analogues have been built; if a problem has not been adequately conceptualized in the first place, then any analogy based on that faulty conceptualization is not likely to be very useful.

A historical review of the uses of analogues in psychological assessment suggests that, indeed, the assessment failures of the past have been more conceptual than methodological (Mischel, 1968). A classic example of how a promising analogue assessment procedure can be rendered invalid by faulty theoretical underpinnings is provided by the experiences of a group of psychologists who were assigned the task during World War II of selecting candidates for an overseas intelligence operation conducted by the Office of Strategic Services (OSS Staff, 1948). In the first stage of developing the assessment program, a task analysis was conducted of the various jobs for which the candidates were being selected. Since the jobs were new and were to be carried out in remote and unknown settings, the results of the analysis were unavoidably speculative and incomplete. Nevertheless, a series of performance tests was developed to assess how the men would respond in situations that presumably were analogous to those that they might encounter in the field. One of these tests, for example, required that a group of candidates plan and execute the capture of an OSS staff member posing as a German officer; another test required that they resist the attempts of "enemy" interrogators to extract secret information; and yet another test was designed as an unobtrusive measure of each candidate's ability to perform tasks under frustrating circumstances. In all, the assessment procedure took three days to administer and yielded a wealth of performance data for each candidate in a range of tasks. Unfortunately, the OSS assessment team then reduced these data to summary scores in 11 trait categories, such as leadership and emotional stability, from which they prepared a general personality description of each candidate. These descriptions subsequently proved to be of little value for predicting which candidates would perform well in the field. In retrospect, it seems that the failure probably was not due to the use of analogue measures, but to the way that the data from these measures were condensed and conceptualized.

Of course, not all historical attempts at psychological assessment have been so unsuccessful. Intelligence testing and job aptitude testing are two positive exceptions. Analogue methods are used in both types of testing, but instead of the test results being interpreted as indirect indices of personality characteristics, they are interpreted straightforwardly as performance samples of the very behaviors that the tests are attempting to predict. The general principle that emerges from an analysis of past successes and failures is that the best measures thus far have been those that were designed to maximize the similarity between the assessment and criterion tasks (Mischel, 1968). Analogue assessment methods based on this principle have been called simulation methods.

SIMULATION METHODS

Simulation methods have been used for years in industrial and educational psychology, but they have been discovered—or rediscovered—only recently by clinical psychologists. This discovery was correlated with the growth of interest in behavioral approaches to treatment, although the development and validation of simulation assessment measures have lagged somewhat behind the development of behavioral treatment techniques. Apparently, it has been difficult—even for behaviorists—to abandon old conceptual habits. In fact, many of the problems with current behavioral assessment methods can be traced to stubborn vestiges of traditional thinking.

Behavioral Avoidance Tests

It was not until the early 1960's that an example of simulation methods gained widespread clinical recognition and use. This occurred with the introduction of the behavioral avoidance test (BAT), which was used in connection with experimental studies of systematic desensitization with snake phobics (e.g., Lang & Lazovik, 1963). Subsequently, similar BAT procedures were developed to assess phobic behavior in relation to a whole array of fear-producing stimuli, including heights, water, spiders, airplanes, rats, public speaking, and test taking (e.g., see Paul, 1969). While these assessment procedures represented a clear improvement over the indirect and highly inferential methods that they replaced, little effort was made to establish their validity for predicting avoidance behaviors in natural settings. In most of the exceptions where investigators sought to demonstrate concordance, either the subjects were asked to report on their own extra-laboratory experiences or reports were obtained from the subjects' friends or family. Direct unobtrusive measures of real-life behaviors were rare. Furthermore, there was no indication that most investigators were even cognizant of the possibility that their laboratory measures might be contaminated by the reactivity of their procedures.

Looking back, it seems reasonable that avoidance behaviors would be the first clinical problems to be assessed routinely by simulation methods. They represent fairly encapsulated problems, the essence of which is the absence of specific approach responses to limited classes of identifiable stimulus objects. Both the problem stimuli and target responses typically lend themselves to objective quantification along dimensions of time, space, frequency, duration, or intensity. Investigators can use simulation methods to assess such avoidance behaviors without being overly concerned with the intricacies of test development and validation; such methodological considerations become far more important, however, when simulation methods are extended to the assessment of more complex social-behavioral problems.

Role-Playing Tests

Over the years, a number of social scientists have advocated the use of role-playing procedures in behavioral assessment. Rotter and Wickens (1948), for example, argued that the predictive accuracy of an assessment method is a function of the degree of similarity between the assessment and criterion situations. They felt that role-playing would be a fruitful method of maximizing that similarity, at least with certain behaviors. In support of their view, they presented evidence showing that observers' ratings of subjects' social aggressiveness in role-played situations accurately predicted subjects' social aggression outside the laboratory assessment situation. Borgatta (1955) also has demonstrated repeatedly that there is a strong association between subjects' role-played behaviors and their analogous "real-life" behaviors.

Despite these early indications of their potential, role-playing methods generally were ignored until the late 1960's, at which time several convergent developments seemed to stimulate a surge of interest. The first development was the behaviorist's shift from studying the circumscribed subject-object relationships typical of fears and phobias to studying the more complicated and difficult-to-assess relationships characteristic of interpersonal problems. Assertive behaviors and heterosexual behaviors are two such problem areas that received particular attention (e.g., Wolpe & Lazarus, 1966). The second development was the publication of Wallace's (1966, 1967) behavioral competence model of personality assessment. This model encouraged investigators to abandon their traditional search for general underlying personality characteristics and to adopt instead the alternative strategy of constructing performance profiles based on assessments of each individual's response to specific critical situations. The third development was Goldfried and D'Zurilla's (1969) presentation of a specific methodological procedure for assessing situation-specific competence. The fourth development was the publication of actual experiments in which role-playing methods had been employed successfully to assess the effects of behavioral treatments for interpersonal problems (e.g., McFall & Marston, 1970; Rehm & Marston, 1968).

Just as the first behavioral avoidance test with snake phobics spawned a host of similar measures for other fears, early versions of behavioral role-playing tests also stimulated the development of many similar measures. Most of the role-playing measures were highly specific, originating in conjunction with experimental studies of specific therapy techniques for specific problems and populations. Unfortunately, many of these measures were not developed very systematically or empirically. Furthermore, there was a tendency for individual investigators to develop their own measures, which meant an unnecessary duplication of effort. When preexisting measures were borrowed, they frequently were modified slightly, thus making it difficult to compare results across studies. Finally, since most of the role-playing measures to date either have not been published at all or have not been published with adequate validational support, a critical evaluation is not possible. At best, behavioral role-playing methods seem to offer a promising approach to behavioral assessment, but require more extensive exploration and development before their real value can be determined.

In the interest of promoting the needed research, the next section examines the strengths and weaknesses of several specific role-playing measures and assesses their implications for future research. The particular examples presented are those that the author knows best—namely, those that he helped to develop and evaluate. The examples chosen, while providing neither a comprehensive overview nor a unbiased sample, illustrate most of the problems that investigators interested in using behavioral role-playing methods of assessment are likely to encounter.

EXAMPLES OF ROLE-PLAYING MEASURES

Assertion was the first behavior that this author and his associates attempted to assess via role-playing methods. The occasion was an experimental evaluation of the effects of behavior rehearsal in assertion training

(McFall & Marston, 1970). Two behavior rehearsal treatments—one with audiotaped playback of rehearsal responses and one without—were compared with two control treatments—a pseudotherapy condition and an assessment-only condition. In addition to several paper-and-pencil self-report measures and a pulse-rate measure, subjects were given a behavioral role-playing test before and after treatment. The test consisted of 16 prerecorded narrative descriptions of interpersonal situations requiring assertive responses; subjects were instructed to role-play responding to each situation as if it were actually happening to them. Their responses were recorded on audiotape for subsequent analysis. Here is a sample situation:

> *Narrator*: In this scene, picture yourself standing in a ticket line outside of a theater. You've been in line now for at least ten minutes and it's getting pretty close to show time. You're still pretty far from the beginning of the line, and you're starting to wonder if there will be enough tickets left. There you are, waiting patiently, when two people walk up to the person in front of you and they begin talking. They're obviously all friends and they're going to the same movie. You look quickly at your watch and notice that the show starts in just two minutes. Just then, one of the newcomers says to his friend in line:
>
> *Newcomer*: "Hey, the line's a mile long. How 'bout if we cut in here with you?"
>
> *Friend*: "Sure, come on. A couple more won't make any difference."
>
> *Narrator*: As the two people squeeze in the line between you and their friend, one of them looks at you and says:
>
> *Newcomer*: "Excuse me. You don't mind if we cut in, do you?" (Bell sounds as cue for subject to respond.)

The final 16 test items were selected out of an initial pool of nearly 2,000 assertion situations that were solicited from college students, condensed, pretested, factor analyzed, condensed again, and cross-validated. Despite these fairly elaborate efforts at test construction, four serious deficiencies in the test and its conceptual foundation became apparent as the study progressed.

First, analyses of pilot subjects' ratings of item difficulty failed to reveal any clear-cut factor structure among the items. Responses tended to be very situation-specific, with little evidence of within-subject consistency or of inter-item correlation. In retrospect, it seems obvious that the test had been constructed as though assertion were a personality trait! The heterogeneous test items had been considered interchangeable stimuli capable of eliciting responses that could be treated as additive indices of a general and consistent personality characteristic—"assertiveness." If the test were actually a measure of behavioral competence in assertion situations, as it was supposed to be, there would have been no assumptions about factor structure, item equivalence, cross-situational consistency, or response additivity.

The second deficiency became apparent when the time came for raters to score the competence (assertiveness) of subject's tape-recorded test responses. The pilot study had identified 16 situations in which college students found it difficult to make satisfactorily assertive responses; however, it had failed to indicate what criteria should be used to determine just how satisfactorily assertive a particular response was. In the absence of such criteria, a paired-comparison method was employed to evaluate treatment effects. Raters were presented with each subject's paired pre- and posttreatment responses, in random order, to each situation, and were asked to indicate which one in each pair they considered to be the most assertive. Analyses of the ratings revealed significant treatment effects, with the two behavior rehearsal conditions showing greater improvement than the two control conditions. However, because the ratings were the product of raters' subjective judgments based on unknown and irretrievable criteria, little could be concluded about the specific nature of the significant group differences. When the raters left at the end of the study, they took the real meaning of the significant results with them. While the measure had proven useful in demonstrating the effectiveness of different treatment methods, it had little or no clinical value because the raters' judgments were not of a kind that clinicians could use to make decisions about a client's specific skill deficits or treatment needs.

The third deficiency was closely related to the first two. Because the test was constructed as though it were measuring a general personality trait that would show cross-situational consistency, and because there were no objective situation-specific scoring criteria for assertive behavior, it was not possible to use the role-playing measure to examine the degree to which there had been specific, as opposed to generalized, training effects. If assertive behavior had been viewed as learned effective responses to specific situations, then the assessment items probably would have been divided into three groups: situations for which subjects had received training; situations for which they received no training, but to which training effects might be expected to generalize; and untrained situations that should show no training effects. This would have permitted a convergent and discriminant analysis of training effects.

The fourth deficiency also was due to the test's structure and scoring: The test results could not be reasonably related to the results of any other assertion measures. The test only provided information concerning the relative quality of each individual's pre- and posttest responses; there was no quantitative measure that permitted comparisons among individuals or between one individual's performance on this test and his/her score on some related measure. This frustrated any meaningful analysis of the test's construct validity.

Summary of Issues

The key issues highlighted by our initial effort to develop a role-playing measure were as follows:

1) We needed to free ourselves from the constraining influence of trait-like assumptions.

2) We needed to develop precise objective definitions of specific skills, rather than relying on the vague subjective definitions provided by judges' ratings.

3) We needed to develop measures that covered a range of target behaviors—including those which were trained, those to which training should generalize, and those which should be unaffected by training—in order to establish the convergent and discriminant validity of our results.

4) We needed to develop measures whose scores could be related to the results of other assessments, for purposes of establishing construct and concurrent validity.

In an effort to overcome the shortcomings of the original role-playing measure, a new measure was developed for use in subsequent assertion training experiments (McFall & Lillesand, 1971; McFall & Twentyman, 1973). Rather than covering a broad, heterogeneous class of assertion situations, it concentrated on a limited, homogeneous, and quantifiable subset—namely eight situations involving unreasonable requests that required subjects to give refusal responses. The choice of these particular situations permitted an *a priori* definition of situation-specific competence and facilitated the development of objective scoring criteria for assertive responses. That is, subjects either refused a request or they did not. Judges could reliably (e.g., $r \geqslant .90$) rate such responses on a five-point scale, ranging from one=unqualified acceptance to five=unqualified refusal. By design, some of the refusal test situations were closely related to the situations covered in the assertion training procedure; these provided a direct assessment of training effects. Other refusal situations that had not been covered in training also were included to assess generalization of training. In addition, a ninth situation that called for a different type of assertive response (i.e., asking the landlord to make promised repairs) was included to assess the extent to which refusal training affected behavior in unrelated assertion situations. Because subjects' responses were evaluated on a criterion-referenced scale, rather than on a relative scale, it was possible to compute the role-playing measure's test-retest reliability (e.g., $r=.76$ over a two-week period for subjects in an untreated control group) and its convergent validity (e.g., $r=.63$ between the measure and the Conflict Resolution Inventory, a paper-and-pencil measure of refusal behavior) (McFall & Lillesand, 1971). An example of one Behavioral Role-playing Assertion Test (BRAT) situation is as follows:

> *Narrator*: Suppose you worked part-time in an office in the afternoon. At 4:30 one afternoon, as you were looking forward to going home and anticipating your evening out at a concert with some friends, your boss asks you if you would mind working overtime that night. What would you say?

The BRAT measure of refusal behavior, or some variant of it, now has been used by a number of different investigators in a number of assertion training experiments (e.g., Eisler, Miller & Hersen, 1973; Kazdin, 1974). While the measure seems to be a significant improvement over previous ones, experience has revealed several serious problems with it. First, the usual BRAT scoring procedure of summing the ratings over individual test items to arrive at a total test score for each subject is an inappropriate holdover from the days of trait measures; there is an assumption of response additivity implicit in this procedure that is inconsistent with a situation-specific view of behavior. An appropriate alternative scoring system needs to be developed that preserves the identity of individual responses while reducing and transforming the test data to a more manageable and digestible form. Perhaps a performance profile analysis, similar to the type used on Wechsler intelligence tests, would be a possible solution to the scoring problem. This possibility deserves to be explored.

It also is apparent that the usual method of assessing interrater agreement—that is, computing the intercorrelation between the total test scores given to individual subjects by different raters—is not appropriate. To be consistent with a situation-specific analysis of behaviors, intercorrelations should reflect interrater agreement for individual responses, not just for total scores. A better approach would be to compare ratings on a response-by-response basis and report the overall percent-agreement between raters. It also would be useful to examine the level of interrater agreement obtained on each of the individual test items. This would indicate which items might be in need of refinement or revision.

Another major weakness in the BRAT role-playing measure is that it usually imposes an artificial constraint on the subject's social behavior by allowing only one brief verbal response to each of the test situations. This constraint may enhance the measure's rigor, but it detracts from the measure's realism and representativeness. Unfortunately, efforts to develop more life-like role-playing measures, in which subjects are permitted to engage freely in more extended interactions, have encountered serious methodological problems. The most significant problem is that it is difficult to exercise satisfactory control over the relevant stimuli in such free-wheeling interactions. Figure 1 illustrates this control problem with a schematic diagram of the branching possibilities for a fairly simple interaction sequence, a sequence in which the subject responds in a binary fashion at each step of the interaction. As can be seen, the first interaction unit, consisting of one stimulus and response, can have only two possible outcomes. If the interaction is carried to the second step, however, with the choice of stimuli determined by the subject's first binary response, then there are four possible outcomes. At the third step there are 8; 16 at the fourth; 32 at the fifth; 64 at the sixth, etc. At the fifteenth step of this seemingly simple model of interactions, the number of theoretically possible outcomes has exploded to 32,768. At the twentieth step it is at 1,048,576! Obviously, it would not be possible to prepare and have accessible for immediate presentation standardized, prerecorded stimuli for all the possible role-playing contingencies in a 20-step interaction; managing even a six-step branching interaction would be a tremendous technological feat. Nevertheless, unless adequate control over the assessment stimuli is maintained, it is difficult to compare the data from any two interactions.

Figure 1 depicts a simple social interaction in which the subject is arbitrarily limited to two possible responses per stimulus; it is more often the case that subjects are not limited to such binary response choices. Even when their behavior is restricted to a brief verbal response at the

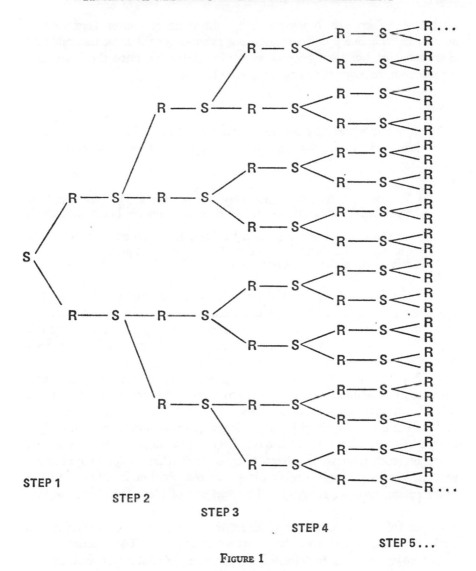

STEP 1

STEP 2

STEP 3

STEP 4

STEP 5 . . .

FIGURE 1

first stage of the interaction, as is usually the case in BRAT-type measures, the resulting responses can be very complex and extremely difficult to codify. Confronted by such complexity, how does the investigator decide which aspects of the subject's behavior to attend to and which to ignore? Under what circumstances should topographically similar responses be treated as equivalent and when should they be treated as different? When are topographically different responses functionally equivalent? These are difficult decisions even under the most favorable of circumstances, but they become virtually impossible once the investigator loses control over the assessment stimuli.

Issues

Again, our continuing research efforts helped bring into focus some of the critical issues involved in using analogue methods for behavioral assessment:

1) We needed to find some way to maximize the "realism" or representativeness of the situations and responses being measured.

2) At the same time, we needed to strive for maximum control over the assessment stimuli in order to insure the standardization and relevance of the assessment task.

A final solution to meeting these two needs has not yet been found, but some promising strides have been made. One of the earlier attempts at a solution was the Extended Interaction Test (McFall & Lillesand, 1971), which was a role-playing measure designed to assess a subject's perseverance at refusing the unreasonable requests of a persistent antagonist. What made the measure possible was the realization that many antagonists are almost totally unresponsive to the specific content of the refusal responses they receive. If their initial request is refused, even if this refusal is accompanied by some logical explanation, they will simply ignore this rejection, stay on the offensive, and counter with yet another, more insistent request. In effect, they seem to have a preprogrammed sequence of increasingly urgent pleas that they will emit either until the other person capitulates or until they run out of pleas, whichever occurs first.

In the following sample of an Extended Interaction Test situation, the subject is confronted with five sequential requests. To experience the extent to which this test format succeeds in simulating an interaction, the reader should assume the subject's role and imagine making a refusal response to each request before reading further.

Narrator: You are feeling really pressed for study time because you have an exam on Friday afternoon. Now, you are studying at your desk, when a close friend comes in and says, "Hi. Guess what. My parents just called and offered to pay for a plane ticket so I can fly home this weekend. Great, huh!? The only problem is, I'll have to skip my Friday morning class, and I hate to miss out on those notes; I'm barely making it in there as it is. Look, I know you aren't in that class, but it'd really be a big help if you'd go to the class Friday and take notes for me so I could go home. Would you do that for me?"

(S responds. If refusal . . .)

"I guess it is kinda crazy to expect you to do it, but, gee, I've got so many things to do if I'm gonna get ready to leave, and I don't want to waste the time asking around. Come on, will you do it for me this once?"

(S responds. If refusal . . .)

"Look, what're friends for if they don't help each other out of a bind? I'd do it for you if you asked. What do you say, will you?"

(S responds. If refusal . . .)

"But I was *counting* on *you* to *do* it. I'd hate to have to call my folks back and tell them I'm not coming. Can't you spare just *one* hour to help me out?"

(S responds. If refusal . . .)

(Sarcastically.) "Now look, I don't want to *impose* on your *precious* time. Just tell me. Will you do it or do I have to call my folks back?"

(S responds.)

Notice that the subject's responses were constrained somewhat by the initial description of the situation—that is, by the need to study for an exam being given later on Friday. This constraint helped make it possible to anticipate some of the subject's likely reasons for refusing. Nevertheless, the antagonist's pleas probably would seem credible no matter how the subject responded because such pleas tend to be basically unresponsive and illogical anyway.

Paralleling the development of the Extended Interaction Test for use in the laboratory and clinic context was the development of a similar measure of refusal behavior for use in the field context. Again, the problem was one of maintaining adequate stimulus control without sacrificing realism and representativeness. The problem was even more acute in the field setting, however. The aim was to obtain a naturalistic sample of refusal behavior that would enable an assessment of the transfer of assertion training effects to the "real world." This meant that the measure had to be unobtrusive, which ruled out the use of ordinary role-playing methods. The method finally selected involved the use of the public telephone as a research tool. The telephone provided relatively easy and inexpensive access to subjects. It imposed some degree of standardization on the assessment conditions. It limited subjects' task-relevant behavior to the verbal channel, which greatly facilitated data recording, analysis, and interpretation. And it enabled the experimenter to pose in the role of someone making an unreasonable request, with subjects being unlikely to detect this deception. Even if subjects should suspect deception, they could not confirm it. In effect, it was a simulation method of assessment, but the subjects were not fully aware of this fact until they were contacted again later and debriefed.

Initial attempts to develop the unobtrusive telephone measure were only marginally successful (e.g., McFall & Lillesand, 1971; McFall & Marston, 1970); however, in three recent experiments an improved version of the telephone measure was capable of differentiating between treatment and control subjects at least one month following assertion training (McFall & Galbraith, 1976; McFall & Twentyman, 1973). A male confederate telephoned subjects five or six days prior to an exam in their introductory psychology course. The confederate was "blind"; that is, he was unaware of subjects' treatment assignments and did not know the experimental hypotheses. Posing as a fellow student in that course, the confederate began by making a vaguely reasonable request for help in the course and then proceeded to escalate both the specificity and unreasonableness of his requests. In all, there was a graded series of seven requests; subjects were scored in terms of the point in this series at which they switched from saying "yes" to saying "no." The confederate's preprogrammed dialogue was as follows:

> "Hi, may I speak to (subject)? (Subject)? You're taking intro psych, aren't you? Well, I'm Tom Blake. I don't think you know me, but I'm in (professor)'s lecture, too. I don't know anyone in the class, so I got your name off the registration list they have in the psych office."

> *Request 1:* "I really hate to bother you, but I have some questions on some of the lecture material. Do you think you could help me for a few minutes?" (*S* responds. If no refusal . . .)

> *Request 2:* "I think all I really need is to look at your notes. Do you think we could arrange that?" (*S* responds. If no refusal . . .)

> *Request 3:* "Actually, I haven't made it to all the lectures, so I'll need to borrow your notes for awhile to fill in what I've missed. Okay?" (*S* responds. If no refusal . . .)

Request 4: "Well, (subject), to tell you the truth, I haven't been to class since the last exam, so I'll probably need your notes for two days. Would that be all right?" (*S* responds. If no refusal . . .)

Request 5: "Let's see now. I have a paper due on Wednesday (five days before exam), so I won't be able to get them before that. Could I get them sometime on Thursday?" (*S* responds. If no refusal . . .)

Request 6: "Oh, wait a minute! I've got a chemistry exam on Friday. Could I get them after that? That would be three days before the psych exam." (*S* responds. If no refusal . . .)

Request 7: "Now that I think about it, I'll probably need a night to recover from the chem exam, so is it all right if I get them Saturday instead, for the two days before the exam? (*S responds.*)

If the subject unequivocally refused any request, the confederate said that he understood and terminated the call. If the subject acquiesced to all seven requests, the confederate began expressing reservations about passing the course and then decided to drop the course, rather than take the exam, thus making it unnecessary for him to borrow the subject's notes after all.

The assessment strategy employed in the Extended Interaction Test and telephone measure was fruitful largely because these measures focused on a very narrow and specific response class, namely, refusal behaviors. It has been difficult to apply the same strategy to the assessment of broader response classes, such as heterosexual skills or other complex social behaviors. Attempts to construct preprogrammed dialogue for the experimenter's half of such dyadic interactions have failed; the dialogue invariably has been either too rigid to be veridical or too flexible to be controllable. Most investigators faced with this measurement dilemma apparently have preferred realism to rigor, choosing to assess their subjects social behaviors via freewheeling simulated interactions. However, for the methodological reasons discussed previously, this choice has been an unfortunate one. Clearly, an assessment strategy combining realism with experimental control over stimuli must be developed before the study of complex social behavior can progress much further.

Two recent developments along this line seem promising and deserve mentioning. The first is an assessment strategy employed in the context of an interpersonal skill-training program for male psychiatric inpatients (Goldsmith & McFall, 1975). In one of the posttreatment measures each subject was asked via audiotaped instructions to meet and carry on a general conversation with a male stranger (a "blind" confederate). The subject was assigned three specific tasks to be accomplished as part of the general interaction: initiate the conversation, ask the stranger to lunch, and terminate the conversation after 10 minutes (a clock was visible). Meanwhile, unknown to the subject, the confederate had been programmed to confront him with three "critical moments": not catching the subject's name when introduced, responding to the lunch invitation with an excuse that left open the possibility of lunch at an alternative time, and saying "Tell me about yourself" at the first convenient pause in the conversation. The six built-in interaction tasks made it possible to evaluate the subject's performance in terms of the number of objectives he satisfactorily accomplished, in addition to evaluating it on the usual overall rating dimensions of skill, comfort, and pleasantness. This simulation measure was based on the concept of *equifinality* in complex social behavior; specifically, it recognized that there may be many different ways to accomplish the same behavioral objective, and that the primary consideration in evaluating any behavior is whether or not it was effective. Only when two or more behaviors are equally capable of producing the desired outcome does it make sense to compare them further on other qualitative dimensions, such as efficiency, elegance, etc. If outcome (function) is more important than process (form), then it is possible to exercise an important amount of control over the stimuli in the assessment situation by assigning the same interactional tasks to all subjects. Within those limits, however, the interaction can be allowed to flow freely, thus enhancing its realism.

Another promising simulation strategy for assessing complex social behavior is the "stop-action" method (see Goldsmith and McFall, 1975). To illustrate how this method works, its contemplated use (by Charlene Muehlenhard and this author) in a study of heterosocial problems among college women will be described. Subjects are asked to observe a prerecorded dramatized interaction between two actors (e.g., between a man and woman) and to imagine that they are in the shoes of one of the actors (e.g., the woman). At a critical moment in the interaction the presentation is halted and the subject is asked to carry the interaction forward by filling in with a role-played response. The subject's response is tape-recorded for subsequent analysis. Following the subject's response, the prerecorded dramatization is resumed from the exact point at which it had been halted. The subject hears how the actress responded to the same critical moment and how the interaction proceeded as a consequence of that response. The interaction continues to the next critical moment, it is stopped again, and the subject fills in with yet another role-played response. This procedure is repeated throughout the presentation of an entire assessment scene, consisting of several critical moments.

The "stop-action" method has several advantages over other simulation methods. First, it provides a high degree of control over the assessment stimuli while managing to give subjects the *subjective* experience of participating in an ongoing interaction. It minimizes the influence of subjects' early responses on their subsequent responses, because the interaction proceeds strictly on a preprogrammed basis. Regardless of how a given subject responds at any particular stopping point, the interaction proceeds in a predetermined manner based on the likely consequences of the scripted responses. Within the limits imposed by the scripted antecedent interaction, however, subjects are given freedom of response at each stopping point. Another advantage is that it provides a mechanism for assessing subjects' performances in highly intimate situations that otherwise would be too sensitive to handle using conventional role-playing methods. For example, in the previously mentioned study of women's heterosocial skills, one of the stop-action scenes involves a dating interaction in which the man makes an inappropriate sexual advance, attempting to unbutton the woman's blouse against her will. This is a realistic problem for many subjects, but one that would be too personal for most subjects to enact directly with a confederate. Using the stop-action method, however, this critical moment can be presented very explicitly to subjects since they only experience the sexual advance vicariously, rather than directly. Finally, the method provides increased control over the variable of *time*. That is, the narrator of the prerecorded interaction can manipulate time almost at will: He can rapidly move ahead in time (e.g., "Suppose it is later that same evening."), or move backward in time to explore other branches of the interaction (e.g., "Let's go back in time. Suppose you *had agreed* to go to his apartment when he invited you . . ."), or change abruptly to an entirely different scene and time ("Now let's change the situation. . . ."). In effect, the method allows the investigator to systematically and efficiently obtain performance samples of the subject's behavior in critical tasks, or in interpersonal "crunch" situations.

Summary of Issues

The discussion in the preceding section highlighted several additional assessment issues:

1) It is important to distinguish between the form and the function of the behaviors being assessed.

2) Role-playing methods are especially useful for assessing performance in highly personal or intimate situations.

3) Role-playing methods offer other potential advantages, such as greater flexibility and more individualization of the assessment stimuli.

4) There has been insufficient research attention devoted to identifying critical assessment tasks and specifying the relevant skills needed for effective functioning in those tasks. The balance of the present paper is devoted to exploring this issue.

IDENTIFYING CRITICAL TASKS AND DEFINING COMPETENCE

Before we can develop valid role-playing measures of competence, we must expirically identify which life tasks are actually critical for our subjects and define what constitutes effective behavior in such tasks. Unfortunately, most investigators have ignored these basic requirements. Many have simply relied on their personal opinions or "clinical intuitions" to determine which problems they will consider most relevant and which responses they will judge as most adaptive. Other investigators have taken a more "democratic" approach, defining situational competence on the basis of the majority opinion among a group of judges. Still others have used the "known-groups" approach, defining competence in terms of the observable performance differences that significantly differentiate between subject groups representing two extremes on some variable (e.g., highly assertive versus very nonassertive subjects). Almost no one has used the most valid—and most time consuming— approach to defining situational competence: Few have taken the trouble to determine experimentally which behaviors actually are most effective for accomplishing subjects' objectives in specific problem situations.

In the early studies on assertive-refusal behaviors, it was possible to finesse the difficulties inherent in defining situational competence. It was taken for granted that unreasonable requests invariably are problematic and that refusal responses usually offer the best solutions. In a subsequent study of heterosocial skills among college-age males (Twentyman & McFall, 1975), however, it became obvious that an empirically-based definition of competence was essential to an understanding of complex social behaviors. The study employed three different simulation measures, each aimed at assessing a different aspect of heterosocial behavior. The measures were administered to two subject groups: "shy" males and "confident" males. Shy subjects were men who dated infrequently (zero or one date in the last month) and reported feeling anxious with women. Confident subjects dated frequently and reported feeling comfortable.

In the first measure, subjects were given the name and phone number of a woman whom they had never met. They were instructed to telephone her and ask for a date. Since subjects were not permitted to complete these calls, this measure only assessed their willingness to initiate heterosocial contacts. The second measure was the Social Behavior Situations test, a series of six role-played interactions with women. The situations had been identified in pilot studies as problematic for many college men. Subjects were instructed to respond out loud as though they were actually engaged in the imaginary situations. In one situation, for example, subjects were told, "You are on a break at your job. You see a girl who is about your age at the canteen. She works in another part of the store and consequently you don't know her very well. You would like to talk to her. What would you say?" If a subject initiated a conversation, then one of two trained female assistants in an adjoining control room engaged him in a role-played conversation over an intercom. This interaction generally lasted for about three minutes or until the subject terminated it. In the third measure, called the Forced Interaction Test, a female assistant entered the subject's room, and engaged him in five minutes of face-to-face role-playing. The subject was told to imagine that she was a girl who had just taken a seat next to him in one of his classes. He was instructed to initiate and carry on a conversation.

The telephone measure yielded a self-report of anxiety and an index of willingness to place the call. Subjects' performances in the Social Behavior Situations and Forced Interaction Test were rated by direct observers, by "blind" raters who listened to audiotapes, and by the subjects themselves. Some of the rating dimensions were quite general (e.g., anxiety and skill), whereas others were fairly specific (e.g., number of speech dysfluencies and total time spent in conversation).

All three measures managed to detect significant differences between shy and confident subjects. On the telephone measure, shy subjects reported being more anxious than confident subjects, although they were no less likely to initiate the call. On the Social Behavior Situations, shy subjects engaged in a higher rate of avoidance behavior and were rated as significantly more anxious and less skillful than confident subjects. They also were rated as more anxious and less skillful on the Forced Interaction Test.

Although the three simulation measures yielded statistically significant results, they did not yield very *informative* results. They failed to reveal, for example, what specific behaviors among the confident subjects had been perceived by raters as "skillful," or what behaviors among the shy subjects had been seen as indicative of "anxiety." None of the specific rating categories (e.g., the frequency of speech dysfluencies) had differentiated between groups. Thus, the study showed that the groups differed, but it contributed little or nothing to our ability to specify the behavioral components of skillful heterosocial behavior.

In the absence of empirically-established behavioral referents for heterosocial competence, it seems premature and presumptuous to design and implement social skill training programs for shy males. To be effective, such programs must teach clients new behaviors that offer valid solutions to their problems. Unless the necessary research has been conducted to identify these genuinely effective behaviors, there is always the likelihood that the clients might be trained to emit new behaviors that actually are ineffective or even counterproductive. For example, investigators have reported skill training programs for shy males in which the clients are taught to increase their rate of eye contact while engaged in conversations with women. Apparently this training is based on the unverified assumptions that competent men show high rates of eye contact, that shy men are deficient in this respect, and that high rates of eye contact contribute to successful interactions. These assumptions, however, are not strongly supported by the evidence (e.g., Arkowitz, Lichtenstein, McGovern & Hines, 1975; Boland, 1973). In fact, the value or appropriateness of eye contact depends on contextual factors. At the extremes, incessant staring is no more appropriate than a total lack of eye contact. What seems to be important is not the absolute *rate* of eye contact, but *when* it occurs. There are certain moments when it is best to look at the other person and certain moments when it is best to look away. Teaching clients to emit a high rate of undifferentiated eye contact, therefore, may actually decrease their effectiveness in certain heterosocial interactions.

Recognizing the necessity of defining competence before attempting to design skill training programs, this author and his associates have undertaken several assessment studies of heterosocial skills among college-age men and women. One study, for example, attempted to determine what actually is an effective way for a person to approach and initiate a conversation with a complete stranger (Twentyman, unpublished data). A number of volunteer undergraduate experimenters, 12 men and 12 women, actually tested the effectiveness of three different opening gambits for approaching same-sex and opposite-sex undergraduates in real-life settings, such as in the lounge at the student union building. The three gambits were: a) asking permission to enter the stranger's personal space ("Hello. Do you mind if I talk to you?"); b) using an indirect approach that might be characterized as a "slick line" ("Hi. Haven't I seen you somewhere before?"); and c) taking a direct approach and admitting to one's awkwardness about meeting people ("Hi. I'm trying to meet people. Do you know of any good ways of doing this?"). Immediately after approaching a stranger with one of these gambits and getting a response, the experimenter handed the stranger a questionnaire and asked the person to rate the attractiveness of each of the gambits. Results of these ratings indicated that the first approach was viewed as significantly more attractive than the second ("line") approach across all sexual combinations of experimenters and strangers (all $p<.05$). The first approach was also rated more favorably than the third approach when males approached either males or females ($p<.01$), but not when females approached either males or females.

These results not only have implications for how shy males and females might be taught to initiate conversations with strangers, but they also tie in to the results of other studies. Specifically, when asked to guess how women might respond to these three gambits, shy males tended to be less accurate than confident males (Twentyman, unpublished data). In general, shy males may be deficient in their ability to interpret interpersonal cues. Consistent with this hypothesis, yet another study (Boland, 1973) found some evidence that shy males tended to be uncertain about how to determine whether a woman was having a good time on a date with them. Confident subjects tended to show less uncertainty; the typical confident male was likely to say, "If I'm having a good time, she's having a good time!"

Although few investigators have taken a systematic, empirical approach toward the development of their social skills training programs, this does not mean that the methods for doing so have been unavailable. On the contrary, Goldfried and D'Zurilla (1969) have provided an excellent set of procedural guidelines for identifying clients' critical problems and defining competent behavioral solutions to their problems. The utility of these guidelines has been demonstrated in two recent studies focusing on two distinct populations and problem areas. The first study (Goldsmith & McFall, 1975) was concerned with assessing the skill deficits of male psychiatric inpatients. The assessment results subsequently served as the foundation for the construction of the treatment content and outcome measures of an experimental social skills training program. The second study (Freedman, 1974) was strictly an assessment study aimed at identifying the skill deficits of institutionalized male adolescent delinquents. To illustrate the procedures involved in conducting a skills assessment, the study focusing on delinquents will be described here in some detail. The study was conducted in five phases.

Phase 1: Situational Analysis. The aim of this first phase was to identify life situations that characteristically pose problems for teenagers in America today. Suggestions of potential problem situations were drawn from a number of sources, including the sociological and psychological literature; interviews with adult authorities on juvenile problems; selected case files of delinquent boys; interviews with nondelinquent adolescent boys; and a questionnaire given to delinquent boys. These sources provided a long list of problem situations, which subsequently was refined, reworded, and condensed to a list of 52 general situations. These were administered in questionnaire form to 22 institutionalized delinquent boys, who were asked to rate the commonness and difficulty of each situation on two four-point scales. These ratings subsequently were used to assign a composite rank to each situation; the more common and difficult a situation was, the better it was for purposes of the study. Forty-one of the situations were ranked as both common and difficult, and thus were retained for subsequent use.

Phase 2: Item Development. This phase was devoted to the development of a pool of specific test items for use in assessing the problem-solving skills of adolescent boys. The 42 general problems identified in the first phase were developed into 90 narrative descriptions of specific problematic incidents, each calling for a role-played response from the subject.

Phase 3: Response Enumeration. In this phase, a sample of role-played responses to each of the 90 test items was obtained from 23 subjects, who were assumed to represent a wide range of problem-solving competence. The subjects were 12 institutionalized delinquent boys, six nondelinquent boys, and five adult authorities on adolescent behavior. The delinquents and nondelinquents were instructed to tell what they would actually say or do if they were in each situation. The adults were asked to tell what they thought would be the most competent response a boy could give in each situation.

Phase 4: Response Evaluation. In this phase, 13 independent raters (four men, nine women) judged the competence of the responses obtained in the preceding phase. For each response, raters indicated whether they considered it "competent," "incompetent," or "neither." In addition, raters were asked to articulate the criteria they used to evaluate the responses to each item. Items with low interjudge agreement were eliminated. In addition, items were eliminated if they were either too easy (i.e., where nearly all responses were considered competent) or too difficult (i.e., where almost none of the responses was considered competent). Of the initial pool of 90 items, 44 were retained. Based on experiences with the items, their wording was refined further in an attempt to clarify any remaining confusions or flaws. The final result was a 44-item, criterion-referenced measure of the problem-solving skills of adolescent boys, called the Adolescent Problems Inventory (API). Accompanying the API was an empirically developed rater's manual derived from the rating criteria articulated by raters in this phase of the research. For each item, the manual presented scoring criteria corresponding to ratings ranging from $0 =$ Very Incompetent to $8 =$ Very Competent. Specific verbatim examples were included of responses meeting the different criterion levels. An illustrative API item and its scoring criteria are as follows:

> You're visiting your aunt in another part of town, and you don't know any of the guys your age there. You're walking along her street, and some guy is walking toward you. He is about your size. As he is about to pass you, he deliberately bumps into you, and you nearly lose your balance. What do you say or do now?
>
>   8—S ignores the boy, says nothing, or walks on (he *may* give the boy a dirty look), *or* gives an assertive, calm response, *or* tries to get to know the other boy.
>
>   6—Polite but conciliatory or apologetic response. *Examples*: "Excuse me." "Sorry about that."
>
>   4—Response is unassertive, wishy-washy, overly wordy, or otherwise ineffective, but not likely to provoke a fight.
>
>   2—Response is insulting, antagonistic, or provocative. *Examples*: "Watch where you're going." "What'd you do that for?"
>
>   0—S pushes or fights the other boy, in any way. (It does not matter what else he says or does. Fighting takes precedence, unless he says he would try to avoid a fight, but if the other boy swung first, he'd hit back. That receives 2.)

Phase 5: Validation. The final step was to determine whether or not the API was a valid measure; that is, did it actually tap performance deficits that were associated with delinquent behavior? The measure was administered individually to subjects in three adolescent groups: institutionalized delinquent boys, nondelinquent boys ("good citizens") matched for age and socioeconomic status, and high school leaders ("superstars") matched only for age. Compared to the nondelinquent subjects, delinquents earned significantly lower overall competence scores. In fact, 42 out of the 44 API items significantly differentiated between delinquents and "good citizens." Assuming that the scoring criteria in the rater's manual actually corresponded to the relative effectiveness in "real-life" of the respective solutions to problems situations, then these results suggest that the delinquents tended to be deficient in certain critical problem-solving skills. Moreover, the research points to the potential clinical value of developing role-playing measures, like the API, along the lines suggested by Goldfried and D'Zurilla (1969) in their behavior-analytic model for assessing competence.

CONCLUSIONS

This paper has explored the use of analogue methods in behavioral assessment, with particular emphasis on the use of simulation and role-playing methods. The research of the author and his associates was critically reviewed in an attempt to illustrate some of the major methodological and conceptual problems associated with developing valid role-playing measures. Hopefully, by openly acknowledging and analyzing past inadequacies, similar problems can be avoided in the future.

On balance, the research indicates that there is good reason to feel optimistic about the potential value of role-playing methods in behavioral assessment. They seem to be preferable to most other available assessment approaches. Except for direct assessments of "real-life" behaviors, no other sampling approach provides a better approximation to the criterion behavior. In fact, role-playing even has a potential advantage over direct assessment in that it often permits significantly better control and standardization.

The future development of better role-playing methods hinges on the development of improved theoretical foundations—foundations capable of dealing with the following unresolved issues: What is the most fruitful way of conceptualizing clients' problems? If problems are viewed as situation-specific performance deficits, as they are within the competence model of behavior, then what are the specific life situations that are most critical for assessment purposes? How should these situations be classified and interrelated? What is the best method of sampling clients' performances in these situations? When obtaining behavioral samples, how should they be codified and interpreted? What is "competent" behavior; how is it to be defined and measured?

In calling for improved theories, we are not suggesting a return to the nonproductive era of grand "armchair" theories based on little more than clinical intuition or speculation. On the contrary, we are calling for the careful and systematic construction of empirically based models capable of integrating available evidence and guiding future research. Platt's (1964) "strong inference" approach to theory building provides a general outline of the approach being advocated here. The present paper provided examples of research employing the strong inference approach in the assessment of clinical problems (e.g., delinquency) in an attempt to illustrate the promise of the approach and in the hopes of encouraging other investigators to adopt it. A concerted effort by a number of investigators employing a common methodology to explore a common set of problems within a common conceptual framework should yield rapid progress toward the behavioral assessment objectives discussed in this paper.

6

PHYSIOLOGICAL ASSESSMENT OF ANXIETY AND FEAR

PETER J. LANG

Once the fact of a contributing, though poorly understood, genetic predisposition is granted, anxiety and pathological fear are presumed to be reactions to stressful stimuli. They may represent a response to a very narrow band of stimulation, occasioned by short but intense exposure, as seems to be the case with many phobias; also, anxiety can be a reaction to pervasive and recurring stimuli. Aversive emotional states, which often develop through successive transactions with the environment, are maintained both by environmental contingencies and by the patient's own self-defeating response patterns, and can thus be woven tightly into the behavioral and physiological fabric of the person we undertake to help.

Assessment for treatment involves two aspects: First, we must specify the stimulus elements in the present context which prompt distress and define the contingencies in the environment that appear to maintain the unwanted behaviors. Second, we need to define the response elements which must be changed or modified in order to effect meaningful treatment. I do not propose in the present chapter to offer a detailed analysis of problems in stimulus assessment, or a guide to locating environmental contingencies that sustain pathological behavior. Stimulus assessment varies considerably for different treatment methods and different problem areas. Thus, if we elect to apply systematic desensitization, the eliciting fear stimuli must be carefully specified and ordered along a dimension analogous to the range of intensity that may be described for a physical stimulus. However, if modeling and/or coaching are used in treatment, we may only need to know the broad context of disturbance, and detailed stimulus specification is held to be less critical. While stimulus considerations cannot be

178

ignored in a practical context, in this chapter I would like to emphasize the analysis of emotional *responding*. My concern will be with response-response relationships as well as stimulus-response events. I will attempt to describe a rough framework in which patterns of emotional responding can be specified, with implications for choice of treatment.

ANALYSIS OF EMOTIONAL RESPONDING

It has become commonplace to refer to emotion as a constellation of response events which can be ordered into three classes: 1) language behavior, 2) motor acts, and 3) changes in the viscera and the level or pattern of muscle tonus. For most psychologists, intense emotional states are defined by the simultaneous or sequential presence of high amplitude behaviors in all three response classes. Thus, when Androcles is first confronted by the lion, we expect him to scream, profess intense fear, go pale in the face, feel his heart to skip a beat or two, perhaps spontaneously vomit or defecate, and freeze into immobility or run away.

The history of the psychology of emotion can be described as a struggle by theorists to define the integration of these differing response systems. Thus, William James (1884) saw the visceral events and motor behavior as primary determinants of verbal report in emotion. Androcles feels afraid because he runs, or because his heart beats rapidly. More recently, Schachter (1964) has proposed that visceral arousal prompts an "evaluative need," and that this need requires logical resolution. If events in the environment favor an emotion interpretation of arousal (as opposed to being aware that we have just jogged three miles), then an emotion will be experienced, with appropriate overt behavior. Cannon (1931) and the physiological psychologists who followed him spurned the phenomenological impurity inherent in such interpretations. They proposed instead that all three components of the emotional response were coincidently determined by structures in the lower brain. The natural science orientation of this approach is appealing. However, it must also be noted that explorations of the hypothalamus and limbic system have neither generated practical treatments for emotional disorders nor provided easy explanations for the mobile patterns and rich variety of human emotional behavior.

It is rare that the emotional states that we see in a treatment context (or, indeed, those of normal subjects) follow the classic pattern. That is to say, when confronted by emotional stimuli, patients seldom show responses in all three systems at comparable levels of intensity. In fact, they often show strong behavior in one system, and perhaps none at all in the others. Furthermore, change in one aspect of the emotional response does not necessarily mean that other response components will also show progress (Lang, 1968; Rachman, 1974; Barlow, Chapter 11). And finally, while everyone speculates about the relationship between responses in emotion, the pool of relevant data is still quite small, and a generally acceptable theory has yet to make an appearance.

Despite the above considerations, it is clear that implicit assumptions about the integration of emotional responses underlie our treatment methods. It was presumed by dynamic therapists that emotional experiences or feelings were the fundamental stuff of emotion and that the three behavior classes that I have described were indicants of some controlling internal state. Their method of treatment was to modify this central feeling state, to help the patient recognize and work through emotional experience. Viewed empirically (the stance I propose here), the dynamic therapist was focusing on the *language* component of the response. His theory led him to assume that if the patient came to talk differently about his feelings, the gross motor and physiological components of the pathology would fade away like old soldiers. A similar general view of treatment is assumed by a number of contemporary behavior therapists. For example, Meichenbaum (1974) and Ellis (1962) emphasize the importance of modifying self-referent language statements in aversive emotional states. While the methodology is different, the assumption is also made that verbalizations about feelings and abilities control other response components, and that language modification will mediate broad change in the organism.

Verbal behavior is not the only focus of therapy for the aversive emotions. A person with social anxiety who seeks help from a general practitioner may be treated with a drug designed to reduce the sympathetic reactivity of his viscera or relax the somatic musculature. The physician assumes that change in the peripheral physiology will prompt the patient to report less anxiety and perhaps also promote positive changes in his social behavior. Clinical psychologists may also reason in this manner when they elect to employ biofeedback therapies (Blanchard & Young, 1974), autogenic training (Schultze & Luthe, 1959), or progressive relaxation (Jacobson, 1938).

Finally, some therapists consider physiological and language behaviors as secondary targets in the therapeutic enterprise. Thus, in treating social anxiety, for example, they would encourage the modification and development of specific social skills (Goldsmith & McFall, 1975). The patient who avoids the opposite sex should be trained in approach behavior. A performance deficit should be replaced with a performance asset. The frightened soldier must put on a brave face and volunteer for hazardous duty. It is presumed that as new functional behaviors replace the disruptive or avoidant behaviors of the emotional state, subjects' verbal reports and visceral reactivity will cease to reflect distress.

In the absence of a clear understanding of behavioral integration in emotion, it is not obvious which of the above approaches is the best general strategy. Certainly, there are many clinical cases to be cited in support of each path. There are startling examples, illustrating how new insights or conceptualizations prompted broad behavior change. Similarly, there are instances in which acquisition of a new coping skill seemed to open up the behavior of a withdrawn or anxious person. Cases can also be cited in which brief relaxation therapy occasioned reports of a new calmness and competency. The failures of a too narrow therapeutic approach are also legion, and they form the basis for most popular psychotherapist jokes, such as the one about a patient who seeks help for spontaneous urination. When interrogated about his condition by a friend after some years of therapy, he admits no change in the urination problem, but reports "Now I don't mind it." Behavior therapists are not immune to the pitfalls of overconcentration on a single system. For example, the frequent failure of their efforts in producing posthospitalization transfer of institutionally trained behaviors (e.g., personal cleanliness or social skills) may result from a neglect of the mediating and conceptual functions of language.

In a previous paper (Lang, 1971), I considered the problem of treating aversive emotional states and proposed that the behavior therapeutic enterprise should be a vigorous multi-system program. That is to say, the patient who shows social performance deficits, the physiology of anxiety and also reports a feeling of dread or helplessness would most likely respond to a program which included the direct modification of each of these behavior sets. I do not mean to deny by this proposal the possibility that a narrower therapeutic program might prove to be more efficient. In fact, I view it as the cardinal weakness of behavior modification that we are constantly coping with pathology in *detail*. We do not yet have a theory of pathological behavior that explains how responses are organized, which would automatically signal targets for intervention commanding many behavioral units. We clearly need this kind of understanding to develop treatments with "leverage," treatments that would be more efficient than the laborious hand work of most behavior modifiers.

A practical approach would be to evaluate the multi-system efficiency of specific therapeutic programs. Presuming that we are in a position to assess behaviors pertinent to the three emotional response systems, we could not only compare treatments for their effectiveness in modifying their target response component, but also note their ameliorative effect on the other two systems. A series of "horse races" between popular therapeutic interventions would tell us which had broad spectrum effects for what problems, and might also offer rough theoretical guidance concerning the fundamental factors controlling integrated emotional responding.

The above discussion is predicated on a postulate that I have already convicted as a fickle truth: All behavioral systems are more or less equally represented in emotional expression across stimuli and subjects. Actually, the responses in emotion are only partially coupled, and only sometimes do they exist in concert in equal strength. Some reasons for their independence are obvious, even in the absence of a good theory. First of all, none of the responses in emotion is unique to say definition of the emotional state. Thus, a verbal report of anxiety can be prompted by many things other than a stressful stimulus. If a young person grows up in a culture in which his peers and elders talk about the "age of anxiety," despair over the "human condition," their sense of "alienation and hopelessness in a world without purpose," it would be a remarkably independent youth indeed who did not also describe at least some of his experience in these terms. However, we would not necessarily expect to find that his "alienation and hopelessness" were correlated with any consistent pattern of visceral events. Similarly, heart rate may be increased in reponse to exercise as well as to emotional stress. Even gross avoidance behavior can be misconstrued, for the student who leaves school in apparent academic panic may be responding positively to the lure of a European vacation.

I appreciate that these examples are gratuitous and facile. However, this only highlights the extent of the problem. When we dig deeper, yet more profound difficulties are uncovered. For example, all response systems are not equally sensitive in their reactance to stress stimuli. They appear to have different scales and one may even be nonresponding at levels of stimulus intensity to which another system makes a palpable and sensitive reply. Furthermore, it would appear that these scale factors vary considerably among individuals. Studies of instrumental conditioning of language behavior (Buss, 1961) show that subjects can generally grade verbal responses to stress in a highly refined manner, making nice distinctions between moderate and less intense stimuli. However, studies of the semantic conditioning of visceral events (Lang, Geer & Hnatiow, 1963) suggest that the gut is not so discriminating. Its response may not appear until higher levels of stimulation are reached and it is not such a connoisseur of subtle stimulus differences.

The above analysis implies that a comprehensive assessment of emotional behavior will not be an easy task. However, some rough guidelines for this enterprise are already apparent, and the implementation of even a gross pattern analysis could be of help in guiding therapeutic intervention. It is clear that verbal, overt motor, and physiological responses in emotion should be assessed separately within a diagnostic evaluation. Furthermore, it is not too farfetched to consider some quantitative rating of their separate contributions to the overall stress response. I am reminded of W. H. Sheldon's somatotypes (1944), and wonder if it would not be reasonable to develop an analogous behavioral typology, which would provide a quick indication of the relative balance between response systems. The reader will recall that Sheldon's three components of body build were each rated on a seven-point scale, and these values were noted sequentially, providing a shorthand description of an individual's physiognomy. Verbal (V), Motor (M), and Physiological (P) responses in aversive emotional states could be assessed on parallel scales. Much basic research would be required to generate optimal measurement in each category. Furthermore, the response characteristics within categories are both complex and idiosyncratic (e.g., a patient whose physiological stress response is predominantly cardiovascular contrasted to one whose reactivity is gastrointestinal).

However, even impressionistic data would be better than our current ignorance of these relationships. It would be very useful to know that an individual with social anxiety was a 7-1-1 (VMP), rather than a 1-1-7. The attention to response characteristics required by such a rating system would mitigate against the easy assumption that a patient's report of anxiety in the context of a problem stimulus is *ipse dixit* accompanied by sympathetic activation. Furthermore, a cognitive restructuring therapy is a more rational treatment choice than biofeedback, in those cases (and I believe there are many) where verbal report of anxiety is indeed independent of any visceral arousal. This orientation would also insure that we did not neglect real visceral distress, while attending exclusively to the modification of language behavior or social skills.

INSTRUCTED IMAGERY AND THE PSYCHOPHYSIOLOGICAL ANALYSIS OF FEAR

In previous reviews (Lang, 1971, 1975) we noted that physiological recording was rarely employed in the assessment of psychotherapeutic process or outcome. However, with the rapid development of biofeedback technology (Beatty & Legewie, 1977), this situation has been modified. Many clinicians are now attempting to use physiological recording in training subjects to relax and cope with stress. Unfortunately, practice is rapidly outstripping its research foundation. There are presently few data which would suggest that biofeedback is more effective than inexpensive and less technically demanding treatments such as instructed muscle relaxation or mediation (Lang, 1977). Nevertheless, irrespective of their value in direct treatment, the availability of physiological recording devices in the clinic now makes it possible for the clinician to study physiological process in a way previously possible only for the laboratory researcher. Thus, there is a real potential to use bioelectric information as part of the diagnostic battery and to broaden our assessment of the emotional response. As we have already noted, it is not yet clear how to use this information to select specific treatments and make meaningful prognostic statements. However, a number of investigators have made useful suggestions (Borkovec, in press; Schwartz, 1976). The final section of this chapter will describe one approach to this problem that is under investigation in our laboratory and some encouraging preliminary data.

Lang, Melamed and Hart (1974) reported that the effectiveness of systematic desensitization as a treatment of phobia covaried significantly with the patients' physiological reactance to fear imagery. In general, they found that subjects who had heightened heart rates while imagining frightening scenes showed more fear reduction at the end of treatment than did subjects who failed to respond autonomically to fearful imagery. This specific relationship is illustrated in Figure 1. The three curves represent groups of three subjects, rank ordered according to degree of post-treatment change on verbal report and behavioral avoidance tests of phobia (most improved: 1-3). The heart rates of each of these subgroups are illustrated, in response to a neutral scene at the beginning of therapy, the scene just preceding one that subjects found so frightening that they requested (by a "fear signal") that it be discontinued, the fear signal scene itself, and two repetitions of this same fear scene after supplemental relaxation instructions. It should be noted that such fear signals are rare in desensitization (the procedure is designed to minimize them),

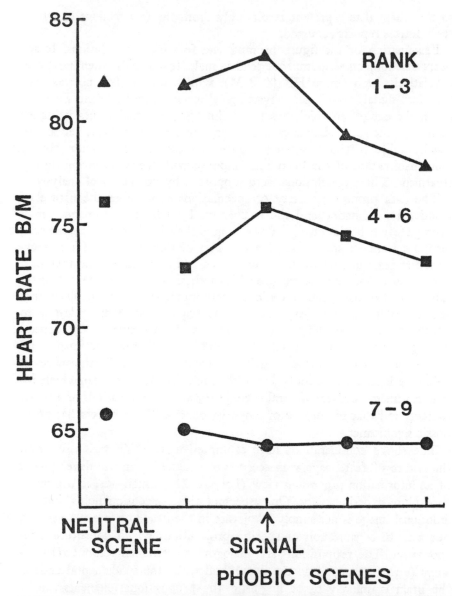

FIGURE 1. Average heart rate response curves for groups of three phobic subjects obtained during fear desensitization. Subjects reported intense distress during the signal scene which, following relaxation instructions, was twice repeated. The ranks represent degree of fear reduction, measured after desensitization. Subjects 1-3 showed the most posttreatment improvement (Lang, Melamed & Hart, 1974).

so that these data represent results only from the few sessions in which
such distress reports occurred.

Examination of the figure prompts the following conclusions. It appears that subjects who improve tend to make fear signals when heart rate
is relatively high (mean HR 80 B/M), while unsuccessful subjects may
give fear signals even when physiological arousal is not evident. Furthermore, the extent to which heart rate during fear signal scenes is higher
than adjacent scenes increases with rating of posttherapy fear reduction.
Finally, subjects who subsequently displayed less phobic behavior showed
more habituation of the heart rate response with scene repetition during
treatment. These conclusions were supported by correlational analysis.

The data prompt a variety of speculations concerning the nature of
emotional imagination and the mechanism by which fear imagery may
prompt fear behavior change. For example, they imply that for some subjects autonomic responses are literally part of their image and are determined at least in part by the instructions administered by the therapist.
They also encourage the reciprocal hypothesis (again for the successful
subjects) that background tonic arousal increases the probability that
subjects will report a fear image to be frightening. More relevant to
assessment, these results suggest that successful treatment may depend
on the fact that visceral events are processed with the fear image, and
that their absence mitigates against behavior change. Furthermore, it
could be inferred that individual differences in the extent to which instructed images control visceral events vary within populations of anxious
subjects and that the degree of language control of the viscera has prognostic significance.

The above considerations have prompted us to think seriously about
the nature of fear imagery in recent years, resulting in the development
of an information processing view (Lang, 1977), which we are beginning
to explore experimentally. One aspect of this conception holds that the
emotional image is not simply a "picture in the head" or internal percept,
but a finite organization of specific propositions which constitute a response set. The propositions are analogous to statements about relationships (e.g., the lamp is on the floor), and while the fundamental code in
the brain is unlikely to be linguistic, the propositional elements can be
stated in a natural language as instructions. We propose that such propositions are of two basic types: 1) stimulus propositions, which are
descriptors of events or relationships; and 2) response propositions, which
are affirmed behaviors. In the case of emotional images, the latter proposi-

TABLE 1

Sample Fear Scripts Which Vary in Response Content

Stimulus Propositions + Filler Material

> While standing in the snake house at the zoo, you notice a large red boa constrictor coiled on a tree branch in a glass cage. You watch the scene closely, with your eyes fixed on the snake. As you watch, the snake moves slowly along the tree branch toward the glass. You are looking from the side as you stand in front of the cage, and have a close view of the whole length of the snake.

Stimulus Propositions + Response Propositions

> Standing in the snake house at the zoo, you notice a large red boa constrictor coiled on a tree branch in a glass cage. You struggle to draw a breath and your heart begins pounding rapidly. As you watch, the snake moves slowly along the tree toward the glass. Your muscles tighten and your mouth goes dry as you begin to sweat heavily. A hollow feeling gnaws at your stomach as you see the snake up against the glass.

tional set might define verbal responses, motor acts, or somato-visceral events.

The scientific study of this conception poses obvious methodological difficulties. The cognitive image is within the brain and presently inaccessible to experimental analysis. However, a "stimulus" image may be defined as the instructions given by the therapist. Furthermore, the propositional structure of this "stimulus" image is readily modified by altering the therapist's script. We presume that the "stimulus" image and the cognitive image may be poorly correlated in individual subjects, because of idiosyncratic responses to instructional control. However, if the size of a subject group is substantial, the signal to noise ratio is greatly improved, and the effect of the stimulus image or instructions should become clear.

In a recent experiment we applied this approach to an exploration of image control over visceral responding. Subjects in this study were college students selected by questionnaire (Klorman, Weerts, Hastings, Melamed & Lang, 1974) and by interview for the presence of small animal and mutilation phobia. The phobic subjects were then trained in relaxation and given practice in imagining affectively neutral scenes. In a final test session subjects were administered, by tape recorder, both neutral and relevant phobic scenes. Heart rate and skin conductance were recorded.

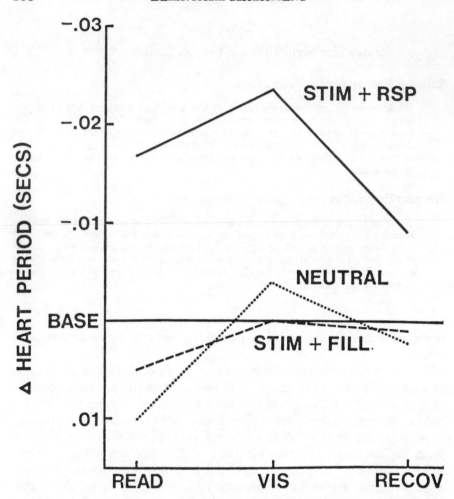

FIGURE 2. Average heart rate responses of 24 phobic subjects during fear imagery. Subjects were administered two types of fear scripts (see Table 1). Data were recorded while the script was read to the subject, during subsequent visualization, and during a following recovery period.

Two groups of subjects participated, balanced for sex of subject and specific phobic content. The experimental procedure involved two types of fear scene instructions. One set of instructions contained only stimulus propositions (descriptive material indicating what the subject "sees," as in Table 1), plus some fear irrelevant filler material that indicated posture or point of view. The second set of instructions included the same stimulus propositions, with the addition of visceral response propositions which are characteristic of emotional reactivity (Table 1). Both groups received three fear scenes of each type (in counterbalanced order) and three neutral scenes.

Heart rate and skin conductance were measured for the last 30 seconds of the reading of imagery instructions, a subsequent 30 seconds while the subject was to visualize the scene, and a 30-second recovery period during which subjects were told to stop imagining and relax.

The results for heart rate are presented in Figure 2. The stimulus plus response instructions clearly generated greater cardiovascular reactivity than did the stimulus propositions alone, and this fact was confirmed by statistical test. A similar but weaker effect was found for skin conductance. It is interesting to note that the two instructional sets did not generate significant differences in post-scene verbal report of fear. As in the Lang, Melamed and Hart experiment (1974) heart rate varied independently of verbal report of fear.

We are presently attempting a replication of this experiment, and conclusions must remain tentative until crossvalidation is demonstrated. However, these data do suggest that for groups of phobics drawn from a normal population visceral responses may be inserted or removed instructionally.

A similar methodology is being employed in a parallel study of clinically neurotic patients, but with particular attention to individual differences in the impact of the "stimulus" image. These patient-subjects are carefully interviewed to determine scene contents relevant to their presenting problems. Audiotapes of these scenes are then constructed and administered as in the student study. All scenes include both stimulus and response propositions. Patients are also administered neutral scenes, in addition to a standard fear scene which describes an automobile accident.

Average curves for heart rate and skin conductance obtained from a sample of four clinic patients are presented in Figure 3. The patients provided similar data to those of student subjects. Visualization of personally relevant fear material generally produced larger heart rate responses than did visualization of neutral material, or of the standard fear stimulus. Similar results were obtained for skin conductance, with the difference that larger responses were obtained during the reading of the instructions, rather than while visualizing.

From the perspective of behavioral assessment, the behavior of individual patients is of considerable interest. While most subjects conform in a general way to the average curve, unique individual patterns

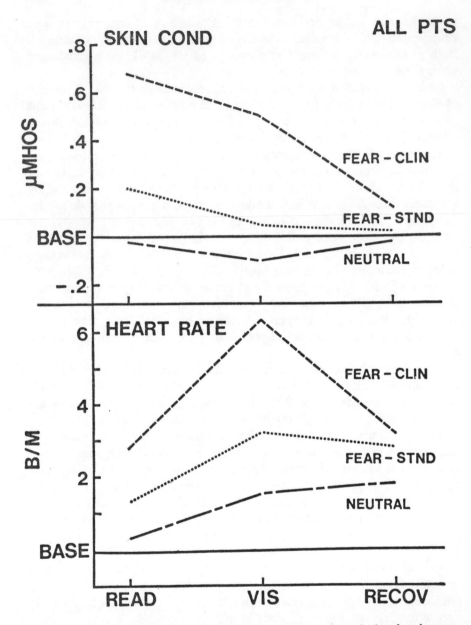

FIGURE 3. Average physiological responses of four clinic patients during fear imagery. The *clinical fear* script was based on their area of anxiety as determined by interview. The *fear standard* described a scene involving human mutilation. The *neutral* scene was non-affect inducing.

were also observed. Data from patient B.W. are presented in Figure 4. This young male sought help at a university clinic for test anxiety. He complained of feelings of panic and associated performance deficits prompted by the demands of a foreign language course. In addition to this admitting complaint, he described during the interview a strong fear of water, of going boating or swimming and of being the victim of an accidental drowning. However, the occurrence of the latter fear was so rare that he did not feel he needed treatment for it. Clinical fear 1 in Figure 4 is the patient's response to a scene describing stressful interaction in language class. Clinical fear 2 is the water phobia. It is clear that this subject does not show autonomic arousal to the language examination scene, but does show such arousal to the water scene. Verbal reports of anxiety while visualizing the two sets of materials were consistent with the physiological analyses. The water scene elicited reports of greater distress.

During the course of one of the later assessment interviews, patient B.W. spontaneously reported a reduction in his academic fears. As is sometimes the case in situation-based anxieties, his decision to seek therapy was part of a more general change in his manner of coping with the problem. He had already begun more intense and systematic study. This change in work habits resulted in improved performance and a concomitant reduction in anxiety felt in the classroom. Thus, the imagery assessment appeared to be consonant with a change in his reported anxiety, or at least in his academic performance, and was useful to both the intake worker and the patient in reaching the decision not to proceed with therapy after an initial few counseling sessions.

Patient M.O. sought treatment for a similar problem to that of B.W., anxiety over academic performance. He had been in private therapy for several months without great success, when he was referred for psychophysiological assessment. His visceral responses to imagery material are presented in Figure 5. This patient also failed to show autonomic arousal to a classroom stress scene (clinical fear), with heart rate and skin conductance changes actually falling below the level for the innocuous, neutral scene. However, unlike B.W., he did report that the classroom scenes were very anxiety arousing and distressing. Thus, in this case there was a specific fractionation of visceral response and verbal report. The relationship between dependent variables is similar to that of low concordance subjects in the analogue study previously described (Lang, Melamed & Hart, 1974). Furthermore, like those subjects, this patient also failed to profit from desensitization and similar therapeutic maneuvers.

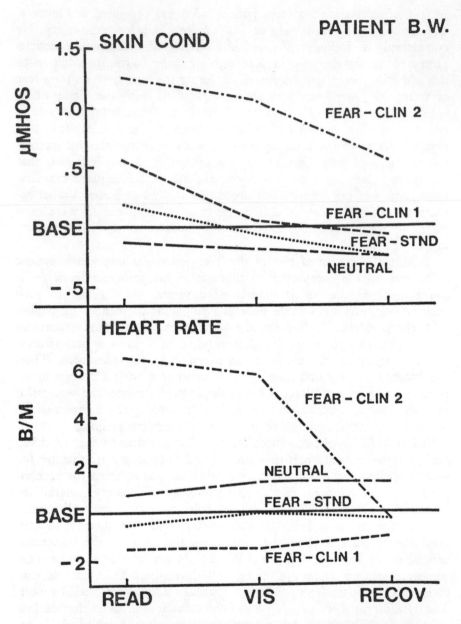

FIGURE 4. Fear imagery responses obtained from a single clinic patient.

He ultimately had to withdraw from school because of his deteriorating condition and continued inability to cope with his academic problems. It is interesting to note that this patient was described as schizoid by his therapist, had previously been hospitalized briefly because of a "breakdown," and that his MMPI profile was elevated on the psychotic scales.

We are just beginning to explore this methodology, and still know little about the factors which produce response concordance or discordance in the imagery situation. However, our pilot studies suggest some general working concepts.

We presume that when an image is reported to be both vivid and fear arousing, yet is unaccompanied by visceral activation, this disjunction occurs for one of the following reasons: 1) The image profile conforms to the subject's response pattern to an objective stimulus of the same class. That is to say, it represents a real pattern discordance. We have suggested elsewhere that such a profile may indicate that overt avoidance responses in the natural environment are also less intense (Lang, 1971; see also Hodgson & Rachman, 1974). Often the subject has learned to report that a stimulus is fear evoking, but the verbal learning was isolated from behavioral avoidance or it is descriptive of an earlier response pattern which has since disappeared. In this instance the therapeutic task is usually not difficult. 2) The image profile is not consonant with the subject's typical response to an objective stimulus in the natural environment. This means that the subject has failed to process the visceral response propositions of the "stimulus image." This could represent uncooperativeness, or a specific avoidance of the image content by the patient, or it could indicate the diagnostician's failure to prepare an adequate script. These possibilities must be explored by interview and testing of alternative materials. However, an absence of visceral activation in the context of fear imagery instructions may also suggest a deficit in the patient's cognitive control of arousal. The use of language to evoke affect is basic to most therapeutic situations. In desensitization, flooding, sensitization, and interview treatments, the content of anxiety is manipulated through language symbols. If visceral events are part of the patient's distress, then language must prompt their activation if affect is to be processed in the treatment. The imagery assessment paradigm permits us to determine how readily this occurs in a given patient. Our previous experiment (Lang, Melamed & Hart, 1974) suggested that a deficit in such language control heralded a poor outcome for desensitization. We speculate that a similar poor result would be anticipated for other imagery or interview therapies. Patients of this type may respond

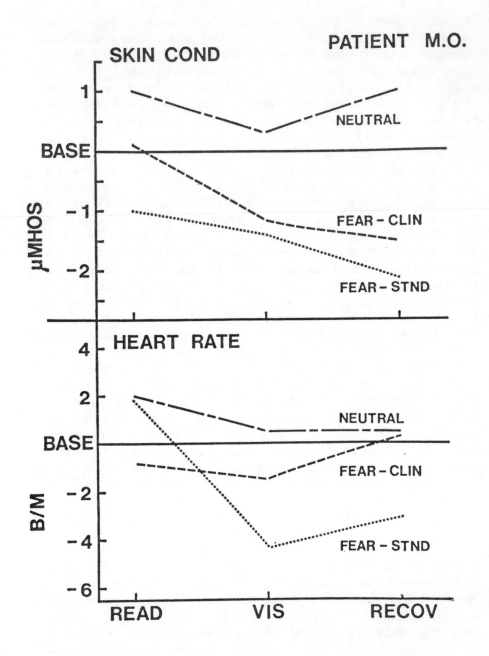

FIGURE 5. Fear imagery responses obtained from a single clinic patient.

best to overt modeling and coaching, which require that the patient work directly with the objective situation.

It is too early for even a preliminary classification system of imagery profiles. However, we are interested both in the relationship of the imagery response to prognosis and its possible covariation with some of the traditional diagnostic categories. Pilot work has been encouraging, and we plan to pursue it vigorously. It suggests a promising path through which psychophysiological analysis may make a significant contribution to behavioral assessment.

7

SEXUAL FUNCTIONING: SOME DATA AND SPECULATIONS ON PSYCHOPHYSIOLOGICAL ASSESSMENT

JAMES H. GEER

The treatment of sexual dysfunctions has been an area in which behavioral approaches have made significant clinical impact. While not all of the apparently successful techniques (e.g., Masters & Johnson, 1970) draw upon behavior modification for their concepts, those that appear to be most successful are characterized by their focusing attention upon the dysfunctional pattern *per se*. As has been true of behavioral asssessment of other clinical phenomena, assessment of sexual dysfunctions has lagged behind modification procedures. In this chapter, there will be a brief review of assessment techniques of sexual dysfunctions that have employed psychophysiological measurement of genital responses; then, some suggestions concerning the directions that continued research in this field might fruitfully follow will be presented.

ASSESSMENT OF SEXUAL DYSFUNCTIONS

It is not the intention of this presentation to imply that assessment of sexual dysfunction is only or even best accomplished by measuring genital responses. However, there are several clear advantages to the use of genital measures. One is the objective nature of the physiological data. While problems of interpretation may occur, the data are objective and

I wish to acknowledge the intellectual stimulation of my colleagues Gerald C. Davison and John H. Gagnon. Our collaborative efforts have generated some of the data and views expressed in this paper. Naturally, responsibility for omissions and errors rests with the author.

scorers do not disagree on such variables as the amplitude or duration of a defined response. A second advantage lies in the importance of the response being measured. As is perhaps less true of many other psychophysiological responses, the genital response often is the foundation of the behavior in question. This is clearest in the male where it can be readily seen that an erect penis is necessary for certain behaviors.

In the present chapter assessment of sexual responding will be limited to research that involves measurement of genital responding. (For a review of some of the technical details of genital measures see Geer, 1975). This limitation reflects the interests of the author and serves the cause of brevity.

A brief issue is: Why limit oneself or focus primarily upon genital psychophysiological variables in sexual arousal? The simple answer is that at the present time nongenital psychophysiological responses do not appear to be as useful as genital responses in assessing sexual interests or behavior (see Zuckerman, 1971, for a review). An exception, as yet unreplicated or followed up, is a study by Kercher and Walker (1973) in which they note that rapists differ from controls on GSRs to sexual stimuli, but not on penile volume responses (PVRs). Other studies have shown that sexual arousal results in nongenital psychophysiological responses; however, the results are not very clear. Measures like GSR and heart rate respond to both nonsexual and sexual stimuli. In their study relating genital and nongenital responses and noting that PVRs are generally not related to nongenital responses, Bancroft and Mathews (1971) suggested that either 1) autonomic arousal and PVRs are independent, or 2) PVRs are an instance of response specificity. By response specificity they mean that effective sexual stimuli reliably evoke genital responses. This compares with responses such as GSRs that occur to a very broad range of stimuli. It appears that in the awake adult male large changes in penile blood volume occur only when the individual is sexually stimulated. Whether vaginal blood volume responses (VBVRs) follow a similar pattern has not yet been determined. It does appear, however, that VBVRs show response specificity similar to PVRs.

Since it has been suggested that genital responses may provide useful assessment data, let us examine the literature that spawns such a view. Most of the work has been with males, since it is only recently that a simple and effective technique for measuring VBVRs (Geer, Morokoff & Greenwood, 1974; Sintchak & Geer, 1975) has become available. We begin by reviewing studies that use PVRs to discriminate among individuals with atypical sexual preferences or sexual dysfunctions. This field of study was first brought to the attention of researchers and clinicians in English-speaking countries by Kurt Freund in his 1963 paper in *Behaviour Research and Therapy*. In that report Freund measured changes in penile volume of subjects with hetero- or homosexual interests. The subjects varied in their sexual preferences for individuals of differing ages. He exposed subjects to sexually arousing photos of either males or females of differing ages. He reported that, in general, he was able to discriminate fairly accurately among his subjects, even detecting those who were deliberately faking. Thus, perhaps not very surprisingly, the field began with the demonstration that males with heterosexual interests show greater increases in penis size in response to erotic photos of females than in response to photos of males, while the reverse was true for males with homosexual preferences. That report was following by a number of others that replicated the finding, often with additional results (Freund, 1967a, 1967b; Freund, Langevin, Laws & Serber, 1974; Freund, Langevin, Cibiri & Zajac, 1973; Mavissakalian, Blanchard, Abel & Barlow, 1975; McConaghy, 1967; Langevin, Stanford & Block, 1975).

A logical extrapolation of the finding concerning homosexual males was to examine individuals with other atypical sexual preferences to see if similar results were obtained. Freund (1963, 1967a) suggested that he could discriminate among both homosexuals and heterosexuals with preferences for children, adolescents, and adults. It should be noted, however, that the number misclassified increased with more detailed discrimination. In a continuing examination of age preferences in "normals" and "offenders," Freund (1967b) found a complicated but interesting relationship between age preference and homosexuality. He reported that sex "offenders" differed from "normals" in the reaction to the *nonpreferred* sex. For normals there were no PVRs to nonpreferred stimuli. In offenders, PVRs occurred to the societal pattern of adult, adolescent, and child in that order of decreased responding. In addition, Freund reported an increase in PVRs to the nonpreferred age-mate of the preferred interest. That is, for the child offender with homosexual preference, there was, first, responding to preferred stimuli, followed by responding to female children, followed by arousal to other nonpreferred stimuli in the societal pattern of adult, with a lesser response to adolescents.

In a recent paper Freund (1975) reported that this finding needs qualification. He now suggests that while bisexuality exists in some homosexuals, as measured by PVRs and verbal report, it is relatively limited to pedophiliac homosexuals. Further, he suggests that in the bisexual pedophiliac homosexual, sexual interest is focused on the genitals more than on general body shape. Quinsey, Steinman, Bergersen and Holmes (1975) reported that PVRs discriminated sex offenders from nonsex offenders and normals. Further, they noted that ranking of preferences, obviously contaminated by need or wish to conceal, did not discriminate among the subject groups. Also, they noted that when individual histories were taken into account, discrimination was improved. Unfortunately, a detailed discussion of that finding is not available.

Other individuals with atypical sexual preferences who have shown increased PVRs to their preferred stimuli are transsexuals (Barlow, Reynolds & Agras, 1973; Barr, 1973), voyeurs, exhibitionists, and a masochist (Abel, Levis & Clancy, 1970). In the Barr study, transsexuals yielded more genital responding toward male stimuli than did homosexuals. In that study, the homosexuals had all presented themselves for treatment and thus, as with many of the studies, probably represent a biased sample of the homosexual population. Finally, as noted earlier, Kercher and Walker (1973) found that PVRs did not discriminate rapists from controls, but that GSRs did so successfully. It should be noted, however, that rapists may or may not belong in a grouping of atypical sexual preferences since there are different kinds of rapists. The act of rape, for many, may not reflect a habitual pattern of sexual preference.

It seems fair to say that PVRs do an acceptable job of discriminating among individuals with different sexual object preferences. It also is clear that, as the assessment becomes increasingly precise, the discrimination becomes more difficult and more incorrect judgments are made. Unfortunately, much of the available research has been limited to individuals who may not be representative of their group as a whole. This is particularly the case for the homosexuals who are candidates for treatment and for convicted sex offenders. It is unfortunate that up to this time there have been no reports of psychophysiological assessment of heterosexual dysfunctions among males. The only minor exception, of which this author is aware, is a report by Britt, Kemmerer and Robinson (1971), in which they noted that some impotent males show abnormal penile blood flow patterns (detected by plethysmography) suggesting a potential organic factor in some cases. We did not find any reported follow-ups to that study.

As we all know, assessment should mean more than sorting into categories. In the case of sexual dysfunctions, there have been a number of reports of using PVRs to provide information for therapeutic decisions. For example, Herman and Presitt (1974) report successfully using biofeedback of PVRs to modify impotence. Quinn, Harbisen and McAllister (1970) used reinforcement of PVRs to female stimuli in treating a homosexual. They reported an increase in penile responding to target stimuli in that case study. However, Barlow, Agras, Abel, Blanchard and Young (1975) found no positive effect of biofeedback upon subsequent clinical behavior. Also, Abel, Levis and Clancy (1970) noted that shocking, contingent upon PVRs, while diminishing the response during treatment, did not maintain the response suppression at follow-up, and Callahan and Leitenberg (1973) reflect concern over the PVR as a treatment target. That type of finding has led Bancroft (1971, 1974) to urge caution in assuming that PVRs and/or their modification necessarily reflect sexual behavior in its more natural setting. It has not been established that penile responses provide, either alone or in combination with other measures, a sufficiently adequate assessment of progress in therapy upon which to base treatment decisions. It is, of course, possible that in the negative findings the treatment procedure and not the assessment was at fault.

A larger number of reports is available in which PVRs were used to assess treatment outcome and progress during treatment (Abel, Levis & Clancy, 1970; Bancroft, 1974; Barlow, Reynolds & Agras, 1973; Herman, Barlow & Agras, 1974; Beumont, Bancroft, Beardwood & Russell, 1972; McConaghy, 1970; McConaghy & Barr, 1973; McCrady, 1973; Tennent, Bancroft & Cass, 1974). In the typical study PVRs are measured while the client is exposed to "relevant" stimuli. It is assumed that the genital responses to the presented stimuli (photos, movies, or audiotapes) reflect sexual interest or preference and thus also index any change in interest or preference that may occur.

The reports, that range from case studies to experimental designs to evaluative therapy procedures, appear to encourage the use of PVRs to assess modification techniques. The data indicate that PVRs have, in general, done an adequate job of tracing therapeutic process. However, before one assumes that genital measures provide the only necessary dependent variable needed to assess progress in therapy, the cautions voiced by Bancroft (1971, 1974) should be observed. For example, he noted that PVRs do not necessarily reflect behavior, but perhaps more directly assess preferences. Certainly, our sex lives reflect reality more nearly than preferences—that may explain the popularity of *Playboy* and *Playgirl* centerfolds that may represent idealized preferences, but seldom represent reality. Further, Bancroft notes the degree to which cognitive mediation plays a role in PVRs. It has been clearly shown (Bancroft, 1971, 1974) that PVRs can readily be elicited by fantasy alone. A brief bit of introspection will add personal verification to that observation. In passing, I might note that in our laboratory (Heiman, 1974, in press) it has been demonstrated that fantasy elicits VBVRs in women. We must, therefore, be cautious when extrapolating from genital responses in the therapy setting to sexual responding in the real world, as we may only be measuring fantasy elicited responses. Barlow (1973) has provided a complete review of papers on increasing heterosexual responding and covers the use of PVRs in assessing therapeutic progress to which this author refers interested parties.

The studies reported thus far have used males, since, as noted, only recently have there been developed simple and reliable measures of genital responding in women. The use of photoplethysmography is a simple yet reliable technique for determination of VBVRs. The procedure permits detection of both vaginal pressure pulse and the pooling of blood in the vaginal walls. These measures have demonstrated considerable validity in assessing sexual arousal in women in a manner that appears analogous to PVRs in males. While the use of VBVRs in assessment does not have an extensive literature, there has been a beginning. Thus far, the work has been limited, to the best of my knowledge, to a preliminary report by Heiman (in press) in which she reported that in pilot work it appeared that VBVRs to erotic films and fantasy in anorgasmic women were smaller than those found in orgasmic controls. It is hoped that the availability of methodology to record VBVRs will result in increased research on female sexuality, including assessment issues. I might note in passing that recent work in our laboratory (Geer & Quartararo, in press) suggests that VBVRs provide, in some women, an unambiguous indication of orgasm. That finding, along with the finding that high levels of arousal are discriminable using VBVRs, greatly broadens the useful areas of study of female sexuality.

DIRECTIONS OF NEW RESEARCH

Let us now turn our attention to considerations of the use of genital responses in more precise assessment than has been the case heretofore. Up to the present, we have noted that assessment has been limited to rather extreme differences in sexual preferences. Some investigators (e.g., Abel, Levis & Clancy, 1970; Bancroft, 1971, 1974; Sanford, 1974) have reported that thematic material may be more useful than presentations of the usual photo or series of photos. For example, in the Abel et al. study, individually tailored tape recordings were selected as effective stimuli for therapeutic intervention on the basis of eliciting PVRs. In that study care was taken to develop the content of the tape so as to be maximally effective in yielding genital responding. David Barlow in Chapter 11 independently suggests such a possibility. Bancroft (1974) suggests that perhaps one could have individuals vary fantasy under directions, and via that procedure examine idiosyncratic responses. Obviously, the control of fantasy or cognition is as yet far from understood and the precise manipulation of cognitions represents a formidable operation. As a manageable alternative we are suggesting that it is both possible and desirable to present subjects with films or tape recordings whose content varies systematically and is designed to sample sexual interests and preferences. These stimuli could be standardized on appropriate control populations and an individual's responses could be compared, for assessment purposes, to both the norms and other components of his or her own responding.

Why deal with norms when considering sexual behavior? There are many ethical and conceptual pitfalls in the use of sexual norms. For example, many question whether sexual norms for women may be harmful to the development of women's potential and rights. Others express concern over whether norms concerning atypical behaviors such as homosexuality might be seen as reasons for condemnation of the behavior. The reason why a normative approach is considered here as a good initial step is a theoretical bias of the author. That bias reflects an interest in the notion of Gagnon and Simon (1973) relating social scripting to sexual behavior. Their suggestions may be briefly, and unfortunately inadequately, summarized as suggesting that much of sexual behavior is guided by internalized norms. These norms or scripts are developed by contacts with the culture and are used by individuals to guide behavior. From that position it is necessary to identify norms for both theoretical and practical reasons. For example, some sexual dysfunctions may have their roots in discrepancies between perceived societal values or norms and an individual's preference. A woman may experience anxiety over her sexual activity if it varies from what she perceives as "normal."

We have begun an approach to developing standardized or normative stimuli in our laboratory. In collaboration with Gerald Davison and John Gagnon we have begun a series of investigations into some of the factors that affect sexual behavior. One of those studies tests an aspect of Gagnon's social scripting theory of sexuality. That model, as noted above, suggests that there are internalized scripts or norms of culturally proscribed model patterns for sexual behaviors. The fact that Bentler (1968a, 1968b) has developed Guttman scales of sexual behavior is consistent with the scripting position. We have been working on a similar project that has as one of its products an erotic tape that contains a set of sexual acts that make up the "most likely" sequence of events in a heterosexual interaction. It is planned to test whether this is, as social scripting theory predicts, the most arousing sequence when compared to other sequences. Should that prediction hold, we would then have a standarized tape against which comparison could be made. Such comparisons, for individuals, would allow the individual to be seen in relation to the cultural norm. Deviation from norms may, for varying reasons discussed above, be of considerable value.

Clearly, developing a standardized tape would not be the end of the story. There would be a need to develop a whole series of tapes that would assess different aspects of sexual preferences and interests. Tapes on atypical patterns would be among the more obvious, along with tapes dealing with supposedly important components of heterosexual dysfunctions such as guilt, anxiety, shame, and particular acts that are of concern. This information would be of value in determining therapeutic strategies and in identifying problems not readily identifiable via other procedures. How valuable these procedures will be with clinical populations remains an empirical question. The point to be made is not that norms are inviolate or necessarily represent ideal states, but rather that in sexual behavior societal values and norms powerfully affect behavior. An early step in assessment may, therefore, require comparison of an individual's behavior to norms and a careful evaluation of what the implications are of any discrepancy. We are currently exploring some of these possibilities and would hope to have some relevant information within the near future. As a practical note, thus far we have described audiotapes. They have the advantage of being readily constructed and modified, and they produce relatively high levels of sexual arousal. It is clear, however, from a number of reports (e.g., Bancroft, 1974; Heiman, in press; McConaghy, 1974) that motion pictures, while technically more difficult to produce, would be even more arousing. Assuming that assessment would be aided by increasing the range of arousal, films would be preferable to audiotapes. The major point, however, is that by careful development of standardized stimuli it would be possible to assess more precisely the preferences, interests, and, to perhaps a somewhat lesser extent, sexual behavior of individuals.

We have collected some data that support our contention that such an enterprise is feasible, and later we wish to draw attention to some of the problems that lie before us in the successful completion of such a task. We have completed and analyzed two experiments that were designed to explore certain questions concerning the role of cognitive factors in sexual arousal. The exact nature of these studies is not important for present considerations; however, both studies consisted of males and females listening to tape recordings of erotic material. The tapes they heard described sexual activities and, since they were in story form, varied in their erotic content throughout. If our suggestion that thematic material provides a method for assessing individual's interests and preferences is valid, we would expect for each sex high correlations for genital responses between and among conditions. To test this prediction the following procedure was used. Every 30 seconds throughout the tape presentation a measure of genital response was obtained for each subject. For males the measure was the increase in penile diameter, expressed in mm of pen deflection on a polygraph, from the level found during a pre-tape resting or basal level. For females the measure was the change from basal or resting level in vaginal pressure pulse.

Our findings from the two studies supported the prediction of high correlations in group responses. In the first study, men and women listened to an identical, mildly erotic tape under two setting conditions. We measured the PVRs and VBVRs every 30 seconds throughout the eight-minute tape. We found that the mean PVRs correlated .933 for the two conditions and VBVRs .803 for the two conditions; both correlations are highly significant. Then we correlated males with females, resulting in four correlations, since there were two conditions for each sex. The correlations ranged from .489 to .749; again all correlations were statistically significant. It does appear, as one would expect, that the within sex correlations were higher than the between sex correlations. However, the significant correlations between the sexes revealed that men and women (college students) were "turning off and on" to a similar content. This was true even though the absolute level of erotic content was relatively low.

In a second study we computed the same correlations on a different sample of subjects, listening to a different, more powerfully erotic tape, and under three different experimental conditions. In a sense, this study provides the opportunity to see if the point by point relationships replicate. We found that the correlations among male's average PVR for the three conditions, using 15 30-second samples, were .94, .92 and .97. For females the same correlations for VBVRs were .85, .89, and .87. The correlation between the sexes, collapsed across the three conditions was .92. All of these correlations, as in the first study, were statistically significant. Again we find that groups show increases and decreases in genital responses at the same points in a tape recording. The correlations were very high in this second study, perhaps as a result of increased erotic value. Thus we find further support for our contention that it is possible to relate content in a thematic presentation to indices of genital responses. We now have evidence that one can plot normative responses against the content of the erotic tape.

This proposal sounds too easy. On a conceptual level the suggestion is relatively simple. All that needs to be done is to develop carefully selected thematic contact and present it to standardization groups so that we can develop profiles of "typical" genital responding. Unfortunately, there are numerous problems facing such a task. Some of these problems are such mundane, yet important, concerns as: the great amount of energy and time that would be required to gather appropriate subjects; the issue of thoughtful and careful selection of stimulus material; and the considerable time and effort that would be required to do an effective job of measuring and analyzing the physiological data. Setting these more practical issues aside for a moment, there are several other concerns that make the task more complex than is at first obvious.

The first issue relates to the use of PVRs and VBVRs to assess sexual arousal and their relationship to subjective judgments of arousal. That is, how confident can we be that genital responses reflect the subjective feelings of the individual, acknowledged, even by those with an operant bias, to be an important component of sexual arousal (Callahan & Leitenberg, 1973). There are several points to be made on the issue of objective vs. subjective measures. First of all, the correlations between genital responses and subjective report are typically higher than is found between most psychophysiological measures and subjective judgments. Bancroft (1974) reported correlations between .67 and .70; Mavissakalian, Blanchard, Abel and Barlow (1975) reported .55 and .74; and Heiman (in press) reported correlations between .60 and .54 for "normal" women and similar, though nonsignificant, correlations for a small sample of anorgasmic women. While not all investigators have found such high correlations (e.g., Quinsey, Steinman, Bergersen & Holmes, 1975), it is likely that the correlation between subjective judgments of sexual arousal and genital responses is substantial and is greater than would be found in most psychophysiological studies.

In our laboratory we are investigating one approach to a more exact definition of the relationship between genital responding and subjective judgments of sexual arousal. In that work, only partially completed, we have drawn upon the concepts and methodologies of psychophysical scaling. In that work subjects were first given the task of setting a tone as loud as a line, projected on a screen, was long. Then lines of differing but known lengths were projected and loudness was set for each one. By this procedure each subject's response bias in judgments was determined. After the bias determining procedure, the subject viewed 10 still photos that varied dramatically in erotic content. Subjects set tone loudness, after 10 seconds of viewing a photo, to match the degree of sexual arousal they felt to the photo. We found the correlation between tone volume and PVR to be .83. When we then adjusted for response bias, the correlation increased to .89. For a more detailed description of that methodology and conceptual issues, see Cross, Tursky and Lodge (1975). This work is continuing and will be applied to a clinical population to determine what differences in the nature of the relationships may occur in a sexually dysfunctional (premature ejaculation) population, as compared to appropriate controls. We also are examining the relationship in females.

Why are the genital response-subjective report correlations so high when other subjective-psychophysiological relationships are relatively low? There are at least two factors that contribute to the high correlations. One, as noted earlier, is the fact that the genital response is directly involved in sexual behavior. The same is not as obviously the case for variables such as GSR and heart rate where the relationship to the specific behavioral acts is less direct. Erections and vaginal lubrication are either necessary for or facilitative of many important sexual acts. This fact is naturally reflected in the correlations. The second factor, particularly relevant to males, is that subjects may be defining sexual arousal on the basis of genital responding. Subjects may use their genitals as a partial indicator of arousal. That notion suggests that some subjects may monitor genital responses and make their evaluation of arousal in part on the degree of genital response present. If that is the case, then high correlations would be expected.

While the relationship between genital responses and subjective judgments of arousal is relatively high, we as yet do not have sufficient information to be able to specify completely the nature of the relationship nor what is producing it. It is likely that the relationship varies along a number of as yet unspecified dimensions, such as the level of arousal (Bancroft, 1971); nature of stimuli; and attributes of the individual, such as dysfunctional state, age and sex. We are encouraged, however, that by utilizing scaling methodologies and by careful analysis of the issues, we shall eventually make considerable progress on these problems. Further, in the process of attacking and solving these problems a great deal will be gained in not only assessment, but also in basic understanding of sexual behavior. For example, one can approach the issue of whether sexual arousal is a continuous variable (prothetic continua) or whether it is made up of discrete processes (metathetic continua). Such a determination has considerable implication for theoretical models of sexual arousal.

A second problem that faces the development of standardized assessment procedures using thematic material and genital responding is the difficulty that one has in controlling the cognitive activity that the individuals may engage in during assessment. We all recognize that fantasy can yield both subjective and physiological indices of sexual arousal (e.g., Heiman, 1974). Bancroft (1971, 1974) also noted the problems generated by this issue in his reviews of assessment using genital responses, and Freund (1971) noted how thoughts and images could present problems. Laws and Rubin (1969), Henson and Rubin (1971), and Rosen (1973) all have noted effects of instructions. They all found that instructions to reduce penile tumescence result in decreased penis size. These data reflect additional cognitive complications in measurement of PVRs. If one can be instructed to inhibit, could not similar effects be found through self-generated instructions?

The degree to which cognitive factors may provide difficulty can be illustrated by reference to work in our laboratory (Geer & Fuhr, 1976). In that paper we reported an experiment in which it was demonstrated that by giving subjects a distracting cognitive task we could essentially obliterate sexual responding to an erotic tape even though the tape was loudly and clearly presented to the subject. The same erotic tape produced high levels of sexual responding when distracting cognitive operations were reduced or eliminated. The point is that such phenomena as attention, distraction, or interfering cognitions could so confound assessment attempts as to make the effort useless. This means that those who undertake the project that has been briefly outlined must develop methods either to insure that unwanted cognitions are reduced or to develop methods to insure that desired cognitions occur. Both Bancroft (1971) and this author (Geer, 1974) have suggested that in humans the lack of appropriate cognitive activity will either block or greatly reduce sexual activity. Fortunately, much of behavior theory has developed sufficiently to recognize the rule of cognitive activity though also recognizing the many complications that such a position entails. We strongly recommend that behavioral assessors, clinicians, and researchers familiarize themselves with the literature of experimental cognitive psychology.

Thus far, this chapter has emphasized the development of assessment procedures for current functioning and has not spoken of the use of genital responses as a guide to therapy or in assessing therapeutic outcome. The determination of outcome is an extrapolation of what has been discussed to include measurement over time. Regarding assessment within therapy in order to make strategy decisions, it would seem again that we are primarily considering differences in the timing of when measures are obtained. This latter concern, of basing therapeutic decisions on "in therapy" assessment, then becomes, to a large extent, the use of genital responses as the treatment target. Biofeedback is an extrapolation of response contingent procedures and would be included in "in therapy" assessment. At this point in time we know much too little about biofeedback to have confidence in its therapeutic power. We would urge research on the relevant questions and suggest caution to clinicians before they adopt and use such procedures. It is very tempting to employ biofeedback to put men and women "in touch with" or "in control of" their bodies, but as yet we do not have evidence that such procedures either work or are therapeutically useful in sexual dysfunctions—let alone in other disorders. The previous discussion should not be interpreted as suggesting that behavioral or cognitive targets are less important than physiological. The suggestion is that in some cases the target of interest may well be genital responding or a combination that involves physiological assessment.

SUMMARY

We have seen how genital responses, almost exclusively in males, have been used to discriminate among individuals with differing sexual preference. We also have seen how such responses have been used to track the course and outcome of therapy and, to a much more limited degree, been employed as the target of therapeutic intervention. Almost all of the work reported thus far has been restricted to the study of individuals with atypical sexual interest or preferences. We have proposed that assessment of sexual functioning could be readily expanded to include the much more common heterosexual dysfunctions and to include the study of women's sexual functioning. We suggested the use of standardized thematic material as a potentially useful direction that assessment of sexual functioning could follow, and we have pointed out some of the major pitfalls of such an approach. It is our feeling that considerable progress is just around the corner in assessment of sexual functioning, understanding of cognitive factors in sexuality, and in knowledge of female sexuality. We believe that the use of genital responses in research will play a major role in advancing our understanding of assessment of, modification of, and conceptualizations of sexual behavior. We agree with Bancroft (1974) when he states, "The problem of developing measures which are both relevant to the individual patient's goals and suitable for the comparison of treatment between individuals and groups is one of the main areas requiring research in the behavior modification field" (p. 205). It is towards solving those problems that this paper is directed.

Part IV

DIRECT METHODS IN NATURAL ENVIRONMENTS

Editors' Comments

The fourth section of this book deals with the method of assessment most valued by behavioral assessors: directly measuring events of interest *in vivo*. Here one need not rely on the verbal report of the client or others, one need not infer from tests how the client behaves in home and work situations and one need not construct office analogues to real life situations, the representativeness of which is unknown. As Hawkins, Peterson, Schweid and Bijou (1966) point out, the clinician can more accurately define the problem and potential solutions by directly observing the client's responses and the natural stimulus conditions under which they occur. If initial assessment and intervention are followed by continuous (e.g., daily) assessment of targeted behavioral and environmental events, one has a maximal opportunity for feedback as to the effectiveness of one's interventions. Such direct assessment in natural environments has been highly characteristic of the work of assessors employing principles of operant behavior exclusively (see any issue of the *Journal of Applied Behavior Analysis*), though it has been much less characteristic of those employing respondent principles in their conception of problems (e.g., in desensitization and flooding).

The validity or generalizability (Cronbach, Gleser, Nanda & Rajaratnam, 1972) issues involved in direct, *in vivo* assessment are quite different from those involved in traditional approaches to assessment. Not only is there no issue as to whether the measures obtained are true measures of a hypothetical personality construct, as typifies traditional assessment (see

211

Chapter 1, by Goldfried), there is even no question whether the measures are related to the real-life events the person is experiencing. One is tempted to think that direct assessment in natural environments involves no validity assumptions (Ebel, 1961); such measurements would appear to be the ultimate criterion by which the validity or generalizability of other measurements is assessed, and certainly they are the appropriate criterion for many generalizability questions.

But even direct, *in vivo* assessment is likely to require certain generalizability assumptions. For example, in deciding to target certain behaviors for change, the clinician may assume that these behaviors were the primary ones that evoked the referral complaint. Even obtaining confirmation of those targets (a verbal report measure) from the client, or significant others, does not fully validate the targeting, as is attested by the observation that clients sometimes report alleviation of the problem when direct observation data show little or no change in the target behaviors (e.g., Lobitz & Johnson, 1975), and by the fact that clients sometimes complain, after target behaviors are changed, that the "real" problem is still present but was unclear to them before.

Another generalizability issue involved in direct assessment in natural environments is whether the data obtained are representative of the client's performance in other, similar situations. Further, when improvement is obtained in the measured situations, there is a question of whether it generalizes to other situations of interest.

Perhaps the most difficult generalizability issue has to do with the functional significance of targeted behavior (Hawkins, 1975). In selecting any behavior for change, and in setting criteria of satisfactory performance, one is assuming that the learner will be better adjusted to the demands of his/her life with the changes in the targeted behavior. An appropriate definition of adjustment, from a behavioral viewpoint, might be that the reinforcement/punishment ratio has been optimized for the individual and for society.* By this definition, behavior changes intended to benefit the client should improve the reinforcement/punishment ratio for that client (and/or others) in his/her natural environment and thus should be maintained by that environment once the client's new behavior

---

* This definition, by including the reinforcers and punishers for society as well as the individual, allows one to include the weakening of certain very profitable criminal or other self-serving behaviors as improving adjustment. An alternative model would be to define two kinds of adjustment—personal adjustment and social adjustment—with the focus of the former being the individual's reinforcement/punishment ratio and the focus of the latter being the reinforcement/punishment ratio of others who are affected by the individual's behavior.

has had ample opportunity to make contact with the contingencies. Thus, if the behavior changes wrought by the clinician are not maintained by the client's natural environment, then the clinician's targeting was of insufficient validity, or the programming of behavior change was inadequate, or both. This was Ayllon and Azrin's (1968) point in stating their "relevance of behavior rule" for institutional token economies: If the behavior will not be maintained once the client leaves the institution, it is not an appropriate target within the institution.

The first chapter in this section, by Rosemery Nelson, presents direct observation procedures in which the client and the observer of the client's behavior are the same person. Direct observation and recording of one's own behavior, or self-monitoring as it is more frequently termed, have enjoyed a good deal of popularity among behavioral assessors seeking precise but inexpensive ways of getting data on clinically relevant behaviors at the time of their occurrence in their natural environment. As Nelson notes, this use of self-monitoring for assessment has been accompanied by an interest in its use as an intervention procedure as well. That is, the act of observing and recording one's own behavior (or stimuli surrounding it) produces changes in that behavior, and this is referred to as the reactivity of self-monitoring.

Nelson nicely reviews the literature dealing with self-monitoring as an assessment method and as a therapeutic one, and presents a table organizing her findings in terms of the effects of 13 classes of independent variables on self-monitoring used in each of these ways. The table should prove heuristically valuable to researchers in the area, as it readily highlights variables that have received extensive investigation and those that have received relatively little.

Explicit attempts to take advantage of the reactivity of self-monitoring for clinical purposes are described by Nelson, and more extensively by Mahoney in the chapter immediately following hers. This use of self-monitoring is in contrast to the use of other direct observation procedures described in this section, which endeavor to minimize the reactive effects of the measurement process itself. Nelson points out that accuracy in self-monitoring does not appear to be consistently correlated with its reactive effects. However, accuracy is obviously important when self-monitoring is used as an assessment procedure. Problems in assessing accuracy are presented along with several suggestions for increasing it.

Widepread use of self-monitoring as an assessment procedure is relatively recent. As a result, little is known about the methodological adequacy of its various forms. After reading Nelson's excellent and comprehensive review of research with self-monitoring, the reader may still wonder about several important questions. For example, what are the differences between the self-monitoring procedures reported in Nelson's chapter and the self-reports described by Bellack and Hersen in Chapter 3? What types of generalizability (Cone, 1977) have been examined for self-monitoring other than between scorers and between human and mechanical data collection modes—that is, are self-monitored data generalizable over time, over settings, and over methods? How does self-monitored responding in one system, e.g., motoric, correspond with self-monitored responding in another, e.g., physiological? Is there differential accuracy and/or reactivity to self-monitoring among the three systems? Interestingly, few studies in Nelson's review dealt with physiological responding; yet, in Chapter 7, Geer reported relatively high correlations between physiological measures of sexual arousal and verbal ones. Perhaps it would be useful to add a third dimension to Nelson's 2 × 13 table, one representing the three response systems. Such a diagram might identify a lifetime's work for a whole generation of behavioral assessors.

The existence of gaps in a relatively new literature is not surprising and neither is the proliferating use of untested self-monitoring procedures in clinical settings, reported by Mahoney in his chapter. Mahoney, drawing on his own clinical experiences, describes practical applications of self-monitoring in changing a variety of client behaviors in a wide range of applied settings. He nicely differentiates the reactive and measurement uses of self-monitoring and concentrates his remarks on the latter. In answering questions regarding when to self-monitor, what to self-monitor, and how to self-monitor, Mahoney provides numerous valuable how-to-do-it tips for the practicing clinician, while simultaneously illustrating issues needing further research. For example, he tells us how to get recalcitrant clients to begin to self-monitor, when self-monitoring should not be used, and why self-monitoring is not coldly analytical and dehumanizing, but rather an essential component of a basically humanitarian effort. He discusses the merits of various modes of self-monitoring, including mechanical counters, diaries, and phone answering devices, and suggests criteria for determining when to use them.

Mahoney emphasizes flexibility in the use of self-monitoring procedures, noting that they should be adjusted to keep pace with client progress in the behavior change enterprise. Perhaps a serious problem with such flexibility should be pointed out: Such changes in instrumentation might make the measure useless in determining client improvement from the initiation of intervention to its end. Presumably the sophisticated clinician will include more consistent collateral measures, as well as the "flexible" self-monitoring ones, in order to be able to document change satisfactorily. How self-monitoring data converge with those from such collateral measures is an important question needing empirical investigation. As the reader goes through Mahoney's informal yet cogent treatment of self-monitoring in applied contexts s/he will doubtless be stimulated to look for answers to questions such as this.

The final chapter in this section of the book presents direct observation procedures in which the client's behavior is observed and recorded by others. Direct measurement of human behavior in natural environments is usually accomplished by human observers, because most significant behaviors cannot readily be recorded by electronic or mechanical instruments, and when instrumentation is possible it is usually very expensive. But the use of human observers adds new opportunity for various types of error. It is a measurement technology of its own, and the development of good, replicable technology for such measurement constitutes a set of methodological problems. The chapter by Wildman and Erickson deals with these methodological problems.

Wildman and Erickson present some historical perspective on the technology of human recording of human behavior. Then they describe several problems, most of which have been subjected to at least some research. The problems they discuss include those of observer training, calculation of interobserver agreement, observers' reactivity to having their agreement checked (or, their decline in performance when it is not being checked), the gradual drift in observer definitions that occurs under certain circumstances, the biasing of observer data by various factors, the choosing or devising of behavioral "codes" (definitions of a set of behaviors to be observed), the selection of an appropriate type of measurement method, agreement, and the effect on the subject of being observed.

Although any one of these topics alone could occupy at least one chapter in a book such as this, Wildman and Erickson have managed to give an excellent, comprehensive overview briefly. They conclude with a very valuable set of recommendations to applied researchers and practitioners.

An issue not discussed in this section of the book is the question, "How much measurement of what quality constitutes responsible, yet cost-efficient clinical or educational practice?" Any practicing clinician or educator knows that the number of target skills measured in a relatively reliable and valid manner never equals the number of skills one hopes to develop in the learner. The cost of obtaining high-quality data on some performances (especially physiological responses) outside a laboratory-clinic setting would be prohibitive. Even direct measurement of motor or verbal behavior can be too costly if the behavior is very infrequent, reactive to observation, or socially defined as too private for observation.

Yet, as a number of behavior analysts have indicated (e.g., Birnbrauer, Burchard, & Burchard, 1970; Hawkins, Axelrod, & Hall, 1976), measurement of our effects is essential. Risley (1970) even defined behavior modification in terms of such measurement. Certainly, if clinical and educational practice is to continue to improve, frequent and high quality measurement is required.

Perhaps the only general rule one can suggest is that clinicians or educators wishing to model responsible professional conduct will at all times be measuring at least some of their effects in relatively reliable and valid ways. As direct measurement technology improves and economical methods are developed, this modeling should set even more responsible norms for professionals.

In addition to these chapters by Nelson, Mahoney, and Wildman and Erickson, the reader interested in direct assessment in natural environments will wish to read the excellent chapters by Livingston, Jones, and White, in Part V of the book. These chapters also deal with direct assessment and raise some new and challenging issues and possibilities.

8

METHODOLOGICAL ISSUES IN ASSESSMENT VIA SELF-MONITORING

ROSEMERY O. NELSON

The technique of self-monitoring consists of a person's discriminating occurrences of some aspect of his or her own behavior and maintaining a record of those occurrences. Self-recording has both therapeutic and assessment utility. It is useful as a therapeutic strategy because the very act of recording aspects of one's own behavior sometimes causes that behavior to change.

As an assessment device, self-monitoring may serve two functions: 1) The first function occurs during the early stages of assessment when the therapist and client are jointly attempting to identify the target behaviors to be modified. The self-recorder may note not only occurrences of a selected behavior but also the situational circumstances surrounding each occurrence. An example (Hay & Hay, personal communication, August, 1975) was the case of a woman who felt that her drug abuse was an attempt to prevent and to alleviate headache pain. During the early stages of assessment, she was asked to keep a diary which noted not only the beginning and end of headache pain, and the frequency and amount of her drug usage, but also other daily events. Since her diary revealed that the headaches were related to household responsibilities and to visits with her in-laws, the target behaviors became her organizational skills and her relationship with her husband. 2) Once the target behaviors have been identified, self-monitoring may serve a second assessment function, that of providing data to serve as a dependent measure in either clinical cases or research projects in evaluating the efficacy of an intervention program.

The increasing popularity of self-monitoring for both assessment and therapeutic purposes is related to other contemporary trends in behavior therapy. First is the emphasis in behavior therapy on empirically verifiable results. While data are often obtained through recordings made by trained observers, the use of such observers is costly and often impractical. As a substitute for trained observers, subjects may collect data on themselves. A second trend is the increasing emphasis on self-control programs, in lieu of externally-arranged controls. Self-monitoring is often integral to self-control programs, either as a therapeutic strategy or as a data collection device. Third, there is a strong interest in the manipulation of covert events. Since, with current technology, the only means of determining the content of covert events is through self-report, self-monitoring may be used to record the occurrence of specific covert behaviors. While covert events are private by their very nature, other behaviors, such as sexual behaviors, are private by convention. Self-monitoring may also be used to record the frequencies of behaviors that would be impractical or infeasible for trained observers to observe.

Research in self-recording is concerned with two central issues: 1) the reactivity and 2) the accuracy of self-recording. *Reactivity* is the occurrence of behavior change initiated by the procedure of self-monitoring. When self-recording is being used as a therapeutic strategy, the goal would be to maximize its reactivity. The *accuracy* of self-monitoring refers to the congruence between self-recorded data and simultaneous data collected by alternate means, such as by another observer or by a mechanical device. When self-recording is being used as an assessment strategy, the goal is to maximize its accuracy. At the same time, the reactivity of self-monitoring must be minimized since behavior change would interfere with assessment of ongoing behavior patterns. The remainder of this chapter deals with the reactivity and accuracy of self-monitoring. Since the chapter stresses the use of self-recording as an assessment device, suggestions are made to minimize the reactivity and to maximize the accuracy of self-monitoring.

REACTIVITY OF SELF-MONITORING

Occurrence of Reactivity

Self-recording has been demonstrated to produce reactive behavior changes in a wide variety of target behaviors which include: time spent in a small dark room by a claustrophobic patient (Leitenberg, Agras, Thompson & Wright, 1968); reported hallucinations (Rutner & Bugle, 1969); the symptoms of Gilles de la Tourette's syndrome (Hutzell, Platzek

& Logue, 1974; Thomas, Abrams & Johnson, 1971); study activities (Johnson & White, 1971; Richards, 1975); teachers' classroom behaviors (Thomas, 1971; Nelson, Hay, Hay & Carstens, in press; Hendricks, Thoreson & Hubbard, 1973); mothers' attention to appropriate child behaviors (Herbert & Baer, 1972); lip and mouth biting (Ernst, 1973); alcoholic drinking (Sobell & Sobell, 1973); a variety of unwanted repetitive behaviors (Maletzky, 1974); swimming practice performance (McKenzie & Rushall, 1974); and time spent outside by agoraphobics (Emmelkamp, 1974; Emmelkamp & Ultee, 1974). While the quality of the above demonstrations varies from case studies to within-subject and between-subject experimental designs, the conclusion reached by these researchers is that at least under some conditions, self-recording causes the behavior being recorded to change.

However, several studies have reported that self-recording did not produce behavior changes (Jackson, 1972; Mahoney, 1971; Mahoney, Moura & Wade, 1973; McNamara, 1972). McFall (1977) has criticized what he labels the "box-score" approach in attempts to integrate these inconsistent findings, that is, simple tallies of the number of studies in which self-monitoring has or has not produced behavior change. A more fruitful strategy appears to be to identify the variables controlling the reactivity of self-monitoring (Table 1).

VARIABLES CONTROLLING REACTIVITY

Motivation

One variable which seems to determine whether self-recording produces behavior change is the motivation of the subject to alter the self-recorded behavior. This suggestion is based on several studies which all happened to use cigarette smoking as the target behavior. The subjects selected by McFall and Hammen (1971) were students who indicated they were motivated to stop smoking. Under these conditions, all four groups of subjects decreased their smoking, regardless of the specific self-recording procedure employed: self-recording of cigarettes smoked; self-recording of unresisted urges to smoke; self-recording of successfully resisted urges to smoke; and self-recording of a minimum of 20 successfully resisted urges to smoke. In contrast, the subjects used by McFall (1970) were students in a class who happened to be smokers and who were not necessarily motivated to reduce their smoking. Under these conditions, self-monitoring of the number of cigarettes smoked actually increased smoking rates, although self-recording of resisted urges did decrease smoking

TABLE 1

Studies Investigating Variables which Affect the Reactivity
and the Accuracy of Self-Monitoring

Variable	Reactivity	Accuracy
Motivation	Lipinski, Black, Nelson & Ciminero, 1975 McFall, 1970 McFall & Hammen, 1971	
Valence	Broden, Hall & Mitts, 1971 Cavior & Marabotto, 1976 Kazdin, 1974a Nelson, Lipinski & Black, 1976a Sieck & McFall, 1976	Nelson, Hay, Hay & Carstens, in press Nelson, Hay & Koslow-Green, 1976 Nelson, Lipinski & Black, 1976a
Experimenter Instructions	Hutzell, 1976 Nelson, Lipinski & Black, 1975 Nelson, Kapust & Dorsey, 1976	
Nature of Target Behavior	Gottman & McFall, 1972 Hayes & Cavior, in press Karoly & Doyle, 1975 McFall, 1970 Peterson, House & Alford, 1975 Romanczyk, 1974	Bailey & Peterson, 1975 Hayes & Cavior, in press Peterson, House & Alford, 1975
Goals, Reinforcement & Feedback	Kazdin, 1974a Kolb, Winter & Berlew, 1968 Lyman, Rickard & Elder, 1975 Lipinski, Black, Nelson & Ciminero, 1975 Nelson, Lipinski & Black, 1976a Richards, McReynolds, Holt & Sexton, 1975	Drabman, Spitalnik & O'Leary, 1973 Fixsen, Phillips & Wolf, 1972 Flowers, 1972 Layne, Rickard, Jones & Lyman, 1976 Lipinski, Black, Nelson & Ciminero, 1975 Lyman, Rickard & Elder, 1975 Nelson, Lipinski & Black, 1976a Peterson, House & Alford, 1975 Risley & Hart, 1968 Seymour & Stokes, 1976 Turkewitz, O'Leary & Ironsmith, 1975
Timing	Bellack, Rozensky & Schwartz, 1974 Nelson, Hay & Koslow-Green, 1976 Rozensky, 1974	

TABLE 1 (*Continued*)

Variable	Reactivity	Accuracy
Concurrent Responses	Cavior & Marabotto, 1976 Thomas, 1971	Cavior & Marabotto, 1976 Epstein, Miller & Webster, 1976 Epstein, Webster & Miller, 1975
Nature of Self-Recording Device	Nelson, Lipinski & Boykin, in press	Nelson, Lipinski & Boykin, in press
Number of Behaviors Concurrently Self-Monitored	Hayes & Cavior, in press	
Schedule of Self-Monitoring	Frederiksen, Epstein & Kosevsky, 1975 Mahoney, Moore, Wade & Moura, 1973	Fredericksen, Epstein & Kosevsky, 1975
Awareness of Accuracy Assessment		Bailey & Peterson, 1975 Lipinski, Black, Nelson & Ciminero, 1975 Lipinski & Nelson, 1974 Nelson, Lipinski & Black, 1975 Santogrossi, 1974
Training in Self-Monitoring	Nelson, Lipinski & Boykin, in press	Nelson, Lipinski & Boykin, in press Peterson, House & Alford, 1975
Social Psychology Manipulations		Bornstein, Hamilton, Carmody, Rychtarik & Veraldi, 1976 Bornstein, Hamilton, Miller, Quevillon & Spitzform, 1976

frequency. A specific comparison of the effects of self-recording number of cigarettes smoked for motivated smokers (subjects who signed up for an experiment specifically designated to reduce smoking) versus non-motivated smokers (subjects who signed up for an experiment generally labeled for smokers) was described by Lipinski, Black, Nelson and Ciminero (1975). Self-recording decreased smoking only for the motivated group.

Valence

While the subject's motivation may determine whether reactive changes occur through self-recording, the valence of the target behavior may determine the direction of the reactive changes. Positively evaluated behaviors tend to increase in frequency during self-recording, while negatively evaluated behaviors tend to decrease. Broden, Hall and Mitts (1971) found that self-recording increased the study behavior of an eighth grade girl and conversely decreased the inappropriate classroom verbalizations of her peer. Using adult retarded subjects, Nelson, Lipinski and Black (1976a) demonstrated that self-recording a positive behavior, conversation in the recreation lounge, increased its frequency, whereas self-recording an undesirable behavior, face-touching, decreased its frequency in three of five subjects.

In addition to these studies conducted in natural settings, Cavior and Marabotto (1976) performed a laboratory experiment in which subjects themselves selected a verbal behavior which they regarded positively or negatively. Self-recording increased the frequency of positive behaviors and decreased the frequency of negative behaviors. In another laboratory study, Kazdin (1974a) experimentally manipulated the valences assigned to self-reference statements in conjunction with a Taffel-type task. Consistent with other findings, self-recording increased self-reference statements if they had been assigned positive valences and conversely decreased the frequency of statements assigned negative valences. In a third laboratory study, Sieck and McFall (1976) attributed either a positive, negative or neutral valence to the eye blink response. Similar to the reports of other studies, self-monitoring of positively valenced blinking increased its frequency, whereas self-monitoring of negatively valenced blinking produced a marginally significant decrease in its frequency.

Experimenter Instructions

In the above experiments, valence was generally assigned to the target behavior by experimenter instructions. These instructions to induce valence were successful in producing differential behavior change during self-monitoring. Other experimenter instructions, however, have not been successful in producing this differential behavior change. Nelson, Lipinski and Black (1975) gave college students different expectancies about the direction of behavior change that self-monitoring would produce in their face-touching. Regardless of whether subjects were told that self-recording would decrease, increase, or not change their face-touching frequency, self-recording clearly decreased the face-touching frequency of all groups of subjects. Similarly, Hutzell (1976) found that all groups of subjects decreased their self-monitored eye-blinking, even though the groups were given differential expectancies that self-monitoring would increase or decrease their eye-blinking.

Orne (1970) and Kazdin (1974b) have suggested that another type of experimenter instructions, namely demand to produce differential behavior change, may contribute to the differential reactivity of self-monitoring. Nelson, Kapust and Dorsey (1976) after a baseline period, gave college students instructions to increase, decrease or not change their frequency of first-person personal pronouns. These instructions were effective in producing the requested behavior rates in the subjects who did not self-monitor. On the other hand, the frequency of the target pronouns decreased for all groups of subjects who self-monitored these pronouns, regardless of the differential instructions. Of all the experimental instructions examined thus far, only valence induction seems to produce differential behavior change during self-monitoring.

Nature of the Target Behavior

Another variable which may determine whether self-recording produces reactive changes is the nature of the target behavior being self-monitored. Hayes and Cavior (in press) compared the relative reactivity of self-recording three negatively valenced target behaviors. Verbalizations containing value judgments changed least via self-monitoring, verbal non-fluencies changed more and face-touching was most reactive. Peterson, House and Alford (1975) suggested that self-recording is more reactive when the target behavior is nonverbal rather than verbal. In their own study, self-monitoring produced greater changes in the frequency of face-touching than of the verbal expressions "you know" and "and all that." Regarding the use of self-recording to produce weight loss, Romanczyk (1974) found that self-monitoring produced greater weight loss if both daily weight and calorie intake were monitored than if only weight was self-recorded.

Other studies have also shown that reactivity may depend on the specific instructions given the self-recorders. McFall (1970) found that instructions to self-monitor resisted urges to smoke decreased smoking rate, whereas instructions to self-record number of cigarettes smoked increased smoking rates. However, Karoly and Doyle (1975) reported equal smoking reductions whether urges or completed cigarettes were self-recorded. Gottman and McFall (1972), using a cross-over design with classroom participation, demonstrated that self-recording instances of classroom participation increased its frequency, whereas self-recording of unfulfilled urges to participate decreased its frequency. In summary, the specific choice of the target behavior to be self-recorded may help determine the reactivity of the results.

Goals, Reinforcement and Feedback

Another set of variables which contributes to the differential reactivity of self-recording seems to be the setting of performance goals and the availability of reinforcement and feedback on the self-recorder's perform- ance. In Kazdin's study (1974a) using a Taffel-type task and self-refer- ence statements, subjects who were provided with a specific goal of the number of self-reference statements to make while self-recording made more such statements than a self-monitoring group who were not pro- vided with a specific goal. Kazdin (1974a) also specifically manipulated the amount of feedback accorded his self-recording subjects by permitting only some of them to view the counter on which they were recording their responses. The subjects permitted to view the counter made more self-reference statements than subjects for whom the counter displays were covered.

The feedback produced by self-recording seems to be an important component of its reactivity, as shown by Richards, McReynolds, Holt and Sexton (1975), who found that students who were relatively un- aware of the amount of time they spent studying (and hence in need of feedback) benefited more from self-recording of study time than stu- dents who were already aware of the extent of their study time. Social reinforcement contingent on self-set behavioral goals also seems to en- hance the reactivity of self-recording. In addition to having all of their subjects set behavioral goals for themselves, Kolb, Winter and Berlew (1968) had half of the subjects discuss their self-recorded progress at weekly meetings. More change was reported for the group receiving social reinforcement on their progress than for the group who met weekly but did not discuss their individual projects. Nelson et al. (1976a) gave edible reinforcers that adult retarded subjects believed were con- tingent on self-recorded changes in response frequency. Compared to the self-monitored baseline, reinforcement in addition to self-recording in- creased the frequencies of talking and touching environmental objects and decreased the frequency of face-touching for four of the five subjects. Lipinski et al. (1975) similarly found that monetary reinforcement con- tingent on decreases in self-monitored face-touching produced decre- ments in the face-touching of college students beyond baseline self-recording levels. Lyman, Rickard and Elder (1975) found improvements in boys' self-recorded tent cleaning when prompt access to breakfast was made contingent on increases in cleanliness. Thus, the reactivity resulting from self-recording seems to be enhanced by the setting of performance goals and by feedback and reinforcement contingent on self-recorded performance.

Timing

The reactivity of self-recording also seems to be affected by the timing of the self-recording response in relation to the occurrence of the target behavior. Kanfer (1970) suggested that self-monitoring prior to, rather than after, the occurrence of an undesirable behavior would produce greater reactivity because the self-recording response interrupts a behavior chain and provides an alternative to the target behavior. In Rozensky's case study (1974), the subject was first asked to self-record the time and place of smoking after smoking the cigarette. In the next phase, she was asked to self-record the smoking data prior to smoking the cigarette. Although the timing conditions were confounded with sequence effects, the results suggested that self-recording before smoking produced greater reactivity than self-recording after smoking.

These results were confirmed by Bellack, Rozensky and Schwartz (1974), who used a group design with the dependent measure of weight loss. The group who self-recorded food intake information prior to eating lost more weight than the group who self-recorded this information after eating. With young children, however, Nelson, Hay and Koslow-Green (1976) found that self-monitoring before or after classroom verbalizations did not differentially affect the reactivity of appropriate or inappropriate verbalizations.

Self-monitoring from videotape seems to affect the frequency of the target behavior in criterion situations, as shown by Thomas (1971) with teachers' praise statements and by Cavior and Marabotto (1976) with college students' conversations. Since self-monitoring is removed in time from the criterion situation, the effective ingredient in this situation may be the fact that self-monitoring is performed when no other incompatible or distracting behaviors are required of the subject.

Nature of the Self-Recording Device

The nature of the self-recording device may also affect reactivity. The device may serve as a discriminative stimulus controlling the frequency of the self-monitored response, as was suggested by Maletzky (1974), who noted that self-recorded undesirable behaviors increased in frequency when the wrist counters used for self-recording were removed. A similar observation was made by Broden et al. (1971), who noted that the presence of slips of papers used to self-record study behavior seemed to cause increased studying, even when the subject forgot to engage in the self-recording response. The effects of the device's obtrusiveness were examined by Nelson, Lipinski and Boykin (in press). When the self-recording counter was held in the hand, retarded subjects tended to produce more appropriate classroom verbalizations than when the counter was kept in a pocket. These data suggest that obtrusive self-recording devices may produce greater reactivity than less obvious devices.

Number of Behaviors Concurrently Self-Monitored

The number of behaviors concurrently self-monitored may also affect reactivity. Hayes and Cavior (in press) had subjects concurrently self-record one, two or three target behaviors. Using a change ratio as a dependent measure, they found that the reactive effects of self-monitoring were greater when only a single behavior was self-recorded. Self-monitoring of two or three behaviors did not produce significantly different results.

Schedule of Self-Monitoring

A final variable which has been demonstrated to affect the reactivity of self-recording is the schedule of self-recording responses. Using college students studying for the Graduate Record Examination by using teaching machines, Mahoney, Moore, Wade and Moura (1973) found that continuous self-recording of correct answers produced longer study sessions than intermittent self-recording—that is, recording after every third correct response. Consistent with this finding were the results of a study by Frederiksen, Epstein and Kosevsky (1975), who reported that continuous recording of each cigarette as it was smoked produced greater reactivity than nightly recording of the number of cigarettes smoked each day or weekly recording of cigarettes smoked the previous week.

In summary, although self-recording may produce inconsistent results, that is, some studies report reactive effects while others do not, these variable findings are not whimsical. Several variables, such as motivation, valence, experimenter instructions, nature of behavior, feedback, timing, nature of self-recording device, number of behaviors self-monitored, and scheduling, have been demonstrated to affect the reactivity of self-recording.

EXPLANATIONS OF THE REACTIVITY OF SELF-MONITORING

The initiation of self-monitoring produces an alteration in the self-recorder's stimulus situation, and this alteration may produce resultant and reactive behavior changes. Similarly, in situations where a person's behavior is being externally observed, the alteration of the stimulus situation may contribute to observee reactivity (e.g., Zegiob, Arnold & Forehand, 1975). The obvious similarity in these two types of reactivity has led several investigators to compare the reactive changes produced by external observation and by self-observation. While neither Kazdin (1974a) nor Cavior and Marabotto (1976) found any difference between the reactive changes produced by self-monitoring and the changes produced by observation by others, Ciminero, Graham and Jackson (1975) and Nelson, Lipinski and Black (1976b) reported greater reactive effects produced by self-recording than by another person's recording.

External observations, even when not compared with self-observation, have been found to produce inconsistent and idiosyncratic results in observees' behavior (Patterson & Harris, 1968; White, 1973). Mash and Hedley (1975) have attempted to account for these findings by emphasizing the discriminative stimulus qualities of the observer. As with any discriminative stimulus, the behavior generated in its presence depends on the subject's past learning history and the perceived consequences signaled by this stimulus. The perceived consequences attributed to the observer may determine the occurrence and the direction of reactive behavior changes produced by external observations. Thus, the inconsistent results reported in the studies comparing self- and external observations may be a function of the specific stimulus qualities of the various external observation procedures employed in these studies.

In addition, two major theories which attempt to account for the reactivity of self-monitoring also stress the perceived consequences of the self-monitored target behavior. The inconsistencies noted above may be due to differential consequences attributed to the self-monitored behavior, as well as to the external observer.

The two major theories which stress the perceived consequences of the self-recorded behavior are Kanfer's mediational model and Rachlin's nonmediational model. Kanfer (1970) proposes a three-stage mediational model to account for the reactivity of self-recording: The self-recorder first observes his or her own behavior, then evaluates the behavior in accordance with norms established during his or her learning history, and finally engages in self-reinforcement for positively evaluated behaviors and self-punishment for negatively evaluated behaviors. In contrast with Kanfer's mediational explanation is Rachlin's nonmediational approach (1974). According to Rachlin, self-monitoring serves to remind or cue the subject about the ultimate environmental consequences accorded the self-recorded behavior. To compare the two approaches, we can consider self-recording of study behavior: According to Kanfer, self-recording of study time may increase its frequency because the self-recorder engages in self-reinforcing verbalizations, such as "It's good that I studied 65 minutes this evening." According to Rachlin, self-recording of study time may increase its frequency because the self-recorder is reminded of the ultimate consequences for studying, such as passing a course, earning a college degree and procuring a well-paying job. The two theories have several common points. Both stress the importance of the consequences—either self-generated or environmentally generated—cued by self-monitoring. As noted earlier, implicit or explicit consequences seem to be necessary in producing differential behavior change through self-monitoring: Valence instructions produced differential behavior change, whereas other types of experimenter instructions did not. Both theories also predict that self-recording will increase the frequency of desirable behaviors and decrease the frequency of undesirable behaviors. As reviewed above, this prediction has been borne out by research findings in a classroom setting (Broden et al., 1971), in a laboratory setting (Cavior & Marabotto, 1976; Kazdin, 1974; Sieck & McFall, 1976), and in an institution for adult retardates (Nelson et al., 1976a).

Thus, both observee reactivity and self-monitoring reactivity may be attributed to a common process. Being observed, either by another person or by oneself, serves as a discriminative stimulus, signaling particular consequences contingent on the observation process and/or the observed target behavior. The reactive behavior changes produced by external observation or by self-observation may be a function of these perceived consequences. This notion receives additional support from a phenomenon which Ciminero, Graham and Jackson (1977) label "reciprocal reactivity." Reciprocal reactivity is the change in the observer's behavior produced by observing another person. This change is specific to the target behavior being observed. Although Ciminero et al. report that reciprocal reactivity is weaker than self-monitoring reactivity, the fact that it occurs at all may be due to the same process described above: Observation serves to cue consequences contingent on being observed and/or the target behavior, hence producing reactive behavior changes.

RELATIONSHIP BETWEEN REACTIVITY AND THE ASSESSMENT FUNCTIONS OF SELF-RECORDING

Self-recording may be used as a therapeutic technique because of its reactive effects, especially since it causes positive behaviors to increase in frequency and negative behaviors to decrease. Thus, when self-monitoring is being used for therapeutic purposes, the variables described above should be considered with the goal of maximizing reactivity.

Conversely, the reactivity of self-recording interferes with its data collection function, since the behavior may be changing as it is being counted. Self-recording for assessment is very useful for a number of reasons: 1) It is costly and inconvenient to use trained observers; 2) some target behaviors are inaccessible to external monitoring; and 3) the subject has access to the entire population of his or her own behaviors which an outside observer may only sample (Kazdin, 1974b). However, when self-recording is being used for data collection purposes, its reactive effects must be circumvented or minimized.

In research projects where dependent measures are collected through self-monitoring, an experimental control is required in order to evaluate separately the reactive effects of self-monitoring and the therapeutic effects produced by other intervention strategies. If a within-subject experimental design is to be used, Jeffrey (1974) has suggested the use of an ABCABC design, in which A is an independently assessed baseline, B is a self-monitoring and C is self-monitoring plus an additional technique. This concept could also be applied to multiple baseline designs in which the ABC procedure is applied sequentially to different subjects, behaviors or situations (Hall, Christler, Cranston & Tucker, 1970). The pre-self-monitoring baseline of condition A may be assessed in several different ways. One procedure is to have independent observers collect data prior to the initiation of the subjects' self-recording. Lipinski et al. (1975), for example, utilized a two-stage baseline. The subjects, who were college students in a classroom setting, were observed by trained observers from behind a one-way mirror in order to obtain a baseline frequency of the subjects' face-touching. The subjects were then asked to self-record their own face-touching. The effects of reinforcement contingent on decreases in face-touching or increases in self-recording accuracy were subsequently evaluated against both the independent observers' and the self-recording baselines. Self-recording produced a decrease in face-touching below levels observed during the independent observers' baseline; differential reinforcement further decreased face-touching below the self-recorded baseline. While an independently assessed pre-self-recording baseline may be ideal, in some situations this procedure may be impractical, and with some target behaviors, such as covert responses, it is impossible. Under these circumstances the initial self-monitored data may be utilized as an artificial baseline against which to evaluate further changes produced by additional intervention strategies. Another alternative is to have the subject estimate the pre-self-recording occurrence of the target behavior. Berecz (1972), for example, had his subjects provide a pre-baseline estimate of the number of cigarettes they smoked per day prior to another baseline where they self-recorded their smoking rates. As might be predicted, the self-recorded levels of smoking were lower than the pre-baseline estimates.

The reactive effects due to self-monitoring versus the effects of other therapeutic techniques may be more readily evidenced through between-group experimental designs. Nelson and McReynolds (1971) and Jeffrey (1974) have suggested the use of a self-monitoring-only control group. By comparing this group and other control groups with groups using treatment procedures, the therapeutic effects of treatment techniques may be assessed while still using self-recording to monitor the dependent variable.

When self-recording is being used to collect day-to-day data in clinical cases, the variables which influence the reactive effects of self-recording should be considered in order to minimize reactivity. Some procedures suggested by these variables which may lessen reactivity during data collection are: having subjects record daily weight but not the number of calories eaten, having subjects record after the target response instead of prior to its occurrence, and not providing reinforcement for self-recorded data which is changing in frequency. Reactive changes may nonetheless occur, but perhaps their occurrence may be minimized.

ACCURACY OF SELF-MONITORING

Is Self-Monitoring Accurate?

The accuracy of self-monitored data is usually evaluated in one of three ways: 1) The self-recorded data are compared with data simultaneously collected by external observers (e.g., Lipinski et al., 1975); 2) the self-recorded data are compared with data simultaneously collected by mechanical means—for example, the teaching machine used by Mahoney, Moore et al. (1973) automatically recorded the answers selected by the subjects while the subjects simultaneously self-monitored their correct answers; 3) the self-recorded data are compared with some measurable by-product, for example, self-recorded calories are compared with actual weight loss (Mahoney, Moura et al., 1973) or self-recorded study time is compared with grades (Johnson & White, 1971).

The procedure most frequently used to assess the accuracy of self-recording is comparing self-recorded data with data simultaneously collected by external observers. This method is similar to the procedure used to evaluate the accuracy of external observations—two observers simultaneously record the same behaviors, and these simultaneous recordings are subsequently compared. In the context of external observations, Johnson and Bolstad (1973) distinguished between interobserver agreement and observer accuracy. When two sets of observations are compared, the result is interobserver agreement. Both observers may agree, however, and nonetheless be inaccurate recorders. Only when there is a more direct measure of "truth," or of the target behavior, is observer accuracy assessed. Similarly, when a self-recorder's data and an external observer's data are compared, interobserver agreement, rather than self-recording accuracy, is being assessed. Even though the external observations are generally used as a criterion against which to measure the self-recorder's data, there is no guarantee that the external observer is any more accurate than the self-recorder. For example, McFall (1970) reported a .61 correlation between self-recorders' and observers' frequencies of number of cigarettes smoked. A closer examination of the data revealed that generally the observers counted fewer cigarettes than the self-recorders. McFall (1970) noted other data which seemed to indicate that the self-recorders were less accurate than the observers, reaffirming that interobserver agreement may not necessarily be a measure of self-recording accuracy. Similarly, Fixsen, Phillips and Wolf (1972) found that boys' reports on the cleanliness of their own rooms agreed with peer reports 76%, but boys' self-reports and their reports on their peers' rooms agreed with adult observers' records 50%. In this case, the "accuracy" of self-monitoring depended on the external observer used as the criterion.

In the remainder of this chapter the term, accuracy of self-monitoring, is used, but, generally, the more correct term would be interobserver agreement of self-monitored data. In the future, the accuracy of self-monitored data may be truly assessed, but currently the yardstick is generally an external observer's recordings. Given this methodology, some studies have found self-recorders to be very accurate, whereas other studies have found them to be relatively inaccurate.

Kazdin (1974b) tentatively suggested that adult subjects may be more accurate self-recorders than children. Ober (1968) reported a correlation of .94 between self-reports and friends' reports of subjects' smoking. A 98% agreement was found by Azrin and Powell (1969) between self-reported pill-taking and hospital employees' records. In Mahoney, Moore et al.'s (1973) comparison of subjects' self-monitored study responses with the unobtrusive reliability measure, a high degree of agreement (.938) was reported. McKenzie and Rushall (1974) concluded that swimmers' and experimenters' counts of the number of laps swam agreed 100%. Shaw, Peterson and Cone (1974) showed that aides' reports of training sessions agreed well with direct checks on the occurrence of these training sessions.

In contrast to these studies demonstrating that adults can be accurate self-recorders, other studies report relatively low agreement between self-recordings and independent observations. McFall (1970) found that college students' records of their smoking rates and simultaneous records taken by their classmates correlated .61. The agreements for two mothers' self-recordings and independent observers' recordings in Herbert and Baer's study (1972) were, respectively, 46% and 42%. Hendricks et al. (1973) reported that the agreement rate between self-monitoring teachers and external observers ranged from 41% to 87.8%. Cavior and Marabotto (1976) found a .37 agreement between trained observers and college students who self-monitored their verbal behaviors in a dyadic situation.

Children, too, have been found to be rather inaccurate self-recorders. By means of a graph, Risley and Hart (1968) depicted the low correspondence between children's self-reports of their nonverbal behaviors and the frequency of their behavior as measured by observers. Broden et al. (1971) found that there were large day-to-day discrepancies in a student's self-recording of her studying and observers' recordings.

Simkins (1971) proposed several reasons why the data collected by self-recorders may be discrepant from data collected by external observers. The contingencies for accurate data collection may differ. The external observers and the self-observers may be using different response criteria in discriminating response occurrence. Finally, the self-recorders may have other prepotent concurrent responses which interfere with their ability to self-record accurately. Some of Simkins' suggestions have been experimentally verified, as described below.

VARIABLES CONTROLLING ACCURACY

Given the varying reports of the accuracy of self-observations as compared with simultaneous external observations, it would seem advisable to consider the variables which have been demonstrated to affect the accuracy of self-monitoring (Table 1). These variables may then be capitalized on to maximize self-recording accuracy, especially when self-monitoring is used for assessment purposes.

Awareness of Accuracy Assessment

One variable which has been shown to affect the accuracy of self-recording is awareness of accuracy assessment. Self-recording is more accurate when self-observers are aware that their accuracy is being monitored than when their accuracy is monitored covertly. Lipinski and Nelson (1974) found that the agreement between self-recorders and trained observers who were simultaneously recording the subjects' face-touching was .86 when the subjects were aware of reliability checks; when reliability checks were made covertly, the self-recorders' accuracy dropped to .52. In two similar studies, Nelson et al. (1975) found that awareness of reliability checks increased the accuracy of self-recorded face-touching from .554 to .810, and Lipinski et al. (1975) found a comparable increase from .46 to .67. Bailey and Peterson (1975) replicated these effects with verbal responses—awareness of accuracy estimates increased agreement for self-recordings and external recordings of praise words from 37.7% to 51.6%. Similarly, Santogrossi (1974) reported that the discrepancies between children's self-recording of correct reading responses and external observers' recordings were decreased when either a teacher or a peer also monitored the children's reading responses. Comparable effects were obtained by either peer or teacher monitoring.

The conclusion that self-recorders are more accurate when they are aware of reliability assessment than when they are unaware parallels results obtained with trained observers. Reid (1970) found that interobserver agreement dropped from a median of .76 to .51 when observers were led to believe that accuracy was no longer being assessed. Taplin and Reid (1973) found that the level of interobserver agreement fell from .81 on the last day of observer training to .65 on the first day of covert reliability assessment. Romanczyk, Kent, Diament and O'Leary (1973) found that the accuracy for trained observers aware both of reliability assessment and of the specific reliability checker was .77. Accuracy dropped to .53 under overt assessment with an unidentified assessor and to .33 when the observers were unaware of reliability assessment.

Reinforcement Contingent on Self-Monitoring Accuracy

A second variable which influences the accuracy of self-recording is reinforcement contingent on self-monitoring accuracy. Risley and Hart (1968) found that the initially low correspondence between children's verbal and nonverbal behavior could be improved when reinforcement was made contingent on correspondence as evaluated by external observers. Fixsen et al. (1972) found that the .76 level of agreement between peer and self-reports of room cleanliness could be enhanced to .86 agreement through contingent reinforcement. The cheating behavior of a sixth grade student was significantly reduced when her weekly grades were made contingent on daily accurate self-evaluation (Flowers, 1972). For two of three target behaviors self-recorded by adult retarded subjects, Nelson et al. (1976a) reported increases in self-monitoring accuracy when reinforcement was made contingent on accuracy: The accuracy of self-recording of touching environmental objects increased from .70 to .92, and the accuracy of self-monitoring of face-touching increased from .45 to .82 (the self-monitored accuracy of talking, however, remained the same, .73). Lipinski et al. (1975) differentially reinforced some college student subjects for increases in the accuracy of their self-recorded face touches and other students for decreases in the frequency of self-recorded face touches. Compared with a baseline self-monitoring accuracy of .67, the former group increased their accuracy to .84 under differential reinforcement for accuracy, while the latter group increased their accuracy to .72 under differential reinforcement for decreases in face-touching. Peterson et al. (1975) similarly found that contingent reinforcement increased their subject's accuracy when self-recording the phrase "you know" from 0% to 50.1%. Although Lyman et al. (1975) obtained improvements in tent cleanliness with their breakfast contingency, the boys' self-recording accuracy remained low until prompt access to breakfast was made contingent on both cleanliness and accurate self-recordings. Punishment, in the form of response cost, has also been shown to prevent self-recorders' overestimation of their desired target behavior, better known as cheating (Seymour & Stokes, 1976).

Given that accuracy of self-monitoring is increased by reinforcement, a related question is whether good accuracy may be maintained while thinning the schedule of accuracy checks and reinforcement for accuracy. Drabman, Spitalnik and O'Leary (1973) and Turkewitz, O'Leary and Ironsmith (1975) reported decreases in the self-monitoring accuracy of schoolchildren when the number of children whose accuracy was checked and reinforced was gradually reduced. On the other hand, Layne, Rickard, Jones and Lyman (1976) found that children's self-monitoring accuracy was maintained when the days on which accuracy was checked and reinforced were thinned on a variable-ratio schedule.

Nature of the Target Behavior

A third variable which may affect the accuracy of self-recording is the nature of the target behavior. Bailey and Peterson (1975) reported that the agreement between college students who self-recorded a class of verbal responses, namely praise statements, and external observers was 51.6% when the self-recorders were aware of accuracy assessment and 37.7% when they were unaware. By comparing their data on verbal responses to Lipinski and Nelson's data (1974) on face-touching (86% when subjects were aware of accuracy assessment, 52% when unaware), Bailey and Peterson proposed that verbal responses may be more difficult to self-record accurately than face touches. This suggestion was confirmed in a subsequent study by Peterson et al. (1975) that demonstrated higher accuracies for self-recorded face touches (64.3% agreement) and lower accuracies for self-recorded verbal responses (0% agreement for the phrase "you know," and 31.4% agreement for the phrase "and all that"). A similar agreement level for self-recorded verbal responses, .37, was reported by Cavior and Marabotto (1976). Hayes and Cavior (in press) similarly reported a higher accuracy for face-touching (87%), than for two classes of verbal responses—value judgments (40%) and non-fluencies (0%). Further research is needed to determine which target behaviors are more amenable to accurate self-recording.

Valence of the Target Behavior

Kanfer (1977) proposed that self-recorders may tend to avoid making self-recording responses for undesirable target behaviors to minimize negative self-evaluation. Thus, self-recording accuracy may be lower for undesirable behaviors than for desirable behaviors. Some confirmation for this suggestion has been reported. In two experiments, teachers tended to self-record their positive classroom verbalizations (.58 and .53) more accurately than their negative classroom verbalizations (.41 and .37) (Nelson, Hay, Hay & Carstens, in press). Children, too, self-recorded their appropriate classroom verbalizations (.81) more accurately than their inappropriate classroom verbalizations (.57) (Nelson, Hay & Koslow-Green, 1976). Adult retardates self-recorded desirable talking more accurately (.73) than undesirable face-touching (.45) or neutral object-touching (.70) (Nelson et al., 1976a). In these studies, accuracy was assessed by having independent observers and self-recorders make simultaneous recordings.

Concurrent Response Requirements

A fifth variable known to influence the accuracy of self-recording is concurrent response requirements. Although Cavior and Marabotto (1976) found the accuracy of self-recording to be .37 when the subjects attempted to self-monitor their verbal behavior while engaging in a dyadic interaction, their accuracy increased to .89 when given the opportunity to self-record their verbal behavior from videotapes. It is possible that the subjects could not accurately self-record during the dyadic interactions because concurrent responses interfered with their accuracy. Three experiments specifically designed to assess the effects of concurrent responses on the accuracy of self-recording confirmed that concurrent responding is detrimental to self-recording accuracy. Epstein, Webster and Miller (1975) in two experiments, and Epstein, Miller and Webster (1976) in an additional experiment found that subjects made fewer errors in their self-monitoring of respiration when they engaged in self-recording alone than when they engaged in a concurrent operant task of lever pressing in addition to self-monitoring. In the three studies, error rates under the former condition were respectively 4%, 28% and 23%, while error rates under the latter condition were respectively 9.5%, 72% and 49%.

Schedule of Self-Monitoring

A sixth variable which influences self-recording accuracy is the schedule of self-monitoring. Frederiksen et al. (1975) found that when subjects self-recorded each cigarette that was smoked, their accuracy of self-monitoring was greater (93.59%) than when they self-recorded the number of cigarettes smoked at the end of each day (85.77%) or at the end of each week (87.32%).

Training in Self-Monitoring

Peterson et al. (1975) attempted to increase their subject's self-monitoring accuracy by training him to self-record from videotapes of his own conversation. Although this procedure increased his accuracy to 62% while he self-monitored from the videotapes, generalization did not occur to the criterion situation where accuracy decreased to 20%. To enhance generalization, Nelson, Lipinski and Boykin (in press) trained four adolescent retarded subjects in self-recording by first having them self-record their appropriate classroom verbalizations from videotape and then by having them self-record the target behavior in the classroom situation. Feedback on the accuracy of the self-recordings was provided by the experimenter in both situations. During the subsequent self-recording periods, observers also recorded the subjects' appropriate classroom verbalizations. The self-recording accuracy for the trained subjects was .914, in contrast with the self-recording accuracy of .784 found for five minimally trained subjects. Training did not, however, affect the reactivity of self-monitoring.

Nature of the Self-Recording Device and Procedure

There has been little experimental investigation of the effects of different self-recording procedures on the accuracy of self-observation. It may be hypothesized that quantitative self-recordings may be less subject to distortion than qualitative self-recordings, as has been found to be true with independent observers (Kent, O'Leary, Diament & Dietz, 1974; Shuller & McNamara, 1976). Future research may well compare the accuracy of numerical self-observation with other forms of self-report. Additionally, if the self-recording procedure suits the target behavior, the subject is more likely to be accurate than if a less suitable procedure is selected. As an example, if the subject is instructed to self-monitor a high frequency behavior by means of a frequency count, the self-recordings may be less accurate than if the high frequency behavior was self-monitored by a time sampling or spot checking method (Kubany & Sloggett, 1973). Also, the self-recorder may be more accurate if the self-recording device is accessible and easy to use. This latter suggestion received some minimal confirmation by Nelson, Lipinski & Boykin (in press) who reported that retarded self-recorders tended to be more accurate when the counter was held in the hand (.845) than when the counter was worn in the belt (.820).

Social Psychology Manipulations

A final class of variables which has been utilized to improve the accuracy of self-monitoring was borrowed by Bornstein and his colleagues from social psychology. A "reliability enhancement package" was found to produce more accurate self-recordings of biofeedback measures than two control procedures (Bornstein, Hamilton, Miller, Quevillon & Spitzform, 1976). This reliability enhancement package consisted of three social psychology manipulations: foot-in-the-door technique, induced self-esteem and guilt induction. In a second study, a different reliability enhancement package consisting of four social psychology manipulations—cognitive consistency, consequence clarification, public commitment, and cueing statements—was similarly found to produce more accurate self-recordings than a control condition (Bornstein, Hamilton, Carmody, Rychtarik & Velardi, 1976).

SUGGESTIONS TO MAXIMIZE SELF-RECORDING ACCURACY

When self-recording is used to collect data, its accuracy is very important. Several suggestions of ways to increase the accuracy of self-recording may be made on the basis of the above studies on variables contributing to self-recording accuracy.

Both self-recorders and trained observers produce more accurate recordings when they are aware of reliability assessment than when they are unaware. O'Leary and Kent (1973) suggested three procedures to capitalize on this phenomenon and to maintain good accuracy in trained observers: 1) have interobserver agreement continuously checked; 2) have interobserver agreement assessed on a random basis; and 3) use mechanical recordings of the target behaviors permitting assessment of interobserver agreement of the codings of these recordings on a continuous or random basis. Parallel procedures may be used with self-recorders. Regarding the first suggestion, Rutner (1967) had someone else in the environment initial each self-recording by his subjects of cigarettes smoked. Regarding the second suggestion, Tokarz and Lawrence (1974) had insomniacs self-record their time of falling asleep and awakening. Roommates were used to assess periodically and covertly the insomniacs' accuracy, with the insomniacs' knowledge of that possibility. Regarding the third suggestion, the accuracy of subjects' self-recordings may also be assessed, with the subjects' awareness, by permanent product data such as weight (Mahoney, Moura et al., 1973) or grades (Johnson & White, 1971; Richards, 1975), or by other unobtrusive and/or mechanical devices (Mahoney, Moore, et al., 1973; Palmer & McGuire, 1973; Schwitzgebel & Kolb, 1974; Webb, Campbell, Schwartz & Sechrest, 1969).

Other procedures to maximize the accuracy of self-recording may include reinforcing the subject for accurate data, having the subject self-record each instance of the target behavior, providing the subject with adequate training and a suitable self-recording procedure, having the subject engage in self-recording when he or she is not overly busy with other behaviors, or using some of the social psychology manipulations suggested by Bornstein.

RELATIONSHIP BETWEEN REACTIVITY AND ACCURACY
OF SELF-MONITORING

Nelson and McReynolds (1971) suggested that even though self-recording may be inaccurate, it may nonetheless produce consistent reactive effects. This suggestion was experimentally corroborated by Broden et al. (1971), Fixsen et al. (1972), Herbert and Baer (1972), and Lipinski and Nelson (1974), all of whom demonstrated that self-monitoring produced reactive effects even though the self-recording itself was inaccurate as compared with external observations. Hayes and Cavior (in press) concluded that the accuracy of self-recording was not correlated with the magnitude of its reactive effects. While reactivity was greatest for face-touching, followed by nonfluencies and value judgments, respectively, accuracy was greatest for face-touching, followed by value judgments and nonfluencies, respectively. Indeed, very small correlations were found between individual subjects' accuracy scores and their ratio change scores for any of the three target behaviors (face-touching, .01; nonfluencies, —.02 and value judgments, .26).

If subjects are inaccurate in self-recording, a mechanism for the reactive effects of self-monitoring must be found. Peterson et al. (1975) suggested that a minimal level of accuracy is necessary before reactivity occurs. This suggestion is based on their data with the self-monitoring of the phrase "you know": When accuracy was .00, no reactivity occurred; only when training and reinforcement increased the level of accuracy did reactivity happen. An alternative suggestion is that subjects self-observe their own behavior but neglect to make the self-recording response. Simkins (1971) noted the distinctiveness of the target behavior and the actual self-recording behavior. Thus, subjects may notice the occurrence of the target behavior, hence cueing behavior change, but not make the self-recording response, hence producing low accuracy.

When self-monitoring is used for therapeutic purposes, its reactivity should be maximized. Conversely, when self-monitoring is used for assessment purposes, it reactivity should be minimized and its accuracy maximized. Some procedures may enhance accuracy without simultaneously increasing reactivity. As an example, Lipinski et al. (1975) reported that reinforcement differentially affected subjects' reactivity or accuracy, depending on whether the reinforcement was contingent on decreases in the frequency of self-recorded face-touching or increases in agreement between the self-recorders and the external observers. On the other hand, some procedures which enhance accuracy also increase reactivity. A continuous self-recording schedule, for example, has been demonstrated to produce both good reactivity and good accuracy (Frederiksen et al., 1975; Mahoney, Moore et al., 1973). Similarly, a highly visible self-recording apparatus may enhance both reactivity and accuracy. In these instances, the researcher or clinician who is using self-recording to collect data must be aware that increases in accuracy may be obtained at the expense of simultaneous increases in reactivity. If self-recording is being used to collect data during treatment, however, these procedures have dual advantages.

SUMMARY

Two main issues in dealing with self-recording are its reactivity and its accuracy. Reactivity is the change in behavior produced by the self-recording procedure. Accuracy is the congruence between self-recorded and externally monitored behavioral recordings. Self-recording has been used to fulfill two central functions. When self-monitoring is used as a therapeutic technique, its reactivity should be maximized. Conversely, when self-monitoring is used to collect data, its reactivity should be minimized, and its accuracy maximized. Variables which influence the reactivity and accuracy of self-recording were reviewed, especially to provide suggestions for enhancing the therapeutic and assessment functions of self-recording.

9

SOME APPLIED ISSUES IN SELF-MONITORING

MICHAEL J. MAHONEY

For me, one of the most pleasurable aspects of preparing a paper for this volume was the realization that the other participants and readers would already value and respect the critical importance of behavior assessment. As many of you are probably aware, the majority of helping professionals still consider the words Rorschach and "assessment" to be synonyms. The idea of defining and/or counting individualized client behavior still rings a sour note in all too many quarters. For some, it connotes a dehumanizing quantification which robs the person of his or her human uniqueness. For me, and hopefully for you, behavior assessment connotes a very different response. It is a critical element in a humanitarian endeavor. As many of the papers in this volume attest, the functional analysis of client problems is not just an element of therapeutic success—it is often its prerequisite. The most efficient therapist is sensitively tuned to the personal data of the client. He is not collecting data for the sake of scientific appearances or because that is what is considered proper. The data in and of themselves are meaningless without being placed in the perspective of a target problem. The effective therapist uses data to guide his or her own efforts at having an impact, and—regardless of theoretical bias or procedural preference—he adjusts therapeutic strategies in tune with that feedback. If the data indicate improvement when an improvement was not anticipated, so much the worse for one's theoretical predictions.

But enough of this. I said earlier that one of the pleasures of contributing to this volume was the fact that I could take it for granted that behavior assessment would be valued. I shall therefore desist in its defense. Let me instead address some of the practical problems which are often faced in clinical applications of behavioral assessment, and specifically where the client is asked to participate as both subject and object of data collection. I am talking, of course, about the process of self-recording or self-monitoring, a procedure which has already been valuably examined in the previous chapter by Rosemery Nelson.

As Nelson has indicated, self-monitoring is a complex undertaking which can serve a variety of clinical purposes. It provides information to both the therapist and client which may be essential for accurate problem diagnosis and continuing assessment. In addition, it often appears to be reactive and may therefore add to one's therapeutic punch by actively contributing to behavior change. The processes which mediate that change are a topic of current research (cf. Kanfer, 1970; Kazdin, 1974a; Thoresen & Mahoney, 1974), and we are beginning to see some regularities in what had formerly been a very unpredictable procedure. Nelson's own work has been responsible for much of our progress.

I should mention in passing that Rosemery Nelson called me several months ago to ask some questions regarding the conference at which this paper was to be presented. She seemed surprised and pleased to hear that I was going to talk about some of the practical problems in self-monitoring, and I soon discovered that she had had the impression that I was anti-self-monitoring. Parts of my early work on obesity had concluded that some forms of self-monitoring are not sufficiently powerful to be used as singular clinical strategies. In two studies we found that self-monitoring alone was not effective in producing weight loss (Mahoney, Moura & Wade, 1973; Mahoney, 1974a). I therefore recommended that therapists not rely solely on the reactive aspects of self-monitoring for their therapeutic gains. Since that time several other researchers have devised alternate self-recording systems which appear to be more powerful and enduring than the ones I employed several years ago (e.g., Romanczyk, 1974; Romanczyk, Tracey, Wilson & Thorpe, 1973). However, to clear up my stance, I would like to say that I have always been a strong advocate of self-monitoring in therapy for assessment purposes. As a matter of fact, after Rosemery's call I tried unsuccessfully to remember the last time I had seen a client without invoking some sort of self-recording. In many ways, this chapter is based on problems I have encountered in my never-ending struggle to squeeze data out of my clients. Unfortunately, many of these problems have yet to receive controlled experimental attention, so many of my remarks and recommendations will have to be filtered and filed as clinical impressions rather than experimental findings.

There are some differences between using self-monitoring for its re-activity versus its assessment functions. My own current opinion is that the latter have been more strongly supported than the former. Despite the recent progress made in self-monitoring technologies, I still think it is fair to say that the reactive effects of self-monitoring are variable (across individuals, target behaviors, etc.) and usually short-lived. In addition, I would argue that these reactive effects, when they do occur, are attributable to more complex variables than simple mechanical recording. For example, standard setting and self-evaluation are probably operative in most instances of reactive self-monitoring (Locke, Cartledge & Koeppel, 1968; Kanfer, 1970; Bandura, 1971; Mahoney, 1974b). Thus, were I forced to choose between its assessment and therapeutic functions, I would presently place more confidence in the former. In practical applications, of course, this dichotomy is seldom enforced, although one may have to choose between procedures which ostensibly serve one function better than the other.

With that qualification in mind, let's take a look at the practical side of self-monitoring. Let us say that you are convinced of the assessment merits of self-recording and would like to begin incorporating this technique more often into your own professional work. Where do you start? How do you go about it? Well, there are several big and small questions which first need attention. Let me begin with the big ones. They can be arbitrarily divided into three parts:

1) *When* to self-monitor;
2) *What* to self-monitor; and
3) *How* to self-monitor.

Let's take each individually.

When TO SELF-MONITOR

This may sound like a contradiction to my earlier contention that self-recorded data may be critically important in successful therapy. However, I do not believe that we should be blinded to the possibility that there may be times and situations during which self-monitoring might better be avoided in some clients. For example, in the initial stages of therapy with someone who is outspokenly opposed to behavior modification, I do not usually begin with a request for some elaborate self-recording. I have encountered several clients who have actively or passively resisted my initial efforts to "quantify their lives." Some have stated their objections by repeatedly failing to comply with my early requests. My way of handling this situation has been roughly divided into a four-stage strategy. First, I try to make the importance of self-monitoring obvious by asking them retrospective questions. For example, a husband recently refused to keep some simple daily rating forms I had provided for the purposes of assessing interactions with his wife. After the second week of noncompliance in self-monitoring, I started asking relatively specific questions which could only have been answered by his consulting a behavior diary. Since he had failed to keep one, he was forced to admit the inadequacy of his memory and I was soon receiving occasionally completed data forms. This was still not satisfactory from my perspective, so I moved into the second phase of my strategy—namely, establish a self-recording assignment which is extremely minimal in its demands. Through a process of shaping, the reluctant self-recorder can gradually be enticed into providing more extensive and valuable personal data. This happened to be sufficient for this particular client. I have had others, however, who were still uncooperative, and my third step is to confront them openly with the fact that they are jeopardizing the success of their treatment (and therefore wasting their own time and mine) unless accurate personal data are provided. Without these critical elements, it is very difficult to offer an accurate problem diagnosis, let alone to guide therapy in a self-corrective fashion toward their desired outcome. If this brief sermon on the merits of behavior assessment does not produce the desired effects, I resort to my final strategy—I make my professional services contingent on their self-recording. In my opinion, I have an ethical obligation to provide the best therapy possible in any given case. However, as a clinical scientist I feel committed to a dependence on data in my therapeutic efforts. If a client refuses to cooperate with me in collecting and analyzing that data, I cannot in all due conscience feel good about my professional assistance. To date, only a couple of clients have gone far enough to earn this ultimatum, and I have occasionally had to abruptly terminate a session on the basis of their uncollected data. In one case, the client saw that I was serious in my seemingly stubborn commitment to data, and her self-monitoring data soon began to arrive. The other terminated therapy.

Before I leave the topic of *when* to self-monitor, I would like to share another clinical impression that may contradict some of the implications of other work in this area. Namely, I believe that there may be times when certain kinds of self-monitoring are contraindicated—that is, when they may actually detract from therapeutic effectiveness. For example, asking a suicidal client to monitor depressive thoughts could—in some clients—exacerbate their depression. Having a tangible record of their deficiencies or focusing on their weaknesses might simply provide perceived corroboration of their shortcomings. Likewise, in the treatment of obesity I believe that—again, for *some* clients—daily monitoring of bodyweight can be catastrophic. If the individual's motivation is riding on a daily weigh-in, he or she may encounter rapid disappointment. Bathroom scales are notoriously unreliable instruments. If the person's continued pursuit of a reduction program hinges upon an observable loss overnight, he is probably doomed for failure. Permanent weight control is a long and effortful undertaking (cf. Mahoney & Mahoney, 1976). Its results are reflected only after weeks or even months. Therefore, I discourage clients from monitoring their weight too often. The principle here is, I think, an important one to bear in mind—namely, that behavioral assessment is a means, not an end in itself. Its contribution to a specific case must be individually evaluated.

How TO SELF-MONITOR

The issue of how to self-monitor takes us into two separate subtopics. The first is instrumentation. A wide variety of devices have been used in clinical applications of self-monitoring—golf counters, pocket diaries, alarm clocks, and so on. With a little imagination, the therapist can usually come up with an appropriate instrument for monitoring specified target behaviors. Each of these devices has certain limitations, however. For example, unless your primary interest is in the *frequency* of a discrete response, many of the mechanical self-monitoring aids are of little use. Golf and wrist counters may reflect changes in the *rate* of responding, but they do not provide information on antecedent or consequent events, response intensity, and so on. Most of my own clinical uses of self-monitoring have incorporated some form of a structured behavioral diary which avoids some of these problems. Before I discuss that diary, however, I'd like to mention some other options which are often overlooked by therapists. One of these is a tape recorder. Although it is less portable than other recording devices, a tape recorder allows greater flexibility in reporting and may be preferable in instances where the client has difficulty with written diary forms. An even more versatile option is a phone answering device. Two years ago we set up a "Self-Monitoring Service" in conjunction with an obesity program at Penn State. Basically, it involved a phone answering device which recorded clients' self-reported data. The device proved to be very beneficial in our program. Clients could call in at any time of the day or night—they were greeted by a prerecorded message, asking them to give their name, the date, and their personal data. Since most individuals are near a phone almost all the time, this made for a very versatile and easy-to-use self-monitoring system. Likewise, from the therapist's perspective, we could play back clients' calls at our convenience and were prepared for their next session well ahead of time.

Generally speaking, your choice of self-monitoring instruments should take the following things into account: 1) simplicity of operation—if it isn't easy to use, the client will be unlikely to provide you with reliable data; 2) reliability; and 3) compatibility—that is, the instrument should be compatible with the kind of self-monitoring you are requesting. If the behaviors being recorded could occur at almost any time and in a variety of geographical locations, then your self-monitoring device should be portable and relatively unobtrusive. These considerations bring me back to the written behavioral diary which, as I mentioned earlier, is one of my preferred methods of self-monitoring.

The behavioral diary is often helpful early in therapy because it need not preclude variables a priori. This means that it may provide you with a broader picture of factors which could have potential relevance for the target problem. In its simplest form, the behavioral diary is comprised of a sheet or card which is divided into columns and rows. Each page in the diary may correspond to a full day, and the client is asked to record not only the occurrence of the target behavior but also its associated events—time of day, physical location, social stimuli (e.g., the presence or absence of specific people), and so on. These associated events are sometimes divided into "antecedent" and "consequent" categories to facilitate assessment of such factors as stimulus control and operant contingencies. With my own penchant for private events, I also request that clients record thoughts and images which are correlated with target behaviors.

The possible variations on this basic format for a behavioral diary are almost infinite. Since my space is not infinite, I shall select only a couple of representative hybrids. One is the time sampling diary, which asks the client to monitor target behaviors only part of the time. For example, a dieter might be asked to monitor problem snacking during the evening only. This strategy can be dangerous, however, because it may give a misrepresentative picture and does not facilitate the complex systems analysis which is often essential in behavioral assessment. A better alternative is one which incorporates representative samples from among a larger time interval. For example, a client may be asked to record the intensity of smoking urges once per hour rather than whenever they occur. Alternatively, the scheduling of monitoring intervals may be spread across variable rather than fixed periods of time. With an asthmatic client, for example, Al Sirota and I asked the woman to carry a portable parking meter timer (Sirota & Mahoney, 1974). She set it for varying intervals which averaged 30 minutes. When the timer signaled, the client monitored her current level of muscular tension—a factor which our earlier assessment had isolated as a treatment target. Sampling diaries such as these are, of course, a compromise. While they may simplify and economize the amount of recording required, they also throw out large amounts of client data which may or may not have important bearing on assessment and changes in therapeutic strategy.

What might be called actuarial diaries are more comprehensive in their content. In these, the client is asked to continuously record occurrences of target behaviors and their associated events. A sample form is shown in Figure 1. Although a continuous actuarial diary may provide a more complete picture, it also has problems of its own. For example, in the area of weight control, many individuals embark on a self-chosen path of counting every calorie they consume. If you have ever tried this feat of masochism, you may have already anticipated some of my comments. The problem with such ambitious undertakings is that they have a large degree of response cost and the clients may be less likely to continue their conscientious performance for a sufficient period of time. In some of our research on obesity at Penn State, we have adopted alternate and supplementary recording systems. For example, obese clients began by giving us daily records of all calories consumed. This request for complete and continual recording is repeated several times during treatment and follow-up to provide us with "probes" against which we can check our assessment impressions. However, during the bulk of their contact with us, they are *not* counting all of their calories. Instead, they may be counting a specific subset of calories (such as sweets or alcohol) which have been suggested as behavioral targets in their earlier and more comprehensive diaries. Alternatively, they may be using a rating scale recording system such as the one illustrated in Figure 2. Here the day is divided into three equal parts—morning (midnight to noon), afternoon (noon to 6 p.m.), and evening (6 p.m. to midnight).

FIGURE 1

Assessment Diary

DATE: .... NAME: ....

Time	Location	Other Persons Present	Preceding Thoughts	Other Preceding Actions or Events	Target Occurrence	Subsequent Thoughts	Other Subsequent Actions & Events
10:15 a.m.	Office	Sandy	Long day ahead of me	Sandy offered me a doughnut	Ate 1 doughnut	Felt guilty; joked about diet	Sandy reassured me I didn't need to lose weight

Figure 2

Daily Rating Form

NAME: .... DATE: ....

Interval	Calories Consumed	Calories Spent	Social Influences	Cognitive Ecology	Comments
Morning	6	3	4	5	Had mild hangover from last night
Afternoon					
Evening					

At the end of each of these three intervals, they assign a score to each of four targets—1) calories consumed, 2) calories spent, 3) social influences, and 4) cognitive ecology (the latter being our label for the person's attempts to clean up what he says to himself). Each of these areas is rated on a seven-point scale, and we discuss the meaning of the various ratings with our clients. This kind of recording is economical in effort while providing general information on several possible patterns and interactions in target areas. It has its own disadvantages though, in that it relies on a subjective rating of performance in a retrospective fashion. Again, the criteria on *how* to self-monitor may require personalization for individual clients. Any recording system is a compromise and must be viewed in a cost efficiency framework. What are the *costs* of the system relative to its *efficiency* in providing valid and relevant clinical data? How can the therapist best minimize the former and maximize the latter? These are not the kinds of questions that can be answered with pat universal generalizations. Rather, they must be addressed in each unique instance and—in a true bootstrapping operation—the therapist must be continually *assessing* his *assessment*.

Before I leave the topic of how to self-monitor, I should perhaps note the usefulness of graphic displays. Gradual trends in behavior change may be overlooked unless the data are transferred to a graph which depicts overall directions and rate of change. For example, one of my depressive clients recently complained about having made little progress in four months of therapy. Indeed, his daily self-ratings showed considerable variability in degree of depression. However, a graph of average weekly ratings showed an unmistakable positive trend and later performance changes corroborated this success. Although I frequently use graphs to give me feedback on therapy progress, they may also serve to illustrate (and perhaps reinforce) client changes. By having the client graph his or her progress, one can invoke some of the processes which seem to be conducive to therapeutic progress. Not only may a chart provide graphic evidence of improvement, but it may become a stimulus for further efforts. When it is publicly displayed, it may invite social feedback (e.g., Rutner & Bugle, 1969). Indeed, before my own writing habits had developed into a comfortable pattern, I used public graphs posted on my office door to enlist the support of friends and colleagues.

What TO SELF-MONITOR

The question of *what* to self-monitor raises a whole series of related issues in behavioral assessment such as the "proper" or preferred targets in therapy. Since several other papers have dealt with these broader topics, I shall restrict my comments to a few practical recommendations dealing with self-monitoring.

First, although the data are still far from conclusive, I tend toward a preference for positive (i.e., accelerative) rather than negative (decelerative) targets whenever this is feasible. This issue was raised several years ago (Kanfer, 1970; Thoresen & Mahoney, 1974) and has yet to be given its experimental due. Basically, it refers to the differential effects of recording desired versus undesired behaviors. The weight watcher for example, can potentially monitor either transgressions or successful instances of self-control, the smoker can count cigarettes consumed or intervals of time without a cigarette, and the depressive can record either negative or positive thoughts. There are probably situations in which monitoring negative behaviors—or both positive *and* negative behaviors—may be more informative and/or therapeutic. However, until we have better evidence on the merits and costs of these different strategies, I opt for emphasizing what is going *right* in a given case rather than what is going *wrong*. This is obviously a subjective clinical bias.

Let me move on here to some other practical recommendations on *what* to self-monitor. One of these deals with the phenomenon of *premature closure* on the part of the therapist. For many clinical scientists, assessment is predominantly a pre-post undertaking. You do it at the beginning of therapy to aid in problem diagnosis, and then again after completion of therapy to measure your impact. In addition to depriving himself of invaluable information in between, the therapist who views assessment in this manner may be more susceptible to being captivated by his first diagnostic impressions. Thus, in the first few sessions he may decide that a child's school adjustment problems stem primarily from inappropriate parental behaviors. Unless his assessment is ongoing, however, his therapy may rest precariously on two risky assumptions: 1) that this first diagnosis is valid, and 2) that the problem will not be influenced by new factors. Many therapists seem to be seduced by such implicit premises. If they find *one* variable which seems to correlate with the target behavior, they eagerly conclude that they have found *the* culprit variable. Likewise, they seem to assume that the problem in question can be approached in a *static* rather than *dynamic* fashion. In many ways, pre-post assessment is like taking two *still* photographs—they capture frozen moments in time without conveying anything about the process of interim change. What I am getting at here is not only the importance of ongoing assessment, but the value of therapist flexibility. The sensitive clinical scientist will be open to a wide range of possible variables—even when they may not have been nominated by his or her preferred theoretical orientation. For example, many behavior therapists neglect such factors as nutrition and sleep because these have been given a minimal role in their own therapeutic training. The problem is that we will never know how important a given variable is until it is included in our clinical assessments.

Related to this issue of flexibility are two corollary points. First, leave room for unsolicited information. That is, don't handicap your own effectiveness by refusing to attend to supplementary input. I have known behavior modifiers who refused to listen to client's spontaneous reports of their dreams, probably because of their attitudes toward psychoanalysis. There is some recent evidence that dreams may be an important consideration even in behavioral therapies (Mahoney, 1974), and who knows what other neglected or prohibited variables will show promise in the next decade? Practically speaking, my point here is that you should not restrict clients to providing you with *only* discrete and quantitative information on their behavior. Give them some room to expand your awareness. In most of the self-monitoring forms I employ, there is an open-ended column for client comments. These comments have often clued me in to factors I had overlooked or totally neglected in my initial assessments.

My second corollary point is that you should not be afraid to change your assessment in any given case. This may seem like a silly point to belabor, but it is my impression that some therapists become captivated by their first analyses of a problem. We all enter the therapy room with unavoidable biases and predilections about what we will find and how we will treat it. Some of us find operant contingencies, others find classical conditioning patterns, and still others "see" cognitive problems. Do not be afraid to modify your assessment or your therapy. There is an old saying that the main difference between wise men and fools is not whether they make mistakes—but whether they persevere in them.

There are a number of other practical problems in the question of *what* to self-monitor, such as the importance of clearly defined targets. It is usually unwarranted to assume that the client knows exactly what you want recorded. You may have described it in great detail and he or she may have nodded understandingly, but there is often some slippage in its execution. I can remember one woman in California who had heard my instructions on how to record her intake of sweets. After going into great detail on what I meant by one instance of snacking, she appeared to be ready to start. As she walked toward the door to leave, however, she turned and said, "But what if I get three pieces of candy in my mouth at once—is that one or three responses?" Since then, I have found it helpful to have clients practice self-monitoring in my presence before they start on their own. My usual sequence is as follows:

1) Give explicit definitions and examples of target events and explain their possible relevance to the problem(s) at hand;

2) Give explicit self-monitoring instructions (i.e., *how* to self-record);

3) Illustrate (model) self-monitoring with a sample form;

4) Ask the client to repeat the target definitions and self-monitoring instructions; and

5) Test their understanding by having them monitor several trial instances described by you.

CONCLUDING REMARKS

I have obviously only skimmed some of the practical issues in applications of self-monitoring. Hopefully, future research on assessment will make us better equipped with data on these topics. For the time being, however, we must settle for the less validated information provided by our own clinical experience and knowledge shared by our colleagues.

I would like to close with three final observations. First, although there is some recent evidence that self-monitoring need *not* be reliable in order to be reactive (cf. Broden, Hall & Mitts, 1971), this does not mean that reliability is not therapeutically valuable. If the therapist is adjusting his or her research strategies on the basis of self-reported information, the reliability and validity of that information are obviously important. For this reason, I recommend that you remain constantly aware of the reliability problems in self-monitoring, and that you obtain clients' permission to seek independent checks on the accuracy of their reports (e.g., Maletzky, 1974).

Secondly, I have not yet addressed the issue of how long to employ self-monitoring. It should be obvious from my earlier comments that I encourage changes in self-recording as they are deemed appropriate. If you end therapy with the identical recording system with which you began, it is either because a) the system was very efficient, or b) you were captivated by the assumption that you should remain faithful to the first system employed. Recall that the purposes of self-monitoring are basically twofold: 1) to provide accurate and relevant information for assessment, and 2) to assist in producing a therapeutic effect. Nowhere do these purposes demand that the system be inviolable. I argued earlier that the assessment function is often best served by a flexible and open-ended recording system. I would also argue that the therapeutic function of self-monitoring may be best served by a graduated series of recording assignments. I may be going out on a speculative limb here, but it is my opinion that the reactive effects of self-monitoring are at least partially accountable in terms of such factors as: 1) focused attention on target events; 2) subsequent self-reactions which are cued by this focused attention and by tangible records of performance; and 3) the provision of a relatively structured and tangibly analytic approach to the problem(s).

Some clients seem to develop a "psychological dependence" on their recording system—they feel that maintenance is contingent upon continued monitoring. Several weight control clients have displayed this pattern and panicked at the thought of not recording their performance. For the last two years, we have therefore been working on a "partial weaning system." Clients are taught to construct a variety of individualized self-recording systems so that they will be proficient in this important skill for future uses. However, during treatment and especially during follow-up, the frequency and the content of self-monitoring are gradually thinned. In our current maintenance phase in the obesity program (Mahoney & Mahoney, 1976), for example, clients eventually attain the status of part-time self-monitorers. Once per month they record their weight. If it is within an acceptable range, they go on about their life as usual. If it begins to trend upward or leaves the acceptable maintenance range, however, they have the previously developed skills to initiate a detailed recording system and a functional behavioral analysis. After determining and correcting problematic patterns, the personal scientist can then return to maintenance spot checks. This cybernetic feedback loop is one which, I think, serves therapeutic purposes very well (Mahoney, 1974b).

. My final comment deals with both a personal and a practical issue in self-monitoring. The evidence on social learning theory and vicarious processes suggests that *modeling* may be one of our most powerful clinical tools. It is for this reason that I often show clients some of my own charts and behavioral diaries from past and current personal change projects. In addition to a permanent monthly chart showing my body weight, exercise habits, and the like, I use temporary recording systems to assist me in the analysis and modification of such things as work patterns and writing. Sharing these personal records need not (and hopefully should not) convey a cold or obsessive penchant to clients. Rather, it should communicate a commitment to being intimately in touch with the factors that are influencing one's life—both in terms of correcting problems and in terms of enhancing personal growth. This kind of practical self-disclosure on the part of therapists is, I think, a valuable multipurpose strategy which will receive more extensive examination in the years to come.

10

METHODOLOGICAL PROBLEMS IN BEHAVIORAL OBSERVATION

BETH G. WILDMAN and MARILYN T. ERICKSON

Reliance on human observers to collect behavioral data has had a long history in psychological research with children. The earliest formal studies were narrative descriptions of children's behavior recorded by adults who had close relationships and continuous contact with them. Although these "baby biographies" provided a wealth of information which was used in subsequent normative research, they have been strongly criticized for their possible lack of objectivity.

Significant attention to the methodological problems associated with the use of human observers in psychological research began during the child development movement of the 1920's and 1930's (e.g., Arrington, 1932b). It was during this period that human observers were utilized to collect data on a wide variety of behaviors; these data, based on both longitudinal and cross-sectional approaches, have provided the foundation for our knowledge of developmental norms. Some of the methodological problems recognized during this early period were observer training, development of codes, synchronization of timing devices and attainment of representative samples of behavior.

Investigators of the 1940's and 1950's generated relatively few observational studies and focused more on data collected in laboratory or clinical, rather than natural, settings. This change of setting served to simplify the task of the observer in that the antecedent stimuli, or materials and cues provided to the child, were substantially controlled. In addition, the behaviors of interest were relatively restricted and easily lent themselves to operational definition. Such was the case for both the research on psychometric testing and the newly emerging research in experimental child

255

psychology. Experimental studies with children, in many cases, bypassed the human observer completely by mechanizing the response (e.g., pushing a button, pulling a lever).

It was not until the 1960's and 1970's that the human observer again had a significant role in the collection of behavioral data. This role was necessitated by the reliance of behavior therapists and behavior analysts on direct observation of behavior in natural environments. Methodological issues related to the use of human observers have increasingly been raised within the context of behavior analysis and therapy. In some cases, the issues are the same as those investigated by the earlier child development researchers, while in others, the issues are more unique to the problems posed by behavioral intervention programs.

In the examination of variables which affect the data collected by human observers, we are usually concerned with either *reliability* or *validity*. The reliability of observational data is generally measured by the extent to which observers agree in their recording of behavior (observer agreement). Research attention has been given to some of the variables which have been hypothesized to influence observer agreement and measures of observer agreement are currently considered to be necessary components of behavioral studies. Validity refers to the extent to which the data collected by observers agree with another criterion. In contrast to the research on reliability, validity research is sparse. Several reasons may be postulated for this relative lack of interest in validity research. First, the researchers may assume that the data obtained via behavioral observations represent the ultimate validity criterion and therefore require no further examination. Second, investigators may not agree on the criteria that should be used to test the validity of behavioral observations. And, third, certain aspects of validity research require permanent records, such as tape recordings and videotapes, which are difficult to obtain in many natural settings. For example, research on accuracy of recording may involve the comparison of behavioral records of observers with records obtained through multiple observations of the same behavorial sequences on videotape. In some cases, research studies approach, but do not directly examine, validity. For instance, studies examining the effects of variables on the frequency of responses recorded by observers may find differences, but we may have no way of determining which of the frequency counts is the "correct" or more valid one.

This chapter will examine the observer, instrumentation and subject variables which are considered to affect the reliability and validity of data collected by human observers. It will be restricted primarily to the research with adult observers and child subjects or clients, their peers and mediators.

OBSERVER VARIABLES

Training

The importance of training procedures for the performance of observers has been recognized by several authors (Johnson & Bolstad, 1973; O'Leary & Kent, 1973), but relatively little research has been devoted to this factor. Two classes of errors—timing errors and interpretive errors—appear to account for many disagreements among observers. Thomas, Loomis and Arrington (1933) found that both types of errors tended to decrease with additional observation experience; however, considerable individual differences among observers were obtained with respect to the number of film repetitions necessary for the most improvement to occur.

Several studies have documented the positive aspects of repeated observations of behavior early in an observer's experience. Arrington (1932b), using movie films to measure the improvement in observer agreement with repeated observations, found that maximum improvement occurred with repeated observations with the same partner by the third or fourth session. Bobbitt, Gordon and Jensen (1966) suggested that observers continue to improve even after reaching criterion. Wildman, Erickson and Kent (1975) also found significant increases in observer agreement over several observation sessions and hypothesized that these increases in observer agreement might have been due to the failure of the observers to reach stable levels of agreement during the brief training phase.

Moustakas, Sigel and Schalock (1956) suggested that one factor which might be responsible for observer disagreements was the observers' lack of familiarity with the behavior categories. However, using a subjective rating scale, Wahler and Leske (1973) found that their *untrained* observers were able to obtain adequate levels of interobserver agreement, but their agreement with a standard protocol was low.

DeMaster and Reid (1973) found that the quality of data collected by observers might be affected by the type of feedback received during training concerning observer accuracy and agreement. They found that the data collected by observers who had discussed their protocols with their partners and with the experimenter, and who had received a report of their agreement with the criterion, were more accurate and had higher agreement scores than observers who had only discussed their protocols with their partners, or who had received no feedback at all.

Wildman, Erickson and Kent (1975) manipulated the standard by which their observers were trained by training one group with a single trainer, while a second group of observers trained itself. No differences in observer agreement were obtained; however, the one-trainer group recorded significantly more behaviors than did the self-training group. In addition, the group trained by one trainer recorded behavior more consistently than did the self-training group (e.g., the variance of the mean number of behaviors recorded per interval was smaller for the one-trainer group than for the self-training group). Another finding of this study was that the agreement percentages obtained within observer-pairs were greater than those obtained when members of different pairs compared their protocols.

Kent, O'Leary, Diament and Dietz (1974) and Hawkins and Dobes (1977) obtained similar results with regard to within pair and between pair reliabilities. These findings may be accounted for by the fact that observers in these studies compared their protocols to their partner's during training and had more experience and greater familiarity with their partner's interpretations of the code than they did with other observers' interpretations of the code. Hawkins and Dobes believe that the development of such implicit definitions between observers who collaborate can be reduced by writing better explicit definitions. The ability of observers to conform to implicit rating standards has also been supported by the Romanczyk, Kent, Diament and O'Leary (1973) study in which observers were found to change their interpretations of the behavior code to conform with the idiosyncratic interpretations of their reliability assessor.

Mash and McElwee (1974) found that the pattern of behavior observed during training may have an effect on the observers' performance during later data collection sessions. Observer accuracy was affected by whether training experiences involved sequences in which one target behavior was followed immediately by another target behavior.

Reactivity

Research has revealed that human observers may change their recording of behavior when they are aware that they are being observed (reactivity). A difference between observer agreement scores obtained with the observers' awareness (overt) and those obtained without the knowledge of the observers (covert) is probably the best documented phenomenon in the observation methodology literature. The research of Reid (1970) on the differences between overt and covert means of reliability assessment initiated a surge of interest in observation methodology, with the result that others have replicated and elaborated on his work (e.g., Romanczyk, Kent, Diament & O'Leary, 1973; Taplin & Reid, 1973; Wildman, Erickson & Kent, 1975).

Observers in the Reid study were informed that their protocols were being compared with a criterion protocol during training (overt assessment). After training was completed, the observers were informed that they would be viewing "unscored" tapes, and that they would be the only ones who would view these tapes (covert assessment). A large decrease in reliability was obtained from the last overt assessment session to the first covert assessment session. These results were important in encouraging further research, even though Reid's design was inadequate for evaluating the differences between overt and covert assessment because of the confound between experimental condition and time.

As part of a larger study, Romanczyk, Kent, Diament and O'Leary (1973) included a more adequate test of the differences between overtly assessed and covertly assessed reliabilities. In this study, reliabilities were assessed overtly and covertly within each session. The results replicated Reid's (1970) finding that reliability was lower during covert assessments than during overt assessments. In addition, observers recorded 25% less behavior during covert assessments than during overt assessments. This study added another manipulation which demonstrated differences related to the person calibrating agreement with an observer. The two reliability assessors adopted idiosyncratic interpretations for four of the nine categories, permitting the authors to obtain data about changes which occurred when assessors with subtle differences in their definitions of certain behaviors were employed. The data indicated that the observers shifted their interpretations of the categories to match the idiosyncratic criteria of the assessors.

In a study designed to expand on Reid's (1970) findings, Taplin and Reid (1973) varied the type of procedure used to assess the reliabilities of three groups of observers. After training, one group was told that its reliabilities would not be checked (no check). Another group was told that its reliabilities would be checked without their advance knowledge 20% of the time (random check). A third group was informed that its reliabilities would be checked on occasion and that it would be told about these sessions in advance (spot check). An immediate and significant drop in reliability was found for all three groups when the observers moved from the training phase to the data collection phase of the study. Although the reliability obtained during spot checks was found to be significantly higher than the reliabilities obtained before and after spot checks, no overall differences were found among the three groups. Thus, no procedure has yet been demonstrated to prevent the serious reduction in observer performance when reliability is not being checked.

Several studies suggest that observer agreement might be affected by the status of the experimenter (Taplin & Reid, 1973) and by motivational factors (Guttman, Specter, Sigel, Rakoff & Epstein, 1971). Taplin and Reid found that observers trained by a high-status trainer (faculty member) obtained significantly *lower* reliabilities than those trained by trainers of lower professional status (graduate students). Since only one faculty member trainer was used, these results are confounded with the personal characteristics of the trainer.

Guttman, Specter, Sigel, Rakoff and Epstein (1971) reported that the motivation of their observers affected the obtained reliabilities. These authors stated that the morale and consistency of the observers were affected by the frustrating, mechanical aspects of coding. They reported that morale improved when regular meetings were held with the observers and problems were discussed. An alternative explanation for the improvement obtained with regular meetings might be that definitions of codes were clarified and reviewed. Regular sessions are held with observers for this purpose at the Oregon Research Institute (Johnson & Bolstad, 1973). Reid, Skindrud, Taplin and Jones (1973) conjectured that motivation might be manipulated with contingent money.

O'Leary and Kent (1973) and Kent, O'Leary, Diament and Dietz (1974) discussed the possibility of observer cheating affecting obtained data. For example, when observer agreement was computed by the observers, the obtained percentages were significantly higher than when agreement percentages were calculated by the investigators on the same data. O'Leary and Kent also reported that observers achieved higher levels of reliability when they observed the subjects' behaviors without the experimenter present, rather than in his presence.

Drift

A problem which confronts most investigators is the maintenance of the accuracy of their measurement devices. Deterioration of the accuracy of these devices due to autonomous changes in the device itself has been referred to as "instrument decay" by Campbell and Stanley (1963). According to these authors, in the case of human observers, changes over time may be due to fatigue or learning, among other variables. Johnson and Bolstad (1973) defined "observer drift" as instrument decay. Both these authors and O'Leary and Kent (1973) used "observer drift" to refer to variations in how observers record behavior over time, and they cautioned that observer drift may render data collected during one experimental condition incomparable to data collected during other conditions.

O'Leary and Kent (1973) and Johnson and Bolstad (1973) also used the term "drift" to describe the finding that data collected by groups of observers who rate together tend to be incompatible with the data of other observers who do not rate with the group, even if all the observers were trained together. This phenomenon, which has been labelled "consensual observer drift" by Johnson and Bolstad, has received empirical support from the findings of Wildman, Erickson and Kent (1975) and Hawkins and Dobes (1977), in which agreement percentages within observer pairs were found to be higher than those obtained between observer pairs.

Finally, "observer drift" has been used to describe the significant decline in observer agreement that may occur from the conclusion of observer training to the beginning of data collection (Taplin & Reid, 1973). However, the decrease in observer agreement obtained by Taplin and Reid, as discussed in the previous section on reactivity, might well be explained by the fact that as observers switched from the training to the data collection phases of the experiment, they also switched from constant, overt reliability assessment to other, less reactive assessment conditions. The results obtained by Taplin and Reid would most clearly be described as reactive effects of testing by Campbell and Stanley (1963), rather than as observer drift.

Bias

Whenever humans are involved in the process of collecting and/or recording data, the effects of their biases must be considered. One source of bias which was considered in the early observation literature, but has not received the attention of modern investigators, is the individual rating tendencies of observers. Rating tendencies include preferences for, or overweighting of, certain categories and tendencies to record events earlier or later than other observers do (Arrington, 1932a). Thomas, Loomis and Arrington (1933), using observations of film characters, found that certain observers tended to record behaviors either one interval earlier or one interval later than the other observers did. The authors also found that different observers tended to favor one category over another category, resulting in consistent errors in the record.

The more common view of bias refers to how observation protocols may be affected by hypotheses the observer may have about what types of behavior the subject should exhibit. These hypotheses may be given to the observer explicitly or implicitly by the experimenter, or the observer may generate his own hypotheses based on prior experience or other stimuli in the observation environment. A great deal of research attention has been focused on ascertaining the effect of an observer's expectations on the frequency of recorded behaviors. Investigations aimed at the study of observer bias have yielded inconsistent results, however.

Recent research on observer bias has generally given observers specific expectations. Skindrud (1973), reviewing the current literature relevant to the issues of observer bias, reported research evidence that observer expectations may result in changes in observation protocols in the direction of expectation (e.g., Azrin, Holz, Ulrich & Goldiamond, 1961).

Although no statistical analyses were performed, Scott, Burton and Yarrow (1967) found that an observer who was aware of the experimental hypotheses recorded different behaviors than did uninformed observers. Since the informed observer in this study was the experimenter, it is probable that factors in addition to expectation may have been involved. The authors suggested that the informed observer might either have been biased or more sensitive to the relevant behaviors than the uninformed observers were.

Skindrud (1972) failed to obtain significant differences between the protocols of observers who were informed of the treatment status of families (normal vs. deviant) and observers who were uninformed of the families' status. He suggested that the slight differences may have been due to differences in the groups, rather than whether or not they were informed of the treatment status of the families. These differences, according to the author, may have been related to such individual factors as the amount of observational experience, attention paid to the subjects' behaviors, age and familiarity with children.

A series of group studies has been conducted in which observers were given specific expectancy instructions concerning changes in the behaviors of target subjects. In the first of these studies, by Kass and O'Leary

(1970), groups of observers were informed that the frequency of disruptive behavior should either increase or decrease during treatment. A third group of observers was told that the experimenters were unsure of the effects of the treatment on the behavior of the subjects. The results of this study indicated that all groups recorded a decrease in disruptive behavior with treatment, but that the decrease was sharpest for the group of observers who were given the expectation that the frequency of disruptive behavior would decrease. However, the Kass and O'Leary study (1970) has been criticized on methodological grounds (Johnson & Bolstad, 1973; Kent, O'Leary, Diament & Dietz, 1974). Since the three groups of observers were trained separately, the percentage of agreement between observers from different groups would probably have been low relative to the agreement percentage of observers within each group.

Skindrud (1972) attempted to replicate the study by Kass and O'Leary (1970). Groups of observers were told that a child was expected to be more deviant, or less deviant, when the father was present than when he was absent. A third group served as a control group and was not given any "expectations" concerning the effect of the father's presence or absence on the child's behavior. Contrary to the results of Kass and O'Leary, no evidence of observer bias was obtained.

Kent, O'Leary, Diament and Dietz (1974) also attempted to replicate the Kass and O'Leary (1970) study. One group of observers was informed that a decrease in disruptive behavior was predicted, and another group was told that no change was expected. Videotapes were selected such that the frequency of behaviors to be observed over time was stable. Although the subjective verbal evaluations of the observers matched the "expectations" that they were given, no significant differences were obtained in the behavioral recordings. This discrepancy between verbal report and other data is much like those described by Barlow in Chapter 11, by Geer in Chapter 7, and by Lang in Chapter 6.

Observers in a study by O'Leary, Kent and Kantowitz (1975) received differential feedback concerning the conformity of their behavior ratings with experimenter expectation. Observers were informed that a decrease was expected in the frequency of occurrence of two categories of behavior, and no change was expected in the frequency of the other two categories. Significant decreases were obtained in the recorded frequency of the categories for which a decrease in frequency was predicted, and no differences were obtained for the other two categories. The results indicated that when no change in frequency actually occurred, the prediction of a decrease in behavior accompanied by differential

experimenter feedback led to biased records. Since the variables associated with observer bias are by no means clear, a group of observers
without feedback should have been included in this study to document
the insufficiency of prediction alone.

A prerequisite to initiating an observational study is the selection of a
behavior code, a sampling procedure, a method for calculating interobserver agreement and a timing device. In choosing a code, the investigator must first consider the clarity of the behavioral definitions and
the number of different behaviors that will be included in the code.
A method for sampling subjects' behaviors must also be chosen, including
selecting the starting time and length of each session, and the order in
which multiple subjects are to be observed. Finally, the investigator must
select what device (e.g., stopwatch, audioprompter) observers will use
to time the observation intervals.

Codes

Although many behavior codes have been devised, few have been used
repeatedly (exceptions are the Disruptive Behavior Code, O'Leary, Kaufman, Kass & Drabman, 1970; and the Family Interaction Code, Patterson,
Ray, Shaw & Cobb, 1969) or researched, resulting in a deficit of information concerning the identification and elaboration of code variables affecting reliability and validity of observational data. However, certain assumptions have been made about various aspects of codes. For example,
an important assumption associated with behavioral observation has been
that clear, objective definitions of behavior are necessary for the collection of reliable and valid data by human observers. Hawkins and Dobes
(1977) obtained results which suggest that carefully constructed,
objective definitions may contribute to improved observer agreement
scores. However, there remains a deficit of empirical data concerning
the relative contribution of objective definitions to observer agreement
scores.

In addition to their concern for supplying observers with adequate
definitions of target behaviors, investigators have also attempted to avoid
overburdening observers by restricting the number of behaviors to be
recorded. Although the research concerning the relationship between
the number of behavior categories in a code and observer agreement is
scant, the assumption has been that the reliability and validity of the

data would decrease as the number of behavior categories was increased. Mash and McElwee (1974), within the context of a larger study, trained observers with either a four-category or an eight-category code. The results indicated that the observers who were trained with four categories achieved high, stable levels of agreement more rapidly than those observers trained with eight categories. However, since the eight-category code was obtained by subdividing each of the categories in the four-category code, the increase in the number of categories also entailed a concomitant change in the discriminability of the behaviors, thus confounding discriminability of individual behaviors with the complexity of the code. The authors reasoned that the differences could not have been influenced by memorization of the definitions alone and that specific demands during the recording process itself might have been involved (e.g., speed of recording, motor skills).

Arrington (1932b) found that for those observers who showed the most consistent improvement and who had achieved high percentages of agreement, no differences in agreement were obtained when two aspects of behavior were observed, in comparison with one aspect. These results suggest that a particular level of complexity may be necessary before a decrease in reliability occurs.

Sampling Procedures

Once a code has been selected, the investigator must decide when these behaviors will be observed. For most clinical studies, subjects are observed at the same time or during the same general activity each day to control variability due to changes in the stimulus environment and, therefore, the opportunity to engage in target behaviors. Observation sessions are usually scheduled during periods when the target behavior is likely to occur.

In addition to choosing the observation period, the investigator must decide what type of data recording procedure would be most appropriate. The most basic recording procedure is a frequency count, in which observers count the number of times the target behaviors occur during each observation session. Although this method may be adequate for some purposes, it has two weaknesses. First, information concerning the time sequence and the correlation between behaviors is lost, and second, observer agreement measures on frequency data cannot take into account when the observers recorded the occurrences of behaviors, unless event recorders are used to record the data. An alternative method which is

often used by behavioral researchers and clinicians and does not have
these weaknesses is an interval recording procedure, in which the observation session is divided into short intervals of equal length, usually
five to 20 seconds long. Observers are usually instructed to simply record
whether or not each target behavior was occurring during the interval,
but frequency of occurrence within each interval can also be recorded.

Although the research is scant, there are certain logical assumptions
about these sampling procedures which may be relevant to choosing a
code. For example, when an interval recording procedure is used in which
a behavior is recorded as either present or absent, low frequency behaviors may be overestimated and high frequency behaviors may be
underestimated when compared to the rate of occurrence that might be
obtained if a frequency count method of recording had been used to
collect the data. Empirical support for this assumption has been obtained
by Powell, Martindale and Kulp (1975) and Repp, Roberts, Slack, Repp
and Berkler (1976). Investigators have hypothesized that the length of
observation intervals may also have an effect on the representativeness
and accuracy of observational data. When the length of the observation
intervals closely corresponds to the duration of the behavior, the data
obtained should be a more accurate representation of both the frequency
and the duration of behavior than when the length of the observation
intervals is either shorter or longer than the duration of the behavior.
Milar and Hawkins (1976) and Powell, Martindale and Kulp (1975)
have obtained data which support this hypothesis.

When observational data are to be collected on multiple subjects, a
procedure for sampling the behavior of each of the subjects must be
established. In one of the few studies concerned with this problem,
Thomson, Holmberg and Baer (1974) compared several methods of
sampling by extracting samples from a continuous 64-minute record on
each of two children and two teachers. They found that records, obtained
by observing each of the four subjects successively for four minutes
each for four rotations through the subjects, matched the continuous
record better than either a procedure which recorded each subject for
16 continuous minutes or a method in which each teacher-subject pair
was observed for 32 minutes, alternating between the teacher and the
child every four minutes until the 32 minutes had elapsed. In another
study, Gonzalez, Martin and Dysart (1973) had observers record interactions between parents and children using seven-second intervals. These
data were well represented by sample data taken from every sixth interval.

Observer Agreement

A widely accepted means of judging the adequacy of observational data has been to measure the extent to which two (or more) observers agree on their recording of behaviors. Behavioral researchers have assumed that agreement on the occurrences and/or nonoccurrences of target behaviors suggests that observers are responding to the same events. Thus, observer agreement is an indication of the replicability of observational data.

One method for calculating observer agreement on interval data has been to divide the number of times observers agree by the sum of the number of times observers agree plus the number of times observers disagree. Although this method has been very popular, considerable discussion has focused on the definition of an agreement (Bijou, Peterson, Harris, Allen & Johnston, 1969; Hawkins & Dotson, 1975; O'Leary & Kent, 1973; Repp, Deitz, Boles, Deitz & Repp, 1974). An agreement can be defined three ways: 1) agreement on occurrences of behavior only; 2) agreement on nonoccurrences of behavior only; and 3) agreement on occurrences and nonoccurrences of behavior. The most conservative method, defining agreements on the basis of occurrences only, has usually been recommended (Johnson & Bolstad, 1973; O'Leary & Kent, 1973). However, other authors have suggested that separate agreement percentages be calculated for agreements defined by occurrences only and for agreements defined by nonoccurrences only (Bijou, Peterson, Harris, Allen & Johnston, 1969; Hawkins & Dotson, 1975). Other, less popular, methods for calculating observer agreement include correlation, and dividing the number of occurrences obtained by the observer who recorded the smaller frequency by the frequency obtained by the observer who recorded the larger number of responses (see Bijou, Peterson, Harris, Allen & Johnston, 1969, and Johnson & Bolstad, 1973 for a discussion of these methods).

A major weakness of the agreements divided by agreements plus disagreements methods of calculating agreement is the lack of criteria for establishing acceptable levels of observer agreement. Johnson and Bolstad (1973) suggested a means for calculating the amount of agreement expected by chance, which could be used as a basis of comparison for the obtained level of observer agreement. This procedure falls short of supplying an adequate criterion (Yelton, Wildman & Erickson, 1977). Alternative methods for calculating observer agreement which have established standards for comparison, such as probability distributions, have been presented by Hartmann (1977) and Yelton, Wildman and Erickson (1977). These authors also review the more conventional methods for computing agreement and discuss the inadequacies of these methods.

Timing Devices

Stopwatches, which have been the most popular means of timing behavior, frequently fail to maintain synchronization. After about one hour of use, Arrington (1932b) reported that stopwatches differed from each other as much as 3.3 seconds. More recently, Bijou, Peterson and Ault (1968) advised that stopwatches be checked periodically in order to assess their agreement. With inexpensive devices available which can signal multiple observers simultaneously, such as cassette recorders or audioprompters (Leifer & Leifer, 1971), experimenters should consider these alternatives before deciding to use stopwatches.

SUBJECT VARIABLES

A frequent goal of direct systematic observation is to obtain data about "typical" behavior. Data are usually collected in naturalistic environments in order to obtain representative samples of behaviors, but even with rigorous controls over the observer and careful consideration of instrumental factors, reseachers may obtain data which do not reflect the typical behaviors of their subjects.

Being observed may create a unique stimulus environment for the subject. That is, subjects' behaviors when they are aware of the observer's presence may not be representative of subjects' behaviors when they are not being observed. Mediators (e.g., parents, teachers) may also respond differently when observers are present, which may, in turn, lead to changes in the behavior of subjects. For example, Zegiob, Arnold and Forehand (1975) found that mothers tended to play more, to be more positive in their verbal behavior and to structure their children's activities more when they were aware that their children were being observed than when they were unaware of the observation. Some of the problems associated with subject and mediator reactivity to being observed may be alleviated after the subjects become "habituated" to the presence of the observers. However, the length of time necessary for the subjects' and mediators' behaviors to stabilize and to resemble behaviors which occur when no observer is present is unknown.

Ideally, observational data should be obtained completely unobtrusively.

Such data would not be contaminated by the reactivity of the subjects to being observed. However, data collection without the consent of subjects (or a responsible adult) presents ethical problems as well as technical difficulties in many settings (e.g., settings without one-way mirrors).

Earlier research on the reaction of subjects to being observed has suggested that the effects may not be strong enough to negate individual differences in children (Jersild & Meigs, 1939) and mediators (Schulman, Shoemaker & Moelis, 1962). More recently, researchers have considered the possibility that the process of being observed might exaggerate or even create individual differences, rather than diminish them. Lobitz and Johnson (1975) conjectured that parents might manipulate their child's behavior when being observed, even though they had been instructed to behave naturally to insure their child's acceptance into a treatment program for problem children. According to the authors, available evidence suggested that during home observation, both parents of problem children and parents of normal children probably attempted to encourage their children to behave in a socially desirable manner.

The reactions of subjects and mediators to being observed may not be determined solely by the fact that their behaviors are being monitored. Subjects' reactions may be controlled by more subtle stimuli, such as the characteristics of the observation situation as well as the observer. The only aspect of the observation situation which has been investigated is the obstrusiveness of the observations. Callahan and Alevizos (1973) found that patients' behavior did not change when television cameras, in addition to observers, were placed in the observation setting. Manipulation of the frequency of observation sessions resulted in only minor changes in patient behaviors when two observations per day were compared with all-day continuous observations. However, the subjects in this study were chronic inpatient adults with low levels of activity.

Samph (1969) and Bales (1950) investigated the effects of the conspicuousness of observers by comparing data obtained when observers were absent to those obtained when observers were present. Samph found that teachers used more praise, accepted student ideas more and criticized students less when observers were present in the classroom than when data were collected unobtrusively with a tape recorder. Bales found no differences in the behavior of adult subjects when observers were present and when observers were behind a one-way mirror, whether or not the subjects were aware that they were being observed. Webb, Campbell, Schwartz and Sechrest (1966) warned that Bales' results should be interpreted with caution, since the experiment was conducted in a laboratory setting, and subjects knew that they were being tested in some ways.

This comment implies that even when the recording apparatus is inconspicuous, knowledge that one is being observed might affect subjects' behaviors. Using small, wireless transmitters which broadcasted to a tape recorder, Johnson, Christenson and Bellamy (1976) found that the behavior of parents and their children who were referred to a clinic for behavior problems changed as a function of knowing that they were being monitored.

In addition to factors related to the obtrusiveness of the observations, personal characteristics of the observer have also been implicated as relevant to subject reactivity. Martin, Gelfand and Hartmann (1971) recorded the amount of imitative aggression engaged in by children in the presence of various types of onlookers. After viewing an aggressive model, children were placed in a playroom alone or with either a male or a female adult or peer onlooker. The onlookers did not attend to the children. The results indicated that both the age and the sex of the onlooker affected the subjects' behavior (e.g., peer onlookers facilitated aggressive responding). In contrast, Callahan and Alevizos (1973) found no differences in the behaviors of their inpatient subjects as a function of sex of the observer. The differences in the behaviors observed, as well as the characteristics of the subjects, might account for the differences in the findings of these two studies.

Several authors have suggested that subjects, especially children, will habituate to being observed and that reactivity may be a problem only during the initial observations (Bijou, Peterson, Harris, Allen & Johnston, 1969; Weick, 1968; Werry & Quay, 1969). Callahan and Alevizos (1973) failed to obtain evidence of habituation with their adult subjects; however, they had found no reactivity to observation and perhaps should not have expected habituation. Purcell and Brady (1966) obtained data supportive of habituation effects when samples of the verbal behavior of adolescents in a cottage setting were obtained with the use of FM transmitters. Subjects and house parents reported that they "forgot" about the transmitters after a few days. In addition, no differences were found in the house parents' ratings of the subjects' behaviors before and with the transmitter. The data from this study were subjective, and the measures were probably not as sensitive to behavior changes as objective measures would have been.

In a more systematic study, Johnson and Bolstad (1975) found no differences in the tape recorded verbal behavior of either parents or their children when observers were present and when they were absent. In addition, no changes in behavior were obtained across the six days of data collection. These results may have been due to the fact that parents were informed that their verbalizations were constantly being recorded.

The behavioral effects of being observed remain largely unknown. Investigators should, and frequently do, allow a period of time for behavior to stabilize before beginning data collection. Since the stimuli present when one's behavior is being monitored are usually different from the stimulus complex when one is unobserved, we cannot assume that behavior during observation, even after it has stabilized, represents "typical" behavior.

Another subject variable of potential importance is the individuality of response topography. Investigators have found that observers do not obtain similar levels of observer agreement for different subjects. That is, individual differences in the topography of behaviors may affect how well observers agree on their occurrence (Arrington, 1932b; Gellert, 1955; Good, 1963; Richards & Irwin, 1936). Those aspects of behavior which have been implicated as factors affecting observer agreement have been frequency (Johnson & Bolstad, 1973; Richards & Irwin, 1936), the number of different behaviors emitted by the subject (Reid, Skindrud, Taplin & Jones, 1973), and the duration of behaviors (Thomas, Loomis & Arrington, 1933). Richards and Irwin reported that infrequent responses tend to be associated with poor agreement; however, this effect depends on how agreement is calculated (Hawkins & Dotson, 1975). Thomas, Loomis and Arrington suggested that, within a category, there may be no consistent relationship between the frequency of behavior and observer agreement. The authors also conjectured that the relative duration of a behavior, without the subject's engaging in an alternative behavior, might be related to the difficulty of the observer's task. That is, the longer the duration of a behavior, the better observer agreement should be.

Rapid, complex interactions might be difficult to observe (Good, 1963). Reid, Skindrud, Taplin and Jones (1973) and Jones, Reid and Patterson (1975) also discussed the possibility of a negative correlation between complexity and observer agreement. Complexity, according to the authors, is the number of discriminations required by an observer during a data collection session and can be measured by the number of different categories rated.

Consideration of the methodological problems associated with behavioral observation can easily lead to a less-than-optimistic view about the status of the area. However, the available research literature does permit us to formulate a number of suggestions for improving the reliability and validity of observational data. Some of these suggestions can easily be incorporated into assessment procedures, while others will require varying amounts of additional resources (e.g., time, equipment, personnel).

The training of observers should include samples of behavioral sequences and environmental settings which closely resemble the behaviors and settings in which data collection will occur. Ideally, all observers should be trained together and their ratings compared with a single standard. The training period should be long enough for the observers to reach an asymptote of agreement for each behavior in the code. Videotapes could be used for both training and the development of a standard rating procedure for extensive programs in the same setting (e.g., elementary schools).

Conditions for assessing observer agreement should be maintained to assure consistent levels of agreement. The research suggests that continuous overt monitoring and randomized, covert monitoring (with the appropriate instructions) generate the most stable levels of agreement. In situations where more than one subject is to be observed, two observers could be independently programmed to observe different subjects during some of the intervals and the same child during the remaining intervals.

One possible way of overcoming the systematic effects of time could be to videotape all sessions and then have the observers rate the sessions in random order. In addition, continuation of training with observers' viewing standardized videotapes intermittently throughout data collection may attenuate observer drift.

Observer bias can be minimized by avoiding the communication of experimental hypotheses to the observers and reinforcement of observers for data supporting experimental hypotheses. It may be that explicit instructions to the observers indicating that the experimenter does not know what is likely to occur during the sessions would be preferable to an avoidance of the topic.

Consideration should be given to previously published codes for which operational definitions have already been developed and data on observer training and agreement presented. However, Hawkins and Dobes (1977) found that some codes' definitions may be less adequate than observer agreement data would suggest. It should be kept in mind that some behaviors are more difficult to rate than others and that pretesting of code variables may save the investigator a large amount of observer training time. The lack of clear research data concerning the effects of the number of categories rated suggests that investigators should be reasonably conservative about the number of variables included in the behavioral code, particularly in situations where the observers do not have a long-term commitment to using the code (e.g., are "volunteer" undergraduates rather than paid employees).

Since being observed may in itself change the behavior of the subject and the subject's mediator, observation should be conducted as unobtrusively as possible. When observation behind a one-way mirror is not possible, observers should position themselves to the back or the side of the subject and avoid both eye contact and interaction with the subject or others in the room. Subject and mediator reactivity may be minimized by alloting a period of time for behaviors to stabilize before data collection is initiated.

Although there are methodological problems associated with the collection of observational data, behavioral observation is clearly the method of choice for many clinical studies. The replicability of these studies would be substantially improved if investigators consistently reported their procedures for training observers, assessing observer agreement and collecting data.

Part V

ISSUES, INNOVATIONS, AND TRENDS IN BEHAVIORAL ASSESSMENT

Editors' Comments

In the introductory chapter of this book several issues were raised for the reader to consider in pursuing the chapters that followed. Some of these issues have been dealt with extensively in the first four parts of the book, some have not been dealt with at all. The present section has been designed to fill in some of the gaps. Unfortunately, few of the issues are resolved. Indeed, additional ones are raised. This part of the book also presents some innovative approaches for conducting assessment in clinical and educational contexts, and for evaluating the adequacy of our measuring devices. Finally, it attempts to characterize the current status of the field and to project future trends.

In the first chapter in this section, David Barlow, whose innovative behavior analyses of various adult outpatient problems are well known among behavior therapists, takes issue with a common practice among behavior analysts: the blanket devaluing of client verbal reports. He illustrates an interesting use of verbal report as one criterion of a compulsive handwasher's success in therapy. At the same time, he also documents excellent case examples illustrating the fact that verbal report data often do deviate markedly from physiological or motoric data. But he goes an important step further and demonstrates *experimenter control* over such deviations, thus exemplifying the very kind of research he is calling for, the analysis of verbal report data.

Barlow describes the development of methods for producing male sexual arousal and compares them for resistance to suppression by verbal instruction. He compares methods for measuring male arousal that will be useful in both laboratory and clinic. He presents data on arousal in populations with differing sexual adjustment problems and thus offers evidence relevant to the measurements employed.

Measures of depression are also compared. Two rating scale measures, which are based primarily on verbal report, are shown to be less accurate in predicting post-hospitalization adjustment than is a non-inferential, behavioral measure. Finally, Barlow presents a study in which 24-hour, automated recording of a clinically significant behavior in a natural environment was accomplished. There have been few such studies. The research presented by Barlow will interest readers, and the issues identified will point the way for much further effort.

The chapter by Livingston on psychometric techniques for criterion-referenced tests is the first of two papers designed to bridge the narrow gap between assessment in clinical and educational contexts. The later chapter by White is the second.

Livingston alerts readers to a recent but widespread movement in educational assessment away from exclusive reliance on norm-referenced measures. The increasing use of criterion-referenced measures in educational contexts has paralleled the emergence of behavioral assessment in clinical psychology, but the two trends have heretofore been independent, with neither benefitting from developments in the other. Livingston draws attention to the similarities between criterion-referenced testing and behavioral assessment, and suggests that newly developed psychometric procedures for evaluating the adequacy of the former may also be applicable to the latter. This chapter and White's have been included in the book because of the editors' belief that assessment in education differs from clinical assessment principally in terms of content, not method, and thus, a book on methodology should have implications for measurement in both contexts. At this point in its development, methodological sophistication in behavioral assessment appears to be lagging behind that in educational assessment, particularly the criterion-referenced testing movement. Thus, behavioral assessors should benefit from papers on criterion-referenced measures generally, and from those attempting to delineate parallels, specifically.

After noting similarities in the basic assumptions of behavioral and criterion-referenced assessors, Livingston suggests measures for evaluating the reliability and validity of devices used by either. The most important interterpretation of test scores in either case will derive from comparisons of individual scores against an absolute criterion rather than against the mean of numerous individual scores. When an absolute criterion is used, traditional measures of reliability and validity need not be modified accordingly. Thus, Livingston offers a criterion-referenced reliability coefficient that serves as a basic measure for evaluating the various forms of score generalizability that are likely to be of interest to educators and clinicians alike.

A distinction between measurement and classification is noted by Livingston, and different ways of determining the reliability with which an instrument measures on the one hand and classifies on the other are described. The alert reader will discover that the procedures suggested for assessing classification reliability (e.g., 2 × 2 contingency tables, *phi* coefficient, Cohen's Kappa) will apply equally in determining interobserver agreement in the use of direct observation procedures. Indeed, behavioral assessors using such methods might benefit from greater use of some of the reliability measures suggested by Livingston.

One problem common to both behavioral and criterion-referenced assessors, and not mentioned by Livingston, is the establishment of the criterion against which to refer individual scores. The traditional assessor does not have this difficulty, of course, since the mean of an appropriate standardization group provides the "criterion." However, in assessing competent behavior in various contexts, the behavioral assessor is faced with definitional problems concerning just what constitutes competence. This issue is addressed directly by McFall in Chapter 5, and again in White's chapter and in the concluding chapter of the book (see also Hawkins, 1975).

Livingston makes some points which should have profound implications for behavioral assessment generally, and they deserve emphasis here. For example, consider the traditional practice of validating new measures against old ones by calculating product-moment correlations. This procedure is reasonable when scores are interpreted against norms or group means. However, the method is inadequate for validating criterion-referenced and behavioral measures since their scores are interpreted against an absolute criterion, and deviations in scores from the criterion should be considered in validating one measure against another. Notice that such criterion-relevant validity coefficients require the definition of criteria for both measures being correlated. Thus, if one were to develop a new, shorter measure of effective interpersonal behavior that was to be validated against a longer, already existing one, both measures would need to have scores above which performance was considered to be competent and below which it was not. Validity for the new measure would be determined by using Livingston's criterion-relevant reliability (validity) coefficient. Similar considerations would apply to establishing the reliability of the new measure as well. To date, we are not aware of any examples of the use of such modified psychometric procedures in the evaluation of behavioral assessment methods. Perhaps their appearance awaits a fuller appreciation by psychologists of the parallels between behavioral assessment in clinical contexts and criterion-referenced assessment in educational ones. Livingston's chapter should go a long way toward producing such an appreciation.

One of the points Livingston makes in his chapter is that developers and users of assessment devices of all kinds are concerned with different sources of variation in scores on the device. Traditionally, scores have been viewed as composites of "true" and error variance, with a variety of factors contributing to the latter. As Livingston notes, and Jones elaborates, an alternative way of viewing scores and influences on them is provided by generalizability theory (Cronbach, Gleser, Nanda, & Rajaratnam, 1972). Rather than view scores as composites of true and error variance, generalizability theory holds that scores belong to various universes of generalization. That is, they may be generalized in various ways, e.g., across different scorers, different times, settings, and so on. Thus, instead of referring to the reliability and validity of a given measure, proponents of generalizability theory merely speak of its scores being generalizable in some ways and not in others.

As Jones notes, the relevance of generalizability theory for behavioral assessment has recently been suggested by several authors (e.g., Cone, in press; Jones, Reid & Patterson, 1975). Jones cautions against an uncritical acceptance of generalizability theory, however, and differentiates between its conceptual aspects on the one hand and its analytical aspects on the other. The former, he says, may have greater utility for behavioral assessment than the latter.

Just as the criterion-referenced reliability and validity coefficients suggested by Livingston may offer new psychometric procedures specifically relevant for evaluating behavioral assessment measures, so might Cronbach's generalizability theory. However, its limitations in this regard are pointed out by Jones, primarily in terms of the inter-individual differences model upon which it is based. As he notes, behavioral assessment procedures, especially the direct observation methods of the applied behavior analyst, seem based upon an intra-individual differences model. Jones clearly describes the assumptions at the base of generalizability theory that would be violated by the application of its analytic procedures to assessment data collected on single subjects. A careful reading of his chapter is important, as the arguments against generalizability theory procedures may apply to other inter-individually based psychometric procedures as well. To what extent, for example, are Jones' criticisms applicable to the criterion-referenced reliability and validity coefficients suggested by Livingston? If they do apply, what procedures are left to behavioral assessors interested in establishing the quality of their measuring devices? Is it possible that the inapplicability of Cronbach's analytical procedures to behavioral assessment includes only measures used to show change over time in single subjects or in groups of subjects treated individually? The answers to these and other questions stimulated by Jones will require additional empirical and conceptual analysis and will undoubtedly have a major influence on the future development of behavioral assessment as a discipline.

Consistent with the intra-individual assessment paradigm emphasized by Jones, and continuing the parallels between behavioral and educational assessment initiated by Livingston, the chapter by White calls attention to some potential contributions from the precision teaching movement. White describes the basic measurement characteristics of precision teaching and emphasizes the value of rate data, or measures combining counts of behavior and the time over which it occurs. Noting that, traditionally, educators have favored accuracy measures, usually in the form of percentage correct, White calls attention to an increasing interest in fluency measures as well. That is, educators are becoming more and more interested in not only whether a child was 100% correct, but also in how long it took the child to complete the work. The more quickly the child works at a given level of accuracy, the more fluent the child is in the behavior. A strong case can be made for the value of rate measures in clinical behavioral assessment as well.

White echoes Livingston's support of criterion-referenced assessment and supplements Livingston's earlier discussion with a number of suggestions for determining criteria or proficiency levels. In addition, White stresses the importance of measuring progress toward these criteria. Thus, it is no longer adequate in education or clinical psychology to establish absolute criteria, goals, or proficiencies toward which to advance pupils or clients indefinitely. It is also necessary to determine the time by which the criterion is to be reached. When the pupil or client's initial performance level, the criterion, and the time by which the criterion is to be met are known, then lines of progress or progress goals can be established (cf. Bushell, Jackson & Weis, 1975). When performance is continually assessed against such progress goals a sensitive measure of the effects of the educational or clinical intervention procedures is provided.

In addition to methods for setting progress goals, White also suggests procedures for describing progress in ongoing programs. Two of these procedures, the quarter-intersect and split middle lines of progress, are easily calculated and could be readily employed by teachers and behavioral assessors alike. The third, the median slope line of progress, requires fairly large computational capacities and could not be used routinely in applied settings. Finally, White shows the applicability of progress measures in the evaluation of programs. He notes that program effects should be evaluated in terms of progress changes (or changes in trends) produced, as well as in terms of changes in absolute levels of performance. It may very well be, for example, that absolute levels of performance produced in an intervention phase would be reached eventually, if the trend or progress in baseline data were merely projected into the intervention phase. The analysis of changes in progress as well as in absolute levels of behavior will undoubtedly become more and more important in both educational and behavioral assessment.

As assessment procedures become more complex and the amount of data they generate becomes increasingly large, the development of more efficient ways of managing those data will undoubtedly result. In this regard, the chapter by Angle, Hay, Hay and Ellinwood presents a very interesting method of obtaining verbal report data for clinical assessment: the computer assisted interview. These authors have developed a broad band initial screening interview, and they are in the process of developing subsequent in-depth interviews that will explore areas identified in the screening interview as problematic. Their conception of the assessment interview is that it, like all initial assessment, involves a series of decisions on the clinician's part, decisions to follow one line of inquiry and not another. Thus, the clinician makes a series of discriminated responses, each response governed by discriminative stimuli in the form of previous client responses. But the decision rules, the stimuli, and the responses they control are generally not stated and many of them are probably unknown even to the clinician conducting the interview. In programming computers to perform interviews, one is forced to make these decision rules explicit—a formidable task, but one with many potential benefits.

Among the benefits available from computer assisted interviewing are the capacity for much more thorough information gathering without fatigue on the clinician's part, and the reduction of numerous interpersonal influence factors such as biased questions, current clinical interests of the assessor, or subtle differential reinforcement or punishment of certain client responses or clinician inquiry. In addition, the computer interview can be made cumulatively more valid as data are obtained pointing out its shortcomings, whereas the human interviewer is not subject to such a reliable "continuing education." In terms of professional training, forcing the specification of decision rules that govern the computer's inquiry throughout the interview is also advantageous. Such specification would make the teaching of interview skills, now accomplished (if at all) almost exclusively by modeling and imitation in most clinical training programs, much easier and more reliable. In terms of research, the computer interview makes possible many of the kinds of studies Linehan called for in Chapter 2, research that is impossible unless the researcher is able to specify just what the interview will involve. For example, it is meaningless to speak of testing the validity of an interview without specifying the questions to be asked. If the pool of possible questions is to be greater than those actually asked, the rules governing the selection of the subset should be specified. Similarly, one cannot profitably study the relative value of different "styles" of interview, independent of individual interviewer characteristics, unless one can specify the stylistic differences in replicable form. Further, the linear sequence of the screening interview used by Angle and his colleagues permits research on an aspect of the validity of verbal reports that has only been touched upon in the several discussions about such validity elsewhere in this text: the situation in which a client reports no problems when asked a general question (e.g., "Are there any problems in your sex life?"), yet reports problems that the clinician considers serious when asked more specific questions in the same area.

Without doubt the computer interview will have certain limitations, though the authors' experience thus far suggests that these may be less extensive than might be expected. One disadvantage is that in the interview designed by Angle and his colleagues, the answer format is limited to multiple choice. This seems unavoidable and has important advantages, but it limits the amount of information any one question can yield, as compared with a format in which an interviewee composes the answer. In addition, any computer interview rules out information from nonverbal communication, a source highly valued by clinicians. However, this may be turned into an advantage, because it can leave the clinician free to *design* a human interaction that will maximize occasions for significant nonverbal communication and for the observation of this behavior without the concurrent requirement that the clinician be obtaining verbal report information. Even if the limitations of computer interviewing were to prevent its extensive use for the clinical purposes intended by Angle and his colleagues, some significant use of computer interviewing seems inevitable as a result of their work.

11

BEHAVIORAL ASSESSMENT IN CLINICAL SETTINGS: DEVELOPING ISSUES

DAVID H. BARLOW

The topics covered in this book form a comprehensive statement of the field of behavioral assessment, and the people involved in this book insure that we are on the very frontiers of recent developments within the various topics to be addressed. It will come as no surprise, however, that most of these developments have yet to be translated into the daily practice of the applied behavior analyst or behavioral clinician. Perhaps this is because there are many more questions than answers concerning procedures and techniques used in behavioral assessment, particularly in clinical settings. The purpose of this chapter is to attempt to put some of these issues and questions into perspective by surveying some of our own recent work with clinical populations. Specifically, some recent developments in the assessment of sexual problems, severe or psychotic depression, and obsessive compulsive behavior will be reviewed.

At least two issues will be addressed throughout this overview and across the various clinical examples. The first will be the use of contrived situations to assess behavior and the relationship of behavior in contrived situations to behavior in the natural environment. The second will be the assessment of self-report, or verbal behavior, and its place in the total behavioral assessment picture in clinical settings.

CONTRIVED SITUATIONS

Behavioral clinicians and researchers would agree that the optimal assessment procedure would be direct and continuous measurement of behavior in the setting where the behavior presents a problem. This setting has come to be known as the natural environment. Everything else is second best. Yet, in applied work we are constantly compromising this principle for practical or ethical reasons. Thus, we seldom measure behavior in the natural environment if that environment is remote from our offices or occurs at very low frequencies (e.g., certain aggressive behavior). For ethical reasons, we also do not observe some behaviors, such as sexual interactions, in the natural environment beyond the very beginnings of this chain of behavior (e.g., initial social approach responses). Instead, we construct contrived situations in order to observe these behaviors at higher frequencies or in more convenient locations. In some cases, we cannot produce behavior even in contrived situations. When this happens, as in the case of sexual behavior, we move back down the behavioral chain and measure responses such as sexual arousal, presumably an earlier component in the chain of sexual behavior. In other cases we rely entirely on what some call indirect measures, such as rating scales or interviews.

These are all very necessary and helpful procedures, but often we have lost sight of the fact that these measures are only as good as their relationship to the behavior in the natural environment. If these measures really reflect the topography or frequency of behavior in the natural environment, they are useful. If not, they are useless. Nevertheless, while reading journals or listening to presentations on therapeutic intervention where "clean" experimental designs demonstrate highly effective therapeutic procedures, few of us may stop to think that the analogue measures so commonly used in these clinical trials may have little or nothing to do with the behavior as it occurs in the natural environment. This observation is particularly applicable to studies in clinical settings.

SELF-REPORT

One of the most important developments in recent years in adult clinical settings is the general acceptance of the importance of assessing all three response systems (Lang, 1968; Leitenberg, Agras, Butz & Wincze, 1971). These response systems, mentioned often in the other chapters, are the *verbal* (or self-report), the *motor* (or behavioral), and the *physiological*. There may still be major disagreement, however, on the relative importance of these response systems in contrived versus natural settings. There seems to be general agreement that one only uses self-report if one cannot measure motoric behavior more directly.

With outpatient, adult clinical problems the relative weight or importance that one places on these three response systems may differ somewhat from assessment of institutionalized populations or children. The difference occurs in the emphasis we must place on the self-report or verbal response system. We have a natural tendency in behavioral assessment to disregard self-report. Most likely, this is a reaction to the overemphasis we perceive as having been placed on it by our psychodynamic colleagues, who often rely exclusively on self-report. When we see that self-report diverges from motoric behavior or that clear discrepancies exist, we say that self-report is unreliable and not a good index of the important behavior. What we often forget is that self-report *is* behavior and, therefore, is just as important as direct observation of motoric or social behavior or physiological responding. This viewpoint may be reflected in our common practice of labelling rating scales, interview data, and such, as "indirect measures." To this, one might respond, "Indirect measures of what?"

Lang (Chapter 6 and 1968) and Leitenberg et al. (1971) among others, have shown that self-report sometimes does and sometimes does not correlate with motor or physiological measures in the assessment of certain clinical problems. Thus, self-report cannot be considered "indirectly" related to these other response systems unless by indirectly we mean that the relationship is unpredictable. It is possible that various types of self-report are under the control of different variables. For example, self-monitoring may correlate highly with observed behavior under certain conditions, as Nelson demonstrates in Chapter 8. Rating scale reports on subjective discomfort, however, may correlate poorly with behavioral measures across a variety of clinical problems (Leitenberg et al., 1971; Mills, Agras, Barlow & Mills, 1973). Determining the different categories of self-report or verbal behavior and the variables controlling each category should be a major focus for future research.

In any case, an argument can be made that self-report is *more* important than motoric or physiological measures in adult clinical settings since self-report of behavioral problems is often the only necessary criterion for entry into treatment (Goldfried & Sprafkin, 1974). In closed environments, such as school or state institutions, intervention is typically initiated without self-report; it begins with the verbal report of people working in these settings. For example, a teacher reports that a student is disruptive in the classroom and a program is begun to deal with the problem, often independent of any complaint by the child. Intervention with noninstitutionalized adults, on the other hand, is usually self-initiated. Similarly, self-assessment of progress is often the major criterion for terminating the intervention. One can show an adult all the behavioral graphs in the world demonstrating that there has been little or no progress, but if the patient says s/he feels better, the chances are that treatment is over.

This is certainly not a plea for a return to exclusive reliance on self-report in assessment. What we do need, however, is a better understanding of those factors which influence self-report during any intervention program, as well as the relationship of self-report to the other response systems. This is particularly important in those cases where self-report diverges from motoric or physiological measures. All of the clinical examples presented in this chapter highlight this issue.

Relationship of Self-Report to Other Response Systems

The assessment of sexual deviation is an area where self-report often diverges from motor or physiological measures. There seem to be at least two reasons for this. First, sexual behavior is still a rather sensitive subject that is difficult for many people to describe. Secondly, it is becoming evident that even people who are quite willing to talk about their sexual behavior often do not accurately report such phenomena as their patterns of sexual arousal.

An example of the difficulty of relying on self-report was presented by a patient who came to one of our outpatient clinics several years ago with complaints of anxiety and some depression. Subsequent, careful interviewing revealed that this anxiety or feeling of uneasiness seemed to be correlated with specific people in his environment, but it was difficult to determine why. After some further discussion it was determined that there were some general social skill deficits and a treatment program to deal with these interpersonal problems was begun. This particular patient came regularly for appointments, weekly at first and then once every two weeks, for almost one year. Although some improvement was evident, the patient continued to report general feelings of unhappiness, anxiety, and depression at intensities which were unchanged since he began treatment; yet, he continued to come, paying the standard $40 a session. It was only by chance, during a routine reevaluation, that the patient finally blurted out that he had overwhelming homosexual attraction and arousal which was "the reason" for his difficulty in interpersonal situations. When asked why he had continued to come to treatment sessions all year long, paying $40 an hour, without mentioning what was really bothering him, he simply said that he had wanted to report these attractions all year but was unable to bring himself to do so.

While this is an extreme case, it is the rule rather than the exception in adult settings that patients will not or cannot tell you what their problem is in an objective or behavioral manner. Usually they present some vague, undefined complaints of being unhappy (Pomeranz & Gold-fried, 1970). While a little functionally analytic "detective work" often nails down the problem in precise, behavioral terms, the techniques of eliciting this information have received little attention in the behavioral literature. Just asking, "What's the problem?" is often not enough. A thoroughly outlined behavioral interview and a validation of self-report from peers or family in the manner outlined by Kanfer and Saslow (1969) is certainly a help, but the interpersonal behavior within an interview, necessary to set the occasion for a complete and accurate description of problems by the patient, is an area of research that has received little attention in behavioral assessment. The work on interviewing is nicely summarized by Linehan in Chapter 2, and the computer conducted interview described by Angle and his colleagues in Chapter 12 may provide a technology for obtaining more thorough verbal reports without an increase in professional time.

A second example of the discrepancy between verbal report and relevant other behavior occurs when the patient is perfectly willing to discuss a problem but seems unable to report accurately the functional relationships involved. You might say the patient really does not know what the problem is. In describing a patient where this phenomenon obtained, I will also describe what I think is one of the more sophisticated approaches to assessment of sexual arousal using direct measures of genital arousal and illustrate its use in a typical, functionally analytic manner. The procedure was devised by Gene Abel (Abel, Blanchard, Barlow & Mavis-sakalian, 1975) and is one we have been using in our labs for several years.

Essentially, the method involves presenting sexual cues by audiotape. These audiotapes are then played back to the patient. While he listens to this recording, the erection responses on the readout are observed. New audiotapes are then made, based on and enlarging the content which was correlated with the greatest penile responses. This new tape will usually elicit erections larger than those noted on the first tape. Then a third tape is made containing elaborations of the content that had elicited erection most effectively on tape number two, and using information from discussions with the client. What emerges is an audiotape which is highly erotic to the particular patient undergoing assessment. It should be apparent that this method of establishing functional relationships between specific audio cues and erection responses might uncover patterns of arousal of which the subject is unaware. Such was the case in the following patient.

The patient was a 22-year-old male who reported being very sexually aroused to white or brown, open-toed sandals. He noted that this pattern of arousal had been bothering him for approximately two years. In his detailed description he also reported fantasies of kissing the girl's feet and even smelling the girl's feet to see how sexy they were. He denied, however, that the woman's feet alone were erotic and noted that the open-toed sandals were the key ingredient. Using the audiotape method, the first tape described an interaction with such a sandal, based on his report of what was erotic:

> You are in a room with a girl, she's got some sandals on, you can see her sandals there. She's very attractive, you see her sandals, the white kind. You see them on her feet there, see the strap between her toes. She's got very pretty feet. You are looking at the white sandals there, very pretty, see how they fit her feet, going in between her toes. See the leather there with the plastic in between her toes, very attractive, white, very attractive, white leather sandals, open-toed, very attractive and white. See them on her, on her feet there, very attractive, and you see the shoes, sandals, white sandals, as you are walking over, and you're feeling the sandal, very white, you can feel it in your hands, the sandal, very white, holding it, you can feel, feel the material (Abel, Blanchard, Barlow & Mavissakalian, 1975, p. 252).

Surprisingly, this scene generated very little arousal, on the order of 20% (see Figure 1). Another tape was developed, excluding the sandal but describing in some detail the girl's foot:

> You are in a room with a girl and you are looking over at her, looking over at her, and you see her feet. She's really got beautiful feet, she's got sandals on, but you are looking at her feet, really beautiful feet, soft skin, very soft skin, very attractive feet, and you are starting to move over there towards her. She's just kind of playing with her sandals there, they drop to the ground. You come over and she's willing to let you play with her feet, to hold her feet, caress them. You have your hands on her feet now, you are licking her feet, you can smell her feet, you are licking her feet. She wants you to do that, she wants you to feel her feet there, get a hold of her foot in your hands, you are licking her foot, kissing it, it's very, very sexy smelling. Really sexy smelling, she really wants you to

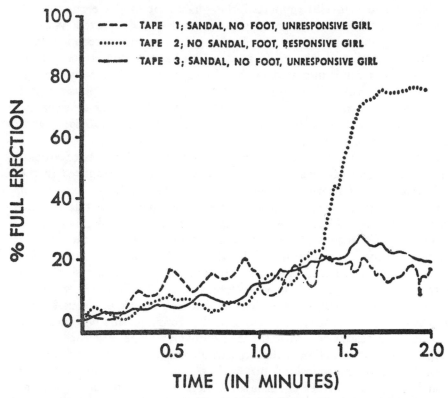

FIGURE 1. Erection responses of possible sandal fetish. (Reprinted from Abel, G. G., Blanchard, E. G., Barlow, D. H., & Mavissakalian, M. Identifying specific erotic cues in sexual deviations by audiotaped descriptions. *Journal of Applied Behavior Analysis*, 1975, 8:247-260.)

hold her foot there. You feel it, you feel the smooth skin, very smooth, smooth skin on her foot, very attractive. You're just kind of holding her foot there, kissing her foot, holding it and kissing it. She's really turned on. Holding her foot, she's really turned on by it. She's really turned on, holding her foot. You're really, really enjoying it. Feeling the skin on her foot, holding her foot, feeling the skin there, very smooth, very smooth skin (Abel et al., 1975, p. 252).

This description generated 75% of a full erection. These data suggested that the foot rather than the sandal was the erotic cue. To confirm this, the patient listened to subsequent tapes containing references only to sandals. These data also supported the girl's foot as the erotic object rather than the sandal, contrary to what the patient had reported. What is really being measured here is a physiological response (erection) in a contrived situation. Furthermore, as mentioned above, only a component of sexual behavior is measured in this situation, arousal, an early step in the behavioral chain. The discrepancy, then, is between a physiological measure of arousal and verbal reports of arousal. When this discrepancy was discussed with the patient, he changed his verbal report to agree with the physiological findings.

Divergence between verbal report and physiological indices of arousal in the assessment of sexual behavior also can be easily *produced* in the laboratory. Several years ago we collected data during an experiment with homosexual patients in which we were examining the role of "expectancy" in an aversive procedure, covert sensitization (Barlow, Agras, Leitenberg, Callahan & Moore, 1972). In covert sensitization the sexually arousing scene, as described by the therapist, is paired in imagination with noxious scenes such as nausea and vomiting or other aversive scenes directly from the patient's experiences. As usual, both arousal, as measured by penile circumference changes, and self-report of arousal were assessed. During the first phase the sexually arousing scene was presented during deep relaxation and without the noxious scene. But the instructions in this phase indicated that this would make them better (thus the term "placebo" is applicable), that is, less aroused. They were told that relaxing would "counteract" arousal. When covert sensitization was administered (second phase) the patients were told that this aversive procedure would actually make them more aroused, due to an increase in general tension that would translate into an increase in sexual arousal. Figure 2 reports the average responding of four homosexual patients. Only the first two phases are relevant for our discussion here. As the data of these two phases indicate, deviant sexual arousal, as measured by penis circumference changes, increased during the relaxation phase but dropped during covert sensitization. Subjective reports of arousal, however, actually dropped considerably during relaxation, but rose during covert sensitization. Three patients said they were much better during the relaxation phase and were ready to stop treatment, and none at any time said he was worse. Conversely, three patients said they were getting worse during covert sensitization although their deviant arousal was dropping daily. These data provide yet another example of divergence among the various response systems comprising sexual behavior, and the seeming ease with which these systems can be made to diverge.

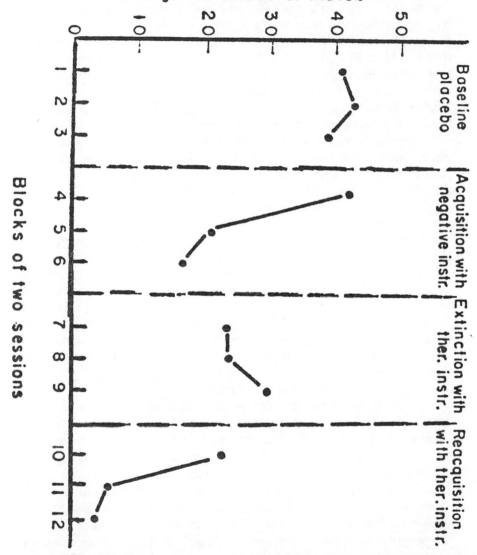

FIGURE 2. Mean penile circumference change to male slides for the four Ss, expressed as a percentage of full erection. In each phase, data from the first, middle, and last pair of sessions are shown. (Reprinted from Barlow, D. H., Agras, W. S., Leitenberg, H., Callahan, E. J., & Moore, R. C. The contribution of therapeutic instruction to covert sensitization. *Behavior Research and Therapy*, 1972, 10:411-415.)

Assessment of Male Sexual Arousal

In Chapter 7, Geer described the increasingly sophisticated equipment recently developed to assess both male and female sexual arousal. Since the apparatus to measure female arousal was only recently developed (Geer, Morokoff & Greenwood, 1974), few data have been collected thus far. Most likely there will be a burst of research in this area in the near future. Since the development of devices to measure male arousal occurred earlier (Barlow, Becker, Leitenberg & Agras, 1970; Freund, Knob & Sedlarcek, 1965), we have refined our assessment procedures and begun to answer some unanswered questions in this area.

One question concerns the relative utility of devices to measure penile circumference (Barlow et al., 1970) and devices which measure penile volume changes (Freund et al., 1965). Recently, Freund and I compared our devices in Freund's lab in Toronto (Freund, Langevin & Barlow, 1974). Independently, McConaghy (1974) also compared volumetric versus circumferential devices in Australia. The general conclusion was that volumetric devices are more sensitive, reflecting smaller changes, and thus they are useful in measuring low levels of arousal of which the patient is often unaware. This device is probably most useful for theoretical studies of sexual arousal and for diagnosis in cases where social contingencies might result in suppression of arousal by the patient (Henson & Rubin, 1971). The problem with volumetric devices is that they are very cumbersome and usually quite expensive. Circumferential measures, on the other hand, are less cumbersome, more sturdy, and relatively inexpensive. They are most effective in measuring large, functionally relevant levels of sexual arousal as a result of treatment.

Another question concerns the optimal stimulus modality in assessing levels of sexual arousal. Various investigators and clinicians have used movies, videotapes, slides, free fantasies, as well as the audiotapes mentioned earlier. A recent project has involved examining the effectiveness of these different modalities in eliciting sexual arousal. A second related question was the ability of patients to voluntarily suppress this arousal in view of findings that this was indeed possible (Laws & Rubin, 1969; Henson & Rubin, 1971). To test this we compared modalities of stimuli in people with different patterns of arousal. In Figure 3 data are presented from a group of 20 voluntary homosexual subjects. All of these subjects were presented with slides, a two-minute videotape depicting homosexual interactions, or an audiotape describing the same homosexual interactions. These three stimuli were presented twice in each of three

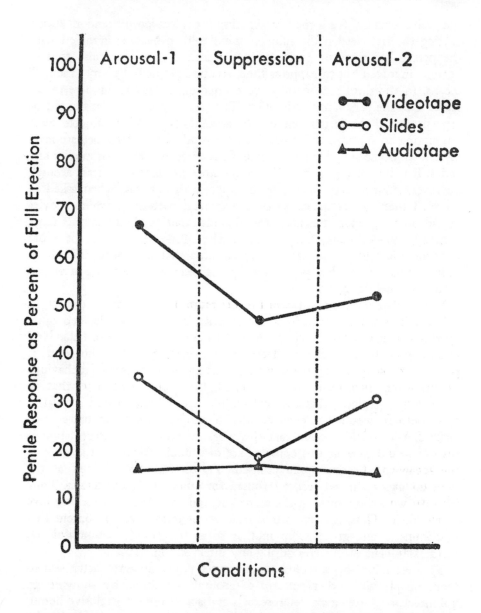

FIGURE 3. Mean penile response for all subjects under all conditions as a percent of full erection. (Reprinted from Abel, G. G., Barlow, D. H., Blanchard, E. B., & Mavissakalian, M. Measurement of sexual arousal in male homosexuals: The effects of instructions and stimulus modality. *Archives of Sexual Behavior*, 1975, 4:623-629.)

successive sessions, for a total of six stimuli per session, in random order. During the first session the subjects were told to become involved with the person described or depicted. In the second they were also told to become involved but to suppress their erection response by any "mental" means. In the third session they were once again told to involve themselves with the person in the situation. The results indicated that the videotape produced the largest amount of arousal, even when subjects were attempting to suppress this arousal. Slides produced an intermediate level of arousal. Some suppression of arousal occurred during both movies and slides. It is interesting to note that audiotapes produced the least arousal; however, subjects seemed unable to suppress this arousal when asked to do so. Other studies indicate that the general pattern in which movies or videotapes produce maximal arousal is also true for heterosexuals (e.g., Sanford, 1974; Freund, Langevin & Zajac, 1974). However, for more idiosyncratic patterns of arousal, or patterns that are more difficult to represent on film, such as pedophilia, audiotapes would seem the preferred method (Abel et al., 1975).

Yet another question concerns the structure of heterosexual arousal. In behavioral assessment we often talk of criterion behaviors decided upon by the patient and the therapist which then become the goal of behavioral intervention. It is difficult to determine criterion behaviors, however, if one is not aware of the population norms for a given set of behaviors. In our sexual assessment we all assumed, for a period of time, that an explicit film depicting heterosexual intercourse, which elicited arousal in heterosexuals, would not elicit arousal in people with other patterns of arousal. We quickly found that this was not true. For instance, homosexuals would look at this complex set of stimuli, focus on the male in the scene and become quite aroused. Transsexuals would look at the same configuration and become aroused for quite a different reason. They identify with the female in the scene and fantasize they are making love to the male. Thus, it is important in assessment to develop content that discriminates one group from another so as to provide meaningful and valid assessment of changes during any intervention.

To determine the stimulus content which discriminates heterosexuals from people with other patterns of arousal, we began by showing six volunteer, exclusive male heterosexuals and six volunteer, exclusive homosexuals four videotapes with different contents. One videotape depicted a single, nude woman assuming various sexual postures. The second depicted a lesbian couple engaged in lovemaking. The third depicted a heterosexual couple engaged in sexual intercourse, and a fourth depicted a

TABLE 1

Mean Values of Percent Full Erection, Percent Subjective Arousal and Subjective Rating of Pleasantness in Six Homosexuals and Six Heterosexual Males Under Four Erotic Stimulus Conditions*

Group	Single girl	Lesbian	Erotic stimuli Heterosexual couple	Homosexual couple
$\bar{x}$ Per cent full penile erection				
Heterosexual	42·83 a²	60·17 a	51·00 a	18·17 b
Homosexual .. · .. · .. · .. ` ..	33·33 a	28·50 a	44·67 b	54·67 b
Level of significance between group comparison	·10	·05	n.s.	·01
$\bar{x}$ Per cent subjective arousal				
Heterosexual ·.	57·67 a	68·67 a	63·17 a	10·33 b
Homosexual	30·33 a	33·67 a	72·33 b	78·17 b
Level of significance of between group comparison ·. .. ·. ·. ..	·10	·05	n.s.	·001
$\bar{x}$ Subjective rating of pleasantness				
Heterosexual .. .. ·. ·..	1·92 a	2·00 a	1·96 a	−1·33 b
Homosexual	0·25 a	0·54 a	2·47 b	2·46 b
Level of significance of between group comparison	·05	·05	n.s.	·001

Note: Within any row, cell means that do not share subscripts are different at least the ·05 level.

male homosexual couple also engaged in lovemaking. Over the course of two sessions, each subject saw examples of each content area four times, for a total of 16 videotapes. These videotapes were counterbalanced for content. Penile circumference changes were measured, along with subjective reports of arousal and verbal reports on a pleasantness-unpleasantness continuum for each tape. The data are presented in Table 1.

It is clear from these data—which are presented in terms of average penile circumference change, based on a zero to 100 scale—that the hetero-

* Reprinted from: Mavissakalian, M., Blanchard, E. B., Abel, G. G. & Barlow, D. H., 1975.

sexual tapes did not discriminate between homosexual and heterosexual subjects. Even the single girl did not discriminate these groups, although there was a trend in that direction. The tapes which clearly discriminated the two groups were those depicting the lesbian couple and the male homosexual couple. Heterosexuals responded with significantly more arousal to the lesbian couple than did homosexuals, and the reverse was true for the homosexual film clip. These data indicate that arousal to lesbian films should be the criterion when one is attempting to instigate heterosexual arousal.

It is also interesting to note another divergence in verbal and physiological measures. Heterosexuals were aroused to homosexual films at a level of 18.2% on the average and yet they rated these films as distinctly unpleasant.

The clinical assessment of patterns of sexual arousal has become more sophisticated in recent years and it is now possible to assess, rather precisely, a variety of patterns. The development of a similar apparatus to measure female sexual arousal (Geer et al., 1974) also opens up a much neglected field of inquiry. Nevertheless, sexual arousal is only one component in a complete clinical assessment of sexual disorders (Barlow, 1974; Barlow & Abel, in press). At least two other components of sexual behavior, in addition to patterns of sexual arousal, require a complete behavioral assessment. These components are 1) the social skills necessary to meet, date, and relate to people of the opposite sex—heterosocial skills; and 2) gender role deviations in which males, for instance, identify to various degrees with the opposite gender. At the extreme of gender role deviations is the transsexual phenomenon where a biologically normal male requests sex change surgery. While we are beginning to develop reliable and valid assessment procedures of these two components of sexual behavior (Barlow, Reynolds, & Agras 1973; Hersen & Bellack, in press), considerably more work is necessary to bring assessment of these components up to the level of assessment of arousal patterns.

Validity of Assessment of Sexual Arousal

As assessment procedures, particularly assessment procedures of arousal in adults with clinical sexual problems, become more sophisticated, some other very basic questions arise which have been overlooked. One question is the relationship of measures of arousal in the laboratory to sexual behavior in the real world. Even within the laboratory setting we are not sure how an erection relates to sexual behavior. Certainly an erection is an early and necessary step in the chain of sexual intercourse. Nevertheless, the fact remains that the external validity of penile circumference measures has not been established. Assumptions of the importance of this assessment procedure have been entirely based on its correlation with subjects' or patients' reports of sexual behavior in the natural environment. A verbal report, as demonstrated in the case at the beginning of the chapter, often has little to do with sexual arousal or behavior.

A clear goal for further development of assessment procedures would be to devise methods of assessing sexual approach behavior more directly. As a first step we might try to create contrived situations in the laboratory where direct sexual approach and the initial stages of contact can be recreated and observed. Some interesting work by Forgione (1974), in which he used mannikins of children to assess the approach behavior of pedophiliacs, seems promising. A second step might be to devise methods of observing sexual approach behavior in the natural environment. The practical and ethical problems inherent in this type of assessment seem overwhelming at the present time. In view of advances in naturalistic observation, however, and in view of the relaxation of attitudes surrounding sexual behavior in our society, something along these lines may be possible. Certainly the increased use of female collaborators in clinical treatment of sexual problems could very possibly be extended to naturalistic studies of sexual approach behavior in males. And I suppose it would not be hard to find male collaborators for similar tasks.

BEHAVIORAL ASSESSMENT OF SEVERE DEPRESSION

In the assessment of sexual deviation, particularly sexual arousal patterns, a behavior occurring very early in the chain is sampled, at most once a day, in a contrived situation. This is necessary because the behavior to be assessed is both low frequency and unlikely to occur in publicly observable settings. A clinical problem more amenable to naturalistic observation is severe or psychotic depression. Despite this state of affairs, there is very little in the way of reliable and valid behavioral strategies for assessing severe depression, although Lewinsohn and his associates (Libet & Lewinsohn, 1973) have recently reported some sophisticated procedures for assessing mild depression.

A few years ago we conducted a study (Williams, Barlow & Agras, 1972) to develop a behavioral checklist based on direct observation of severely depressed patients in a hospital setting. We then compared data collected with this behavioral checklist to some well-known rating scale measures of depression, the Beck Depressive Inventory and the Hamilton Rating Scale (Beck, Ward, Mendelson, Mock & Erbaugh, 1961; Hamilton, 1960). This study suggested some interesting relationships between these directly observed behavioral indices of depression and the rating scale measures of depression, which are essentially a method of quantifying self-report. Again, divergencies in response systems appeared, in this case verbal-motoric discrepancies.

The study was conducted with 10 patients on the psychiatric unit of a university hospital. These patients were the first 10 who met very strict behavioral and self-report criteria defining the category of severe, or psychotic, depression:

1) Feelings of hopelessness and worthlessness;

2) Suicidal thoughts or attempts;

3) Loss of interest in life;

4) Self-reproach or guilt;

5) The physiological signs of deep depression, including:
   a) Anorexia,
   b) Weight loss,
   c) Sleep pattern disturbance,
   d) Impotence,
   e) Constipation,
   f) Anergia;

6) The usual motoric signs of depression, such as:
   a) Depressed facies,
   b) Slow, monotonous speech,
   c) Psychomotor retardation.

The two well-known rating scales of depression, the Beck and the Hamilton, were administered to these patients upon admission. The Beck Depressive Inventory consists of 21 items describing various behaviors or feelings related to depression. The patient answers each question by circling a number from zero to three; zero indicates a less depressed patient, three the most depressed state. The Hamilton Rating Scale, on the other hand, is really a method of quantifying an in-depth interview. Typically, two experienced clinicians will independently interview the patient and fill out the scale. Thus, the score actually represents the rater's quantified estimate of the degree of depression, based not only on self-report, but also the clinician's observations during the interview. Thus, the Beck represents the patient's own estimate of depression, while the Hamilton quantifies the rater's estimate of depression.

Development of the behavioral measures involved choosing behaviors which were easily observable and occurred at a reasonably high frequency. Thus, we purposely avoided low frequency behaviors, such as sighing, which are often described as an integral part of a severely depressed behavioral constellation. After some preliminary observations, it seemed that in addition to a series of subtle behaviors, depressed patients talked little, avoided social interaction (usually by withdrawing to their rooms), smiled infrequently, and exhibited diminished motor activity. Definitions were worked out for these behaviors and subsequent recordings, based on these definitions, yielded high rates of agreement between independent raters, with a reliability coefficient of 96%, based on 20 independent observations (agreements over agreements plus disagreements, times 100) during the hospital course of each patient.

Psychiatric aides time sampled depressed behaviors on variable interval, half-hour schedules from 8:00 a.m. to 4:00 p.m. each day, resulting in 16 observations. The four behaviors sampled were highly correlated. Because of this correlation the behavioral measures were summed in daily totals and treated as a single datum for the analysis. The total behavioral score for each day was plotted across the course of the patient's hospitalization and correlated with rating scale measures. Generally, the measures correlated reasonably well. The two rating scale measures correlated .82, based on Pearson product moment correlations. The Hamilton and the checklist measures correlated .71, while the Beck and the checklist measures correlated .67. One should remember that the Hamilton was a bit closer to the behavioral checklist measures in that some behaviors occurring during the interview were observed and quantified by the rater. The Beck Inventory, on the other hand, was based entirely on the patient's self-report.

The most interesting findings from this study, however, are some hints on the relative predictive validity of these measures. In view of the high correlation between behavioral and self-report measures, it is tempting to discard behavioral measures which require observation throughout the day and utilize the simpler self-report measures. There are some hints in these data, however, that behavioral measures predict the post-hospital course of these patients more accurately than the other rating scales. This is best illustrated in five patients whom we followed for one year. After a period of one year, three of these five patients had serious relapses of their severe depression and were rehospitalized. When they were in the

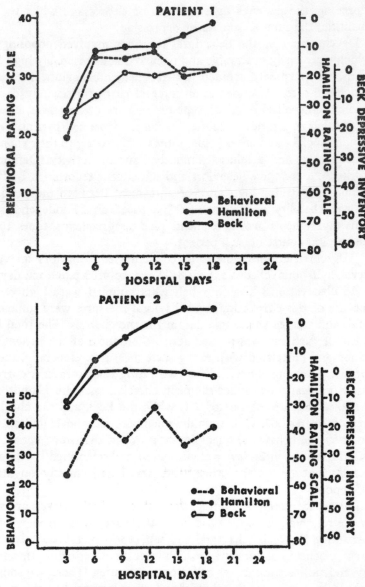

FIGURE 4 (see caption, p. 301)

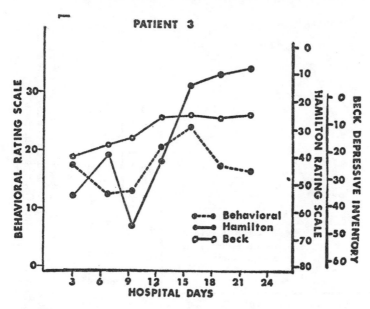

FIGURE 4. Changes in the behavioral rating scale, the Beck Depressive Inventory and the Hamilton Rating Scale over the course of hospitalization for patients 1, 2, and E. Each point for the behavioral score represents the mean over a three-day period blocked around the Hamilton Rating Scale. Each point on the Hamilton Rating Scale and Beck Depressive Inventory represents the score on that day. (Reprinted from Williams, J. G. Barlow, D. H., & Agras, W. S. Behavioral measurement of severe depression. *Archives of General Psychiatry*, 1972, 27:330-334.)

hospital their behavioral scores would improve initially, plateau midway during their course in hospital, and then worsen somewhat just prior to discharge (see Figure 4). The two rating scales, on the other hand, tended to improve rapidly and remain improved, suggesting that these patients were completely over their depression within the first week or two after hospitalization. On the other hand, the two patients who showed clear upward trends in their behavioral measures prior to discharge both remained well at the end of one year (see Figure 5).

An interesting finding in one case, not represented in the figures, was the lag in the behavioral measures relative to the rating scales. While rating scales reflected rapid improvement, behavioral measures reflected a much slower improvement. After six days, both rating scale scores were essentially within normal limits. On the other hand, the behavioral meas-

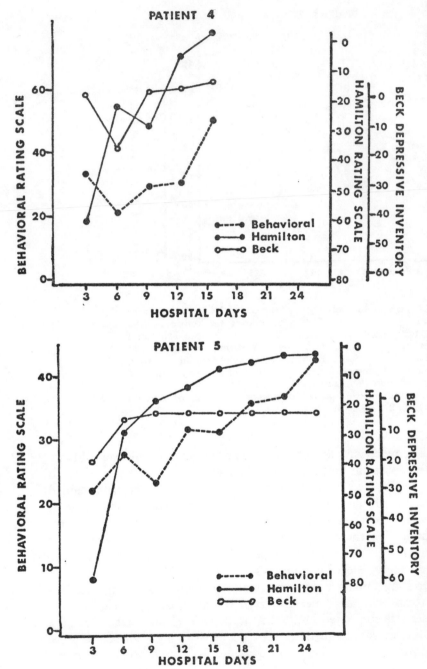

FIGURE 5. Changes in the behavioral rating scale, the Beck Depressive Inventory, and the Hamilton Rating Scale over the course of hospitalization for patients 4 and 5. Each point for the behavioral score represents the mean over a three-day period blocked around the Hamilton Rating Scale. Each point on the Hamilton Rating Scale and the Beck Depressive Inventory represents the score on that day. (Reprinted from Williams, J. G., Barlow, D. H., & Agras, W. S. Behavioral measurement of severe depression. *Archives of General Psychiatry*, 1972, 27:330-334.)

ures on this patient did not even begin to improve until the sixth day, although improvement continued fairly steadily for about three weeks. This particular patient had been treated for depression in another hospital before admission to our unit. During the first hospitalization he was discharged after approximately a week and shortly thereafter cut his throat and anticubital veins in a serious suicide attempt, leading to admission to our hospital. It seems likely that his pattern of quick recovery, based on the verbal response system, was responsible for this premature discharge, whereas the behavioral measures provided a more conservative measure of depression.

Validity of Behavioral Measure of Depression

This behavioral measure seems a useful development in that concurrent or convergent validity was established by direct comparison with two well-known and tested rating scales. The interrater reliability was satisfactory, and the measure also seems to be cost effective in that it can be administered by the psychiatric aide rather than by a more highly trained professional. Finally, it is useful in the assessment of severe depression since this particular clinical problem must be treated in a hospital setting, due to the danger of suicide.

Nevertheless, much like procedures for assessing sexual arousal, some very important questions remained unanswered. The predictive validity of these measures remains essentially untested since the number of patients was really very small and the purpose of this study was not to test the relative predictive validity of these measures. While the post hoc analysis seemed to reveal a pattern in these few cases, our criteria for judging post-hospital course were very gross in that rehospitalization or lack of rehospitalization, and status based on an interview at the end of one year were the indices of the post-hospital course. Thus, we are left with a similar problem as in the assessment of sexual deviation, since the ultimate purpose of any behavioral assessment that does not occur in the natural environment is to predict behavior in the natural environment of that patient. Obviously, the prediction of serious suicidal attempts would be a very valuable contribution if this finding were confirmed.

ASSESSMENT OF SEVERE OBSESSIVE-COMPULSIVE BEHAVIOR

It is clear that we are becoming more sophisticated in direct observation of behavior, either in contrived situations or in the natural environment. Nevertheless, the use of observers in these naturalistic or contrived situations has led to a host of problems unforeseen a few years ago (Romanczyk, Kent, Diament & O'Leary, 1973; Jones, Reid & Patterson, 1975). Problems such as observer drift and observer decay are not surprising, given the number of possible factors that can influence the accuracy of human observation. But, in fact, these issues are forcing the establishment of a new sub-area within the field of behavioral assessment which might be called the social psychology of human observation.

In view of these difficulties, there would be wide agreement that the automatic recording of behavior, if possible, would be preferable to direct observation of the same behavior in many situations. The sophisticated use of equipment and apparatus is, of course, widespread when assessing the physiological response system, but there have been fewer innovations in the assessment of the motoric response system without the use of observers, probably because observers are usually readily available and cheaper, particularly in universities or psychiatric wards. One exception has been the very nice work on "behavioral engineering" by Azrin and his colleagues (e.g., O'Brien & Azrin, 1970).

In our own research we have turned to the use of mechanical assessment of behavior in at least one instance—the assessment and treatment of severe-obsessive-compulsive behavior. This research also illustrates again an interesting divergence between motor behavior and self-report.

The patient was a 25-year-old woman with a three-year history of compulsive handwashing. The situations which produced handwashing were associated with illness and death. If an ambulance passed near her or she found herself near a funeral home, she would feel quite contaminated and engage in cleansing rituals. This involved washing and disinfecting all clothes worn in such situations. Prior to hospitalization she had become progressively more isolated, restricting herself to her safe, disinfected home. However, even newspaper reports, magazines, and television pictures of injury or death produced the urge to wash her hands, which she did more than 30 times a day prior to hospitalization, based on her report. She also feared hospitals because of the potential contamination therein. Therefore, it was only with some reservation that she agreed to enter the hospital.

The behavioral measure of handwashing was called a "washing pen." This was a railing with a single gate, completely surrounding a six-by-eight-foot board on the floor. Eight switches, wired in series, on the underside of the board were connected to a cumulative recorder in another room. These switches were tripped by the patient's approaching the sink in her room, which activated the recorder. This provided a 24-hour, daily record of the frequency and duration of approaches to the sink to perform her washing ritual. The door to the patient's room remained open during waking hours so that the nurses could observe and record handwashings. This provided a check on the reliability of the apparatus. The correlation coefficient was .96 between the nurses' reports of hand-washing and the frequency as recorded by the instrument. The self-report measure in this case was the patient's record of urges to perform the washing ritual, presumably a somewhat earlier component in the chain of behavior.

The particular procedure we were testing was a response prevention technique described in some detail in the published study (Mills, Agras, Barlow, & Mills 1973). The introduction of this treatment was preceded by a baseline and a placebo phase. During these phases the patient washed her hands from 40 to 60 times per day. The introduction of the treatment essentially eliminated the handwashing, as demonstrated in placebo and baseline phases following the treatment (see Figure 6). However, as in previous examples reported in this chapter, the patient's self-report di-verges from her motor behavior in that she continued reporting a high frequency of urges to wash her hands, on the order of 20 to 30 times a day. At this time the patient would say, "I'm not washing my hands now, but I still would like to. I still feel contaminated." As an indication of the importance we attach to self-report in adult clinical situations, we then proceeded to extend treatment despite the fact that the motor behavior, objectively measured, was no longer occurring. At a point not represented in Figure 6, reports of urges to wash dropped to a clinically insignificant level.

This particular apparatus was not difficult to build and the advantages of this apparatus, as well as similar instrumentation, are obvious. The elimi-nation of human observers and the efficient and reliable 24-hour recording of the target behavior would be desirable goals in any assessment pro-cedure. It is a much broader and more complete assessment of behavior than the usual sampling procedures and allows more confidence in the accuracy of results, assuming the reliability and durability of the apparatus.

CONCLUSIONS

The cases presented in this chapter illustrate three different assessment strategies with adults in clinical settings:

1) The assessment procedure for sexual deviations measured a physio-

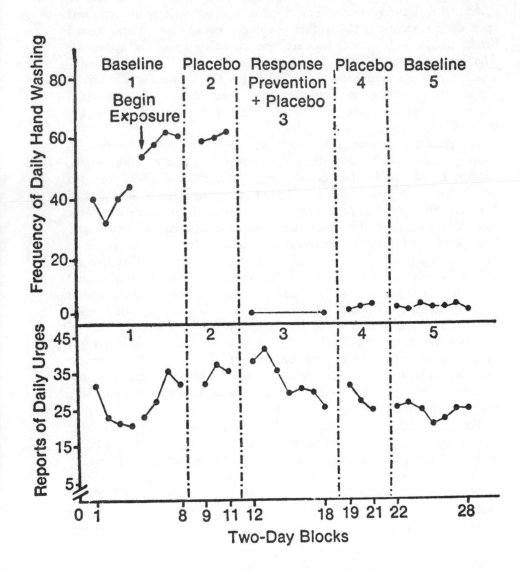

FIGURE 6. Top: Frequency of hand washing across treatment phases; each point represents average for two days. Bottom: Total urges reported by patient. (Reprinted from Mills, H. L., Agras, W. S., Barlow, D. H., & Mills, J. R. Compulsive rituals treated by response prevention. *Archives of General Psychiatry*, 1973, 28:524-529.)

logical response early in the chain of sexual behavior. The measure was administered in a contrived situation, a maximum of once a day.

2) The behavioral checklist assessment of severe depression employed direct, time-sampled observation of motor behaviors over an eight-hour period in a hospital situation. If one allows that treatment of severe depression must be carried out in a hospital, then hospitals qualify as a natural situation for a short period of time. Nevertheless, depressive behavior was not measured in the home or work environment.

3) The assessment procedure for compulsive behavior goes two steps further. First, human observers were eliminated since target behaviors were measured mechanically. Second, behavior was measured 24 hours a day, eliminating the need for sampling. Once again, behavior was not measured in the home.

These three procedures comprise a gradual approximation to the goal of direct and continuous measurement in the natural environment, mentioned at the beginning of the chapter. Indeed, progress towards this goal is occurring in many clinical settings.

In view of this progress, it might be tempting to drop all work on rating scales, interviews, checklists, behavioral sampling, and contrived situations and concentrate on development of direct and continuous measurement of behavior in the natural environment. This would be a mistake. Rating scales, interviews, behavioral checklists, and measures in contrived situations will, in fact, be used. Complicated and expensive measures will not be used. What we need is information on the kinds and levels of validity we can expect from these simpler, less expensive measures. Development of measures in the natural environment is essential, if only to validate these measures in contrived situations. Of course, many of the more direct, naturalistic assessment methods will prove useful in their own right, as they have already.

Furthermore, it is important to stop considering self-report as only an indirect measure and to begin collecting data on this response system across all situations, contrived or natural. Only in this way will the nature and variety of self-report and its relationship to other response systems be elucidated.

12

PSYCHOMETRIC TECHNIQUES FOR CRITERION-REFERENCED TESTING AND BEHAVIORAL ASSESSMENT

SAMUEL A. LIVINGSTON

This chapter is about criterion-referenced testing, an educational concept, and behavioral assessment, a psychological concept. The chapter is intended to serve four purposes:

1) To present and explain the concept of criterion-referenced testing to readers who are not familiar with it;

2) To point out similarities between the criterion-referenced approach to educational testing and the behavioral approach to psychological assessment;

3) To discuss the implications of these approaches for the traditional psychometric concepts of reliability and validity;

4) To suggest ways of describing in quantitative terms the reliability and validity of criterion-referenced tests and behavioral assessment procedures.

Notice the use of the word "suggest," rather than "prescribe." At the present time there is considerable disagreement among educational measurement theorists as to what psychometric techniques are appropriate for criterion-referenced tests. Therefore, the recommendations made in this chapter should be regarded as the author's best efforts, not as the consensus of the educational measurement profession.

I wish to thank John D. Cone, John J. Fremer, Marvin R. Goldfried, Michael M. Ravitch, Julie S. Vargas, and Lawrence E. Wightman for their helpful comments on earlier drafts of this paper.

CRITERION-REFERENCED TESTING

Possibly the most popular and most controversial topic in the field of educational measurement in the past few years has been criterion-referenced testing. Measurement specialists disagree with each other even about the meaning of the term. And yet few would deny that it has influenced their thinking about measurement problems—or that it has had a tremendous impact on the way educators think about and talk about the tests they use.

The term "criterion-referenced" was coined by Robert Glaser in 1963 to refer to a type of measurement which had for many years been de-emphasized in American education: measurement of students' skills in absolute, rather than relative terms, with the intention of providing a score that can be interpreted without reference to the performance of other examinees. Glaser also coined the term "norm-referenced" to refer to measurement for the purpose of comparing examinees with each other or with a norm group. He presented the distinction as follows:

> The scores obtained from an achievement test provide primarily two kinds of information. One is the degree to which the student has attained criterion performance, for example, whether he can satisfactorily prepare an experimental report, or solve certain kinds of word problems in arithmetic. The second type of information that an achievement test score provides is the relative ordering of individuals with respect to their test performance, for example, whether Student A can solve his problems more quickly than Student B. The principal difference between these two kinds of information lies in the standard used as a reference. What I shall call criterion-referenced measures depend upon an absolute standard of quality, while what I term norm-referenced measures depend upon a relative standard (p. 519).

Obviously, the distinction pointed out by Glaser had long been recognized by students and teachers, in less formal terms (e.g., "grading on the curve" vs. "straight percentage grading"). Among measurement specialists, the practice of interpreting test scores in relative terms had by far the greater respectability. Why relative (i.e., norm-referenced) test score interpretations were emphasized to the exclusion of absolute (i.e., criterion-referenced) interpretations is a matter for speculation. Certainly, the basic statistical concepts and methods that have recently been applied to criterion-referenced testing are not new. Whatever the reason, few attempts were made to establish procedures for evaluating tests and interpreting scores in ways that do not depend on comparisons between persons.

Two serious efforts to deal with this problem before Glaser's much-quoted statement deserve to be mentioned. In 1954 Leo Nedelsky proposed a method for establishing absolute grading standards for multiple-choice tests. The technique was based on judgments by experts (possibly the course instructors) as to which multiple-choice options "the lowest D-student should be able to reject as incorrect." And in 1962 Robert Ebel proposed what he called "content standard test scores," a system by which a student's score on a test was interpreted in terms of his expected performance on a small number of sample items. The actual sample items were to be presented, along with the students' test score and a frequency distribution relating the test score to the sample items.

Not much interest in the issue of absolute vs. relative grading seems to have been aroused by Nedelsky's and Ebel's ideas. Even after Glaser provided a set of new and appropriately technical-sounding names for the two concepts, the issue seems to have lain dormant for a few years. Perhaps in the late 1950's and early 1960's—the days of the space race, with its emphasis on competition and excellence—criterion-referenced measurement was an idea whose time had not yet come. Suddenly, in the late 1960's, the educational measurement community discovered criterion-referenced measurement, and measurement specialists began to deal seriously with the problems of interpreting test scores *without* measuring each student against the others. This explosion of interest may have been set off by an article by Popham and Husek (1969) entitled "Implications of Criterion-Referenced Measurement." In it they identified the main barrier to the use of traditional psychometric procedures with criterion-referenced tests:

> With criterion-referenced tests, variability is irrelevant. The meaning of the score is not dependent on comparison with other scores; it flows directly from the connection between the items and the criterion. It is, of course, true that one almost always gets variant scores on any psychological test; but that variability is not a necessary condition for a good criterion-referenced test . . . although it may be obvious that a criterion-referenced test should be internally consistent, it is not obvious how to assess the internal consistency. The classical procedures are not appropriate. This is true because they are dependent on score variability. A criterion-referenced test should not be faulted if, when administered after instruction, everyone obtained a perfect score. Yet, that would lead to a zero internal consistency estimate, something measurement books don't recommend (pp. 3, 5).

When measurement specialists began to try to solve the problems that Popham and Husek had laid out, they soon discovered that they needed a more precise definition of a criterion-referenced test than anyone had yet provided. Glaser's original definition left considerable room for disagreement about specifics, as did Popham and Husek's definition:

> Criterion-referenced measures are those which are used to ascertain an individual's status with respect to some criterion, i.e., performance standard. It is because the individual is compared with some established criterion, rather than with other individuals, that these measures can be described as criterion-referenced (p. 2).

The result of this ambiguity was that each writer who proposed a solution to the problems of test construction, reliability and validity estimation, and score interpretation created his own more precise definition. A brief sampling of these definitions should illustrate the points of difference.

> A criterion-referenced test is a test based on a set of specific learner objectives stated in terms of the behavioral change to be expected in the examinee as a result of instruction toward these objectives. . . . There is no assumption of an underlying continuum of achievement on a particular objective, but rather there is the simple assumption that each student either has mastered the objective or that he has not mastered the objective (Roudabush & Green, 1972, p. 1).

> Rather than sample performance across a hypothetical population of pupils, it is more appropriate to measure the individual's behavior on a random sample of problems drawn from a clearly defined population of tasks. The individual's relative score (i.e., percentage score) can then be interpreted as an estimate of his *proficiency*. . . . I define tests constructed to provide proficiency measures, as described above, [as] criterion-referenced tests or CRT's (Kriewall, 1972, p. 3).

> [T]he term "criterion-referenced" will be used to refer to any test for which the criterion score is specified without reference to the distribution of scores of a group of examinees. . . . When we use norm-referenced measures, we want to know how far a student's score deviates from the group mean. When we use criterion-referenced measures, we want to know how far his score deviates from a fixed standard, the criterion score (Livingston, 1972, pp. 13-14).

> [T]here is no quota on the number of individuals who can exceed the *cut-off score* or *threshold* on a criterion-referenced test. A cut-off score is set for each subscale of a criterion-referenced test to separate examinees into two mutually exclusive groups. One group is made up

of examinees with high enough test scores ($\geqq$ the cut-off score) to infer they have mastered the material to a desired level of proficiency. The second group is made up of examinees who did not achieve the minimum proficiency standard (Hambleton & Novick, 1973, p. 163).

Notice that these definitions reveal a lack of agreement on at least three fundamental issues:

1) Does criterion-referenced measurement imply an attempt to classify persons into two groups? If so, is this classification considered as an attempt to reproduce a natural, existing dichotomy on some underlying variable?

2) Does criterion-referenced measurement imply either random or representative sampling of items from a specified item domain?

3) Does criterion-referenced measurement imply comparison of scores with a prespecified score level? If so, is the size of the difference of interest, or only its direction?

The different positions taken by these and other authors on these issues reflect their differing approaches to the problems of constructing, interpreting, and evaluating criterion-referenced tests.

Fundamental as the above differences are, they are far less important than the differences between these criterion-referenced approaches to testing and the traditional, norm-referenced psychometric approach. Consider the following list of five assumptions of traditional psychometrics:

1) A test has no intrinsic importance; it is of interest only as an indicator of some underlying variable.

2) The purpose of a test is to reveal differences between individuals.

3) What a test measures is indicated by its pattern of correlations with other tests.

4) The distribution over persons of a variable underlying a test score can be assumed to be normal unless there is some specific reason to believe otherwise (e.g., pre-selection on the basis of a similar test).

5) The score of a person on a test derives its meaning by comparison with the scores of other persons.

Every one of these assumptions would be challenged by at least some of the advocates of criterion-referenced testing, and assumption 5 would be rejected by all of them. It would not be possible to draft a single set of corresponding assumptions for criterion-referenced testing that would satisfy all those who have written on the subject, but a combined list of criterion-referenced alternatives to these assumptions would probably look like the following:

1) A criterion-referenced test is a sample of the behaviors of interest.

2) The purpose of a criterion-referenced test is a) to estimate a person's level of skill or achievement in absolute terms, or b) to classify a person as a master or nonmaster of a specified behavior.

3) What a criterion-referenced test measures is indicated by a) the specification of the domain from which items are selected, or b) the extent to which it classifies persons in the same way as other classification procedures.

4) The distribution over persons of a variable underlying a criterion-referenced test score a) is not of interest, or b) is a Bernoulli (two-point) distribution, since the variable is dichotomous, or c) cannot be assumed to have any particular form.

5) The score of a person on a criterion-referenced test a) is a direct estimate of his absolute level of proficiency, or b) derives its meaning from a conditional probability distribution of some related variable (e.g., the probability of mastery, given the person's test score), or c) derives its meaning by comparison with a pre-specified reference point.

Table 1 presents a juxtaposition of these contrasting assumptions.

BEHAVIORAL ASSESSMENT

The basic differences between behavioral assessment and traditional psychometric practice (as outlined by Goldfried & Kent, 1972) all seem to be consequences of the acceptance or rejection of assumption 1: that a test should be interpreted as an indicator of one or more underlying variables. Psychologists who accept this assumption will view behavior as the outward manifestation of inner personality traits. They will interpret test performance as a "sign" rather than a sample, and they will select test items so as to make the "sign" clearer. Psychologists who reject this assumption will interpret test performance as a sample, and they will select items to be representative of some universe of behaviors.

The rejection of assumption 1 (concern with underlying variables) calls into question the other four assumptions as well. If we are interested in observable behavior, rather than latent traits, then we can talk in terms

TABLE 1

Assumptions of Traditional and Criterion-Referenced Approaches
to Educational Measurement

	Traditional	Criterion-Referenced
1. A test is ...	An indicator of some underlying variable.	A sample of the behaviors of interest.
2. The purpose of a test is ...	To reveal differences between individuals.	To estimate a person's level or skill or achievement in absolute terms, or To classify a person as a master or nonmaster of a specified behavior.
3. What a test measures is indicated by ...	Its pattern of correlations with other tests.	The specification of the domain from which items are selected; or The extent to which it classifies persons in the same way as other classification procedures.
4. The distribution over persons of a variable underlying a test score ...	Can be assumed to be normal unless there is a specific reason to believe otherwise.	Is not of interest; or Is a two-point distribution; or Cannot be assumed to have any particular form.
5. The score of a person on a test derives its meaning from ...	Comparisons with the scores of other persons.	Its interpretation as a direct estimate of the person's absolute level of proficiency; or A conditional probability distribution of some related variable; or Comparison with a pre-specified reference point.

of probabilities or frequencies of observing specified behaviors under specified conditions. These probabilities or frequencies are meaningful in themselves even without comparisons between individuals. Therefore, we may be inclined to reject assumptions 2 (emphasis on individual differences) and 5 (interpretation in terms of group norms). If our test consists of observations of the behavior we are interested in, we do not need patterns of correlations to tell us what it measures. Hence, we will be likely to reject assumption 3. And if we are not interested in underlying variables, we have no reason to assume anything about their distribution. Hence, assumption 4 is irrelevant.

Behavioral assessors, then, may find themselves confronted with the problems of assessing the validity and reliability of their observation procedures *without* using techniques derived from the assumptions of classical psychometrics. These are the problems that educational testers interested in criterion-referenced measurement have been attempting to solve, and some of their attempts may be of interest to behavioral assessors.

RELIABILITY

The concept of test reliability is quite familiar to most, if not all, psychologists. Still, I would like to suggest a fairly precise definition of test reliability—one which clearly reveals the ambiguities in the concept: *The reliability of a test is the level of agreement between test scores that would be the same if there were no errors of measurement.*

This definition clearly implies that the first step in establishing the reliability of a test or other behavioral measurement is to specify which sources of variation (or inconsistency) are to be considered errors of measurement. For example, if we have several subjects observed by several observers on several occasions in each of several situations, we have four "naturally occurring" sources of variation. In addition, we will also have variation within a single observation period, which we could estimate by creating an "artificial" source of variation, by dividing the observation period into two or more sub-periods. How should we decide which of these sources of variation to consider as measurement error? Cronbach, Gleser, Nanda and Rajaratnam (1972) have pointed out that the key question is one of "generalizability": *Over which sources of variation do we intend to generalize our results?* For example, if we intend to generalize across observers, then differences between observers must be considered as measurement error.

The second source of ambiguity in the concept of reliability—one which is not always recognized—is the way in which the level of agreement between scores is to be measured. Classical psychometric theory avoids this question by means of statistical conventions. Variation is measured by the variance (or standard deviation); similarity of two variables is measured by the product-moment correlation (or by other correlations based on the product-moment correlation). These established practices have both the advantages and disadvantages of other sorts of conventions. They have the advantage of familiarity; we are accustomed to using them, and when results are reported in these terms we can more easily relate them to other results with which we are familiar. The disadvantage is that the very familiarity of these common statistical procedures may cause us to use them when they are not appropriate—when they do not answer the questions we want to ask. The next few pages will suggest some alternatives which may be more appropriate in some of the measurement situations which criterion-referenced testers and behavioral assessors may encounter.

Before we can talk technically about the reliability of a criterion-referenced test or a behavioral assessment device, we have to decide whether we are talking about the reliability of *measurement* or the reliability of *classification*. Measurement means assigning numbers to things in some meaningful way; classification means arranging things into groups. Of course, we could first assign numbers to things and then arrange the things into groups on the basis of those numbers. Consider, for example, a procedure that classifies persons as high or low in the frequency of a certain type of behavior, as recorded by an observer using a checklist. This is a classification procedure, and we might be interested in the reliability of the classification it produces. But the classification is based on frequency scores, and the assigning of these scores to persons is a measurement procedure. We might be interested in the reliability of this measurement procedure itself.

The statistics used to describe the reliability of measurement can be classified into two types: those that describe the amount of measurement error in absolute terms and those that describe it in relative terms. In the classical psychometric approach these would be the standard error of measurement and the reliability coefficient. The standard error of measurement describes measurement error in absolute terms—in the same units as the test (e.g., questions answered correctly, or number of times a certain behavior is observed). The reliability coefficient describes measurement error in relative terms; it tells us what proportion of the information contained in a group of test scores can be considered reliable information.

When is the classical reliability coefficient appropriate for behavioral assessment? It is appropriate whenever we want to know the reliability of a group of scores and we are interested only in differences between subjects, or between occasions, or between observers. The key question in applying classical psychometric methods is whether the absolute level of the scores is of interest. If not, then the classical methods are perfectly appropriate. A good test to use is to add a constant—10, or 50, or 100—to each score and ask whether the meaning of the scores has also changed. If not, then we can estimate their reliability in the traditional way.

Now, suppose we are interested not only in differences between scores, but also in the absolute level of the scores *in relation to a particular point* on the score continuum. This point might be zero, or it might be the target level for training in a certain type of behavior, or it might be a cutoff score for classification. It can be any point, as long as we have some reason for wanting to know how far each score is above or below that level. In this situation we can describe the reliability of a group of scores by using the "criterion-referenced reliability coefficient," which is simply a generalization of the classical reliability coefficient (Livingston, 1972). The classical reliability coefficient implicitly uses the variance in a group of scores as a measure of the amount of information they contain. The criterion-referenced reliability coefficient generalizes this approach by using, instead of the variance, the average squared distance of the scores from whatever point the test user selects as a reference point.

The criterion-referenced reliability coefficient is based on the concept of "criterion-referenced correlation" (Livingston, 1972). This concept can perhaps best be explained by means of an example such as that presented in Figure 1. The ellipse represents the outline of a scatterplot of data points; the horizontal and vertical lines represent the reference points for the two variables. Notice that the shape of the scatterplot indicates a negative correlation. Yet all the data points lie above the reference point *on both variables*, so that it makes sense to say that the two variables are positively related, though not as strongly as if the shape of the scatterplot indicated a positive correlation. The criterion-referenced correlation takes into account both the shape and the location of the scatterplot, by correlating the distance of each data point from the reference points on the two variables, rather than from the means.

The criterion-referenced reliability coefficient is the criterion-referenced correlation between two "parallel measurements"—that is, between two variables that differ only because of measurement error, with the amount of error the same for both variables. There is a simple formula that ex-

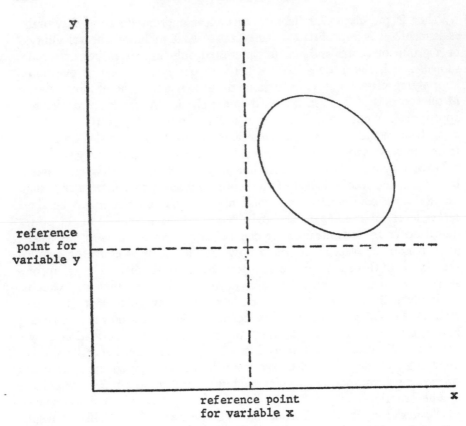

FIGURE 1. Conventional correlation is negative; criterion-referenced correlation is positive.

presses the relationship of the criterion-referenced reliability coefficient to the conventional reliability coefficient for the same set of scores. If r is the conventional reliability coefficient, m is the mean score, s^2 is the variance of the scores, and C is the reference point, the criterion-referenced reliability coefficient is given by

$$k = \frac{r\, s^2 + (m - C)^2}{s^2 + (m - C)^2}$$

You can see from this formula that k is generally larger (and cannot be smaller) than r for the same set of scores. The reason for this relationship is that the conventional reliability coefficient disregards part of the reliable information in the scores—their absolute level. Notice that when the reference point is equal to the mean, then k equals r. That is exactly what we should expect, since conventional reliability theory is based on the use of the mean as a reference point.

Like the conventional reliability coefficient, the criterion-referenced reliability coefficient can be a measure of internal consistency, of stability over time, of interobserver agreement, or of more than one of these things at the same time. The Spearman-Brown formula for the relationship between reliability and test length (i.e., number of independent observations) applies to the criterion-referenced reliability coefficient exactly as it does to the conventional reliability coefficient. In general, the most convenient way to compute a criterion-referenced reliability coefficient is to compute the conventional reliability coefficient and apply the formula given above.

Even when our reference point for measurement is not the mean, the standard error of measurement remains appropriate for expressing measurement error in absolute terms. There is also an alternative statistic which is more intuitively appealing but has less desirable mathematical properties. This is simply the expected size of the difference between two scores that would have to be equal if there were no measurement error. For example, if we consider differences between subjects and changes over time to be true differences, but differences between halves of an observation period and between observers to be measurement error, we could take the mean absolute difference between scores for the same subjects observed by different observers in different halves of the same observation period. This average difference size would be an absolute measure of the reliability of our observation and scoring procedure.

The reliability of classification can be estimated by having the same subjects classified by two independent observations that would produce identical results if there were no measurement error. The researcher must decide for himself which sources of possible differences in classification are to be considered as measurement error (e.g., different observers, differences over time, etc.). This procedure would yield a contingency table such as the following, which shows hypothetical data for two observers classifying the behavior of 20 subjects as normal or pathological:

		Observer 1:	
		Normal	Pathological
Observer 2:	Normal	16	2
	Pathological	2	0

There are several ways to summarize this information into a single statistic. The simplest is the proportion of agreement, which is simply the proportion of the subjects who were classified the same way by both observers. In the above example the proportion of agreement is $(16 + 0)/20$ $= .80$. Critics of this approach claim that this way of summarizing the data is misleading when most of the subjects fall into the same category. Notice that in the example, while the two observers each classified two subjects as pathological, they disagreed completely as to *which* two subjects should be classified as pathological.

Another way to summarize the data would be to disregard the subjects who were classified as normal by both observers and compute the proportion of agreement for only those subjects who were classified as pathological by at least one observer.

Another approach is to compute the correlation between the two observers. The correlation computed from this type of data is called the *phi* coefficient.

An approach with a different rationale from the phi coefficient but which yields similar results is that proposed by Cohen (1960), in the form of a statistic which he called *kappa*. Kappa is defined by the formula

$$\frac{p_o - p_c}{1 - p_c}$$

where p_o is the observed proportion of agreement and p_c is "the proportion of agreement expected by chance." Cohen's formula for computing p_c implicitly assumes that each observer will tend to classify a certain fixed proportion of the subjects into each category. Under this assumption, we would assume that each of the observers in our example tended to classify 90% of the subjects he observed as normal. The proportion of agreement expected by chance would then be $(.90)(.90) + (.10)(.10)$ $= .82$, and the value of kappa would be $(.80 - .82)/(1.00 - .82) = -.11$. When the two observers agree on the proportion of subjects classified into each category (as in the example), kappa will be exactly equal to phi.

Cohen's formula for p_c seems to imply that each observer has decided, before he begins the classification process, what proportion of the subjects he will classify into each category. If we prefer to assume that each observer begins with no idea of the proportion of subjects he will classify into each category, we should set $p_c = .50$, since we would expect the two observers to agree on half the subjects and to disagree on the other half. Under this assumption, the formula $(p_o - p_c)/(1 - p_c)$ becomes simply $2(p_o - .50)$, which is the "G index" recommended by Holley and Guilford (1964). For the data in the example, this statistic would be $2(.80 - .50) = .60$.

Clearly, the different ways of summarizing the data in the classification table can lead to very different conclusions about the reliability of the classification process. For this reason it is a good idea to present the full classification table whenever possible.

Now suppose that instead of only two independent observation procedures (e.g., observers, time periods, etc.), we have many. Rather than computing the agreement between each possible pair of observation procedures, we would like to compute a single overall index of consistency of classification. This situation is analogous to the case of many persons' taking a test of several questions. The different test questions might correspond to different observers, or different times of observation, or different specific situations of the same general type. What we are looking for is a measure of internal consistency that treats the test as a classification device. One solution is simply to split the test in half and compute the proportion of agreement between the two half-tests. There are two obvious problems with this method. First, the particular split of questions may give us misleading results. For example, if we happened to get all the most difficult questions in one half of the test, the agreement between halves would be misleadingly low. This problem can be solved by computing the average proportion of agreement over all possible ways of splitting the test into two halves. Some formulas to reduce the computational labor of this task have been derived by Marshall and Haertel (1975).

The second problem is that the average proportion of agreement between half-tests can be expected to underestimate the proportion of agreement between the full test and an equivalent form of the full test, since an increase in test length should produce an increase in reliability. Marshall and Haertel (1975) have devised a correction formula on the basis of empirical results with simulated data. If b is the average proportion agreement between half-tests, then the proportion of agreement between the full test and an alternate form is estimated by

$$\frac{b \, (3 + b)}{2 \, (1 + b)}$$

This formula produces a correction about half the size of the corresponding Spearman-Brown correction for a conventional reliability coefficient.

For example, a split-half reliability coefficient of .50 corrects to .67 with the Spearman-Brown formula. An average split-half proportion of agreement of .50 corrects to .58 with Marshall and Haertel's formula.

A somewhat different approach to the reliability of classification—one that may be more directly relevant to behavioral assessment procedures—is the "coefficient of agreement" proposed by Fricke (1972). This approach treats each test question as a separate classification device. The overall agreement among them is described by the statistic

$$U = \frac{\sum\limits^{n} d^2}{n\, k^2}$$

where n is the number of students, k is the number of questions, and d is the difference between the number of questions a student gets right and the number he misses. The sum is over all students. In behavioral assessment terms, d might be the difference between the number of observers who classify a subject's behavior in a certain way and those who do not; then n would be the number of subjects, and k would be the number of observers. When U is computed for a single subject, $n = 1$, and U becomes simply d^2/k^2. Notice that in the case of perfect consistency—when a subject's behavior is classified the same way by all k observers—the difference (d) will equal the number of observers (k). Therefore, if all k observers agree about all n subjects, U will equal one. When the observers are equally divided on how to classify a subject's behavior, d will equal zero, so that if the observers are equally divided on every subject, U will equal zero.

For an example of a situation in which U would be appropriate, suppose we have a subject observed by 10 observers. And suppose that nine of the observers classify the subject's behavior as normal, while one classifies it as pathological. Then d for this subject would equal 9 minus 1, or 8, and U would equal $8^2/10^2 = .64$. Now suppose we had a second subject, and all 10 of the observers classifies the second subject's behavior as pathological. Then d for this subject would equal 10 minus 0, or 10. And U for the group consisting of these two subjects would equal $(8^2 + 10^2)/2(10^2) = 164/200 = .82$.

Fricke (1972) also shows that U can be interpreted in terms of variance. Let p represent the proportion of questions a student answers correctly (the proportion of observers classifying a subject's behavior in a certain way), and let $q = 1 - p$. Let $S = \Sigma pq$ (the sum is over the n students). Then

$$U = 1 - \frac{S}{S_{max}}$$

where S_{max} is the maximum possible value of S, given the marginal totals for the test questions (observers). Presumably, this interpretation in terms of variance is the reason the differences (d) and the number of students (k) in the previous formula for U are squared. A perfectly legitimate index of agreement could be defined using the absolute values of d and k instead of their squares—or the absolute value of *any* positive power of d and k.

These internal-consistency procedures are quite flexible. The "test questions" need not actually be different observers; they might be time intervals in an observation period, or different specific situations across which we wish to generalize. Similarly, the "subjects" need not actually be different persons; they could be the same person in different situations across which his behavior could be expected to differ.

VALIDITY

The concept of test validity is even more ambiguous than the concept of test reliability. Most psychologists would probably agree with Cureton's (1951) concise statement that "the essential question of test validity is how well a test does the job it is employed to do." This definition implies that the first step in establishing test validity is to specify the job the test is being employed to do. Is the test being used to describe a person's present behavior, to predict some future event, or to indicate the person's status on some unobservable variable? Our answer to this question will indicate whether we are primarily concerned with content validity, criterion-related (i.e., concurrent or predictive) validity, or construct validity. Once we have answered this question, we must specify in detail the category of behaviors the test is intended to describe, or the future events it is to predict, or (insofar as possible) the other observable indicators of the unobservable variable it is to indicate.

The second source of ambiguity in the concept of validity, as in that of reliability, is the way in which the "how well" portion of the question is to be answered. In the case of validity, the established statistical conventions are not quite as firmly established as those for reliability, and their limitations are more often recognized.

With criterion-referenced tests, as with behavioral assessment, the type of validity with which we are most concerned is content validity. The purpose of a criterion-referenced test is to describe the student's level of mastery of a particular skill or body of knowledge. The question of content validity is how well the items on the test represent the knowledge or skills we are interested in testing. In the case of behavioral assessment, we are interested in describing the subject's behavior in a particular set of circumstances. The question of content validity is how well the circumstances under which the subject's behavior is actually observed represent all those sets of circumstances we are interested in.

Some authors have claimed that only random sampling from a well-defined domain of items can produce a content-valid criterion-referenced test. However, the specification of item domains is a laborious task and one which is frequently bypassed in actual practice. A more common means of assuring content validity is to subdivide the knowledge or skill to be tested into several specific areas of knowledge or skill application, and to make sure that the test items do not overrepresent some of these areas at the expense of others. (Of course, this technique applies to norm-referenced tests as well as criterion-referenced tests.) For behavioral assessment, instead of specific knowledge or skill areas, we might list specific sets of circumstances in which we are interested in observing behavior, and make sure that these are properly represented in the assessment procedure.

Unfortunately, there does not seem to be any completely satisfactory statistical procedure for describing the content validity of a test. Content validity differs from the other types of validity in that it is a characteristic of the test itself, rather than of the responses of a group of persons taking the test. There are two complementary aspects of content validity that must be considered. The first concerns the possible failure of the test to *exclude irrelevant* influences on the subject's behavior. The second concerns the possible failure of the test to *include* all *relevant* influences. Anyone attempting to devise a method for quantifying content validity will have to decide first whether to measure these two aspects together (i.e., in a single statistic) or separately. He/she will then have to decide what type of data to use as input to the method. A start in this direction has been made by Lawshe (1975), but his suggested method deals only with the problem of excluding irrelevant content and does not seem easily applicable to behavioral assessment.

Criterion-related validity is usually considered irrelevant for criterion-referenced testing and for behavioral assessment, since the test or the assessment itself is assumed to be as good a criterion as can be provided.

Nevertheless, a criterion-referenced test user might want to know (for example) whether he can substitute a less expensive, group-administered test for a more expensive, individually administered test. Similarly, a behavioral assessor might want to know whether he can use observations of behavior in a laboratory situation as indicators of behavior in a naturally occurring situation of some kind. These are questions of criterion-related validity.

The statistics that can be used to describe criterion-related validity are similar to those that can be used to estimate reliability from two independent observations. As in the case of reliability, we must specify whether we are interested in the validity of measurement or the validity of classification. If we are interested in the validity of *measurement*, we must decide whether we are interested in the absolute level of the scores or only in differences between scores. If we are interested in the absolute level of the scores, and if we can specify meaningful reference points for both the predictor and the criterion measure, we can use the criterion-referenced correlation coefficient described in the previous section. Probably the least cumbersome way to compute this coefficient is by means of the formula

$$k_{xy} = \frac{r_{xy} s_x s_y + (m_x - C_x)(m_y - C_y)}{\sqrt{[s_x^2 + (m_x - C_x)^2][s_y^2 + (m_y = C_y)^2]}}$$

where x and y are the two variables, m_x and m_y are their means, s_x and s_y are their standard deviations, C_x and C_y are their reference points, and r_{xy} is the conventional correlation between x and y. Notice that the reference points for the predictor and the criterion measure need not be the same.

If we are interested in the validity of *classification*, we can use the phi coefficient, or the proportion of agreement, or some conditional probability estimate, based on observed classifications in the predictor and criterion situations. Two conditional probabilities that may be of particular interest are the probability of success (or high frequency of behavior, etc.) on the predictor for those successful on the criterion variable, and the probability of failure (or low frequency of behavior, etc.) on the predictor for those who fail on the criterion variable. These correspond to the "sensitivity" and "specificity" indices that physicians use to describe the effectiveness of a test for the presence of a disease.

When we want to describe criterion-related validity in more detail than a single statistic can provide, we can use an expectancy table such as Table 2. This table answers the question, "Given that a person's score

TABLE 2

Sample Expectancy Table

		0-1	2-3	4-5	6+
	6+	.00	.10	.20	.40
Frequency of behavior in outside world	4-5	.10	.10	.30	.30
	2-3	.20	.50	.30	.20
	0-1	.70	.30	.20	.10
		0-1	2-3	4-5	6+

Frequency of behavior
in laboratory

on the predictor is within a certain interval, what is the probability that his score on the criterion measure will fall within a certain interval?" For example, in Table 2, a subject with a laboratory behavior frequency score of six or more would have a 40% probability of having a behavior frequency score of six or more in the outside world. The entries in an expectancy table are estimates based on actual observations. The intervals for the scores should be broad enough to provide a substantial number of observations in each row and in each column (though not necessarily in each cell; if the relationship is strong, some of the cells may well be empty).

Construct validity would seem to be only peripherally relevant to criterion-referenced testing and to behavioral assessment. However, as Johnson and Bolstad (1973) have pointed out, "As we begin to talk about such broad categories as appropriate vs. inappropriate behavior, deviant vs. non-deviant behaviors in children, or friendly vs. unfriendly behaviors, we are labeling broader behavioral dimensions. At this level we are dealing with constructs, whether we like to admit it or not, and the importance of establishing the validity of these constructs becomes crucial" (pp. 51-52, references omitted). Johnson and Bolstad advocate the use of the "multitrait-multimethod" technique of Campbell and Fiske (1959), in which each of two or more traits (i.e., categories of behavior) is measured by two or more methods. The resulting matrix of correlations—or other measures of relationship—is then analyzed for patterns of "convergent and discriminant validity." Notice that this technique does *not* necessarily require the use of a conventional correlation as the measure of strength of relationship. It will work with any statistic that describes the strength of a relationship between two variables, as long as the same statistic is used for all pairs of scores in the matrix. Applications of multitrait-multimethod matrices in behavioral assessment have recently been addressed by Cone (1976a).

BAYESIAN METHODS

Another recent development in educational testing is the application of Bayesian methods to the problem of using test scores to make decisions about what type of instruction to assign to a student. These methods may be useful with behavioral assessment when the assessment is used as a diagnostic tool. The problem is one of assigning subjects to treatment categories on the basis of an assessment, taking into account additional information about the subject population and the relative costs of the various types of errors possible in making the wrong assignment. The solution is a straightforward application of statistical decision theory; it has been presented in educational measurement terms by Swaminathan, Hambleton and Algina (1975). The procedure can be briefly outlined as follows:

1) Use population data to estimate the prior probability (in the absence of any assessment data) that a randomly selected subject will fall into each category (e.g., needs treatment/does not need treatment).

2) Find the distribution of assessment scores among subjects in each category.

3) Apply Bayes' theorem (described below) to get the posterior probability that a subject randomly selected from among those with a given assessment score will fall into each category.

4) For each possible assessment score, find the category that yields the lowest expected cost of misclassification. This expected cost is found by multiplying the cost of each possible misclassification times the probability of making it, and summing the products.

As an example of step 4, suppose the cost of withholding treatment when it is needed is twice the cost of giving it when it is not. And suppose that among persons with a certain assessment score, 40% actually need the treatment. Then the cost of withholding treatment from persons with this score is $2(.40) = .80$, while the cost of giving them the treatment is $1(.60) = .60$. Therefore we would give the treatment to persons with this assessment score.

Bayes' theorem, which forms the basis for step 3, can be expressed in the following formula:

$$P(Y \mid X) = \frac{P(X \mid Y) \; P(Y)}{\sum_{\text{all } Y} [P(X \mid Y) \; P(Y)]}$$

where $(P(Y/X)$ is the posterior probability that a subject is in a particular category Y, given that his assessment score is X; $P(X/Y)$ is the probability that a subject in category Y will receive assessment score X; and $P(Y)$ is the prior probability that a subject selected at random, without knowledge of his assessment score, will be in category Y.

Steps 1 and 2 require information that may not be readily available. Step 2 in particular requires that there be some means (other than the assessment) of identifying a group of subjects who truly belong in each category and whose scores on the assessment are like those of all subjects who belong in that category. In some cases this information may not be too hard to find; we may need only to administer the assessment to a sample of the subjects and then observe their behavior over an extended period of time, to determine which category each subject truly belongs in.

The use of these Bayesian methods suggests a natural statistic for evaluating the usefulness of the assessment. Let C_1 be the total expected cost of all misclassifications we would make if we classified on the basis of the *prior* probabilities. Let C_2 be the total expected cost of the misclassifications that would result from our using the assessment scores and the posterior probabilities. Then the usefulness of the assessment is indicated by the ratio $(C_1 - C_2)/C_1$. This ratio varies from one, for an assessment that classifies perfectly, to zero, for an assessment that is perfectly worthless. In a situation where the necessary information is available and the relative costs of the different types of classification errors can be established, this ratio provides a more important piece of information than any conventional validity coefficient.

CONCLUSION

This chapter has presented a variety of quantitative techniques for describing the reliability and validity of behavioral assessment procedures. I have avoided labeling a few of these techniques as the "correct" ones; the correct technique for a behavioral assessor depends on the type of data to be presented, the way it was collected, and the use to be made of it. In choosing from the catalog of techniques presented here, the behavioral assessor must consider the type of reliability or validity information provided by each technique and then decide which technique is most useful and appropriate.

13

CONCEPTUAL VS. ANALYTIC USES OF GENERALIZABILITY THEORY IN BEHAVIORAL ASSESSMENT

RICHARD R. JONES

Assessment in behavioral intervention studies has contributed to the birth (or rebirth, depending on one's age or perspective) of measurement techniques which focus on observed behavior as samples of other behaviors, rather than signs of underlying trait dispositions (Wiggins, 1973). Renewed concern with the quality of measures (i.e., reliability and validity of scores) has accompanied the proliferation of techniques classified under the rubric of behavioral assessment. The variety of behavioral assessment techniques is well documented by Linehan (Chapter 2), Bellack and Hersen (Chapter 3), and Walls et al. (Chapter 4) in this volume, and concern with reliability and validity issues is mentioned by most other authors.

The current concern of behavioral assessors with reliability and validity issues represents a potentially beneficial shift away from reliance on singular techniques such as interobserver agreement and toward more inclusive approaches based on traditional reliability and validity theory (Cronbach, 1970; Gulliksen, 1950; Lord & Novick, 1968) or Generalizability Theory (Cronbach, Gleser, Nanda & Rajaratnam, 1972). While this renewed interest of behavioral assessors in traditional psychometrics is certainly laudable, only the naive will assume that traditional psychometric theory provides a panacea for issues concerned with the quality

I would like to thank John D. Cone for suggesting the conceptual vs. analytic distinction to me.

330

of behavioral assessments. In anticipation of possibly uncritical use of traditional psychometric methods by behavioral assessors, certain assumptions or limitations in applying traditional reliability theory to behavioral assessments should be noted.

Nothing in this chapter is intended to dissuade behavioral assessors from their legitimate concern with the reliability and validity of behavioral scores. The intention is to identify limitations of psychometric procedures, as expressed by the measurement specialists themselves. In so doing, behavioral assessors may be prevented from overzealously applying sophisticated measurement methodology in situations for which available techniques are either inappropriate or not yet developed.

We will concentrate on Generalizability Theory (Cronbach et al., 1972) which seems to be the most comprehensive contemporary approach available for appraising the quality of behavioral assessments (Cone, 1977; Jones, Reid & Patterson, 1975). We will focus on behavioral assessments, as defined herein, and the way in which they tend to be used in intra-subject research or behavioral intervention programs.

The main argument of this chapter is that Generalizability Theory holds clear implications conceptually for appraising the quality of behavioral assessments used in both inter-subject (group designs) and intra-subject (individual organism designs) research, but that the analytic models (i.e., statistical assumptions and procedures) employed in Generalizability Theory are more suited for inter-subject than intra-subject research. Much of the following discussion, therefore, is focused on reviewing the limitations of Generalizability Theory for analysis of scores for a single subject. But to temper the possibly critical tone of this discussion, the clear conceptual value of Generalizability Theory for studying the dependability of behavioral assessments will be argued first. To set the stage for these discussions, behavioral assessment will be defined for the purpose of this chapter, and later, the critical differences between inter-subject and intra-subject research strategies will be outlined.

BEHAVIORAL ASSESSMENT DEFINED

Behavioral assessment is defined for the purpose of this chapter as assessment done by researchers, clinicians, and other practitioners whose goal is to measure aspects of people's overt, publicly observable behavior, rather than covert, private events of constructs like thoughts, attitudes, or personality attributes. Thus, behavioral assessment is distinguishable from trait assessment by the content of what is assessed. Behavioral assessment methods may, but do not necessarily, differ from trait assessment methods.

This definition excludes self-report of behavior which cannot be publicly verified. Hence, self-report of behavior from the distant past, which cannot be publicly verified, is excluded by this definition. True, past behavior is still behavior, verified or not. But the behavioral assessor's concern with reliability of behavioral scores (i.e., agreement between two or more independent, but simultaneous, recordings of the behavior) precludes from behavioral assessment events which cannot be publicly verified. While this limitation may seem profound, it simply serves to delineate the acceptable domain of events to be considered as behavioral assessments. One certainly can assess other "things," like traits or unverifiable behaviors, but these are excluded from the domain of behavioral assessment.

A crucial distinction logically is in the difference between behavior and non-behavior. Behavioral assessors would classify attitudes, opinions, thoughts, or traits as non-behaviors. The report of these is behavior, but since only the report, not the actual construct, is publicly observable, only the report would be included as an assessment of behavior by our definition, i.e., the assessed behavior is the report, not the content of the report. And, the report itself is probably of trivial interest. A score of 20, meaning that a subject reported *something* 20 times, is of little interest. Only the content of the reports would be of interest, but the above definition excludes such content as attitudes, traits, etc., from the domain of behavioral assessment.

But, if the report is about behavior, not private constructs, then it may be a behavioral assessment, but if, and only if, the reported behavior can be publicly verified by another reporter in addition to the self-reporter. By exclusion, then, unverifiable or private events are in the domain of some other kind of assessment. To label this other kind of assessment, an admittedly awkward phrase like nonbehavioral assessment could be proposed. Nonbehavioral assessment would include the measurement of thoughts, attitudes, opinions, traits, *and* unverifiable behavior. Nothing in this precludes the assessment of these "things." All that is proposed is that assessment of constructs and unverifiable behaviors not be included in the defined domain of behavioral assessment.

This definition of behavioral assessment incorporates several tenets of behavioral research in general. It uses the standard of reliability (agreement between independent, simultaneous observations) as a basis for excluding any events, including behavior, which cannot be publicly verified. The definition is nonspecific regarding method of assessment, i.e., any kind of instrument or data collection procedure can be used so long as the verifiability requirement is met. The discussion will proceed, assuming that this definition of behavioral assessment is at least workable, but recognizing that some assessors, behavioral or otherwise, may take exception to its exclusions.

CONCEPTUAL IMPLICATIONS OF GENERALIZABILITY THEORY

In simple language, Generalizability Theory provides the behavioral assessor with a way of thinking about an assessment problem. This can become a very general and useful style for approaching an assessment task, which typically will enhance the assessor's design decisions. A Generalizability Theory approach usually will provide a broadening of the problem conceptually, such that aspects of the assessment plan never previously considered become primary concerns. In particular, Generalizability Theory forces the behavioral assessor to consider various influences on behavioral scores, influences which may be critical for generalization of measures to conditions other than those under which the behavioral scores are actually obtained. Before expanding this point, consider some background information about Generalizability Theory.

Statistical developments over the past 30 years have greatly broadened the conceptualizations of reliability and validity of tests or other kinds of assessment. Currently, the most notable summarization and incorporation of these developments is Generalizability Theory (Cronbach et al., 1972), in which various lines of statistical thinking and development have been collected into a body of theory which refers to the dependability or generalizability of psychological measures of all kinds—test scores, ratings, behavioral observations, etc. A complete review of Generalizability Theory is beyond the scope of the present chapter. The reader is referred to the original source material, such as the book by Cronbach et al. (1972). For an illustration of Generalizability Theory applied to behavioral observations, Jones, Reid and Patterson (1975) used these procedures with a behavioral coding system developed to assess family interactions. Other examples of generalizability approaches to analysis of observational data can be found, for example, in Medley, Mitzel, and Doi (1956).

Generalizability Theory, as an extension of reliability theory and sampling theory, has its main goal in identification of various influences on the dependability or generality of scores. Generalizability Theory is based on an individual differences or correlational paradigm and has been developed largely, although not exclusively, to deal with the dependability of scores derived from psychological testing instruments. The theory recognizes that psychological measures are obtained under a variety of assessment conditions which can influence errors of measurement, or the generalizability of scores. The generalizability approach seeks estimates of the extent to which obtained scores, measured under particular sets of assessment conditions, may be generalized to the universe of conditions, from which the actual conditions of measurement were sampled.

Psychological assessments used in the individual differences paradigm for classification and prediction of behavior are readily evaluated using Generalizability Theory. The salient characteristics of this paradigm, recently called the multivariate trait research design (Wiggins, 1973), include multiple subjects, two or more facets which describe the universe to which scores may be generalized, and two or more conditions within each facet which are randomly sampled from all conditions possible within each facet. The crucial obligation of investigators using Generalizability Theory is to make an "explicit choice of universe" (Cronbach et al., 1972, p. 352), which means that the universe must be clearly characterized so that facets and conditions within facets may be adequately described and sampled. Perhaps the main point is that various facets, i.e., influences on the variability of behavioral scores, can be appraised simultaneously in the generalizability approach.

In contrast, consider the usual approach to reliability appraisal of behavioral scores. In many studies, the reliability of behavioral scores is based solely on inter-coder agreement, which is only one kind of reliability. Inter-coder agreement of behavioral scores tells nothing about variance in scores due to occasions, to different assessment methods, or to settings. Yet occasions, methods, and settings clearly influence the variance in behavioral scores. The generalizability approach permits appraisal of these and any other identified sources of variance in behavioral scores that can be specified in an appropriate assessment study.

This last statement summarizes the conceptual implications of Generalizability Theory for studies which use scores based on behavioral assessments. More specifically, Generalizability Theory draws the behavioral assessor's attention to conditions of the assessment situation which might influence the generalizability of scores. Said differently, Generalizability Theory highlights the fact that any one score is a sample of many scores which could be obtained by the behavioral assessor. The one score is obtained under a set of assessment conditions which are specified by the measurement operations actually used to obtain the score. But there are many possible sets of assessment conditions under which scores may be obtained. Assessors implicitly accept some assessment conditions and reject others when designing an assessment study. Given that different sets of assessment conditions will produce different behavioral scores, the conditions actually used should be viewed as a sample of the possible conditions that could have been used. It is unlikely that the assessor is interested only in a specific set of scores obtained under specific assessment conditions. Other scores obtained under other assessment conditions may be just as acceptable. In fact, the influence of these other conditions on scores may be critical for the planned use of the obtained measures. Assessors usually wish to generalize from obtained scores to assessment situations with conditions different from those under which the sample scores were obtained. For example, behavioral observation scores representing pupils' deviant behavior in math class on Monday morning are a sample of possible scores for the pupils which could be obtained under other assessment conditions. That is, deviant behavior scores could also be obtained for the same pupils on Tuesday, Wednesday, Thursday, or Friday, in the morning or the afternoon, and in language arts, music, social studies, or physical education classes. Two crucial issues for the behavioral assessor are highlighted by this example. First, does the assessor plan to generalize from the Monday morning math data to other days, times of day, or classes? Probably so. And second, are the deviancy scores of pupils likely to vary when different days, times of day, and classes characterize the assessment conditions? Again, probably so. Generalizability Theory forces the assessor's attention to these other conditions, to which the obtained scores might be generalized.

So, the implications of Generalizability Theory conceptually for behavioral assessment seem clear. The two issues raised in the preceding paragraph are very important concerns in designing an assessment study. Simply by asking these questions about influences on the behavior to be assessed and the generalization plan for the assessed behavior, researchers' attention will be drawn to influences on behavioral scores which might be otherwise neglected. Researchers who take these issues seriously will frequently realize that their initial assessment plan was more limited than they really intended it to be. And, by expanding the sets of assessment conditions under which behavioral scores are obtained, the researcher will learn more about the influences on behavioral scores and will be better able to support claims for generalizability from obtained scores than would have been possible with a more limited assessment approach.

These conceptual implications from Generalizability Theory apply to all kinds of research designs. That is, regardless of whether behavioral assessments are to be used with groups of subjects or with an individual subject, assessors should determine the possible influences on scores which in turn will specify the universe for generalization of scores. The universe includes all of the possible assessment conditions under which scores acceptable for the purpose of the assessment study could, or might, be obtained.

LIMITATIONS OF GENERALIZABILITY THEORY

While the conceptual benefits and implications of Generalizability Theory for behavioral assessment are clear, its analytic assumptions and procedures appear to be more limited, especially for individual subject research. More detail will follow, but to preface this point, it will be argued that the statistical assumptions and mathematical developments of reliability theory and Generalizability Theory are not suitable currently for uncritical use with data collected for individual subjects over ordered time samples. These kinds of data, it will be recognized, are typical of many behavioral intervention studies. Before describing the analytic limitations of Generalizability Theory, it is necessary to review the differences between inter-subject and intra-subject research paradigms.

Inter- and Intra-Subject Designs

The analytic procedures of Generalizability Theory are suitable for inter-subject research strategies but not for intra-subject studies. Inter-subject designs use multiple cases, typically assessed as groups and at the same time. Intra-subject designs use individual cases, assessed separately, i.e., not necessarily at the same time or in the same settings as other individual cases. While intra-subject designs may use multiple cases, as do inter-subject designs, the distinction involves the assessment conditions under which the data are collected and the methods used to analyze the behavioral scores. In inter-subject designs, all cases should be assessed under the same conditions, i.e., settings, time, and assessment methods should be the same for all cases in a study. These three facets, unless held constant across all subjects, could produce unwanted variance in scores. Intra-individual designs do not require that all individual cases be assessed under the same conditions. Individual cases are assessed at different times, in different settings, although often with the same assessment method. Data analyses also differ between inter- and intra-subject designs. In the former, both descriptive and inferential group statistics are used, e.g., means, variances, t-tests, chi-squares, F ratios, etc. In intra-subject designs, statis-

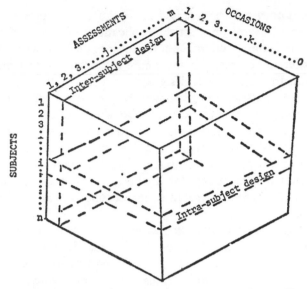

FIGURE 1. Three-dimensional schema showing prototypic inter-subject and intra-subject research approaches.

tics may or may not be used, but due to the focus on individual cases, repeatedly assessed over time, group statistics, particularly inferential ones, are often inappropriate (Jones, Vaught & Weinrott, 1976).

Figure 1 shows these differences between inter-subject and intra-subject designs schematically. The three dimensions represent subjects, assessments, and occasions. In any one study, there may be one or more subjects, assessed with one or more instruments, on one or more occasions. For example, a study which involved each of the three dimensions could include 1,000 persons, assessed with a battery of 10 instruments (tests, interviews, naturalistic observations, etc.), during each of 100 successive days. A typical inter-subject study, however, is less extensive, e.g., 100 persons assessed with a single personality inventory during two successive months to appraise the short-term stability of personality attributes. In contrast, a prototypical intra-subject study would involve a single subject assessed with a behavioral observation coding system during each of 10 successive days to establish a baseline of behavior rates. Other single subjects could be similarly assessed, but usually not on the same occasions or in the same settings, particularly if naturalistic observations are being collected. Without getting into all the possible variations of subjects, assessments, and occasions represented in Figure 1, the important distinction to understand has to do with the replications of scores in the inter-subject and intra-subject designs. In inter-subject designs, scores are replicated over different subjects, for any single assessment instrument on any single occasion. In intra-subject designs, scores are replicated over occasions, for any single assessment instrument for an individual subject. These two cases are shown schematically as two slices in Figure 1, each of which retains two of the three dimensions, but collapses or eliminates the third. Obviously, these two cases are idealized illustrations of inter-subject and intra-subject designs, but are presented to highlight the difference in score replications. Scores are replicated over subjects in the idealized inter-subject design. Scores are replicated over occasions in the idealized intra-subject design.

The importance of this difference in source of score replications, i.e., over subjects vs. over occasions, for the inter-subject and intra-subject designs, respectively, has to do with the adequacy of Generalizability Theory methodology for handling behavioral scores which are likely to be non-independent. We will return to this point later in the discussion of analytic limitations of Generalizability Theory for intra-subject data. For now, note that replicated scores over subjects are independent, in that one subject's score has no bearing, influence, or connection with any other subject's score. Said differently, knowledge of one subject's score does not allow prediction of any other subject's score, except under very limited and trivial circumstances. This is not likely to be true of replicated scores for a single subject. Scores from earlier occasions for a single subject could very well predict scores for later occasions. Hence, single subject scores replicated over occasions are likely to be non-independent. The term serial dependency describes the absence of independence often encountered in temporally ordered behavior scores for single subjects.

Generalizability Theory and Intra-Subject, Behavioral Intervention Studies

Behavioral intervention programs using intra-subject research designs possess characteristics which limit satisfactory application of Generalizability Theory's analytic methods. First, and perhaps most importantly, there is a steady state assumption underlying Generalizability Theory. Trends or order effects in behavioral scores are not satisfactorily accommodated by the model (Cronbach et al., 1972, pp. 22, 363-364). Using their words, Generalizability Theory does not adequately deal with scores on "successive observations in a changing situation" (p. 294). In intra-subject, behavioral intervention studies, the assessor or therapist is often, in fact, dealing with successive behavioral assessments in a changing situation and is concerned with assessment conditions (loosely, the universe) which stretch over a period of time when the client's behavior is changing. This, after all, is the goal of a behavioral intervention program, to change the client's behavior and to measure that change via some kind of behavioral assessment. In effect, the steady state assumption underlying Generalizability Theory is not met by the very nature of behavioral interventions in intra-subject studies.

A second major concern in applying Generalizability Theory is that the model does not adequately handle the situation where ". . . the universe of generalization may be unique to the individual, covering his behavior settings or his friends, etc." (Cronbach et al., 1972, p. 364). In intra-subject behavioral interventions, the universe of conditions to which one might generalize behavioral scores is, in fact, nested within the individual subject. The universe for generalization is, necessarily, subject-specific.

Analytically, Generalizability Theory is essentially an inter-subject model, where conditions to which scores may be generalized apply across all individuals. Individual subject studies, where conditions are nested within each subject, are not appropriate for analysis with analytic tools provided by Generalizability Theory. In brief, then, the two major characteristics of intra-subject behavioral intervention studies, i.e., a) the goal of changing behavior over time, and b) the individual subject focus of the analyses, seem to preclude the satisfactory application of Generalizability Theory.

To expand these arguments, consider the possible application of Generalizability Theory to behavioral assessments as used in a single case, behavioral intervention study. First, the universe for generalization must be specified. The universe is defined when the researcher tells what assessments would be equally acceptable for the purposes of the study; that is, what assessments would provide the same information as those actually obtained. For intra-subject, behavioral intervention programs, this requirement of Generalizability Theory might be rephrased as follows. Are there any conditions other than those under which the assessments are actually obtained, to which the obtained scores could be usefully generalized? To answer this question, we must further clarify the concept of facet.

A facet is an allowable condition of measurement and must be described when applying Generalizability Theory to behavioral scores. Facets describe the various aspects of the assessment situation within which behavioral assessments are obtained. For example, three facets which are relevant to many behavioral intervention studies are observers, time, and settings. The generalizability of scores among different observers is certainly a reasonable goal, since reliability of measurement between two or more independent but interchangeable observers is a canon of reliability theory. In many intra-subject studies, this form of generalizability is represented by indices of interobserver agreement.

The generalizability of behavioral observation scores to different time periods and to different settings for a single subject seems to pose a logical problem. Time periods and settings are inextricably confounded in an intra-subject, behavioral intervention study, since one person cannot behave in more than one setting at any one time. Thus, we argue that measurement dependability or generalizability does not apply separately to time and setting facets. Here we shall discuss time periods only, with the realization that different time periods could also be defined as different settings.

The Steady State Assumption: Intervention Phases as a Facet

What are the time periods used in typical behavioral intervention studies for the single case? Essentially they are defined by the assessment procedures used to obtain behavioral scores. For example, naturalistic observations may be obtained for one hour each day for 10 consecutive days (10 time periods). Alternatively, 15-minute behavioral interviews might be obtained in a clinician's office each week over a five-week treatment period.

Taking the example of 10 one-hour naturalistic observations, the generalizability of behavioral scores to other time periods, i.e., other one-hour daily observation sessions, might be of interest. The issue involves the generalizability of the measures obtained for these 10 time periods to other time periods that might have been used but were not. What might those other time periods be? Or, what is the universe of time periods from which these 10 have been selected?

Recall the definition of universe in Generalizability Theory. The universe is defined when the observations that would be equally acceptable for the purposes of the study or intervention are specified. In effect, what time periods other than those actually used would be equally suitable?

Would, for example, one hope to generalize observation scores obtained during a baseline phase to time periods during an intervention phase or to time periods during a follow-up phase?* In effect, are the time periods during intervention or follow-up time periods for which the behavior analyst would obtain the same information as during baseline time periods? We submit that the answer to this question is no, because the conditions in the single subject's life are supposedly changed during intervention and follow-up from those which existed during baseline. In fact, one would not logically substitute observation time periods from intervention or follow-up phases for those actually used during a baseline phase. Our point is supported by the authors of Generalizability Theory.

> Because our model treats conditions within a facet as unordered, it will not deal adequately with the stability of scores that are subject to trends or to order effects arising from the measurement process. This is a limitation common to all reliability theory. A large contribution will be made by the development of a model for treating ordered facets (Cronbach et al., 1972, p. 364).

In other words, Cronbach et al. indicate that Generalizability Theory as presently developed is limited with regard to the basic measurement and design features of intra-subject, behavioral intervention studies. In such studies, the subject's status is supposedly changing over a period of time running from baseline through intervention and into follow-up. These three phases are ordered conditions within what could be described as a time or treatment facet. Generalizability Theory treats such conditions as if they were unordered. Further, it is a goal of the intervention that scores for the single subject will show a trend or order effect across the three phases. Considering treatment as a facet and the phases within treatment as conditions does not fit the assumptions of Generalizability Theory. Phases are naturally ordered in time, while the theory treats them as unordered.

The Steady State Assumption: Serial Dependency

Another typical characteristic of behavioral scores for single subjects which exists within, and across, phases is a problem for Generalizability Theory.

---

* Of course, a different and legitimate question could involve the suitability of other time periods within a phase. Generalizability within a phase is an appropriate question, but one which does not address the steady state issue, the main concern of this section.

For many variables, adjacent scores agree more closely than scores
that are further separated. Some kind of growth or decay function
will be needed in place of the present universe score to describe *a
process that is strongly time dependent.* A development along these
lines will amplify, not replace, our model (Cronbach et al., 1972, p.
364, emphasis added).

Typically, behavioral scores close together in time are more related
than those further separated. That is, scores in a single subject's time
series tend to be time dependent, or in time series terminology, tend to be
serially dependent or auto-correlated (Jones, Vaught & Weinrott, 1976).
A universe score obtained from a series of auto-correlated scores will not
adequately represent the time-dependent character of the observations.
While subsequent developments of Generalizability Theory to handle
time-dependent scores may remove this analytic problem, at present the
model does not appear to be suitable for use with such scores.

Generalization Within the Person

The last, and perhaps most difficult, problem for Generalizability
Theory in assessing the quality of behavioral assessments is due to the
individual subject focus of many behavioral intervention programs. Cases
are treated one at a time, and thus the assessment and intervention activities are idiosyncratic to individual subjects. This point remains even if
behavioral researchers choose to collect several treated cases into a group
for purposes of analysis (e.g., Patterson, 1974). If behavioral treatment
were typically conducted by applying all assessment and intervention
procedures in a very similar manner to groups of cases at the same time,
then the problem of within-person generalization would not exist.

Again, the problem is well stated by the authors of Generalizability
Theory.

> Moreover, we have given no consideration to universes where all the
> admissible conditions are nested within the person. That is, the uni-
> verse of generalization may be unique to the individual, covering his
> behavior settings or his friends, etc. . . . To pursue measurements in
> this vein appears to require different questions for (or about) each
> individual and a personalized universe of generalization. Generaliza-
> bility Theory should nevertheless be readily adaptable to such meas-
> uring procedures (Cronbach et al., 1972, p. 364).

The universe of admissible conditions in intra-subject behavioral intervention programs is very much nested within the person. Conditions of

assessment and treatment are peculiar to the individual case. Generalizability Theory appears to require conditions of assessment, which define the universe for generalization, that are relevant to, and similar for, multiple subjects. In single subject methodology where individual differences are of little interest, Generalizability Theory seems to have limited analytic usefulness.

14

DATA-BASED INSTRUCTION: EVALUATING EDUCATIONAL PROGRESS

OWEN R. WHITE

INTRODUCTION

It is the purpose of education to provide each child with those experiences which will foster the development of behavioral patterns and skills requisite to the highest possible degree of independent and productive action in the adult community. In short, it is the job of education to change learners from, for example, nonreaders to readers, or from destructive or disruptive influences to "socially adapted" individuals. In this basic concern, there is very little difference between the fields of education and clinical psychology. Specific targets of concern might vary, and certain intervention or instructional procedures might differ, but to the extent that both education and psychology are interested in behavioral change, their technologies should have certain basic approaches in common. This chapter has been prepared in hopes that an investigation of the latest educational assessment procedures might foster a type of cross-disciplinary interaction of interest and benefit to both the psychological and educational communities.

THE MOVEMENT CYCLE: TARGET OF ASSESSMENT

It is axiomatic in any behavioral approach that reliable and easily interpreted assessments must be based on the measurement of directly observable behavioral events. In the experimental analysis of behavior, where most studies are conducted under highly controlled and complex system-supported laboratory conditions, the precise specification of behavior is rarely a problem (e.g., Stiers & Silverberg, 1974; Christman, 1974; Wright

344

& Nevin, 1974; Flory & Lickfett, 1974; Gonzalez & Waller, 1974; Selekman & Meehan, 1974; Cohen, 1975; Baum, 1975; Rashotte et al., 1975).
With the application of behavioral technology to education, however,
special guidelines were found necessary to assist the teacher in identifying
appropriate behavioral targets which are easily measured and amenable to
educational intervention. Lindsley (1964) was the first to formulate a set
of just such guidelines with the teacher in mind. Since that time, those
guidelines have been expanded, modified, and redefined several times (e.g.,
White & Liberty, 1976; White & Haring, 1976) and have proven of tremendous help to teachers in selecting appropriate behavioral targets.
Briefly, those guidelines are:

1) *The behavior must involve some directly observable movement.*
   This insures that the target is, in fact, behavior in the original
   sense of the term (i.e., any transposition of the organism or part
   thereof through space [White, 1971a]); and avoids the problems
   of working with phenomena which represent the absence of behavior (e.g., "sitting still").

2) *The behavior must have a definite cycle, with a clearly defined
   beginning and end.* Being able to precisely define the beginning
   and end of a behavioral event greatly facilitates the collection of
   precise and reliable data. This criterion, for example, forces the
   teacher to define the difference between "disruptive episodes" and
   "disruptions."

3) *The behavior must be repeatable in easily identified instances of
   uniform importance.* The behavior must be repeatable, of course, if
   it is to be changed. The rationale for uniform importance of each
   repetition, however, is somewhat less obvious. Essentially, the logic
   goes like this: If each repetition of a behavior is of uniform importance, then a simple count of its occurrence will suffice for
   behavioral assessment. If, on the other hand, the importance of
   each repetition changes (e.g., as a function of its duration, latency,
   or some other behavioral dimension), then a simple behavioral
   count will *not* suffice to define the progress of the child. Given
   that simple behavioral counts are the easiest form of data to collect
   in an educational situation, it also follows that assessments based
   on that form of data will be more reliable and take less of the
   teacher's time away from instructional activities. In order to pinpoint behaviors which are of equal educational importance with
   each repetition, it is necessary to "calibrate" the movements of
   children (White and Liberty, 1976; White & Haring, 1976). For
   example, instead of counting *answers* written in responses to addition problems (which might vary in length), the teacher will count
   the number of *digits* in each answer—thereby calibrating problem

length, at least in terms of the actual physical requirements for responding to each problem.

Reflecting the first two criteria for acceptance as a behavioral target, any behavior which meets all of the requirements specified above is called a *movement cycle*. Experience has shown that well pinpointed and calibrated movement cycles serve as excellent foci for instructional activities (concentrating the effort of the teacher on behaviors which are, in fact, amenable to instructional intervention) and lead to more precise and easily interpreted assessments.

ASSESSING THE MOVEMENT CYCLE: BEHAVIORAL COUNTS

As mentioned earlier, one of the prime reasons for the specification of instructional targets in terms of movement cycles is the facilitation of assessment. If each instance of the behavioral phenomena is, by definition, of equal educational importance, then assessments can be based on simple behavioral counts. If a child reads more words today (under equivalent conditions) than he read the day before, then some assumption of progress is justified. Behavioral counts might be rather restricted (e.g., counts of correct and error words only) or more descriptive (e.g., breaking "errors" down into counts of omissions, substitutions, mispronunciations, insertions, and repetitions), depending upon the information needs of the teacher. In either case, however, the results of assessment are immediately interpretable and directly related to the behavioral phenomena in question. By specifying how often a behavior *should* occur during each assessment, and then keeping track of the actual behavior counts from day to day, the progress of the child and effects of various intervention strategies are easily documented.

Other forms of data, e.g., durations or latencies, have also proven of some utility in monitoring the development of certain behaviors, but have been avoided in education for a very simple reason: They are more difficult to collect. In order for a teacher to collect duration data, for example, each and every instance of the behavior must be timed (usually with a stopwatch). If the behavior has been defined in a manner which allows simple behavior counts to suffice, on the other hand, it is usually possible to provide the child with a number of opportunities to move (e.g., a math-fact sheet) and then tally the results at some later time. If the movement is not dependent upon opportunities provided by the teacher (e.g., "out of seat" behavior), the advantages of a behavior count are even greater. It is likely, for example, that a teacher will notice that a child is out of his seat *sometime* during the out of seat episode—thus prompting a tally of the behavior to be made. It is *less* likely that a teacher will notice exactly when the behavior was initiated and terminated —obviating the possibility of reliable duration statements. That is not to say that duration statements would not be of some value (see, for example, Walker & Buckley, 1968), only that those data would have a lower probability of being accurate and, therefore, could mislead a teacher in educational decisions.

Research to date has indicated that assessments based on simple behavioral counts tend to be quite reliable. In one case, for example, teachers involved in classes with up to 27 pupils were able to monitor behaviors on several students at once with 84% to 100% reliability when compared with trained professional observers (Hall, et al., 1971). Self-recording and peer-recording studies have also demonstrated the potential advantages of this data type (e.g., Broden et al., 1971; Risley & Hart, 1968). The implication for clinical psychology, of course, is that the client and/or another untrained observer (spouse or parent) might be expected to collect reasonably accurate behavioral data on the performance of the client outside of the counseling situation. If the required data were more complex than simple behavioral counts, however, the data might be more misleading than helpful.

ADJUSTMENT IN COUNTS

Simple behavioral counts only lend themselves to valid comparison when collected under equivalent conditions from one day to the next. In many situations, however, either the time allowed for assessment or the number of opportunities for the behavior to occur changes from day to day. To correct for these inconsistencies and to provide a "universal base" against which the results of our observations might be interpreted by others, percentage or rate statements have often been employed to "adjust" behavioral counts.

Percentage statements are most commonly employed to correct for differences in opportunity for the behavior. If, for example, a child completes five out of 10 items on one day and nine out of 20 items on the next, the behavior counts *per se* would lead one to believe that the child has improved. Since there were more opportunities for the behavior to occur on the second day, however, the results can be misleading. Percentage statements hold behavior counts relative to a hypothetical 100 opportunities, i.e., *if* the child had been given *100* opportunities for the behavior, how many movements might the child have made? For the first day, $(5 \times 100) \div 10 = 50\%$; and for the second day, $(9 \times 100) \div 20 = 45\%$. It is now apparent that the child actually performed a little more poorly on the second assessment.

Rate statements are used to correct for differences in assessment times. If a child reads 125 words correctly during a two-minute assessment on one day, and 35 words during a 30-second timing on the next day, has he improved? As with percentages, each count is adjusted to reflect the expected behavior count for a standard base—in this case, a standard assessment time. In most situations a time base of one minute is employed. To find the number of words read *per minute* of assessment, the behavior count is divided by the number of minutes over which the assessment was conducted. For the first day, 125 words $\div$ 2 minutes equals 62.5 words per minute; and for the second day, 35 words $\div$ 0.5 minutes (i.e., 30 seconds) equals 70 words per minute. It would appear that the child improved slightly.

The calculation of either percentages or rates allows comparisons to be made between counts collected under different assessment conditions. It should be noted, however, that the adjustment is *artificial*, and that the differences in assessment conditions still exist. It could be, for example, that the child's average rate per minute is higher in a 30-second timing because he is less fatigued. Had the child been timed for a full two minutes on the second day, his actual performance might have turned out no better than his performance on the first day. Rate and percentage statements will not pinpoint *why* performances differ; they will only help to identify cases in which they *do* differ.

THE RECORD FLOOR

To clarify the existence of differing assessment conditions and help in their meaningful analysis, many educators have adopted the procedure of calculating and reporting *record floors* (White & Liberty, 1976; White & Haring, 1976). The record floor, in any given assessment situation, is the mathematically lowest non-zero performance value which can possibly be recorded. Since the lowest non-zero behavior *count* is one (assuming that only whole movement cycles are counted), the lowest non-zero percentage or rate which can be recorded will be that value based on a count of one. For the examples provided above, 10 opportunities would yield a record floor of $(1 \times 100) \div 10 = 10\%$; 20 opportunities produces a record floor of $(1 \times 100) \div 20 = 5\%$; a two-minute timing will produce a record floor of $1 \div 2 = 0.5$ movements per minute, and a 30-second timing has a record floor of $1 \div 0.5 = 2$ movements per minute.

The record floor makes two statements: It tells us the lowest limit of our measurement (i.e., we can only measure performances equal to or greater than the value of the record floor), and it defines the smallest amount of behavioral *change* which we will be able to assess accurately (i.e., unless the performance increases or decreases by a value equal to or greater than the value of the record floor, we cannot measure the change). By comparing apparent changes in performance against the value of our assessment record floors, therefore, we are able to decide whether all of that apparent change might be due only to the differences in mathematically *possible* values. Going back to the example concerning percentages which was presented earlier, we find that the differences between the two percentage statements was $(50\% - 45\%) = 5\%$. But the record floor for the first day's assessment was $(1 \times 100) \div 10 = 10\%$, a value larger than the apparent change, so we must conclude that all of the observed change might be due only to differences in assessment procedures. The calculation and use of record floors help immensely in distinguishing real performance differences from those differences which are only a function of the way in which we choose to collect, adjust, and present our behavior counts. The importance of record floors to the meaningful analysis of behavior change cannot be overestimated.

CHOOSING BETWEEN PERCENTAGES AND RATES

Percentage statements have been used with far greater frequency than rate statements in traditional educational and psychological literature. That tendency appears to be reversing itself for many reasons, however. Percentage statements are used primarily to explicate the proportion of one particular behavioral phenomena in relation to some larger set of possible phenomena. In education, the most common example would be a statement of percentage correct behavior. The relative accuracy of a student's performance is certainly important, but many educators are rapidly coming to the conclusion that *fluency* (how rapidly the child works) is equally important. For example, if a child reads with perfect accuracy but at a rate of only 25 words per minute, he is likely to be far less successful in school than a child who reads with only 95% accuracy at a rate of 125 words per minute. Also, many management or social problems are almost exclusively a problem of frequency. All children will get out of their seats from time to time, but it is the child who does so with a rate of 0.10 movements per minute (i.e., one movement every 10 minutes) who will come to the attention of the teacher.

Secondly, correct and error percentages are ipsative (that is, the value of one determines the value of the other). If a child's percentage of correct movements increases, his percentage of error movements *must* decrease. In fact, however, the actual *number* of both types of behavior might increase or decrease on any given day (assuming that the total number of behaviors is not fixed). Since rate statements do not mix correct and error counts, they allow the analysis of either form of behavior independently of the other—something which can prove quite useful in determining where a child's real problems lie.

Third, percentage statements have a definite ceiling: A child cannot be more than 100% accurate or take advantage of more than 100% of all behavioral opportunities. Just because a child reaches the magic level of 100% does not mean that his performances can no longer change, however. The child can still improve the fluency and ease with which he performs his movements—something which only raw behavior counts or rate statements can reflect.

Since accuracy and fluency are both important parameters of a child's performance, one might be tempted to collect and calculate *both* types of data. In fact, rate statements alone will usually suffice. Since rate statements still contain information about the correct and error movement cycle counts, one may combine them to find percentage statements whenever necessary. Percentage statements do not contain any information about the assessment time, however, so they cannot be used to calculate rates. To save time, therefore, it is suggested that one collect rated information, and convert to percentages only when statements of relative accuracy are desired.

FREQUENCY OF ASSESSMENT

Learning, or behavior change of any type, is rarely a "one-trial" phenomenon. Generally, behavior changes take place continuously, over time. To be most reactive to the needs of a pupil or client, therefore, it is essential that our *assessments* of behavior are as nearly continuous as possible. In most educational situations that will mean the scheduling of short, daily probes for each of the child's academic skills. In the counseling situation, that might mean the structuring of special self-observations or assessments at selected points during each day. In either case, our ability to offer consistently appropriate assistance to a client or pupil is directly limited by the frequency with which we assess the behavioral phenomena of concern. Of course, frequent assessments will be of little or no value unless we know exactly how to interpret and *use* the results of those assessments. To begin, we must know the *aim* of our interventions.

AIMS: NORMS, CRITERIA, AND PROFICIENCIES

If we are to be consistently successful in altering the behavior of our pupils and clients, it follows that we must know the aim or goal of our work. In general, we will want our charges to become "proficient" in some task, to "master" certain skills, or to reach some predetermined "terminal level of performance." Just how levels of proficiency, mastery, or terminal performances are set, however, is a matter of some debate.

Until recently, *norm-references* were the most commonly employed aims. That is, we attempted to make each child as much like other children as possible. Norms are established by measuring the performances of a child's chronological peers and then taking the average of those measures as the performance level to which we will strive to bring each child. At one time in the history of education, there were only enough resources to provide a limited number of children with complete educational services. Measuring each child in terms of his relative prowess made sense. Only the "fittest" were allowed to proceed up the educational ladder. Now legislative and judicial mandates have made it quite clear that *all* children will be provided whatever services are appropriate to meet their individual needs. Knowing whether one child is superior to another is no longer important in and of itself. It is more important to determine whether each child is ready for particular educational service and, if not, to identify those services and experiences which are appropriate.

In response to this shift in the purpose of assessment, a second type of referent has emerged: the *criterion*. Supposedly, a criterion-referenced assessment is one in which the child's performance is compared against that level of performance required to be "successful" in a task. Unlike norm-referenced assessment, with criterion-referenced assessment all children could presumably fail to reach a criterion or all children could pass. Although many criteria in use today are simply the result of "armchair" revelation" (reflecting only what one or more persons "feel" is an acceptable performance), successful task completion *should* be determined as that which results in one or more of the following conditions:

1) A performance on one task in a sequential task hierarchy which insures a high probability of continued progress on subsequent tasks in the hierarchy;

2) A performance which insures the maintenance of a skill over time, or successful transfer of the skill from one situation to another; or

3) A performance which meets the requirements for acceptable skill demonstration in "real world" situations.

CRITERIA FOR PROGRESS

Criteria designed to insure a pupil's continued progress through the curriculum are generally the most immediately important to the classroom teacher. What levels of accuracy and fluency should a child reach in two-term, single-digit addition problems, for example, before he is really prepared to tackle two-term, double-digit problems successfully? Moving on too soon could result in difficulties with later curriculum, and moving on too late will waste time, at the very least, and could potentially result in loss of pupil interest.

There are essentially two methods for the determination of intracurricular criteria. First, all children could be moved from one level of the curriculum to the next at some predetermined time. This is a common programming tactic in any event. After the children have been working at the next level of the curriculum for some time, their performances are examined to see which of them have maintained or improved their rate or accuracy in the new material and which have done more poorly than in the preceding step. By reexamining their performances at the time of the program change, the minimum acceptable levels for advancement can then be deduced. This type of discriminate analysis (i.e., discriminating between successful and unsuccessful pupils on the basis of the performance they achieved in earlier parts of the curriculum) can either be performed at a simple paper and pencil level (e.g., Liberty, White & McGuigan, 1975), or (where a great deal of data is concerned) with the aid of sophisticated computer analysis techniques.

Alternatively, all children are advanced to the next step in the curriculum whenever they reach that level of performance which one *believes* to be an appropriate criterion. The success and failure of all students in the next step of the curriculum are then examined. If most students *are* successful in each succeeding step, then it is assumed that the present criterion for advancement is appropriate. If a number of children fail or get progressively worse, then the criterion for earlier performances is increased (to better prepare future pupils fo the material which lies ahead). This method for the determination of progress criteria should really only be employed after some reasonable estimate of an appropriate criterion has been established, perhaps through the method described above.

CRITERIA FOR MAINTENANCE AND GENERALIZATION

The procedures for determining those criteria which insure maintenance or generalization of a skill are essentially the same as those for determining criteria for progressing though a curriculum. Frequently, however, maintenance and generalization can only be achieved if "overlearning" occurs. For example, if one wishes a child to maintain a reading rate of at least 100 words per minute, experience indicates that initial instruction will probably have to bring the child to a level of fluency in *excess* of that eventual goal (say, *125* words per minute).

CRITERIA FOR SUCCESSFUL APPLICATION IN THE "REAL WORLD"

Eventually, we want our pupils or clients to apply skills in their everyday lives. It is often difficult, if not impossible, however, to conduct follow-up studies to see whether application has occurred. As an alternative to the methods described above, therefore, we are often forced to seek out persons who already possess a skill at an obviously proficient level or to deduce what the real world working requirements will be for a skill, and use that information for the formulation of our performance criteria. For example, the criterion for oral reading might be set as the rate at which newscasters read prepared scripts on the television. Newscasters must read quickly and accurately, but must not read *so* rapidly that intonation and inflection suffer. In short, newscasters must be highly proficient oral readers. By setting their performance level (which, by the way, is surprisingly consistent from one newscaster to another) as our ultimate criterion, we are not likely to go wrong. A slightly different approach might be taken with silent reading. If the child with whom we are working is likely to go on to college, we might seek out estimates of the amount of reading required for college students and the time they typically spend studying and, with that information, deduce the required reading rate. If the child is only likely to reach the level of sheltered workshop employment, then a list of required "survival" words (men, women, poison, stop, go, etc.) might be compiled by actually watching such people and noting the situations which they encounter.

Regardless of the approach we take in setting our criteria, it is likely to be a long and demanding task. Furthermore, as the requirements of our society change, recalibration of criteria will be necessary at regular intervals. Nevertheless, criteria are well worth the effort. Criterion-referenced assessments offer a pupil or client a chance for meaningful advancement and eventual success. Norm-referenced assessments only guarantee that a certain proportion of the children will look like relative failures, because their performances fall below the norm.

CRITERIA IN CLINICAL PSYCHOLOGY

The establishment of meaningful criteria in clinical psychology will be much more difficult than in education. Problems tend to be more individual in nature (so there are fewer clients with similar problems to use as a group for discriminate analyses), and the "curriculum" through which a client must pass is far less well defined than that in the typical classroom. Even so, the potential advantages of empirically derived criteria remain, so the attempt should be made.

Progress criteria in clinical psychology should be established to indicate those performances which the client must display before the nature of therapy or counseling progresses from one phase to the next. When is a client ready for a group session? When can sessions be reduced from daily to weekly meetings? When can parents begin to reduce the amount of artificial consequation (e.g., tokens for free time or candy) they use in the home? At first, the criterion selected will be more the product of guesswork than empirical evidence, but if the attempt is made to quantify the basis of program decisions, the cumulative results of those data over time should begin to point out some consistencies. Of course, if several clinicians share their data, the process can be accelerated considerably.

Maintenance and generalization criteria can be tested by having the client or a member of his family keep records of the frequency of key behaviors outside of the counseling or therapy setting. How well must the client be made to behave in the special setting before the effects of that work begin to appear outside of that setting? Even if not all clients can be relied upon to produce accurate records, the results of work with those who can should eventually begin to provide some guidelines for work with those who cannot.

Application criteria might be estimated through the observation of persons deemed to be socially or psychologically adapted. What, for example, is the rate of negative statements with people who are not considered to be overly negative? In a way, the establishment of criteria based on the performances of other people can be construed as "norms." It must be noted, however, that only people who are considered to be *successful* are included in the sample, so the average performance does *not* necessarily reflect the "normal" performance of people in general.

Knowing where a pupil or client should end up, either before moving on to the next step in our interactions with them or before terminating services altogether, is only part of the answer to the full utilization of daily progress assessments. In order to be truly reactive to the individual needs of each person, we must be able to identify on a daily basis whether the pupil or client is progressing at an acceptable rate toward the criterion. Most people assume that a simple graph or chart of the daily assessments will suffice to meet this need. If the rates of the pupil or client are going up when they should go up, then all is fine. We leave the program alone. If the rates are going in the wrong direction, the program is changed. It is *not* as simple as all that! Most people will not progress evenly from one day to the next. Little patterns of ups and downs are likely to emerge which can obscure any overall, general pattern of growth or progress. Even if progress is continuously in the appropriate direction, there still remains the question of whether the progress is adequate to reach the goal *in time* (i.e., within the time available). Recently, an excitingly simple and effective method for daily progress assessment has been developed for use in education.

Minimum 'Celeration*

Given that we have decided the minimum fluency and accuracy which we desire of a behavior, the client or pupil's present level of performance, and the time which is available to reach our aim, it should be possible to draw a line on a chart which describes how rapidly the performances must increase or decrease each day, on the average, to reach that aim. Then, by simply noting whether the client's or pupil's performance meets or exceeds that expectancy each day, we can tell at a glance if the program must be modified or changed to *avoid* a potential failure. Specifically, the procedures for using a minimum 'celeration line are as follows:

---

* The term *'celeration* derives from the terms *acceleration* and *deceleration*, the two different types of changes which we might want to achieve in the rate of a behavior. *Minimum 'celeration*, then, would be the least acceptable rate of change for any given behavior.

1) Draw an *aim-star* on the performance chart to represent the performance level you wish to achieve and the day by which that aim should be met.*

2) Assess the performance of the pupil or client for three successive days (or sessions, whichever is most appropriate).

3) Determine the pupil's or client's *start-mark* by finding the intersection of the mid-date (or session) and mid-rate for those first three assessments. Entry performance might be estimated with only a single assessment, but generally it is better to use the median of several assessments to account for initial adaptation factors and other sources of error variance. The intersection of the mid-day and mid-rate is used so that the estimate of the person's entry behavior can be located in terms of both time and initial level of performance.

4) Draw a line between the person's start-mark and the aim-star. That line will represent how rapidly the performance must change over time, on the average, in order to reach the aim.

5) Continue to work with and assess the behavior at regular intervals. Record the result of each assessment on the appropriate day-line of the chart.

6) Whenever the results of three successive assessments fall below the line, the probability that the person will reach the aim in time must be assumed to be unacceptably low, so the program must be changed in some way (to more frequent sessions, a different type of instruction or counseling, etc.). Some people have employed the criterion of *two* successive failures to reach the minimum 'celeration line, and in cases where it is extremely important that the subject have every chance of success, one might even change the program whenever any *one* of the assessments fails to reach the criterion. In general, experience has shown that a criterion of two or three days below the minimum 'celeration line will catch most programming errors and avoid most unnecessary program changes.

7) If and when a change becomes necessary in a program, there are several options for determining a new minimum 'celeration line

---

* It makes some difference which type of chart is employed. In general, a chart which provides space for each calendar day will be best, since it takes into account both the time when we can work with the pupil or client and the time during which we cannot (but during which progress might still occur); a chart should be selected which also makes the progress of the subject appear as linear as possible (i.e., the growth pattern should look like a straight line). Semilog charts or log/log charts are usually more satisfactory in this last respect, since most human performance changes are usually *proportionally*, rather than absolutely, equivalent to the size of previous changes occurring at higher or lower rates.

(Liberty, 1972; White & Liberty, 1976; White & Haring, 1976). It is recommended, however, that the following procedure be employed:

a) Establish a new start-mark by drawing a line from the mid-rate of the last three assessments to the day on which the new program will begin.

b) Reevaluate the aim-star. If possible, leave it as it is. If there is some doubt that the subject will be able to overcome the original program problem prior to the date originally set for the aim, however, the aim-star can be adjusted to allow more time.*

c) Draw a new minimum 'celeration line from the new start-mark to the (original or adjusted) aim-star.

Continue the new program, the regular assessments and charting, and evaluate the subject's progress in accord with the rules specified above. The procedures for using minimum 'celeration are illustrated in Figure 1.

The general procedures for employing minimum 'celeration techniques have been well documented, including certain cautions about a "blind" adherence to those rules (Liberty, 1972; White & Liberty, 1976; White & Haring, 1976). More importantly, evidence exists that the implementation of those rules for program evaluation can result in dramatically improved pupil progress and aim attainment. In a study involving 15 special education teachers and 74 learning disabled children, Bohannon (1975) found that when teachers employed simple, daily assessments and minimum 'celeration program change rules, they spent less time with pupils and yet were able to promote much higher rates of progress than when they tried to work without the daily data or rules. Starting with reading deficits of between one and three years, all of the children who were working under minimum 'celeration rules achieved a level of reading performance equal to or greater than the twenty-fifth percentile of their normal peers within 28 days, while only two members of the con-

---

* In a surprising number of cases, the information gained from the first program failure is sufficient to prompt the development of a new program which *is* effective in helping a child to reach his aim within the time originally allowed (i.e., necessitating a rate of progress *higher* than originally expected). Since most immediate objectives are scheduled for completion within a period of one or two months, however, there is usually sufficient time left in the school year to readjust the aim-date if that is felt to be more practical than the demand for even greater rates of progress.

FIGURE 1

Minimum 'Celeration Line

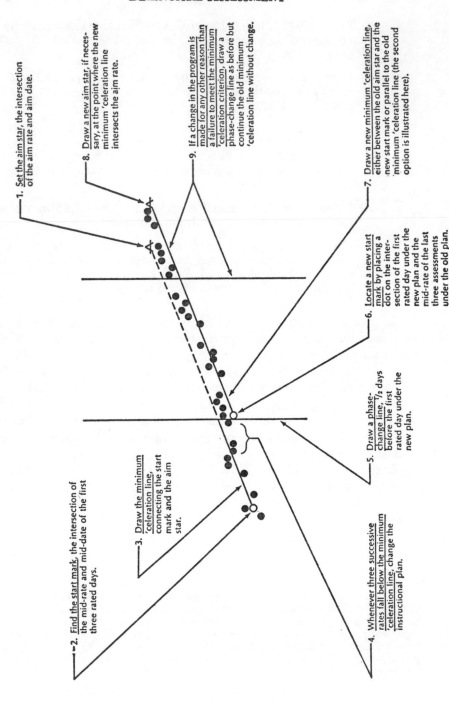

1. Set the aim star, the intersection of the aim rate and aim date.

8. Draw a new aim star, if necessary, at the point where the new minimum 'celeration line intersects the aim rate.

9. If a change in the program is made for any other reason than a failure to meet the minimum 'celeration criterion, draw a phase-change line as before but continue the old minimum 'celeration line without change.

7. Draw a new minimum 'celeration line, either between the old aim star and the new start mark or parallel to the old minimum 'celeration line (the second option is illustrated here).

2. Find the start mark, the intersection of the mid-rate and mid-date of the first three rated days.

3. Draw the minimum 'celeration line, connecting the start mark and the aim star.

6. Locate a new start mark by placing a dot on the intersection of the first rated day under the new plan and the mid-rate of the last three assessments under the old plan.

5. Draw a phase-change line, 1/2 days before the first rated day under the new plan.

4. Whenever three successive rates fall below the minimum 'celeration line, change the instructional plan.

From White & Haring, 1976, p. 380.

trast group achieved similar progress. Moreover, teachers in the regular classes (who were unaware of which children were receiving which treatments) were able to identify members of the experimental group as having achieved better gains in *all* subject areas (presumably, as a result of their increased fluency in reading) and much better "affective" development in general.

Although no specific research has been conducted on the application of daily data decision rules in clinical psychology, the implications are no less exciting. Since the rules are simple to follow and direct, it would be possible, for example, to have a client or parent chart the progress of a behavior and use that information to identify precisely when additional counseling or therapy is needed. In this way, clients could assume more of the responsibility for their own treatment, a desirable state of affairs in any event, and reduce the work load of the psychologist at the same time. Successes with procedures involving client collected data have already been reported (e.g., Patterson & Gullion, 1968; Diebert & Harmon, 1970; Knox, 1971; Stuart, 1971). It can only be assumed that rules which assist clients and managers in the more efficient and effective use of those data will be of tremendous benefit.

THE DESCRIPTION OF PROGRESS

The minimum 'celeration line does not describe how the pupil or client is *actually* progressing; it only defines how he *must* progress in order to reach a level of proficient or acceptable performance within the time available. That will be all the information one requires when making daily programming decisions. It may be useful, however, to describe the actual progress of the subject for purposes of reporting or prediction. Three methods have been developed to do just that. The first two can be accomplished without special tools or extensive training. The third method will produce more reliable and predictively valid results, but usually requires the use of a computer. All three methods are based on the properties of the median, since that statistic tends to reduce the influence of the dramatic and non-random shocks to which all human learning curves are subject (e.g., days in which the subject is sick or is under the influence of some drug or emotional experience). Studies have indicated that mean-based descriptions of progress (e.g., regression) overemphasize the performance of the subject on unusual days, and the predictive validity of those descriptions suffers accordingly (White, 1972a, 1972b; Koenig, 1972).

The Quarter-Intersect Line of Progress

The quarter-intersect line of progress is a simple description of how rapidly the median performance of the pupil or client is changing over time (Koenig, 1972). After dividing the data to be summarized into two equal halves, one simply finds the intersection of the mid-rate and mid-date in the first half (counting only those days on which assessments were conducted) and the intersection of mid-rate and mid-date in the second half. A line is then drawn through those intersections to describe how rapidly the rates of the subject are increasing or decreasing over time.*

The Split-Middle Line of Progress

The quarter-intersect line of progress will represent a reasonable description of the subject's overall rate of progress. The line may, however, be a little high or low on the chart for an accurate description of the subject's average *level* of performance on any given day. The split-middle line of progress corrects for this problem by moving the quarter-intersect line up or down (keeping it parallel to its original slope) until 50% of the data fall on or above the line and 50% of the data fall on or below the line (i.e., until the properties of a median are achieved). By correcting for an imbalance of data above and below the line of progress, the split-middle will be somewhat more accurate in predictions and a more reasonable description of the child's performance. It should be noted, however, that this final adjustment might take more time than all preceding steps combined, and so is usually reserved only for those cases in which the most precise description is required.** The procedures for finding the quarter-intersect and split-middle lines of progress are illustrated in Figure 2.

---

* References here are made to "rates" simply for the sake of convenience. While it is true that most of the research concerning the predictive validities of lines of progress has been conducted on rated information, there is no reason to believe that these procedures cannot be applied with success to other forms of data as well (e.g., duration or latency times). If an ipsative datum is used, however (e.g., percentages), one must take care to account for any mathematical limits imposed by the measurement scale (e.g., a ceiling of 100%).

** I do not mean to imply that the time required to find either of these lines is very great. With practice, one should be able to find the quarter-intersect line for 20 data points in about 10 seconds and the split-middle line in 20 or 30 seconds.

FIGURE 2

The Split-middle
Line of Progress

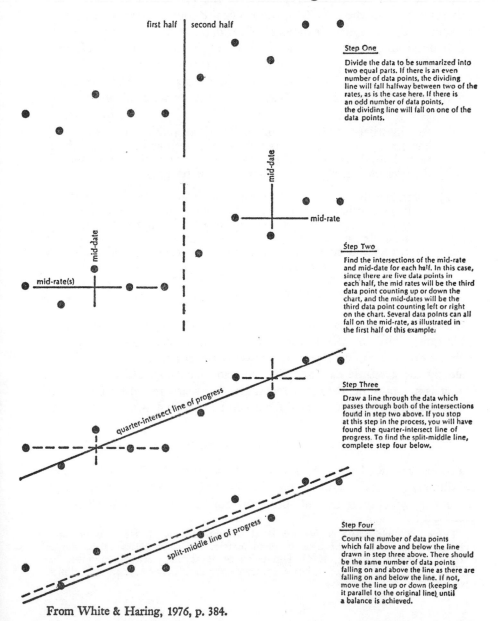

first half | second half

Step One

Divide the data to be summarized into two equal parts. If there is an even number of data points, the dividing line will fall halfway between two of the rates, as is the case here. If there is an odd number of data points, the dividing line will fall on one of the data points.

mid-date

mid-rate

Step Two

Find the intersections of the mid-rate and mid-date for each half. In this case, since there are five data points in each half, the mid rates will be the third data point counting up or down the chart, and the mid-dates will be the third data point counting left or right on the chart. Several data points can all fall on the mid-rate, as illustrated in the first half of this example:

mid-date

mid-rate(s)

quarter-intersect line of progress

Step Three

Draw a line through the data which passes through both of the intersections found in step two above. If you stop at this step in the process, you will have found the quarter-intersect line of progress. To find the split-middle line, complete step four below.

split-middle line of progress

Step Four

Count the number of data points which fall above and below the line drawn in step three above. There should be the same number of data points falling on and above the line as there are falling on and below the line. If not, move the line up or down (keeping it parallel to the original line) until a balance is achieved.

From White & Haring, 1976, p. 384.

The Median Slope Line of Progress

The quarter-intersect and split-middle lines of progress describe how a subject's median performance is changing over time. They do *not*, however, yield a line which actually displays the properties of the median with respect to all the data (i.e., those lines do not necessarily minimize the sum of the unsigned deviations of all data about it). Finding a line which does possess the properties of a dynamic median will result in a more valid and predictively useful description (White, 1971a, 1971b, 1974). Unfortunately, to find such a line requires a great deal more time and effort on the part of the analyst. Two methods are available.*

1) All lines between all possible pairs of data (that is, $\frac{1}{2}n(n-1)$ lines) are generated, and the sums of the unsigned deviations about each line determined. The line which minimizes the sum is then selected as the median slope line of progress.

2) Alternatively, a set of decision rules can be used to find the median slope line of progress without generating all possible lines. Based on certain geometric relationships which must exist between the possible lines of progress in a data set, these rules *can* reduce the time required to find a solution. The rules are quite difficult to program, however, so the development of appropriate software is usually undertaken only when large data sets are to be analyzed in great number (White, 1972b).

On occasion, more than one line of progress will satisfy the mathematical requirements for the median slope. In such situations, it must be assumed that the subject's performance characteristics are not clearly defined by the available data and that additional data should be collected. If that is not possible, then it is recommended that the most conservative of the alternative lines be selected for use in further analyses.

THE PREDICTION OF PROGRESS

Having described a subject's rate of progress under a set of program conditions, one may wish to predict the level of future performances (assuming, of course, that all program conditions remain unchanged).

---

* There are multivariate equivalents to the procedures which are described here that have been used in the field of econometrics for some years called the L, criterion (Sposito & Smith, 1974). Discussion of these multivariate techniques has been eliminated from this paper, however, since they have little application in clinical practice.

Such predictions are useful in making prognostic statements and a detailed analysis of program change effects (to be discussed later).

To accomplish a prediction, one simply lays a straight-edge along the line of progress and draws an extension of it out to the date in question. Mathematical predictions may also be made, but rarely increase the accuracy of prediction to a degree which warrants the extra work in a clinical setting. Of course, predictions should never be allowed to exceed the limits of measurement (e.g., go above 100% when using percentage data, or below the record floor with either percentage or rate data).

The predictive validity of the quarter-intersect, split-middle, and median slope lines of progress has been investigated on several large data sets (White, 1972a, 1972b; Koenig, 1972). In all cases, semilog transformations of the data were employed, and only rate data have been analyzed in sufficient number to allow meaningful conclusions to be drawn. Empirically derived estimates of successful prediction (over varying periods of time, given varying amounts of data to use in formulating the prediction) are provided in Table 1 for the split-middle and median-slope methods of deriving a line of progress.* As can be seen in that table, levels of predictive validity acceptable for research purposes are not really reached until nine or 11 data points are available to draw the line of progress. Reasonable confidence might be placed in predictions based on as few as seven data points, however, for most clinical purposes. Also, note that although the median-slope procedure is consistently superior to the split-middle procedure, practical differences become quite small when nine or 11 data points are used.

It would seem reasonable that certain behavior types or performances

---

* All predictions studied were conducted within phases of actual classroom programs, i.e., over periods during which program variables were held constant. In each case, the first few data points in each phase were used to formulate a prediction of the pupil's performance later in the same phase. Criteria for successful prediction were based on "envelopes" drawn about the line of progress in the predictor data set. One envelope was drawn to contain 50% of the data, another to contain 75%, and a third to contain 100% of the data used to formulate the line of progress. These envelopes were then projected into the predicted data set (along with, and parallel to, the line of progress). If the distribution of predicted performances within those projected envelopes equalled or exceeded 50%, 75%, and 100% respectively (i.e., attained the same distribution about the predicted line of progress as the original predictor data set), then prediction was considered sufficiently precise for experimental purposes. Criteria for success were also tested in which 25% of all predicted data were allowed to exceed expected deviations from the projected line of progress. Predictions meeting these criteria were judged acceptable for most clinical applications where somewhat less accurate predictions might still be considered functional.

TABLE 1: Percent of successful predictions using the split-middle and median-slope lines of progress

		Number of days over which prediction is extended									
		2	4	6	8	10	12	14	16	18	20
5	Split-Middle	62-64%	54-60%	48-56%	41-54%	41-48%	34-44%	31-41%	26-37%	24-32%	24-30%
	Median-Slope	68-71%	66-70%	63-69%	61-67%	59-66%	57-64%	54-63%	53-62%	52-61%	50-59%
7	Split-Middle	74-87%	71-84%	70-82%	64-78%	60-74%	60-70%	56-66%	51-63%	50-67%	50-67%
	Median-Slope	78-90%	76-88%	75-86%	73-85%	72-83%	70-81%	69-80%	67-78%	66-77%	65-75%
9	Split-Middle	93-96%	91-95%	83-93%	80-91%	77-89%	71-86%	70-83%	70-81%	70-79%	70-78%
	Median-Slope	88-96%	88-96%	87-96%	87-96%	87-96%	86-96%	86-97%	85-97%	85-97%	85-97%
11	Split-Middle	96-99%	94-99%	91-98%	87-92%	84-92%	82-92%	81-92%	81-92%	81-92%	81-92%
	Median-Slope	97-99%	96-99%	96-98%	95-98%	94-98%	94-97%	93-97%	93-96%	92-96%	92-96%

Number of days used to draw the line of progress

NOTE: The low percentage in each case is the actual percentage of predictions in which the distribution of predicted data about the line of progress was initially the same as the distribution of data about the line of progress in the predictor data set. The high percentage in each case is the percentage of predictions in which 25% of the predicted data exceeded the limits of the distribution defined by the predictor data set. All percentages are based on a sample size of 1,150 predictions of actual classroom data. All percentages are rounded to the nearest whole value.

with certain characteristics would be more predictable than others. Preliminary studies concerning behavior type (with behaviors ranging from simple pointing responses to complex reading behavior), performance variability, and initial rate of progress have failed to identify any differences in predictive validity, however. Thus far, it would seem that all general performance types are equally predictable, albeit, within a considerable range of predictability which applies to all performances (White, 1971c, 1972a). Despite these encouraging results, one must bear in mind that the prediction of future events cannot be mathematically or theoretically justified in the same sense that the appropriate application of an F-test can be justified. There is always some unknown probability that new variables or continued exposure to old variables will affect the performance of the subject in some unexpected manner and invalidate any prediction. It is suggested, therefore, that an attempt be made to validate predictions empirically whenever possible, and that a table of successful prediction probabilities be constructed which matches the behaviors and situations which you will encounter. Also, there will be occasions when a single line of progress will not serve as an adequate descriptor of a subject's progress during any given phase of a program. Perhaps the line intersects a record floor or ceiling, or perhaps the subject's reaction to treatment variables changes with increases or decreases in performance. By selecting the appropriate chart, one which produces a visually linear pattern of growth,* many problems in description and prediction can be avoided, but under certain conditions, it will be necessary to divide a single phase of a program into two or more parts with a separate line of progress for each (White & Haring, 1976). Of course, in such a case, only the last line in a phase would be used for actual predictions.

THE ANALYSIS OF PROGRAM CHANGE EFFECTS

Although the line of progress and predictions based upon that line will be useful in estimating prognoses for program success or failure, the primary use of lines and predictions is in the analysis of program change effects. Data collected on a single individual over time represent a sequentially dependent time series. That is, each data point can be expected to influence, to some extent, the value of succeeding data points. As such, these data cannot be treated in the usual manner (e.g., with simple F or t tests) when it comes to estimating the magnitude and significance of changes in performance attributable to program alteration (e.g., see Glass,

---

* Usually a semilog or log/log chart is best (White & Liberty, 1976).

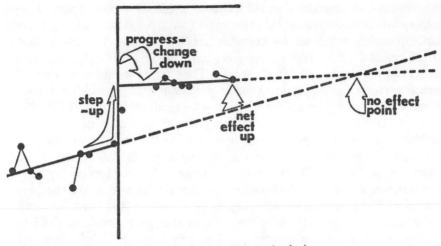

FIGURE 3. Between Phase Analysis.

Willson & Gottman, 1975). Although several valid statistical treatments have been devised to correct for sequential dependency (e.g., Bartlett, 1935; Anderson, 1942; Box, Jenkins & Bacon, 1967; Coutie, 1962; Gottman, McFall & Barnett, 1969; Glass, Willson & Gottman, 1975), none of these traditional procedures yields a description of performance changes which can assist the practitioner in interpreting the meaningfulness of results. By describing the growth which occurred within each phase of a program with a line of progress, however, and then extending each line into the next treatment phase, an excellent and easily interpreted picture of performance trends and changes can be achieved. Figure 3 illustrates the use of lines of progress for a between phase analysis.

A heavy vertical line is drawn on the chart to indicate the day on which the program was changed. A line of progress (in this case, the split-middle line) is drawn through the data in each condition to describe daily growth and progress. Dotted lines are drawn as extensions of each line of progress to indicate where we might predict the subject would have gone if conditions were left unchanged. The analysis of changes then proceeds as follows:

> 1) *The immediate impact of the new program is determined by* examining where the first line of progress ends and the next line begins. This "step" change has often been equated with a Hawthorne

or novelty effect, but may represent a true and permanent change in the subject's behavior.

2) *The change in rate of learning or behavior change* is determined by comparing the slope of the first line of progress with the slope of the second line of progress. In the example provided, the subject has changed from an upward trend to virtually no trend at all. A progress change will continue to affect performances for as long as the condition which produced it remains in effect.

3) *The net effect* of the program change is determined by comparing the value of the new line of progress and the value of the predicted line of progress (i.e., the prediction based on the line of progress in the first phase) at the time the program is terminated or changed once more. In the example provided, the net effect is "up," since the child's actual level of performance exceeded that which we would have predicted on the basis of his old line of progress. Note, however, that if the second treatment had not been terminated when it was, we might expect that the child would eventually be performing *below* the predicted line of progress. The progress change *down* would eventually cancel out the effects of the step change *up* (note where the two prediction lines cross). If step and progress changes are in opposite directions, therefore, a program change cannot be considered either all good or all bad. It will depend on the location of the *no-effect point* (the place where the step and progress changes cancel out), and whether we terminate or change the program again before or after that point.

An analysis of lines of progress and their projections enables a detailed analysis to be made of changes within and between program phases that would not otherwise be possible. More detailed discussions of such analyses are beyond the scope of this manuscript, but may be found elsewhere (e.g., White, 1972a, 1972b, 1974; White & Haring, 1976). Procedures for the application of inferential statistics to the question of the significance of step, progress change, and overall net effect of changes have also been developed (White, 1972b), but if significance of change statements are desired, it is suggested that the more powerful traditional time-series statistics be employed (e.g., Glass, Willson & Gottman, 1975). Usually, significance statements will be of secondary concern to the clinical practitioner or teacher. The simple description of changes in the precise manner described above will be sufficient for the interpretation of program value, identifying which programs might be expected to produce which types of changes, for developing an expectancy table of initial effects (so an initial effect detrimental to the overall aim will not necessarily result in program alteration if an appropriate progress change can be expected to follow), and for determining how long different programs must be left in effect to achieve or avoid an overall combined effect of step and progress changes.

CONCLUSION

The technology of data collection and analysis in education is advancing rapidly. Educational practitioners are, for the first time, beginning to realize the true potential of systematic, data-based instruction. I have only been able to scratch the surface of the available technology in this manuscript. But if I have been successful in pointing out some of the procedures and practices which might be of value in clinical psychology, then I have achieved my purpose. Availing oneself of the referenced literature will fill in the details needed to actually begin the implementation of an advanced data-based program.

15

COMPUTER ASSISTED
BEHAVIORAL ASSESSMENT

HUGH V. ANGLE, LINDA RUDIN HAY, WILLIAM M. HAY
and EVERETT H. ELLINWOOD

The original purpose of the evaluation program described in this chapter was to investigate the abuse of prescribed psychoactive drugs in 25-to-65-year-old individuals. In the study of drug abuse, research has been marked by an almost exclusive emphasis on demographic information. Until recently, the present project similarly emphasized demographic variables, plus the assignment of diagnostic labels to clients abusing drugs. We found this information to contribute little to the understanding of drug-taking behavior or to the design of treatment plans.

As an alternative to conventional procedures, the project committed itself to the behavioral assessment approach in order to examine the variables controlling drug behavior. These variables necessarily cover a wide range of life areas, especially since drug abuse is often not the drug client's presenting problem.

The present program has adopted features of the comprehensive behavioral assessment described by Kanfer and Saslow (1969). The current assessment system is divided into three stages: 1) identification of behavior excesses and deficits over a broad spectrum; 2) clarification of situational events surrounding each problem behavior; and 3) integration of assessment information into a functional analysis. The immediate difficulty with implementing these stages was the general unavailability of detailed and specific assessment procedures. Although Kanfer and Saslow have outlined broad categories of behavioral information, they do not specify the pro-

This project was supported by a NIDA grant 1H81 DA 01665.

cedures for collecting this information. The following describes a set of procedures for obtaining such information in a highly systematic fashion.

COMPREHENSIVE ASSESSMENT DATA

Traditional and behavioral assessment approaches are distinguished by the content of the information collected and by the way that this information is processed. The strategy of traditional assessment is to condense information to a few relevant personality dimensions, while the behavioral approach expands the information base until events are clearly differentiated into precise and manipulable units. Specifically, the many stimuli and responses that may be controlling the occurrence of the problem behavior are enumerated and the parameters of the behavior under *each* situation are detailed.

At the level of a single behavioral problem, the data gathered in an assessment are large but still clinically manageable. But clients usually have problems which extend over a wide range of life situations, and the assessment of just a few such problems represents a data base of huge proportions. The extent of the data and the effort necessary to gather them have caused many to view behavioral assessment as impractical, infeasible and much too costly (Wiggins, 1973). The demand on the clinician to observe or inquire about the specifics of behaviors on a broad spectrum is overwhelming.

A major source of data for a comprehensive behavioral assessment is the client's self-report, particularly through an interview. As Linehan points out in Chapter 2, the interview method allows considerable flexibility for assessing many behavior problems that would tax the limits of more direct observation procedures. One aspect of this flexibility is the interviewer's freedom to inquire about relevant information and to ignore irelevant infomation. However, the sequential decision process, in which the interviewer decides to follow one line of inquiry at one point and another line of inquiry at a subsequent point, greatly reduces interview reliability. Not every interviewer branches from one particular line of inquiry to another line on the basis of the same stimuli. Even the same interviewer would probably make different decisions at different times, yet based on irrelevant influences. Further, the rules for the decisions are generally unknown or unstated. Finally, interview questions vary with different interviewers and within the same interviewer on separate occasions.

The interview reliability can be improved by specifying the total pool of interview questions, by insuring that the same questions are asked under the same conditions, and by defining the sequential decision rules in branching from prior information to subsequent questioning. Although approximations to such reliability can be achieved by careful training of human observers, computer assisted interviewing can go much further in achieving reliability. Computer assisted interviewing may also be the only feasible means to collect and organize the vast data base of a comprehensive behavioral assessment. Further, it makes possible a variety of research that is otherwise virtually impossible.

COMPUTER ASSISTED INTERVIEWING

In the last two decades, the computer has often been used to give knowledge or information to individuals in the form of computer assisted instruction. It is a simple matter to reverse the direction of information flow and to emphasize the gathering of knowledge from individuals who, for example, are clients in a clinical setting. In this way, the computer can be used to conduct part of the clinical interview.

Computer assisted interviewing is performed with a CRT (cathode ray tube) video terminal that displays multiple choice questions to the client. The client reads the question displayed on the CRT screen and selects an appropriate multiple choice answer. The number associated with the answer is entered by the client into a typewriter keyboard, and this answer is stored permanently by the on-line computer. On the basis of the answer, the computer then displays a new question on the CRT screen. It will not advance to the next question until the client answers the currently displayed material; and if the client leaves the task unfinished and returns later, the computer will restore the interview at the point of interruption.

The task is so simple that a client learns the computer interview operation in a very few minutes. The client then operates the terminal alone and at a self-paced rate. When a client has completed the computer interview, there is an immediate printout of critical responses. If the client has not indicated that certain behaviors are causing difficulties, then the statements related to these problems are not printed.

In the present program, a mini computer Digital PDP 11/40 is used to perform the interview. The computer's software operating system is a multi-user, time sharing system (Digital RSTS). The approximate costs of the computer and software systems are $50,000 and $5,000, respectively. The cost of CRT terminals average $1,000 to $2,000. The present computer system is capable of interviewing 16 clients simultaneously.

Presently the program's computer is dedicated to interviewing and is available 24 hours a day, seven days a week. Other programs, such as mental health clinics and drug programs, are using the computer interview over telephone lines. Each program is assigned a separate computer account, a unique account password and its own data files. A number of terminals can operate under one account.

The computer assisted interview is used to gather two types of information: the client's problem behaviors and the situational events associated with these problems. The information is gathered in two stages. First, the client's problem behaviors are identified across a broad spectrum of life areas. This initial interview system has been termed the Computer Problem Screen. Following the completion of the Computer Problem Screen, the client is to receive a series of in-depth computer interviews that cover the problem areas identified by the Problem Screen. Currently the program has only begun the development of the in-depth computer interviews.

Computer Problem Screen

The Computer Problem Screen is organized in three sections: 1) client characteristics (e.g., demographics), 2) problem behaviors (i.e., excess and deficit responses), and 3) motivation. Within the problem behavior section, there are 26 problem areas, such as marriage, sex, childrearing, employment, social isolation, assertion, sleep, and tension. The number of specific questions in a problem area may range from 20-90 items. The entire Problem Screen contains over 3000 questions.

Content validity is stressed in developing the Computer Problem Screen (see Goldfried, Chapter 1). The initial item pool was gathered through a combination of procedures. First, questionnaires emphasizing behavioral rather than intrapsychic variables were reviewed for appropriate items. Second, clinical case histories were reviewed and the question was asked whether the Computer Problem Screen would have revealed the problem described in each history. If not, appropriate items were systematically added to the item pool. Third, clinical assessment procedures employed subsequently to the Problem Screen (e.g., human interview, self-recording, role playing) often suggested items currently not in the Problem Screen. The computer list of questions is continually expanding.

The primary purpose of the Computer Problem Screen is to enumerate problem behaviors across a broad spectrum. Thus, there is very little conditional branching as a function of prior information, this being more appropriate to in-depth interviewing. The presentation of questions is mostly in linear sequence, taking four to eight hours in total. Problem areas are excluded, however, when the client lacks the demographic characteristics to make the presentation of the area appropriate (e.g., marriage, childrearing). The linear presentation of Computer Problem Screen questions circumvents the difficulties associated with the loose association between abstract problem labels and the concrete problem behaviors represented by the abstractions. We have found that some clients will say "No" to a general question (e.g., "Do you have any sexual problems?") and then indicate serious difficulties in that area when asked specific and detailed questions.

Each excess or deficit behavior identified in the Problem Screen contributes to the conditional branching of the in-depth computer interview. Thus it is crucial that the Problem Screen be thorough, because interviewing that is based on incomplete data will take an inappropriate line of inquiry. While the human interviewer may be fortunate enough to later discover an omitted fact and then simply return to an earlier point in the interview to resume the proper line of inquiry, the computer interview must be successful the first time. The linear or nonbranching development of the Problem Screen, in contrast with the strategy of branching with each positive response to in-depth questions, helps to make the interview thorough and promotes the systematic evolution of the computer interview.

In-Depth Computer Interviewing

Currently the Problem Screen printout is used by a human interviewer as a base from which to then question the client about the situational events surrounding each listed behavior, but the computer can also serve this interview function. The plan is to develop an in-depth computer survey for each of the 26 Problem Screen areas. An in-depth survey will require considerably more computer branching capabilities than was utilized in the Problem Screen. This branching can be depicted as a hierarchy of branching levels, the highest level representing information that may apply equally to almost everyone, the content of the Problem Screen. At the lowest hierarchial level, there is only information which describes the uniqueness of a single individual.

In the present application, the client's Problem Screen responses of excess and deficit behaviors indicate life areas that require more thorough assessment. For example, the Problem Screen item of premature ejaculation is a relatively specific problem behavior, but at least a hundred questions can be asked about this one problem. The decision to follow up a set of screening items with a particular in-depth computer survey represents a transition from a higher to lower branching level. Within an in-depth survey, behaviors are defined in greater detail (e.g., behavior-in-a-situation) and this specificity creates additional levels of branching. At any branching level, a positive answer means that the inquiry must extend on that level to the description of antecedents, consequences, parameters of these events, and parameters of the behavior. This description may require branching to lower levels, to more idiographic information. The in-depth computer survey can approach a more individualized assessment than is currently available outside the human interview setting.

Presently, the evaluation program is operating with a single in-depth computer survey, although several others are being written and programmed. This single computer survey covers the problem area of sexual arousal. The decision to put the client through the in-depth Sexual Survey is based on the client's answers in the sexual area of the Computer Problem Screen. The in-depth computer survey of sexual arousal currently consists of over 1000 questions and adds approximately two hours of computer interviewing. With the completion of other in-depth computer surveys that are in development, we anticipate that a typical client will answer in the neighborhood of 10,000 computer questions and spend two or more days at the computer terminal. This raises questions about the feasibility of the computer assisted interview.

FEASIBILITY OF COMPUTER INTERVIEWING

Recent reductions in mini-computer costs make the advantages of computer-assisted interviewing available to today's therapist. While hardware costs are not a serious obstacle, other factors may limit the acceptance of computer assisted interviewing. A primary factor is that computer interviewing departs from traditional ways of conducting the evaluation process. To change tradition, two things must be demonstrated. First, it must be shown that the therapist will benefit substantially from the information supplied by the computer interview. Second, it must be shown that clients will accept the computer interview format. This latter question is often an important concern of clinicians seeing the computer interaction for the first time.

Computer versus Human Interviewing

The first and most obvious computer benefit is that clinicians are saved valuable time in the assessment process. In computer assisted interviewing, clinicians are relieved from asking many routine questions, leaving more time for analyzing the information obtained and for planning treatment. Some clinicians may take issue with any suggestion that the computer interview can qualitatively approach that of the clinician. However, such arguments must weigh certain disadvantages associated with human participation in the interview process. Schwitzgebel and Kolb (1974) have identified three sources of interviewer error that can affect the quality of interview data. These sources of error can be redefined as errors of input, output, and stimulus control. Input errors include the omission of critical questions and, to a lesser extent, the asking of irrelevant questions. Output error refers to the inaccurate recording of client information. Errors of stimulus contol are commonly referred to as interviewer bias. Computer assisted interviewing may reduce substantially the influence of these interviewer errors.

The computer controls input errors by consistently presenting the same questions to each client. The importance of consistency was evidenced in the present project when the computer assumed the human interviewer role. The case records of 28 married clients who had been seen pior to the use of the computer assisted interviewing were reviewed by three raters to determine whether there was any evidence of sexual adjustment problems. Evidence of sexual difficulties was found by one or more reviewers in 29% of these cases. By contrast, 86% of the first 14 married clients interviewed by the Computer Problem Screen revealed sexual difficulties. Although this is by no means an adequate experimental analysis, it suggests that the computer interview may be capable of greater sensitivity to problems. Of course, similar results might have been obtained had earlier clients been given printed questionnaires or had the interviewer followed a structured interview guide. Investigation is currently underway to compare the computer interview and interviews by human interviewers. In a systematic and counterbalanced research design, the computer and each human interviewer will identify problems in the same clients.

The computer prevents output errors by automatically recording client data. The computer will not advance to the next question frame until the client makes a response and this information has been recorded. In contrast, clinicians are faced with the concurrent clinical behaviors of analyzing client statements, planning the next question and transcribing client statements. In many instances, clinicians delay the recording of client responses, which only compounds output error by relying on memory (Guest, 1947; Payne, 1949).

A number of stimulus control factors may bias the client information gathered by a human interviewer. Factors correlated with interviewer and client demographics such as age, sex, racial background and socioeconomic status may affect the questions posed, the responses given, and the actual answers recorded during the interview process. Computer assisted interviewing eliminates these factors and prevents the shaping of client responses by differential reinforcement (e.g., selective recording, verbal conditioning) of certain response content by the interviewer's behavior.

On the other hand, one advantage the human interviewer brings to the interview process is flexibility. The human interviewer can react to the give and take of information during the clinical interview by composing new lines of inquiry contingent upon client responses. In contrast, the client cannot direct the computer to ask questions that are not already a part of the Computer Problem Screen. Computer questions must be developed beforehand. However, this is both an advantage and a disadvantage. It means that the computer interview will cover topics that a human interviewer might not think of covering, and it means that the computer interview cannot be led into trivial, irrelevant topics by interpersonal manipulation. It also means that topics important to a particular case may not be explored because the computer does not have appropriate programming. On the other hand, through systematic procedures of program development, the computer's oversight with one case will be detected and corrections will be made in the program so that oversight does not occur with subsequent cases of similar types. Thus, the computer program "learns" from its error and, unlike the human interviewer, retains this learning indefinitely. Such increments in content validity may raise the level of systematic and comprehensive computer interviewing to approach that of the most highly skilled interviewer, and grossly deficient interviewing might become a thing of the past.

Client Reaction to Interactive Computer

In the clinical field computer usage is primarily devoted to standard psychological testing, such as scoring and interpreting the MMPI. There are very few reports of computer interviewing, but Slack and Van Cura

(1968) have interviewed medical patients and Greist, Klein and Van Cura (1973) have interviewed mental patients with the interactive computer. In both instances, positive acceptance of the computer task by all patients was reported. Similar client acceptance has been the typical case in the present project. Acceptance has ranged from client reports that the computer interaction was enjoyable to reports that it was preferred over that of the human interviewer.

A variable that might adversely affect client acceptance is the length of the computer task. Previous reports of client-computer interaction have involved considerably fewer items than the present 3000 screening questions. The Computer Problem Screen normally takes four to eight hours for clients to complete. Our initial concern was whether clients would object to this task, but experience with over 400 clients who have completed the interview has revealed this concern to be unfounded. Few clients have criticized the interview length, and most have expressed a willingness to engage in additional computer interviewing. The clients whose Computer Problem Screens indicated sexual arousal difficulties have been asked to take the computer Sexual Survey and were told that another hour or more is added to the interview length. These clients have agreed to the additional computer interview and all have completed the Sexual Survey.

We suspect that a number of reinforcing variables are present in computer interviewing that contribute to positive acceptance of the computer by clients. First, there is the fact that when the client enters a response, the environment immediately changes—a new question is presented. Second, the computer questions are relevant to individuals who seek to express and describe their difficulties and such expression may be reinforcing. Further, the computer task is novel. Finally, a delayed but significant consequence for clients is the receipt of a printout copy of their answers to keep. Although the output is only that which the client has put in, many clients have stated that their printout provides them with a clearer and more organized picture of their problems.

Perhaps the most important factor contributing to client acceptance of the computer task is the absence of negative consequences for disclosing private information: The computer is a neutral, nonjudgmental interviewer which will not react adversely to the content of the interview.

Although Kleinmuntz (1972) is concerned about the dehumanizing effects of the computer interview, we have been unable to detect any negative effects. In fact, the mechanical aspect of the computer seems to facilitate the client's accuracy of self-report. Some clients have verbally expressed this view without any prompting or suggestions from the program staff.

Alternative to Computer Assessment

A variety of further questions about computer interviewing will be raised as this technology develops. For example, Stuart (1970) has suggested that the approach of attempting such a behavioral assessment as described here or by Kanfer and Saslow (1969) may not be parsimonious, and Linehan, in Chapter 2 of this text, recommends that a narrow band assessment be generally applied to the client's presenting problem, although she concedes that the relative cost, risk, and benefits of broad versus narrow band assessment are empirical questions. Such comparisons cannot be investigated, however, until the comprehensive assessment is a reality. While it is within the ability of the human interviewer to follow the Kanfer and Saslow outline, we suspect that the enormity of the task discourages any attempt. With the exception of human interviewers, who may be overwhelmed by the task, we doubt that the same length and detailed information could be routinely gathered by non-computer means.

One alternative that some may propose is the pencil-and-paper questionnaire. Even though on an item by item basis the Computer Problem Screen and an equivalent pencil-and-paper questionnaire are the same, when the computer questions and multiple-choice answers are printed in a very compact manner, the result is a 275-page document. We view this questionnaire form to be physically unmanageable for client, clinician, and data technician. In addition, the in-depth surveys, with their branching questions, cannot be duplicated easily in the pencil-and-paper format, because the conditional branching must be communicated to the client by rather complex instructions, such as the following: If questions 122 = "sometimes," 307 = "no" and 408 = "spouse," then answer question 1017. The paper questionnaire would contain more instructions than questions!

FUNCTIONAL ANALYSIS

Client information is a set of discriminative stimuli controlling the clinician's decisions regarding treatment. In decision-making, different information usually leads to different treatment responses. In some non-behavioral therapies, the discriminative quality of the information is often quite low because the treatment decision is little more than treat or do-not-treat and the treatment itself is generally the same for different clients.

FUNCTIONAL ANALYSIS DIAGRAM
CLIENT #104

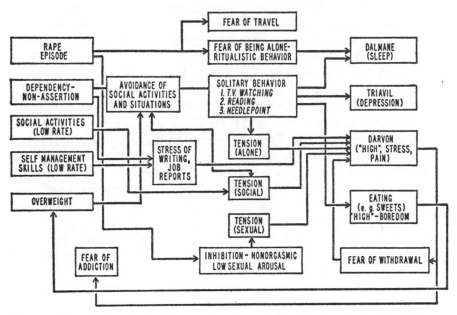

FIGURE 1. Functional analysis diagram of major problem behavior chains. The diagram summarizes the client's assessment report and assists both client and therapist in making treatment decisions.

This does not seem to be the case in most behavior therapies. The behavior therapy field has developed a great variety of treatment techniques, or differential responses, aimed at the modification of many kinds of client problem behaviors under many different situations. The challenge for behavioral assessment is to establish the relation between assessment information and the differential responses of treatment.

The computer can collect a vast body of client data, but the crucial question is how to translate this information into appropriate therapeutic action for each client. First, it is procedurally important to distinguish between initial and ongoing assessment. In the present program, the initial behavioral assessment begins with the Computer Problem Screen and ends with an estimated functional analysis. This analysis is estimated from data obtained in the client's computer interview, a human interview, self-recordings and role-playing sessions. The reason that it is termed "estimated" is that the relationships have not been subjected to experimental analysis (Wiggins, 1973); they are only hypothesized. During ongoing assessment, some of the independent variables identified in initial assessment are manipulated, thus their actual functional relationship may be discovered.

In the present program the estimated functional analysis of the comprehensive behavioral assessment is summarized in the form of a diagram (Figure 1). In the diagram, the connecting lines between broad categories of problem behaviors and events indicate the various hypothesized relationships. This summary diagram aids the clinician and client in selecting points of treatment intervention that are likely to produce greatest benefit at least cost and risk (for detailed treatment planning, the clinician must refer to the comprehensive assessment data). In the client's diagram depicted here, for example, planning for better weight control might consider the client's solitary behavior that is yielding few social reinforcers ("depression"). If effective treatment operations are applied to this activity or to earlier chain members (e.g., avoidance of social activities), then the client should be able to follow a structured weight control routine, a routine at which the client has repeatedly failed. On the other hand, increasing the client's frequency of social reinforcement should have no influence on the client's sexual arousal problem. The examples illustrate the use of the diagram to represent a set of specific hypotheses.

If any prediction stemming from the estimated analysis and tested in ongoing assessment is wrong, then the assessment that specifically relates to that prediction must be reviewed. Isolating assessment errors is a complex undertaking, for many factors can contribute to the discrepancies between estimated and actual analyses. Inaccuracy of the assessment data, the misapplication of general behavioral principles, and insufficient information about the individual are three sources of error. The computer interview reduces at least the latter of these sources of error.

The greatest weakness in the current assessment procedures is the gap between the assessment data and the estimated analysis. The construction of the estimated functional analysis is more art than science. Clearly, there is an urgent need to formalize the rules for this analysis, but, without data of sufficient scope and detail, the construction of such rules will be impossible. A data base is needed that provides specific information representing antecedent events, concrete behaviors, and consequences of behavior. Computer assisted interviewing has shown great promise in approaching this information goal, and the present program has only begun to tap the potential of this data collecting technique.

16

CURRENT STATUS AND FUTURE DIRECTIONS IN BEHAVIORAL ASSESSMENT

JOHN D. CONE and ROBERT P. HAWKINS

It is tempting to suggest, after carefully reading the preceding pages, that behavioral assessment is here to stay. However, mindful of a similar statement made by Campbell 20 years ago, to wit, "to judge from the pages of this and similar journals, the projective test movement is here to stay" (Campbell, 1957), we have decided against such untempered optimism. Campbell went on to suggest that such a heterogeneous variety of measures was being included under the general rubric "projective" that the term was rapidly losing a good deal of its denotational value.

Perhaps unbridled diversity is characteristic of the early stages of any intellectual movement. It is certainly true of behavioral assessment, where there is presently such a heterogeneous collection of measures referred to by that term that it, too, is in danger of losing much of its denotational value. It would seem that the time is ripe to evaluate the state of the behavioral assessment movement and offer suggestions and predictions as to its future development. In the chapters preceding this one the reader has been given a reasonably comprehensive view of the field, including much of its diversity. The purpose of this final chapter is to summarize the status of some major issues, suggest ways of ordering the field so as to restore some of the meaning to the term "behavioral assessment," and suggest directions for future research, development, and clinical assessment practice.

Any attempt to produce more order in the field will eventually have to clarify some of the terminologic confusion that currently exists. As was mentioned in the introductory chapter, terms such as "behavior analysis," "functional analysis," and "behavioral assessment" are often used interchangeably, creating confusion for the naive as well as the sophisticated. The problem is created partly by the fact that a behavioral approach to assessment requires that the assessor employ empirically established principles describing *functional* relations between responses and stimuli, and between responses themselves. Thus the term "functional analysis" seems appropriate. Unfortunately that term is also used as a label for experimental tests of the effects or "functions" or various events, particularly when those tests are done through a time-series design with single subjects (cf. Skinner, 1966, regarding the experimental analysis of behavior). "Behavior analysis" is used for this same type of research, but it is also used as the name for a school of thought based on the writings of Skinner. In addition, "behavior analysis" is sometimes used to denote a *conceptual* analysis of the problem using empirically established principles. Clearly we do need a term for such a conceptual analysis, and perhaps the term used by Angle et al. in Chapter 15—tentative behavior analysis— will do. Or perhaps "conceptual functional analysis" will serve the needed stimulus control (meaning).

Another term occasionally mentioned in the previous chapters is "behavioral diagnosis." As it has been used in the literature (e.g., Kanfer & Saslow, 1969), the term is essentially the same as the first three phases of behavioral assessment described in the Introduction, those in which the problem is defined and data for treatment planning are obtained. It should be noted that this view of diagnosis, like Ferster's (1965) view of the "classification of behavioral pathology," is not simply the assignment of behaviors or persons to particular categories, as the traditional use of the term "diagnosis" implies. Though such classification can serve a useful administrative and epidemiological function for even the behavioral assessor, we are aware of only one formal effort to develop a diagnostic and classification system for behavioral assessors that serves functions similar to those of the Diagnostic and Statistical Manual of the American Psychiatric Association (1968). In that scheme (Cautela & Upper, 1975), 21 major behavioral categories are used, such as "fears," "self-injurious behavior," "sex," and "inappropriate habits of daily living." These categories are further differentiated into subcategories, some of which are divided into specific behaviors. A total of 283 behaviors are classified in this Behavioral Coding System. A client would be diagnosed as having certain responses needing alteration, and would be classified by listing the Behavioral Coding System numbers of these behaviors. Thus, "John Doe 2-12.2" would be a client needing change in some area of sexual functioning (2), specifically transvestism (12), with particular attention to cross dressing in public (.2).

Such a behavioral diagnostic system might eventually include information as to the relative effectiveness of various intervention strategies, as well as probable etiology (for prevention purposes). The development of taxonomies such as the Behavioral Coding System could help organize the field of behavioral assessment and facilitate its continued development.

In the meantime it might be useful to differentiate the term behavioral diagnosis from behavioral assessment. The latter seems to be the process one goes through in producing the former. That is, behavioral diagnoses, the listing of responses needing change, are products of behavioral assessment. The determination of these responses is accomplished by using various assessment methodologies, including interviews, self-reports, and observations by others.

A different kind of terminologic confusion exists concerning so-called "triple response mode" assessment. As is apparent from the previous chapters, it has become axiomatic in behavioral assessment to speak of measuring responses in three different systems: cognitive, motor, and physiological. Triple response mode assessment is a logical outgrowth of the repeated observation (Arkowitz, Lichtenstein, McGovern & Hines, 1975; Borkovec, Stone, O'Brien & Kaloupek, 1974; Lang, 1968, 1971) that measures of different types of behavior that have been assumed to be components of the same phenomenon (e.g., anxiety, hostility) are not highly correlated. Lang (1971) indicated that we should:

> confine ourselves to measurable behaviors in all systems, and discover the laws that determine their interaction. The data suggest that we must deal with each behavior system in its own terms. Treatment programs will have to be tailored to each behavior, in the light of what we know about its educability . . . (p. 109).

Obviously, dealing with each "behavior system in its own terms" requires assessing each of those systems as well; thus it has been considered desirable for behavior change efforts to include measures of cognitive, motor, and physiological responses.

This seems a reasonable strategy if, in fact, responding of the three types is independent. However, the evidence for such independence is very sparse (Cone, 1976a). First, comparisons of the three systems have confounded *method* of assessment with behavioral *content*. For example, self-report measures of cognitive activities are frequently compared with direct observation measures of motor or physiological ones, as when a man with an erection reports that he does not feel aroused (see Chapter 11). Resulting low correlations may be due to content differences, method differences, or both. The use of multicontent-multimethod-multibehavior matrices by behavioral assessors has been proposed as a way of sorting out these confounds (Cone, 1976a). Within such matrices, correlations between behavioral contents (e.g., cognitive, motor, physiological) would have to be based on a common method (e.g., self-report, ratings by others, direct observations), and it would be necessary to show that such multicontent-monomethod-multibehavior comparisons produced correlation magnitudes appreciably lower than those resulting from monomethod-multibehavior comparisons within a single content area. If they did not, of course, it could not be concluded that the systems are in any way independent.

In making such comparisons, the importance of using measurement devices that are content-homogeneous has also been emphasized (Cone 1976b). If the method used is, itself, not restricted to one type of content, then the "monocontent-monomethod-multibehavior" analysis would not be legitimate, and subsequent comparisons with the multicontent-mono-method-multibehavior values would be inappropriate for establishing the independence of the content areas.

This discussion, like much of that in the literature, assumes there is general agreement on the definition of the three response systems. Unfortunately, there appears to be no such consensus. When Lang (1968, 1971) referred to response systems he did so in the context of measuring fear, a complex, hypothetical characteristic *presumed to underlie* various types of escape and avoidance behavior. Because it was thought that a person might "manifest" fear in one or more of three different ways, the term "triple response mode" was coined. Such a view of three-response system assessment is closely related to traditional views of "personality" and behavior, in which hypothetical constructs such as traits or inner dynamics determine responding. Even among behavioral assessors these hypothetical constructs are still in use, as when one attempts to measure "anxiety" or "assertiveness" (Hawkins, 1976a; McFall, Chapter 5). We believe a more neutral, inductive approach is called for, one in which no a priori assumptions are made regarding interrelationships between or within the three types of responses: cognitive, motor and physiological (cf. Cone, 1975, 1976b). That is, given a particular stimulus context a person may respond cognitively, motorically, and/or physiologically. The type of behavior displayed will depend largely on the stimulus arrangements experienced by the person for various types of response in the same or similar situations in the past. For example, to the extent that behavior of the three types or contents has been followed by functionally different consequences for different persons, their responding will be dissimilar.

It should be noted here, that "cognitive" is not synonymous with vocal verbal behavior as it appears to be in some tripartite systems (e.g., Lang, 1968, 1971; Staats, 1975). Verbal behavior in and of itself is a motoric event. It may *refer* to other actions, however, and these may be cognitive, motor, or physiological. If reference is made to an internal, publicly unverifiable activity such as a thought, wish, want, feeling, need, etc., that *referent is cognitive* (Cone, 1976b). The self-report, "I feel nervous in the presence of strangers," refers to a cognitive event, a "feeling," the truth or falsity of which cannot be publicly established. The report itself is not a cognitive event but a motoric one. The private, cognitive behavior is nonetheless important, and requires serious effort at measurement by behavioral assessors. If reference is made to activities of the striate musculature or to activities of the autonomic nervous system, those referents are motoric and physiological, respectively. Thus, verbal behavior is unique in the human repertoire because, though it is motoric it can also represent other events as well. It is this status, plus the low effort of verbal behavior, that provides the great flexibility of assessment methods based on verbal report.

A good deal of the terminologic confusion in behavioral assessment could be clarified by serious efforts at developing some sort of taxonomic system (Cone, 1976b). One such system results from the simultaneous consideration of response systems or content areas and methods of measuring behavior within them. The contents ($N = 3$) have been described above. The methods ($N = 8$) include interviews, self-reports, ratings by others, self-observation (self-monitoring), direct observation by others in controlled or analogue environments, and direct observation by others in natural environments. By including instructions to role play (versus to behave "as you normally would") the direct observation methods are increased to four in number since these instructions may be included or omitted in both controlled and natural environments. The organization of the previous chapters of this book has been based on the eight methods just described.

The content × method juxtaposition results in a $3 \times 8 = 24$-category system referred to as the Behavioral Assessment Grid (BAG). Of course, at present it is only a theoretical possibility that cognitive content can be assessed using ratings by others and the four direct observation methods. Hence, there are currently exemplars for only 19 of the 24 categories.

The BAG clarifies the points made earlier regarding the independence of the three content areas since it demonstrates the possibility of using a variety of different methods for assessing responding within each. Thus, for example, physiological behavior may be assessed using self-report measures of the "true-false" type, or using direct observation measures aided by sensing, amplifying, and recording apparatus. Similar possibilities exist for motor behavior, and, at least theoretically, for cognitive behavior as well.

The two-dimensional BAG provides a way of classifying existing measures and also has implications for the development of new ones. In more complete descriptions of the BAG (Cone, 1975, 1976b) a third dimension, representing the psychometric adequacy of each classified measure, is included. This dimension represents different ways in which scores on the measure have been shown to generalize. Six universes of generalizability (Cronbach et al., 1972) are included: 1) scorer, 2) item, 3) time, 4) setting, 5) method, and 6) dimension. Thus, a self-report measure of heterosocial motor behavior classified as S-R: M, 1, 3, 4 is one that has been shown to be scored accurately, to be stable over time, and to generalize to more than one situation or setting. The inclusion of the universes of generalizability provides users with an objective way of comparing the measurement characteristics of various assessment devices.

The addition of the third dimension to the BAG presupposes the existence of acceptable tools for establishing the various types of generalizability. However, as Jones noted in Chapter 13, the ANOVA procedures suggested by Cronbach et al. (1972) for use in generalizability analyses are based on an inter-individual differences model. The same is true for nearly all procedures commonly used to establish the reliability and validity of measuring devices. Each requires a group of persons to be administered a measure on which they receive different scores. Measures of central tendency and variability are then calculated and further analyses, usually correlations, are performed to determine the stability of the individual scores relative to one another. Thus, for example, a measure is said to be internally consistent, and thus measuring the same trait throughout, if a group of persons' scores on one-half of it bear the same position relative to one another on the second half. Similarly, a measure is temporally stable if a group of persons obtain the same scores relative to one another on two different administrations. The fact that their absolute scores may change is unimportant so long as their scores relative to one another remain relatively the same.

This type of analysis makes sense when the meaning given scores is based on comparing them against a group average or norm. If a score is significant only in comparison with the average for a group of persons, it is reasonable to examine its stability within a distribution of scores around that average.

However, if the significance of scores derives from comparing them against some absolute standard or performance criterion, then the stability of positions within distributions must be established viz that standard. This is what was pointed out clearly by Livingston in Chapter 12. It should be noted though, that merely switching from norm-referenced to criterion-referenced testing does not escape the inter-individual differences model. It merely changes the point of reference. That is, rather than speaking about differences in scores relative to other persons, we now speak of differences in them relative to some criterion performance. The criterion-referenced correlation coefficient suggested by Livingston is clearly based on an inter-individual differences model.

It can be argued that group-based, inter-individual difference procedures are useful in evaluating behavioral assessment devices just as they have been for traditional trait-oriented measures. If one is interested in the accuracy with which an instrument measures differences between individuals relative to some norm or absolute criterion, the usual reliability indices or Cronbach et al.'s (1972) generalizability procedures will probably serve very well. However, if one is interested in the characteristics of devices used for single-subject analyses, especially those involving repeated measurement over time, the usual psychometric procedures may not apply, as Jones noted in Chapter 13.

The extent to which traditional, individual difference-based psychometric procedures can be used to establish the quality of behavioral assessment devices is currently a hotly debated issue, and will continue to be so for some time (cf., Hartmann, 1976; Linehan, 1976; Nelson & Hay, 1976). Our own current view is that these procedures are often applicable, and will continue to be so for most types of behavioral assessment, but that their use should be quite different from their use in developing traditional assessment devices. For example, in constructing the Social Avoidance and Distress Scale and the Fear of Negative Evaluation scale, Watson and Friend (1969) stated "One of the major goals was to foster scale homogeneity" (p. 453), so they were pleased by the high correlation between answers to specific items and total scale scores. But such high correlations indicate that the items are not measuring very different behaviors, and a preference for such correlations suggests that the authors are hoping to measure a rather homogeneous trait rather than a variety of independent or semi-independent performances. This goal was also evident in their selection of items, for they discarded items endorsed by fewer than 10% of the subjects sampled. A behavioral approach would suggest that if those discarded items reflect situations of significant practical (functional) importance in daily living, they should be retained. In fact, those items may be endorsed by only the most anxious or least anxious client and thus may be especially valuable!

A similar selection procedure was used by Geer (1965) in designing the Fear Survey Schedule II. Of the 111 different fears listed by the undergraduate student subjects, he discarded 60 because only one person listed them. If the purpose of the device is to plan specific treatment of individuals (Hawkins, 1976b), this procedure reduces the Fear Survey Schedule II's value, for it can detect 60 fewer fears, some of which may have great functional importance.

However, traditional procedures for evaluating the quality of measuring devices could assist in standardizing the administration and use of many behavioral assessment devices. Perhaps because of the chaotic diversity and insufficient conceptualization of the field, many investigators appear to find it easier to construct new measures for local purposes rather than use already existing ones. The result is a continued proliferation of new measures and the deferred standardization and evaluation of those already available. Perhaps a widespread adoption of the BAG as a basis for development and evaluation of assessment devices would slow this proliferation and encourage development of standardized administration.

In addition to the applicability of traditional psychometric procedures for appraising the quality of assessment devices, the more specific question of the value of norms has also received considerable attention in the behavioral assessment literature (see the chapters by Geer, Livingston, McFall, and White in this volume). As suggested above, it has long been customary in clinical and educational contexts to attach meaning to scores in terms of their deviation from the average scores of an appropriate reference group. It has only recently been recognized that the group's average may, itself, deviate from some optimum value. Thus, for example, the average silent reading rate for graduating high school seniors may be 250 words per minute in technical materials. However, the optimum rate for mastery of typical college freshman courses may be 350 words per minute. It would be more important to interpret a college-bound high school senior's reading proficiency against the latter "criterion" than against the former "norm." A less obvious example comes from the assessment of human sexual performance. It is nearly always the case that scores on measures of sexual behavior derive significance in terms of their deviation from a group "norm." But, there are surely other criteria that are equally if not more important. For example, what is the optimum frequency of intercourse in terms of cardiovascular-pulmonary functioning for a 45-year-old male? What is the optimum intensity? Duration?

However, some behavioral assessors have found norms very useful at times in determining optimum performance. The rationale is as follows: As several authors in this volume have noted (e.g., McFall, White), some performances are highly effective in achieving certain goals (reinforcers) for the performer. Other performances are less effective. A functional analysis of behavior would suggest that good adjustment is behaving effectively, performing in ways that optimize reinforcement for the performer and for society (Hawkins, 1976b). Assessment research should increasingly focus on determining the functional utility of behavior, in this sense, and discovering what level and topography of performance are most effective (Hawkins, 1975). Norms can be useful in this effort for two reasons. First, for many behaviors the optimal topography or level is socially defined in terms of norms. For example, a male's walking or sitting in a particular "masculine" manner will receive social acceptance (reinforcement) because it is the *norm*, while walking or sitting in a feminine fashion will reduce the overall reinforcement available to the male (cf. Barlow, Reynolds & Agras, 1973). Where social norms thus *define* what is effective, assessment in terms of norms will be very valuable.

Second, norms can provide suggestive evidence as to what is effective (Hawkins, 1975). Using Webster's (1970) first definition of the term "norm"—an authoritative standard; model—one might classify the use of exemplary models of performance for setting performance criteria as a use of norms. For example, Jones and Eimers (1975) studied the behavior of highly successful teachers and used that as a criterion in modifying the behavior of less successful teachers, with the result that the second group became more successful (thus, by definition, more competent). Similarly, Arkowitz, Lichtenstein, McGovern and Hines (1975) compared actual heterosexual interactions of high-frequency daters with those of low-frequency daters to determine relevant and irrelevant skills. Again a normative assessment was valuable. Another common use of norms has been for predictive purposes, the IQ score being the most obvious example. Prediction has a definite place in behavioral assessment (Hawkins, 1976b), and it seems likely that normative data will be useful for this reason as well as the above two. However, norms will no longer be the exclusive reference points for interpreting individual scores as they have been in the past. This is one reason why traditional psychometric procedures will have different uses in behavioral assessment.

As behavioral assessors go about refining existing instruments and developing better ones they will undoubtedly turn more attention to sources of unwanted variance in their scores. In self-report methodology, they will address issues of reactivity, response sets, and discriminant validity. In ratings by others, the problems of halo and generosity effects, response styles, and response bias will get attention. In self-observation, accuracy and reactivity will continue to be studied and attention may be given the effects of response sets. Some terminologic sorting out may occur, with examination of the separate contributions of merely observing and noting one's own behavior on the one hand, and graphing and tracking (monitoring) it on the other.

Consistent with its position as the *sine qua non* of behavioral assessment, direct observation methodology can be expected to receive the most thorough evaluation and development in the next few years. Many of the unwanted influences on its data pointed out by Johnson and Bolstad (1973) and by Wildman and Erickson in Chapter 10 of this volume will continue to be studied, including observer biases and expectancies, observer drift, and the reactivity of both observers and observees. The complexity variable noted by Jones et al. (1975) will receive additional attention, as will the development of more sophisticated ways of establishing the generalizability of data collected from direct observation procedures. In terms of generality, the comparability of data collected by different observers will continue to receive extensive study, and increasing attention will be given the convergence of data obtained by direct observation and by self-report and other assessment methods.

It is likely that more development of environmental assessment methods will occur, as Mash and Terdal (1976) have suggested. Whether these will be comparable to the procedures developed by Moos (1975) is not clear, but certainly such verbal report measures seem to have the same assets and liabilities as most social validity measures (Wolf, 1976).

Hopefully, more behavioral assessors will begin to look at the functional utility of behavior and develop devices on this basis (Goldsmith & McFall, 1975; Hawkins, 1975). This should result in more task analytic approaches to assessment (Hawkins, 1976a; Schwartz & Gottman, 1976).

Since the skills needed for effective adjustment in our society are innumerable, it seems inevitable that the number of assessment devices needed by the behavioral assessor will be vastly more than the traditional clinician has been getting by with. Not only will yearbooks like those of Buros (1972) reviewing behavioral assessment devices be valuable, but computerized clearinghouses for behavioral assessment devices and even local sources where numerous devices can be obtained on short-term loan may be needed.

Other trends one can expect to see are greater concern with the teaching of behavioral assessment (e.g., Evans & Nelson, 1974) and with ethical issues involving its use. As more and more knowledge is amassed in the area, it is likely that more graduate training programs will include course offerings in behavioral assessment. Where trait-oriented and behavioral assessment content compete in the same course, one can expect to see the former pushed more and more into the background. Moreover, second-generation teachers of behavioral assessment now infiltrating our graduate programs will be less and less familiar with traditional, group-based inter-individual measurement approaches and are likely to see less and less value in them. These second-generation assessors are likely to be radically separatist initially, just as their counterpart generation in the behavior modification movement has been. It would not be too surprising to see a *Journal of Behavioral Assessment* spring up. The third and fourth generations will likely be more moderate, and an integration of traditional and behavioral views will probably be attempted. Meanwhile, present teachers of behavioral assessment will continue to struggle with questions such as how much emphasis to place on conceptual-methodological issues versus how-to-do-it skills, and the importance of teaching trait-oriented measures such as the I-E Scale (Rotter, 1966) and the MMPI. Hopefully, more and more attention will be given to the teaching of task analytic skills and the development of inventories based upon them.

Ethical issues in assessment can be expected to center around the use of direct observation procedures. To obtain highest fidelity, such methods must be minimally reactive. To be minimally reactive they will have to restrict observee awareness as much as possible. Is it ethical to observe and record another's behavior without that person's knowledge? If not, how much of an effect does knowledge of observation produce? How can the last be answered without unobtrusive observation? Other ethical issues, including safeguarding the results of behavioral assessments, communicating these to other agencies, and assuring competent administration of the procedures, are similar to those involving traditional assessment and behavior change practices as well, and will undoubtedly receive extended discussion in the years ahead.

Finally, one can expect to see a more satisfactory definition of behavioral assessment emerge as the field develops. Presently it is largely defined by contrasting it with traditional, trait-oriented assessment. We are told that behavioral assessors focus on what a person *does* rather than on what s/he *is* (Mischel, 1968, p. 10); that they observe samples of clinically relevant behavior rather than signs of underlying dispositions (Goldfried & Sprafkin, 1974); that they explain behavioral consistency or lack thereof in terms of contemporary environmental influences rather than generalized dispositions or traits formed in early childhood (Mischel, 1969); and that they observe specific, discrete responses (e.g., "hitting") rather than general or global characteristics (e.g., "aggression"). Perhaps definitions by contrast are inevitable for endeavors that develop largely in reaction to the perceived shortcomings of already existing ones, especially when those existing definitions are a part of the general culture as well as the professional disciplines involved.

REFERENCES

ABEL, G. G., BARLOW, D. H., BLANCHARD, E. B., & MAVISSAKALIAN, M. Measurement of sexual arousal in male homosexuals: The effects of instructions and stimulus modality. *Archives of Sexual Behavior,* 1975, 4, 623-629.

ABEL, G. G., BLANCHARD, E. B., BARLOW, D. H., & MAVISSAKALIAN, M. Identifying specific erotic cues in sexual deviations by audiotaped descriptions. *Journal of Applied Behavior Analysis,* 1975, 8, 247-260.

ABEL, G. G., LEVIS, D. J., & CLANCY, J. S. Aversion therapy applied to taped sequences of deviant behavior in exhibitionism and other sexual deviations: A preliminary report. *Journal of Behavior Therapy and Experimental Psychiatry,* 1970, 1, 59-66.

AKUTAGAWA, D. A study in the construct validity of the psychoanalytic concept of latent anxiety and test of a projection hypothesis. Unpublished dissertation, University of Pittsburgh, 1956.

ALLPORT, G. W. *Personality: A Psychological Interpretation.* New York: Holt, 1937.

AMERICAN PSYCHIATRIC ASSOCIATION. *Diagnostic and Statistical Manual of Mental Disorders,* II. Washington, D.C.: American Psychiatric Association, 1968.

AMERICAN PSYCHOLOGICAL ASSOCIATION, AMERICAN EDUCATIONAL RESEARCH ASSOCIATION, & NATIONAL COUNCIL ON MEASUREMENT IN EDUCATION. *Standards for Educational and Psychological Tests.* Washington, D.C.: American Psychological Association, 1974.

ANASTASI, A. *Psychological Testing,* (2nd ed.). New York: Macmillan, 1961.

ANDERSON, R. L. Distribution of the serial correlation coefficient. *Annals of Mathematical Statistics,* 1942, 13, 1-13.

ARKOWITZ, H., LICHTENSTEIN, E., McGOVERN, K., & HINES, P. The behavioral assessment of social competence in males. *Behavior Therapy,* 1975, 6, 3-13.

ARRINGTON, R. E. Interrelations in the behavior of young children. *Child Development Monographs,* (No. 8). New York: Bureau of Publications, Teachers College, 1932 (a).

ARRINGTON, R. E. Some technical aspects of observer reliability as indicated in studies of the "Talkies." *The American Journal of Sociology,* 1932, 38, 409-417 (b).

AYLLON, T., & AZRIN, N. *The Token Economy: A Motivation System for Therapy and Rehabilitation.* New York: Appleton-Century-Crofts, 1968.

AZRIN, N. H., HOLZ, W., & GOLDIAMOND, I. Response bias in questionnaire reports. *Journal of Consulting Psychology,* 1961, 25, 324-326.

AZRIN, N., HOLZ, W., ULRICH, R., & GOLDIAMOND, I. The control of conversation through reinforcement. *Journal of the Experimental Analysis of Behavior,* 1961, 4, 25-30.

AZRIN, N. H., & POWELL, J. Behavioral engineering: The use of response priming to improve self-medication. *Journal of Applied Behavior Analysis,* 1969, 2, 39-42.

393

BAER, D. M., WOLF, M. M., & RISLEY, T. R. Some current dimensions of applied behavior analysis. *Journal of Applied Behavior Analysis*, 1968, 1, 91-97.

BAILEY, M. I., & PETERSON, G. L. Reactivity and accuracy on self-monitored verbal responses. Unpublished manuscript, Ohio University, 1975.

BALES, R. F. *Interaction Process Analysis*. Cambridge: Addison-Wesley, 1950.

BANCROFT, J. The application of psychophysiological measures to the assessment and modification of sexual behavior. *Behaviour Research and Therapy*, 1971, 9, 119-130.

BANCROFT, J. *Deviant Sexual Behavior: Modification and Assessment*. Oxford, England: Clarendon Press, 1974.

BANCROFT, J. A comparative study of aversion and desensitization in the treatment of homosexuality. In L. E. Bem, and J. L. Worsly (Eds.), *Behavior Therapy in the 1970's*. Bristol, England: Wright, 1975.

BANCROFT, J., & MATHEWS, A. M. Autonomic correlates of penile erection. *Journal of Psychosomatic Behavior*, 1971, 15, 159-167.

BANDURA, A. *Principles of Behavior Modification*. New York: Holt, Rinehart and Winston, 1969.

BANDURA, A. Vicarious and self-reinforcement processes. In R. Glasser (Ed.), *The Nature of Reinforcement*. New York: Academic Press, 1971, pp. 228-278.

BANDURA, A., BLANCHARD, E. B., & RITTER, B. Relative efficacy of desensitization and modeling approaches for inducing behavior, affective, and attitudinal changes. *Journal of Personality and Social Psychology*, 1969, 13, 173-199.

BARLOW, D. H. Increasing heterosexual responsiveness in the treatment of sexual deviation: A review of clinical and experimental evidence. *Behavior Therapy*, 1973, 4, 655-671.

BARLOW, D. H. The treatment of sexual deviation: Toward a comprehensive behavioral approach. In K. S. Calhoun, H. E. Adams, & K. M. Mitchell (Eds.), *Innovative Treatment Methods in Psychopathology*. New York: John Wiley & Sons, Inc., 1974.

BARLOW, D. H., & ABEL, G. G. Recent developments in assessment and treatment of sexual deviation. In W. E. Craighead, A. E. Kazdin, & M. J. Mahoney (Eds.), *Behavior Modification: Principles, Issues, and Applications*. Boston: Houghton Mifflin, 1976, pp. 341-360.

BARLOW, D. H., AGRAS, W. S., ABEL, G. G., BLANCHARD, E. B., & YOUNG, L. D. Biofeedback and reinforcement to increase heterosexual arousal in homosexuals. *Behaviour Research and Therapy*, 1975, 13, 45-50.

BARLOW, D. H., AGRAS, W. S., LEITENBERG, H., CALLAHAN, E. J., & MOORE, R. C. The contribution of therapeutic instructions to covert sensitization. *Behaviour Research and Therapy*, 1972, 10, 411-415.

BARLOW, D. H., BECKER, R., LEITENBERG, H., & AGRAS, W. S. A mechanical strain gauge for recording penile circumference change. *Journal of Applied Behavior Analysis*, 1970, 3, 73-76.

BARLOW, D. H., REYNOLDS, J., & AGRAS, W. Gender identity change in a transsexual. *Archives of General Psychiatry*, 1973, 28, 569-576.

BARR, R. F. Responses to erotic stimuli of transsexual and homosexual males. *British Journal of Psychiatry*, 1973, 123, 579-585.

BARTLETT, M. S. Some aspects of time correlation problems in regard to tests of significance. *Journal of the Royal Statistical Society, Series B*, 1935, 24, 297-343.

BAUM, W. M. Time allocation in human vigilance. *Journal of the Experimental Analysis of Behavior*, 1975, 23, 45-54.

BEATTY, J., & LEGEWIE, H. (Eds.). *Biofeedback and Behavior*, Proceedings of the NATO Symposium on Biofeedback and Behavior, Munich, July 1976.

BECK, A. T. *Depression: Causes and Treatment.* Philadelphia: University of Pennsylvania, Pa., 1972.

BECK, A. T., WARD, C. H., MENDELSON, M., MOCK, J., & ERBAUGH, J. An inventory for measuring depression. *Archives of General Psychiatry*, 1961, 4, 561-571.

BEGELMAN, D. A., & HERSEN, M. An experimental analysis of the verbal-motor discrepancy in schizophrenics. Unpublished study, 1971.

BEGELMAN, D. A., & HERSEN, M. An experimental analysis of the verbal-motor discrepancy in schizophrenia. *Journal of Clinical Psychology*, 1973, 29, 175-179.

BELLACK, A. S., ROZENSKY, R., & SCHWARTZ, J. A comparison of two forms of self-monitoring in a behavioral weight reduction program. *Behavior Therapy*, 1974, 5, 523-530.

BELLACK, A. S., & SCHWARTZ, J. Assessment for self-control programs. In M. Hersen & A. S. Bellack (Eds.), *Behavioral Assessment: A Practical Handbook.* New York: Pergamon Press, 1976.

BERECZ, J. Modification of smoking behavior through self-administered punishment of imagined behavior: A new approach to aversive therapy. *Journal of Consulting and Clinical Psychology*, 1972, 38, 244-250.

BEM, D. J., & ALLEN, A. On predicting some of the people some of the time: The search for cross-situational consistencies in behavior. *Psychological Review*, 1974, 81, 506-520.

BENTLER, P. M. Heterosexual behavior assessment—I. Males. *Behaviour Research and Therapy*, 1968, 6, 21-25 (a).

BENTLER, P. M. Heterosexual behavior assessment—II. Females. *Behaviour Research and Therapy*, 1968, 6, 27-30 (b).

BERNSTEIN, D. A. Behavioral fear assessment: Anxiety or artifact? In H. E. Adams & I. P. Unikel (Eds.), *Issues and Trends in Behavior Therapy.* Springfield, Ill.: Charles C Thomas, 1973.

BERNSTEIN, D. A. Manipulation of avoidance behavior as a function of increased or decreased demand on repeated behavioral tests. *Journal of Consulting and Clinical Psychology*, 1974, 42, 896-900.

BERNSTEIN, D. A., & NIETZEL, M. T. Procedural variation in behavioral avoidance tests. *Journal of Consulting and Clinical Psychology*, 1973, 41, 165-174.

BERNSTEIN, D. A., & NIETZEL, M. T. Behavioral avoidance tests: The effects of demand characteristics and repeated measures on two types of subjects. *Behavior Therapy*, 1974, 5, 183-192.

BERNSTEIN, D. A., & PAUL, G. L. Some comments on therapy analogue research with small animal "phobias." *Journal of Behavior Therapy and Experimental Psychiatry*, 1971, 2, 225-237.

BERSOFF, D. M., & MOYER, D. Positive reinforcement observation schedule (Pros): Development and use. In E. J. Mash and L. G. Terdal (Eds.), *Behavior Therapy Assessment: Diagnosis, Design, and Evaluation.* New York: Springer, 1976.

BEUMONT, R., BANCROFT, J., BEARDWOOD, C., & RUSSELL, G. Behavioral changes following treatment with testosterone: A case report. *Psychosomatic Medicine*, 1972, 2, 70-72.

BIJOU, S. W., & PETERSON, R. F. Functional analysis in the assessment of children. In P. McReynolds (Ed.), *Advances in Psychological Measurement* (Vol. 2). Palo Alto: Science and Behavior Books, Inc., 1971.

BIJOU, S. W., PETERSON, R. F., & AULT, M. H. A method to integrate descriptive and experimental field studies at the level of data and empirical concepts. *Journal of Applied Behavior Analysis*, 1968, 1, 175-191.

BIJOU, S. W., PETERSON, R. F., HARRIS, F. R., ALLEN, K. E., & JOHNSTON, M. S. Methodology for experimental studies of young children in natural settings. *The Psychological Record*, 1969, 19, 177-210.

BIRNBAUER, J. S., BURCHARD, J. D., & BURCHARD, S. N. Wanted: Behavior analysts. In R. H. Bradfield (Ed.), *Behavior Modification: The Human Effort.* San Rafael, Ca.: Dimension Publishing Co., 1970.

BLANCHARD, E. B., & YOUNG, L. D. Clinical application of biofeedback training: A review of evidence. *Archives of General Psychiatry,* 1974, 30, 573-589.

BOBBITT, R. A., GORDAN, B. M., & JENSEN, G. D. Development and application of an observational method: Continuing reliability testing. *The Journal of Psychology,* 1966, 63, 83-88.

BOHANNON, R. *Direct and Daily Measurement Procedures in the Identification and Treatment of Reading Behaviors of Children in Special Education.* Doctoral dissertation, College of Education, University of Washington, 1975.

BOLAND, T. B. A social skills assessment of nondating college males. Unpublished doctoral dissertation, University of Wisconsin, Madison, 1973.

BOLSTAD, O. D., & JOHNSON, S. M. Self-regulation in the modification of disruptive classroom behavior. *Journal of Applied Behavior Analysis,* 1972, 5, 443-454.

BORGATTA, E. F. Analysis of social interaction: Actual role playing and projective. *Journal of Abnormal and Social Psychology,* 1955, 51, 394-405.

BORKOVEC, T. D. Physiological and cognitive processes in the regulation of fear. In G. E. Schwartz & D. Shapiro (Eds.), *Consciousness and Self-regulation: Advances in Research.* New York: Plenum Publishers Corp., in press.

BORKOVEC, T. D., STONE, N. M., O'BRIEN, G. T., & KALOUPEK, D. G. Identification and measurement of a clinically relevant target behavior for analogue outcome research. *Behavior Therapy,* 1974, 5, 503-513.

BORKOVEC, T. D., WEERTS, T. C., & BERNSTEIN, D. A. Behavioral assessment of anxiety. In A. Ciminero, K. Calhoun, & H. E. Adams (Eds.), *Handbook of Behavioral Assessment.* New York: John Wiley & Sons, 1977.

BORNSTEIN, P. H., HAMILTON, S. B., CARMODY, T. P., RYCHTARIK, R. G., & VERALDI, D. M. Reliability enhancement: Increasing the accuracy of self-report. Unpublished manuscript, University of Montana, 1976.

BORNSTEIN, P. H., HAMILTON, S. B., MILLER, R. K., QUEVILLON, R. P., & SPITZFORM, M. Reliability and validity enhancement: A fidelity of self-report. Unpublished manuscript, University of Montana, 1976.

BOULOUGOURIS, J. C., MARKS, I. M., & MARSET, P. Superiority of flooding (implosion) to desensitization for reducing pathological fear. *Behaviour Research and Therapy,* 1971, 9, 7-16.

BOX, G. E., JENKINS, G. H., & BACON, D. W. Models for forecasting seasonal and non-seasonal time-series. In B. Harris (Ed.), *Special Analysis of Time-Series.* New York: Wiley, 1967.

BRAUKMAN, C. J., & FIXSEN, D. L. Behavior modification with delinquents. In M. Hersen, R. M. Eisler, and P. M. Miller (Eds.), *Progress in Behavior Modification.* Vol. I. New York: Academic Press, 1975.

BRAUN, P. R., & REYNOLDS, D. N. A factor analysis of a 100-item fear survey inventory. *Behaviour Research and Therapy,* 1969, 7, 399-402.

BRITT, D. B., KEMMERER, W. T., & ROBISON, J. R. Penile blood flow determination by mercury strain gauge plethysmography. *Investigative Urology,* 1971, 8, 673-678.

BRODEN, M., HALL, R. V., & MITTS, B. The effect of self-recording on the classroom behavior of eighth-grade students. *Journal of Applied Behavior Analysis,* 1971, 4, 191-199.

BROWN, G. L., & ZUNG, W. W. K. Depression Scales: Self or physician-ratings? *Comprehensive Psychiatry,* 1972, 13, 361-367.

BUROS, O. K. (Ed.), *The Seventh Mental Measurements Yearbook.* Highland Park: Gryphon Press, 1972.

BUSHELL, D., JR., JACKSON, D. A., & WEIS, L. C. Quality control in the Behavior Analysis approach to Project Follow Through. In W. S. Wood (Ed.), *Issues in Evaluating Behavior Modification*. Champaign, Ill.: Research Press, 1975.

BUSS, A. *The Psychology of Aggression.* New York: Wiley, 1961.

CALLAHAN, E. J., & ALEVIZOS, P. N. *Reactive Effects of Direct Observation of Patient Behaviors.* Paper presented at the meeting of the American Psychological Association, Montreal, August, 1973.

CALLAHAN, E. J., & LEITENBERG, H. Aversion therapy for sexual deviation: Contingent shock and covert sensitization. *Journal of Abnormal Psychology*, 1973, 81, 60-73.

CAMPBELL, D. T. A typology of tests, projective and otherwise. *Journal of Consulting Psychology*, 1957, 21, 207-210.

CAMPBELL, D. T., & FISKE, D. W. Convergent and discriminant validation by the multitrait-multimethod matrix. *Psychological Bulletin*, 1959, 56, 81-105.

CAMPBELL, D. T., & STANLEY, J. C. *Experimental and Quasi-Experimental Designs for Research.* Chicago: Rand McNally, & Co., 1963.

CAMPBELL, J. P., DUNNETTE, M. D., ARVEY, R. D., & HELLERVIK, L. V. *Journal of Applied Psychology*, 1973, 57, 1, 15-22.

CANNELL, C. F., & KAHN, R. L. Interviewing. In G. Lindzey & E. Aronson (Eds.), *The Handbook of Social Psychology*, (2nd ed.). Reading, Mass.: Addison-Wesley Co., 1968.

CANNON, W. B. Again the James-Lange and the thalamic theories of emotion. *Psychological Review*, 1931, 38, 281-295.

CAUTELA, J. R., & KASTENBAUM, R. A reinforcement survey schedule for use in therapy, training, and research. *Psychological Reports*, 1967, 20, 1115-1130.

CAUTELA, J. R., & UPPER, D. The process of individual behavior therapy. In M. Hersen, R. M. Eisler, and P. M. Miller (Eds.), *Progress in Behavior Modification*, Vol. 1. New York: Academic Press, 1975.

CAVIOR, N., & MARABOTTO, C. M. Monitoring verbal behaviors in a dyadic interaction: Valence of target behaviors, type, timing, and reactivity of monitoring. *Journal of Consulting and Clinical Psychology*, 1976, 44, 68-76.

CHAPLIN, J. P., & KRAWIEC, T. S. *Systems and Theories of Psychology.* New York: Holt, Rinehart and Winston, 1960.

CHRISTMAN, C. L. A digital sequential generator for implementing reinforcement schedules. *Journal of the Experimental Analysis of Behavior*, 1974, 22, 577-580.

CIMINERO, A., GRAHAM, L., & JACKSON, J. A comparison of obtrusive- and self-recording procedures. Paper presented at the meeting of the Southeastern Psychological Association, Atlanta, March 1975.

CIMINERO, A. R., GRAHAM, L. E., & JACKSON, J. L. Reciprocal reactivity: Response specific changes in independent observers. *Behavior Therapy*, 1977, 8, 48-56.

COHEN, I. L. The reinforcement value of schedule-induced drinking. *Journal of the Experimental Analysis of Behavior*, 1975, 23, 37-44.

COHEN, J. A coefficient of agreement for nominal scales: *Education and Psychological Measurement*, 1960, 20, 37-46.

COHEN, J. Weighted Kappa: Nominal scale agreement with provision for scaled disagreement or partial credit. *Psychological Bulletin*, 1968, 70, 213-220.

CONE, J. D. What's relevant about reliability and validity for behavioral assessment? Paper presented at the meeting of the American Psychological Association, Chicago, September 1975.

CONE, J. D. Multitrait-mulimethod matrices in behavioral assessment. Paper presented at the meeting of the American Psychological Association, Washington, D.C., September 1976 (a).

CONE, J. D. The behavioral assessment grid (BAG): A taxonomy for behavioral assessment. Paper presented at the meeting of the Association for the Advancement of Behavior Therapy, New York, December, 1976 (b).

CONE, J. D. The relevance of reliability and validity for behavioral assessment. *Behavior Therapy*, 1977, 8, 411-426.

COOKE, G. The efficacy of two desensitization procedures: An analogue study. *Behaviour Research and Therapy*, 1966, 4, 17-24.

COOPER, A., FURST, J. B., & BRIDGEN, W. H. A brief commentary on the usefulness of studying fears of snakes. *Journal of Abnormal Psychology*, 1969, 74, 413-414.

COUTIE, G. A. Commentary on paper by Box and Jenkins. *Journal of The Royal Statistical Society*, Series B, 1962, 24, 345-346.

COWDEN, R. C., REYNOLDS, D. J., & FORD, L. I. The verbal-behavior discrepancy in schizophrenia. *Journal of Clinical Psychology*, 1961, 17, 406-408.

COZBY, P. C. Self-disclosure. *Psychological Bulletin*, 1973, 79, 73-91.

CRONBACH, L. J. *Essentials of Psychological Testing*. (2nd ed.). New York: Harper & Row, 1960.

CRONBACH, L. J. *Essentials of Psychological Testing* (3rd ed.). New York: Harper and Row, 1970.

CRONBACH, L. J., GLESER, G. C., NANDA, H., & RAJARATNAM, N. *The Dependability of Behavioral Measures*. New York: Wiley, 1972.

CRONBACH, L. J., & MEEHL, P. E. Construct validity in psychological tests. *Psychological Bulletin*, 1955, 52, 281-302.

CRONBACH, L. J., RAJARATNAM, N., & GLESER, G. C. Theory of generalizability: Liberalization of reliability theory. *British Journal of Statistical Psychology*, 1963, 16, 137-163.

CROSS, D., TURSKY, B., & LODGE, M. The role of regression and range effects in determination of the power function for electric shock. *Perception and Psychophysics*, 1975, 18, 9-14.

CURETON, E. E. Validity. In E. F. Lindquist (Ed.), *Educational Measurement*. Washington, D.C.: American Council on Education, 1951.

CURRAN, J. D., & GILBERT, F. S. A test of the relative effectiveness of a systematic desensitization program and an interpersonal skills training program with date anxious subjects. *Behavior Therapy*, in press.

DAVISON, G. C., & STUART, R. B. Behavior therapy and civil liberties. *American Psychologist*, 1975, 30, 755-763.

DeMASTER, B., & REID, J. B. *Effects of Feedback Procedures in Maintaining Observer Reliability*. Eugene, Oregon: Oregon Research Institute (cited in Johnson, S. M. & Bolstad, O. D. Methodological issues in naturalistic observation: Some problems and solutions for field research. In L. A. Hamerlynck, L. C. Hardy, & E. J. Mash (Eds.), *Behavior Change: Methodology, Concepts and Practice*. Champaign, Ill.: Research Press, 1973).

DICKSON, C. R. Role of assessment in behavior therapy. In P. McReynolds (Ed.), *Advances in Psychological Assessment* (Vol. 3). San Francisco: Jossey-Bass, 1975.

DIEBERT, A. N., & HARMON, A. J. *New Tools for Changing Behavior* (2nd ed.). Champaign, Ill.: Research Press, Inc., 1970.

DINOFF, M., RAYMAKER, H., & MORRIS, J. R. The reliability and validity of the minimal social behavior scale and its use as a selection device. *Journal of Clinical Psychology*, 1962, 18, 441-444.

DIXON, J. J., DE MONCHAUX, C., & SANDLER, J. Patterns of anxiety: The phobias. *British Journal of Medical Psychology*, 1957, 30, 34-40.

DMITRUH, O. M., COLLINS, K. W., & CLINGER, D. L. The "Barnum Effect" and acceptance of negative personal evaluation. *Journal of Consulting and Clinical Psychology*, 1973, 41, 192-195.

DOLLARD, J., & MILLER, N. E. *Personality and Psychotherapy: An Analysis of in Terms of Learning, Thinking, and Culture*. New York: McGraw-Hill, 1950.

DRABMAN, R. S., SPITALNIK, R., & O'LEARY, K. D. Teaching self-control to disruptive children. *Journal of Abnormal Psychology*, 1973, 82, 10-16.

EBEL, R. Must all tests be valid? *American Psychologist*, 1961, 16, 640-647.

EBEL, R. L. Content standard test scores. *Education and Psychological Measurement*, 1962, 22, 15-25.

EISLER, R. M., HERSEN, M., & MILLER, P. M. Effects of modeling in components of assertive behaviors. *Journal of Behavior Therapy and Experimental Psychiatry*, 1973, 4, 1-6.

EISLER, R. M., HERSEN, M., MILLER, P. M., & BLANCHARD, E. B. Situational determinants of assertive behaviors. *Journal of Consulting and Clinical Psychology*, 1975, 43, 330-340.

EISLER, R. M., MILLER, P. M., & HERSEN, M. Components of assertive behavior. *Journal of Clinical Psychology*, 1973, 29, 295-299.

ELLIS, A. *Reason and Emotion in Psychotherapy*. New York: Lyle Stuart, 1962.

EMMELKAMP, P. M. G. Self-observation versus flooding in the treatment of agoraphobia. *Behaviour Research and Therapy*, 1974, 12, 229-237.

EMMELKAMP, R. M. G., & ULTEE, J. A. A comparison of "successive approximations" and "self-observation" in the treatment of agoraphobia. *Behavior Therapy*, 1974, 5, 606-613.

ENDLER, N. S., HUNT, J. McV., & ROSENSTEIN, A. J. An S-R inventory of anxiousness. *Psychological Monographs*, 1962, 76 (Whole No. 536).

ENDLER, N. S., & OKADA, M. A multidimensional measure of trait anxiety: The S-R Inventory of General Trait Anxiousness. *Journal of Consulting and Clinical Psychology*, 1975, 43, 319-329.

EPSTEIN, L. H., MILLER, P. M., & WEBSTER, J. S. The effects of reinforcing concurrent behavior on self-monitoring. *Behavior Therapy*, 1976, 7, 89-95.

EPSTEIN, L. H., WEBSTER, J. S., & MILLER, P. M. Accuracy and controlling effects of self-montoring. *Behavior Therapy*, 1975, 6, 654-666.

ERNST, F. A. Self-recording and counter-conditioning of a self-mutilative compulsion. *Behavior Therapy*, 1973, 4, 144-146.

EVANS, I. M., & NELSON, R. O. A curriculum for the teaching of behavior assessment. *American Psychologist*, 1974, 29, 598-606.

FARINA, A., ARENBERG, D., & GUSKIN, S. A scale for measuring minimal social behavior. *Journal of Consulting Psychology*, 1957, 21, 265-268.

FARLEY, F. H., & MEALIEA, W. L. Dissimulation and social desirability, in the assessment of fears. *Behavior Therapy*, 1971, 2, 101-102.

FAZIO, A. Verbal and overt behavioral assessment of a specific fear. *Journal of Consulting and Clinical Psychology*, 1969, 33, 705-709.

FERSTER, C. B. Classification of behavior pathology. In L. Krasner and L. P. Ullmann (Eds.), *Research in Behavior Modification*. New York: Holt, Rinehart, & Winston, 1965, pp. 6-26.

FERSTER, C. B. A functional analysis of depression. *American Psychologist*, 1973, 28, 857-870.

FIXSEN, D. L., PHILLIPS, E. L., & WOLF, M. M. Achievement place: The reliability of self-reporting and peer-reporting and their effects on behavior. *Journal of Applied Behavior Analysis*, 1972, 5, 19-30.

FIXSEN, D. L., PHILLIPS, E. L., & WOLF, M. M. Achievement Place: Experiments in self-government with pre-delinquents. *Journal of Applied Behavior Analysis*, 1973, 6, 31-47.

FLORY, R. K., & LICKFETT, G. G. Effects of Lick-contingent timeout on schedule-induced polydipsia. *Journal of the Experimental Analysis of Behavior*, 1974, 21, 45-55.

FLOWERS, J. V. Behavior modification of cheating in an elementary school student: A brief note. *Behavior Therapy*, 1972, 3, 311-312.

FOREHAND, R., KING, H. E., PEED, S., & YODER, P. Mother-child interactions: Comparison of a non-compliant clinic group and a non-clinic group. *Behaviour Research and Therapy*, 1975, 13, 79-84.

FORGIONE, A. G. The use of mannequins in the behavioral treatment of "Child molesters." Paper presented at the meeting of the Association for Advancement of Behavior Therapy, Chicago, November, 1974.

FOSTER, F. G., & KUPFER, D. J. Psychomotor activity and serum creatine phosphokinase activity. *Archives of General Psychiatry*, 1973, 29, 752-758.

FRANKEL, A. J. Beyond the simple functional analysis. *Behavior Therapy*, 1975, 6, 254-260.

FREDERIKSEN, L. W., EPSTEIN, L. H., & KOSEVSKY, B. P. Reliability and controlling effects of the procedures for self-monitoring smoking. *The Psychological Record*, 1975, 25, 255-264.

FREEDMAN, B. J. *An Analysis of Social-Behavioral Skill Deficits in Delinquent and Non-Delinquent Adolescent Boys*. Unpublished Doctoral Dissertation, University of Wisconsin, 1974.

FREUND, K. A laboratory method for diagnosing predominance of homo and heteroerotic interest in the male. *Behaviour Research and Therapy*, 1963, 1, 85-93.

FREUND, K. Diagnosing homo- or heterosexual and erotic age-preferences by means of a psychophysiological test. *Behaviour Research and Therapy*, 1967, 5, 209-228 (a).

FREUND, K. Erotic preference in pedophilia. *Behaviour Research and Therapy*, 1967, 5, 339-348 (b).

FREUND, K. Bisexuality in homosexual pedophilia. Paper delivered at 1975 International Academy of Sex Research Meetings, Stony Brook, N.Y.

FREUND, K., KNOB, K., & SEDLARCEK, F. Some transducer for mechanical plethysmography of the male genital. *Journal of the Experimental Analysis of Behavior*, 1965, 8, 169-170.

FREUND, K., LANGEVIN, R., & BARLOW, D. Comparison of two penile measures of erotic arousal. *Behaviour Research and Therapy*, 1974, 12, 355-340.

FREUND, K., LANGEVIN, R., CIBIRI, S., & ZAJAC, Y. Heterosexual aversion in homosexual males. *British Journal of Psychiatry*, 1973, 122, 163-169.

FREUND, K., LANGEVIN, R., LAWS, R., & SERBER, M. Femininity and preferred partner age in homosexual and heterosexual males. *British Journal of Psychiatry*, 1974, 125, 442-446.

FREUND, K., LANGEVIN, R., & ZAJAC, Y. A note on erotic arousal value of moving and stationary human forms. *Behaviour Research and Therapy*, 1974, 12, 117-119.

FRICKE, R. Test g ü tekriterien bei lehrzielorien tierten Tests. *Zeitschrift für Erziehungswissenschaftliche Forschung*, 1972, 6, 150-175.

GAGNON, J. H., & SIMON, W. *Sexual Conduct: The Social Sources of Human Sexuality*. Chicago: Aldine, 1973.

GALASSI, J. P., DeLo, J. S., GALASSI, M. D., & BASTIEN, S. The college self-expression scale: A measure of assertiveness. *Behavior Therapy*, 1974, 5, 165-171.

GALASSI, M. D., & GALASSI, J. P. The effects of role playing variations on the assessment of assertive behavior. *Behavior Therapy*, 1976, 7, 343-347.

GAMBRILL, E. D., RICHEY, C. A. An assertive inventory for use in assessment and research. Unpublished manuscript, University of California at Berkeley, 1975.

GAY, M. L., HOLLANDSWORTH, J., & GALASSI, J. P. An assertiveness inventory for adults. *Journal of Counseling Psychology*, 1975, 4, 340-344.

GEER, J. H. The development of a scale to measure fear. *Behaviour Research and Therapy*, 1965, 3, 45-53.

GEER, J. H. Effects of fear arousal upon task performance and verbal behavior. *Journal of Abnormal Psychology*, 1966, 71, 119-123 (a).

GEER, J. H. Fear and autonomic arousal. *Journal of Abnormal Psychology*, 1966, 71, 253-255 (b).

GEER, J. H. Cognitive factors in sexual arousal: Toward an amalgam of research strategies. Paper read at 1974 American Psychological Association Meetings, New Orleans, La.

GEER, J. H. Direct measurement of genital responding. *American Psychologist*, 1975, 30, 415-418.

GEER, J. H., & FUHR, R. Cognitive factors in sexual arousal: The role of distraction. *Journal of Consulting and Clinical Psychology*, 1976, 44, 238-243.

GEER, J. H., MOROKOFF, D., & GREENWOOD, P. Sexual arousal in women. The development of a measurement device for vaginal blood volume. *Archives of Sexual Behavior*, 1974, 3, 559-564.

GEER, J. H., & QUANTARARO, J. Vaginal blood volume rseponses during masturbation and resultant orgasm. *Archives of Sexual Behavior*, in press.

GELLERT, E. Systematic observation: A method in child study. *Harvard Educational Review*, 1955, 25, 179-195.

GLASER, R. Instructional technology and the measurement of learning outcomes. *American Psychologist*, 1963, 18, 519-521.

GLASS, G. V., WILLSON, V. L., & GOTTMAN, J. M. *Design and Analysis of Time-Series Experiments*. Boulder, Co.: Colorado Associated Press, 1975.

GOFFMAN, E. *Asylums*. Garden City, New York: Doubleday, 1961.

GOLDFRIED, M. R., & DAVISON, G. C. *Clinical Behavior Therapy*. New York: Holt, Rinehart & Winston, 1976.

GOLDFRIED, M. R., DECENTECEO, E. T., & WEINBERG, L. Systematic rational restructuring as a self-control technique. *Behavior Therapy*, 1974, 5, 247-254.

GOLDFRIED, M. R., & D'ZURILLA, T. J. A behavioral-analytic model for assessing competence. In C. D. Spielberger (Ed.), *Current Topics in Clinical and Community Psychology*. New York: Academic Press, 1969.

GOLDFRIED, M. R., & GOLDFRIED, A. P. Cognitive change methods. In F. H. Kanfer & A. P. Goldstein (Eds.), *Helping People Change*. Elmsford, N.Y.: Pergamon Press, 1975.

GOLDFRIED, M. R., & KENT, R. N. Traditional versus behavioral personality assessment: A comparison of methodological and theoretical assumptions. *Psychological Bulletin*, 1972, 77, 409-420.

GOLDFRIED, M. R., & LINEHAN, M. M. Basic issues in behavioral assessment. In A. R. Ciminero, K. S. Calhoun, & H. E. Adams (Eds.), *Handbook of Behavioral Assessment*. New York: Wiley-Interscience, 1977.

GOLDFRIED, M., & POMERANZ, D. Role of assessment in behavior modification. *Psychological Reports*, 1968, 23, 75-87.

GOLDFRIED, M. R., & SPRAFKIN, J. N. *Behavioral Personality Assessment*. Morristown, N.J.: General Learning Press, 1974.

GOLDFRIED, M. R., & SPRAFKIN, J. N. Behavioral personality assessment. In J. T. Spence, R. C. Carson, & J. W. Thibaut (Eds.), *Behavioral Approaches to Therapy*. Morristown, N.J.: General Learning Press, 1976.

GOLDFRIED, M. R., STRICKER, G., & WEINER, I. B. *Rorschach Handbook of Clinical and Research Application*. Englewood Cliffs, N.J.: Prentice-Hall, 1971.

GOLDSMITH, J. B., & McFALL, R. M. Development and evaluation of interpersonal skill-training program for psychiatric inpatients. *Journal of Abnormal Psychology*, 1975, 84, 51-58.

GOLDSTEIN, A. P. *Therapist-Patient Expectancies in Psychotherapy*. New York: Pergamon Press, 1962.

GOLDSTEIN, A. P., & STEIN, N. *Prescriptive Psychotherapies*. New York: Pergamon Press, 1976.

GONZALEZ, F. A., & WALLER, M. B. Handwriting as an operant. *Journal of the Experimental Analysis of Behavior*, 1974, 21, 165-176.

GONZALEZ, J., MARTIN, S., & DYSART, R. A comparison of various methods of recording behavior using the Patterson scoring system. Proceedings of the 81st Annual Convention of the American Psychological Association, Montreal, Canada, 1973, 8, 53-54.

GOOD, C. V. *Introduction to Educational Research*. New York: Appleton-Century-Crofts, 1963.

GOODENOUGH, F. L. *Mental Testing*. New York: Rinehart, 1949.

GOTTMAN, J. M., & McFALL, R. M. Self-monitoring effects in a program for potential high school dropouts: A time-series analysis. *Journal of Consulting and Clinical Psychology*, 1972, 39, 273-281.

GOTTMAN, J. M., McFALL, R. M., & BARNETT, J. T. Design and analysis of research using time-series. *Psychological Bulletin*, 1969, 72, 299-306.

· GRIEST, J. H., KLEIN, M. H., & VAN CURA, L. J. A computer interview for psychiatric patient target symptoms. *Archives of General Psychiatry*, 1973, 29, 247-254.

GUEST, L. A study of interviewee competence. *International Journal of Opinion Attitude Research*, 1947, 1, 17-30.

GUILFORD, J. P. *Personality*. New York: McGraw-Hill, 1959.

GULAS, I., McCLANAHAN, L. D., & POETTER, R. Phobic response factors from the fear survey schedule. *Journal of Psychology*, 1975, 90, 19-25.

GULLIKSEN, H. *Theory of Mental Tests*. New York: John Wiley & Sons, 1950.

GUTTMAN, H. A., SPECTOR, R. M., SIGAL, J. J., RAKOFF, V., & EPSTEIN, W. B. Reliability of coding affective communications in family therapy sessions: Problems of measurement and interpretation. *Journal of Consulting and Clinical Psychology*, 1971, 37, 397-402.

HALL, R. V., CRISTLER, C., CRANSTON, S. S., & TUCKER, B. Teachers and parents as researchers using multiple baseline designs. *Journal of Applied Behavior Analysis*, 1970, 3, 247-255.

HALL, R. V., FOX, R., WILLARD, D., GOLDSMITH, L., EMERSON, M., OWEN, M., DAVIS, F., & PORCIA, E. The teacher as an observer and experimenter in the modification of talking out behavior. *Journal of Applied Behavior Analysis*, 1971, 4, 141-150.

HAMBLETON, R. L., & NOVICK, M. R. Toward an integration of theory and method for criterion-referenced tests. *Journal of Educational Measurement*, 1973, 10, 159-170.

HAMILTON, M. A rating scale for depression. *Journal of Neurology, Neurosurgery and Psychiatry*, 1960, 23, 56-62.

HAMILTON, M. Development of a rating scale for primary depressive illness. *British Journal of Social and Clinical Psychology*, 1967, 6, 278-296.

HARTMANN, D. P. Must the baby follow the bathwater? Psychometric principles—behavioral data. Paper presented at the meeting of the American Psychological Association, Washington, D.C., September 1976.

HARTMANN, D. P. Considerations in the choice of interobserver reliability estimates. *Journal of Applied Behavior Analysis*, 1977, 10, 103-116.

HAWKINS, R. P. Who decided that was the problem? Two stages of responsibility for applied behavior analysits. In W. S. Wood (Ed.), *Issues in Evaluating Behavior Modification*. Champaign, Ill.: Research Press, 1975.

HAWKINS, R. P. Relevance for what? It depends on the assessment goal. In D. H. Barlow (Chair), *Behavioral Assessment: The Relevance of Traditional Psychometric Procedures*. Symposium presented at the meeting of the American Psychological Association, Washington, D. C., September, 1976 (a).

HAWKINS, R. P. The role of assessment in behavioral intervention: Cut the umbilical cord, but save the baby. In M. R. Goldfried (Chair), *Issues in Behavioral Assessment*. Symposium presented at Association for Advancement of Behavior Therapy convention, New York, December, 1976 (b).

HAWKINS, R. P., AXELROD, S., & HALL, R. V. Teachers as behavior analysts: Precisely monitoring student performance. In T. A. Brigham, R. Hawkins, J. W. Scott, and T. F. McLaughlin (Eds.), *Behavior Analysis in Education: Self-control and Reading*. Dubuque, Ia.: Kendall/Hunt, 1976.

HAWKINS, R. P., & DOBES, R. W. Behavioral definitions in applied behavior analysis: Explicit or implicit. In B. C. Etzel, J. M. LeBlanc, and D. M. Baer (Eds.), *New Developments in Behavioral Research: Theory, Method and Application. In Honor of Sidney W. Bijou*. Hillsdale, N.J.: Lawrence Erlbaum Assoc., 1977.

HAWKINS, R. P., & DOTSON, V. A. Reliability scores that delude: An Alice in Wonderland trip through the misleading characteristics of interobserver agreement scores in interval recording. In E. Ramp & G. Semb (Eds.), *Behavior Analysis: Areas of Research and Application*. Englewood Cliffs, N.J.: Prentice-Hall, 1975.

HAWKINS, R. P., PETERSON, R. F., SCHWEID, E., & BIJOU, S. W. Behavior therapy in the home: Amelioration of problem parent-child relations with the parent in a therapeutic role. *Journal of Experimental Child Psychology*, 1966, 4, 99-107.

HAYES, S. C., & CAVIOR, N. Effects of multiple teaching and target difficulty on the reactivity of self-monitoring: I. Negative behaviors. *Behavior Therapy*, in press.

HAYES, S. C., JOHNSON, V. S., & CONE, J. D. The marked item technique: A practical procedure for litter control. *Journal of Applied Behavior Analysis*, 1975, 8, 381-386.

HEIMAN, J. Facilitating erotic arousal: Towards sex-positive sex research. Paper presented at the meeting of the American Psychological Association, New Orleans, September 1974.

HEIMAN, J. Use of the vaginal photoplethysmograph as a diagnostic and treatment aid in female sexual dysfunction. *Psychophysiology*, in press.

HENDRICKS, C. G., THORESEN, C. E., & HUBBARD, D. R. Effects of behavioral self-observation on elementary teachers and students. Unpublished manuscript, Stanford University, 1973.

HENSON, D. E., & RUBIN, H. B. Voluntary control of eroticism. *Journal of Applied Behavior Analysis*, 1971, 4, 37-44.

HERBERT, E. W., & BAER, D. M. Training parents as behavior modifiers. *Journal of Applied Behavior Analysis*, 1972, 5, 139-149.

HERMAN, S. H., BARLOW, D. H., & AGRAS, W. S. An experimental analysis of exposure to "explicit" heterosexual stimuli as an effective variable in changing arousal patterns of homosexuals. *Behaviour Research and Therapy*, 1974, 22, 335-345.

HERMAN, S. H., & PRESITT, M. An experimental analysis of feedback to increase sexual arousal in a case of homo and heterosexual impotence: A preliminary report. *Journal of Behavior Therapy and Experimental Psychiatry*, 1974, 5, 271-274.

HERSEN, M. Fear scale norms for an in-patient population. *Journal of Clinical Psychology*, 1971, 27, 375-378.

HERSEN, M. Self-assessment of fear. *Behavior Therapy*, 1973, 4, 241-257.

HERSEN, M., & BARLOW, D. H. *Single Case Experimental Designs: Strategies for Studying Behavior Change*. New York: Pergamon Press, 1976.

HERSEN, M., & BELLACK, A. S. Assessment of social skills. In A. R. Ciminero, K. S. Calhoun, & H. E. Adams (Eds.), *Handbook for Behavioral Assessment*. New York: John Wiley & Sons, 1977.

HERSEN, M., & BELLACK, A. S. Social skills training for chronic psychiatric patients: Rationale, research findings, and future directions. *Comprehensive Psychiatry*, in press.

HERSEN, M., EISLER, R. M., MILLER, P. M., JOHNSON, M. B., & PINKSTON, S. G. Effects of practice, instructions and modeling on components of assertive behaviors. *Behaviour Research and Therapy*, 1973, 11, 443-451.

HODGSON, R., & RACHMAN, S. Desynchrony in measures of fear. *Behaviour Research and Therapy*, 1974, 12, 319-326.

HOLLAND, C. An interview guide for behavioral counseling with parents. *Behavior Therapy*, 1970, 1, 70-79.

HOLLEY, J. W. & GUILFORD, J. P. A note on the G index of agreement. *Educational and Psychological Measurement*, 1964, 24, 749-753.

HULL, H. G. Interobserver variation in recording behavior: Random or systematic error? *Dissertation Abstracts International*, 1971, 31 (11-B), 6904.

HUTZELL, R. R. Effects of self-recording and expectancy on a neutral valued behavior. Unpublished manuscript, University of North Carolina, Greensboro, 1976.

HUTZELL, R. R., PLATZEK, D., & LOGUE, P. E. Control of symptoms of Gilles de la Tourette's Syndrome by self-monitoring. *Journal of Behavior Therapy and Experimental Psychiatry*, 1974, 5, 71-76.

JACKSON, B. Treatment of depression by self-reinforcement. *Behavior Therapy*, 1972, 3. 298-307.

JACOBSON, E. *Progressive relaxation.* Chicago: University of Chicago Press, 1938.

JAMES, W. What is emotion? *Mind*, 1884, 19, 188-205.

JANIS, I. L., MAHL, G. F., KAGAN, J., & HOLT, R. R. *Personality: Dynamics, Development, and Assessment.* New York: Harcourt, Brace and World, 1969.

JEFFREY, D. B. Self-control: Methodological issues and research trends. In M. J. Mahoney, & C. E. Thoresen (Eds.), *Self-control: Power to the Person.* Monterey: Brooks/Cole, 1974.

JEGER, A. M., & GOLDFRIED, M. R. A comparison of situation tests of speech anxiety. *Behavior Therapy*, 1976, 7, 252-255.

JERSILD, A. T., & MEIGS, M. F. Direct observation as a research method. *Review of Educational Research*, 1939, 9, 472-482.

JOHNSON, S. M., & BOLSTAD, O. D. Methodological issues in naturalistic observation: Some problems and solutions for field research. In L. A. Hamerlynck, L. C. Handy, and E. J. Mash (Eds.), *Behavior Change: Methodology, Concepts, and Practice.* Champaign, Ill.: Research Press, 1973.

JOHNSON, S. M., & BOLSTAD, O. D. Reactivity to home observation, a comparison or audio recorded behavior with observers present or absent. *Journal of Applied Behavior Analysis*, 1975, 8, 181-185.

JOHNSON, S. M., CHRISTENSON, A., & BELLAMY, G. T. Evaluation of family intervention through unobtrusive audio recordings: Experiences in "bugging" children. *Journal of Applied Behavior Analysis*, 1976, 9, 213-219.

JOHNSON, S. M., & WHITE, G. Self-observation as an agent of behavioral change. *Behavior Therapy*, 1971, 2, 488-497.

JONES, E. E., DAVIS, K. E., & GERGEN, K. J. Role playing variations and their information value for person perception. *Journal of Abnormal and Social Psychology*, 1961, 63, 302-310.

JONES, F. H., & EIMERS, R. C. Role playing to train elementary teachers to use a classroom management "skill package." *Journal of Applied Behavior Analysis*, 1975, 8, 421-433.

JONES, R. R., REID, J. B., & PATTERSON, G. R. Naturalistic observation in clinical assessment. In P. McReynolds (Ed.), *Advances in Psychological Assessment* (Vol. 3). San Francisco: Jossey-Bass, Inc., 1975, pp. 42-95.

JONES, R. R., VAUGHT, R. S., & WEINROTT, M. R. Time series analysis in operant research. *Journal of Applied Behavior Analysis*, 1977, 10, 151-166.

KANFER, F. H. Self-monitoring: Methodological limitations and clinical application. *Journal of Consulting and Clinical Psychology*, 1970, 35, 148-152.

KANFER, F. H. The many faces of self-control. In R. B. Stuart (Ed.), *Behavioral Self-Management: Strategies, Techniques, and Outcome.* New York: Brunner/ Mazel, 1977.

KANFER, F. H., & GOLDSTEIN, A. P. (Eds.), *Helping People Change.* New York: Pergamon Press, 1975.

KANFER, F. H., & GRIMM, L. G. Promising trends toward the future development of behavior modification: Ten related areas in need of exploration. In W. E. Craighead, A. E. Kazdin, & M. J. Mahoney (Eds.), *Behavior Modification: Principles, Issues, and Applications.* Boston: Houghton Mifflin, 1975.

KANFER, F. H., & SASLOW, G. Behavioral diagnosis. In C. M. Franks (Ed.), *Behavior Therapy: Appraisal and Status.* New York: McGraw-Hill, 1969, 417-444.

KAROLY, P., & DOYLE, W. W. Effects of outcome expectancy and timing of self-monitoring on cigarette smoking. *Journal of Clinical Psychology*, 1975, 31, 351-355.

KASS, R. E., & O'LEARY, K. D. The effects of experimental bias in field experimental settings. Paper presented at the Behavior Analysis in Education Symposium, University of Kansas, Lawrence, Ks., April 9, 1970.

KAZDIN, A. E. Reactive self-monitoring: The effects of response desirability, goal setting and feedback. *Journal of Consulting and Clinical Psychology*, 1974, 42, 704-716 (a).

KAZDIN, A. E. Self-monitoring and behavior change. In M. J. Mahoney, & C. E. Thoresen (Eds.), *Self-Control: Power to the Person.* Monterey: Brooks/Cole, 1974 (b).

KAZDIN, A. E. Effects of covert modeling and model reinforcement on assertive behavior. *Journal of Abnormal Psychology*, 1974, 84, 240-252 (c).

KAZDIN, A. E. *Behavior Modification in Applied Settings.* Homewood, Ill.: Dorsey Press, 1975.

KENT, R. N., O'LEARY, K. D., DIAMENT, C., & DIETZ, S. Expectation biases in observational evaluation of therapeutic change. *Journal of Consulting and Clinical Psychology*, 1974, 42, 774-780.

KERCHER, G. A., & WALKER, C. E. Reactions of convicted rapists to sexually explicit stimuli. *Journal of Abnormal Psychology*, 1973, 81, 46-50.

KLEINMUNTZ, B. *Computer in Personality Assessment.* Morristown, N.J.: General Learning Press, 1972.

KLORMAN, R., WEERTS, T. C., HASTINGS, J. E., MELAMED, B. G., & LANG, P. J. Psychometric description of some specific-fear questionnaires. *Behavior Therapy*, 1974, 5, 401-409.

KNOX, D. *Marriage Happiness: A Behavioral Approach to Counseling.* Champaign, Ill.: Research Press, 1971.

KOENIG, C. H. *Charting the Future Course of Behavior.* Unpublished doctoral dissertation, Department of Education, University of Kansas, 1972.

KOLB, D. A., WINTER, S. K., & BERLEW, D. E. Self-directed behavior change: Two studies. *Journal of Applied Behavioral Science*, 1968, 4, 453-471.

KRIEWALL, T. E. Aspects and applications of criterion-referenced tests. Technical Paper No. 103. Downers Grove, Ill.: Institute for Educational Research, 1972.

KUBANY, E. S., & SLOGGETT, B. B. Coding procedure for teachers. *Journal of Applied Behavior Analysis*, 1973, 6, 339-344.

LACEY, J. I. Individual differences in somatic response patterns. *Journal of Comparative and Physiological Psychology*, 1950, 113, 338-350.

LACEY, J. I. The evaluation of autonomic responses: Toward a general solution. *Annals of the New York Academy of Sciences*, 1956, 67, 123-164.

LACEY, J. I. Psychophysiological approaches to the evaluation of psychotherapeutic process and outcome. In F. Rubenstein & M. B. Parloff (Eds.), *Research in*

Psychotherapy. Washington, D.C.: American Psychological Association, 1962.

LACEY, J. I., & VAN LEHN, R. Differential emphasis on somatic response to stress. *Psychosomatic Medicine,* 1952, 4, 71-81.

LANG, P. J. Fear reduction and fear behavior: Problems in treating a construct. In J. M. Shlien (Ed.), *Research in Psychotherapy,* Vol. III. Washington, D.C.: American Psychological Association, 1968.

LANG, P. J. The application of psychophysiological methods to the study of psychotherapy and behavior modification. In A. E. Bergin and S. L. Garfield (Eds.), *Handbook of Psychotherapy and Behavior Change.* New York: John Wiley, 1971.

LANG, P. J. Psychophysiological analysis in psychotherapy research. In I. E. Waskow & M. B. Parloff (Eds.), *Psychotherapy Change Measures.* Report of the Clinical Research Branch Outcome Measures Project DHEW Publication No. (ADM) 74-120. Washington, D.C.: U.S. Government Printing Office, 1975.

LANG, P. J. Research on the specificity of feedback training: Implication for the use of biofeedback in the treatment of anxiety and fear. In J. Beatty & H. Legewie (Eds.), *Biofeedback and Behavior,* Proceedings of the NHTO Symposium on Biofeedback & Behavior, Munich, July, 1976. New York: Plenum Press, 1977.

LANG, P. J., GEER, J., & HNATIOW, M. Semantic generalization of conditioned autonomic responses. *Journal of Experimental Psychology,* 1963, 65, 552-558.

LANG, P. J., & LAZOVIK, A. D. Experimental desensitization of a phobia. *Journal of Abnormal and Social Psychology,* 1963, 66, 519-525.

LANG, P. J., MELAMED, B. G., & HART, J. H. Automating the desensitization procedure: A psychophysiological analysis of fear modification. In M. J. Kietzman (Ed.), *Experimental Approaches to Psychopathology.* New York: Academic Press, 1974.

LANGEVIN, R., STANFORD, A., & BLOCK, R. The effect of relaxation instruction in erotic arousal in homosexual and heterosexual males. *Behavior Therapy,* 1975, 6, 453-458.

LANYON, R. I., & MANOSEVITZ, M. Validity of self reported fear. *Behaviour Research and Therapy,* 1966, 4, 259-263.

LAWLIS, G. F. Response styles of a patient population on the fear survey schedule. *Behaviour Research and Therapy,* 1971, 9, 95-102.

LAWS, D. R., & RUBIN, H. B. Instructional control of an autonomic sexual response. *Journal of Applied Behavior Analysis,* 1969, 2, 93-99.

LAWSHE, C. H. A quantitative approach to content validity. *Personnel Psychology,* 1975, 28, 563-575.

LAYNE, C. C., RICKARD, H. C., JONES, M. T., & LYMAN, R. D. Accuracy of self-monitoring on a variable ratio schedule of observer verification. *Behavior Therapy,* 1976, 7, 481-488.

LAZARUS, A. A. Multimodel behavior therapy: Treating the "Basic Id." *Journal of Nervous and Mental Disease,* 1973, 156, 404-411.

LAZARUS, A. A. *Multi-model Behavior Therapy.* New York: Springer, 1976.

LEIFER, A. D., & LEIFER, L. J. An auditory prompting device for behavior observation. *Journal of Experimental Child Psychology,* 1971, 11, 376-378.

LEITENBERG, H., AGRAS, S., BUTZ, R., & WINCZE, J. Relationship between heart rate and behavioral change during the treatment of phobias. *Journal of Abnormal Psychology,* 1971, 78, 59-68.

LEITENBERG, H., AGRAS, W. S., THOMPSON, L. E., & WRIGHT, D. E. Feedback in behavior modification: An experimental analysis in two phobic cases. *Journal of Applied Behavior Analysis,* 1968, 1, 131-137.

LENTZ, R. J., PAUL, G. L., & CALHOUN, J. F. Reliability and validity of three measures of functioning with "hard-core" chronic mental patients. *Journal of Abnormal Psychology,* 1971, 78, 69-76.

LEWINSOHN, P. M., BIGLAN, A., & ZEISS, A. M. Behavioral treatment of depression. In

P. O. Davidson (Ed.), *The Behavioral Management of Anxiety, Depression and Pain*. New York: Brunner/Mazel, 1976.

LEWINSOHN, P. M., & GRAF, M. Pleasant activities and depression. *Journal of Consulting and Clinical Psychology*, 1973, 41, 261-268.

LEWINSOHN, P. M., & LIBET, J. Pleasant events, activity schedules and depressions. *Journal of Abnormal Psychiatry*, 1972, 79, 291-295.

LEWINSOHN, P. M., & SHAFFER, M. The use of home observations as an integral part of the treatment of depression. Preliminary report and case studies. *Journal of Consulting and Clinical Psychology*, 1971, 37, 87-94.

LIBERTY, K. A. *Data Decision Rules.* University of Oregon, Regional Resource Center for Handicapped Children, Working Paper No. 20, 1972.

LIBERTY, K. A., WHITE, O. R., McGUIGAN, C. *A Discriminate Analysis Procedure for Determining Proficient Performance Levels.* A working paper available from the Experimental Education Unit, Child Development and Mental Retardation Center, University of Washington, Seattle, WA., 1975.

LIBET, J. M., & LEWINSOHN, P. M. Concept of social skill with special reference to the behavior of depressed persons. *Journal of Consulting and Clinical Psychology*, 1973, 40, 304-312.

LICHTENSTEIN, E. Techniques for assessing outcomes of psychotherapy. In P. McReynolds (Ed.), *Advances in Psychological Assessment* (Vol. 2). Palo Alto: Science and Behavior Books, Inc., 1971.

LINDSLEY, O. R. Direct measurement and prothesis of retarded behavior. *Journal of Education*, 1966, 9, 27-36.

LINEHAN, M. M. Content validity in behavioral assessment. Paper presented at the meeting of the American Psychological Association, Washington, D.C., September, 1976.

LINEHAN, M. M., & GOLDFRIED, M. R. Assertion training for women: A comparison of behavior rehearsal and cognitive restructing therapies. Paper presented at the Association for Advancement of Behavior Therapy Convention, San Francisco, 1975.

LIPINSKI, D. P., BLACK, J. L., NELSON, R. O., & CIMINERO, A. The influence of motivational variables on the reactivity and reliability of self-recording. *Journal of Consulting and Clinical Psychology*, 1975, 43, 637-646.

LIPINSKI, D., & NELSON, R. The reactivity and unreliability of self-recording. *Journal of Consulting and Clinical Psychology*, 1974, 42, 110-123.

LIVINGSTON, S. A. Criterion-referenced applications of classical test theory. *Journal of Educational Measurement*, 1972, 9, 13-26.

LOBITZ, G. K., & JOHNSON, S. M. Normal versus deviant children: A multimethod comparison. *Journal of Abnormal Child Psychology*, 1975, 3, 353-374.

LOBITZ, W. C., & JOHNSON, S. M. Parental manipulation of the behavior of normal and deviant children. *Child Development*, 1975, 46, 719-726.

LOCKE, E. A., CARTLEDGE, N., & KOEPPEL, J. Motivational effects of knowledge of results: A goal-setting phenomenon? *Psychological Bulletin*, 1968, 70, 474-485.

LONDON, P. *The Modes and Morals of Psychotherapy*. New York: Holt, Rinehart and Winston, 1964.

LORD, F. M., & NOVICK, M. R. *Statistical Theories of Mental Test Scores*. Reading, Ma.: Addison-Wesley, 1968.

LORR, M., & KLETT, C. J. *Inpatient Multidimensional Psychiatric Scale Manual*. Palo Alto: Consulting Psychologists Press, 1966.

LORR, M., KLETT, C. J., & McNAIR, D. M. *Syndromes of Psychosis*. New York: Pergamon Press, 1963.

LORR, M., KLETT, C. J., McNAIR, D. M., & LASKY, J. J. *Inpatient Multidimensional Psychiatric Scale. Manual*. Palo Alto, Ca.: Consulting Psychologists Press, 1962.

LUBIN, B. Adjective checklists for the measurement of depression. *Archives of General Psychiatry*, 1965, 12, 57-62.

LUBIN, C. Fourteen brief depression adjective checklists. *Archives of General Psychiatry*, 1966, 15, 205-208.

LUBIN, B., HORNSTRA, R. K., & LOVE, A. Course of depressive mood in a psychiatric population.

LYMAN, R. D., RICKARD, H. C., & ELDER, I. R. Contingency management of self-report and cleaning behavior. *Journal of Abnormal Child Psychology*, 1975, 3, 155-162.

MACCORQUODALE, K., & MEEHL, P. E. On a distinction between hypothetical constructs and intervening variables. *Psychological Review*, 1948, 55, 95-107.

MACDONALD, M. L. *A Behavioral Assessment Methodology, Applied to the Measurement of Assertion.* Unpublished doctoral dissertation, University of Illinois, 1974.

MACPHILLAMY, D. J., & LEWINSOHN, P. M. Measuring reinforcing events. *Proceedings of the 80th Annual Convention, American Psychological Association*, 1972.

MACPHILLAMY, D. J., & LEWINSOHN, P. M. Depression as a function of levels of desired and obtained pleasure. *Journal of Abnormal Psychology*, 1974, 83, 651-657.

MCCONAGHY, N. Penile volume change to moving pictures of male and female nudes in heterosexual and homosexual males. *Behaviour Research and Therapy*, 1967, 5, 43-48.

MCCONAGHY, N. Penile response conditioning and its relationship to aversive therapy in homosexuals. *Behavior Therapy*, 1970, 1, 213-221.

MCCONAGHY, N. Penile volume responses to moving and still pictures of male and female nudes. *Archives of Sexual Behavior*, 1974, 3, 565-570.

MCCONAGHY, N., & BARR, R. F. Classical, avoidance, and backward conditioning treatments of homosexuality. *British Journal of Psychiatry*, 1973, 122, 151-162.

MCCRADY, R. E. A forward-fading technique for increasing heterosexual responsiveness in male homosexuals. *Journal of Behaivor Therapy and Experimental Psychiatry*, 1973, 4, 257-261.

MCFALL, R. M. Effects of self-monitoring on normal smoking behavior. *Journal of Consulting and Clinical Psychology*, 1970, 35, 135-142.

MCFALL, R. M. Parameters of self-monitoring. In R. B. Stuart (Ed.), *Behavioral Self-Management: Strategies, Techniques, and Outcome.* New York: Brunner/Mazel, 1977.

MCFALL, R. M., & GALBRAITH, J. R. Two experiments on the contribution of response feedback to assertion training. Unpublished manuscript, University of Wisconsin, 1976.

MCFALL, R. M., & HAMMEN, C. L. Motivation, structural and self-monitoring: Rate of non-specific factors in smoking reduction. *Journal of Consulting and Clinical Psychology*, 1971, 37, 80-86.

MCFALL, R. M., & LILLESAND, D. B. Behavior rehearsal with modeling and coaching in assertive training. *Journal of Abnormal Psychology*, 1971, 77, 313-323.

MCFALL, R. M., & MARSTON, A. R. An experimental investigation of behavior rehearsal in assertive training. *Journal of Abnormal Psychology*, 1970, 76, 295-303.

MCFALL, R. M., & TWENTYMAN, C. T. Four experiments on the relative contributions of rehearsal, modeling, and coaching to assertion training. *Journal of Abnormal Psychology*, 1973, 81, 3, 199-218.

MCKENZIE, T. L., & RUSHALL, B. S. Effects of self-recording on attendance and performance in a competitive swimming training environment. *Journal of Applied Behavior Analysis*, 1974, 7, 199-206.

McNamara, J. R. The use of self-monitoring techniques to treat nail biting. *Behaviour Research and Therapy*, 1972, 10, 193-194.

Mager, R. F., & Pipe, P. *Analyzing Performance Problems*. Belmont, Ca.: Lear Siegler, Inc., Fearon Publishers, 1970.

Mahoney, M. J. The self-management of covert behavior: A case study. *Behavior Therapy*, 1971, 2, 575-578.

Mahoney, M. J. Self-reward and self-monitoring techniques for weight control. *Behavior Therapy*, 1974, 5, 48-57 (a).

Mahoney, M. J. *Cognition and Behavior Modification*. Cambridge, Ma.: Ballinger, 1974 (b).

Mahoney, M. J., & Mahoney, K. *Permanent Weight Control*. New York: W. W. Norton, 1976.

Mahoney, M. J., Moore, B. S., Wade, T. C., & Moura, N. G. M. The effects of continuous and intermittent self-monitoring on academic behavior. *Journal of Consulting and Clinical Psychology*, 1973, 41, 65-69.

Mahoney, M. J., Moura, N. G. M., & Wade, T. C. The relative efficacy of self-reward, self-punishment, and self-monitoring techniques for weight loss. *Journal of Consulting and Clinical Psychology*, 1973, 40, 404-407.

Mahoney, M. J., & Thoresen, C. E. (Eds.), *Self-Control: Power to the Person*. Monterey, Ca.: Brooks/Cole, 1974.

Maletzky, B. M. "Assisted" covert sensitization in the treatment of exhibitionism. *Journal of Consulting and Clinical Psychology*, 1974, 42, 34-40.

Mandler, G., & Sarason, S. B. A study of anxiety and learning. *Journal of Abnormal and Social Psychology*, 1952, 47, 166-173.

Manosevitz, M., & Lanyon, R. I. Fear survey schedule: A normative study. *Psychological Reports*, 1965, 17, 699-703.

Mariotto, M. J., & Paul, G. L. A multimethod validation of the inpatient multidimensional psychiatric scale with chronically institutionalized patients. *Journal of Consulting and Clinical Psychology*, 1974, 42, 497-508.

Marks, I., Boulougouris, J., & Marset, P. Flooding versus desensitization in the treatment of phobic patients: A cross over study. *British Journal of Psychiatry*, 1971, 119, 353-375.

Marshall, J. L., & Haertel, E .H. A single-administration reliability index for criterion-referenced tests: The mean split-half coefficient of agreement. Madison, Wisconsin: University of Wisconsin Research and Development Center for Cognitive Learning, 1975.

Martin, M. F., Gelfand, D. M., & Hartmann, D, P. Effects of adult and peer observers on boys' and girls' responses to an aggressive model. *Child Development,* 1971, 42, 1271-1275.

Mash, E. J., & Hedley, J. Effect of observer as a function of prior history of social interaction. *Perceptual and Motor Skills*, 1975, 40, 659-669.

Mash, E. J., & McElwee, J. D. Situational effects on observer accuracy: Behavioral predictability, prior experience, complexity of coding categories. *Child Development*, 1974, 45, 367-377.

Mash, E. J., Terdal, L. G. Behavior-therapy assessment: Diagnosis, design, and evaluation. *Psychological Reports*, 1974, 35, 587-601.

Mash, E. J., & Terdal, L. G. (Eds.). *Behavior Therapy Assessment: Diagnosis, Design and Evaluation*. New York: Springer, 1976.

Masters, W. H., & Johnson, V. E. *Human Sexual Inadequacy*. Boston: Little, Brown and Co., 1970.

Mavissakalian, M., Blanchard, E. B., Abel, G. C., & Barlow, D. H. Responses to complex erotic stimuli in homosexual and heterosexual males. *British Journal of Psychiatry*, 1975, 126, 252-257.

MEDLEY, D. M., MITZEL, H. E., & DOI, A. N. Analysis-of-variance models and their use in a three-way design without replication. *Journal of Experimental Education*, 1956, 24, 221-229.

MEICHENBAUM, D. H. A cognitive-behavior modification approach to assessment. In M. Hersen & A. Bellack (Eds.), *Behavior Assessment: A Practical Handbook*. New York: Pergamon, 1976.

MEICHENBAUM, D. H., & CAMERON, R. The clinical potential of modifying what clients say to themselves. In M. Mahoney & C. Thoresen (Eds.), *Self-Control: Power to the Person*. Monterey, Ca.: Brooks/Cole, 1974, 263-290.

METCALFE, M., & GOLDMAN, E. Validation of an inventory for measuring depression. *British Journal of Psychiatry*, 1965, 111, 240-242.

MILAR, C. R., & HAWKINS, R. P. Distorted results from the use of interval recording procedures. In T. A. Brigham, R. Hawkins, J. W. Scott, & T. F. McLaughlin (Eds.), *Behavior Analysis in Education: Self-control and Reading*. Dubuque, Ia.: Kendall-Hunt, 1976.

MILLER, B. V., & BERNSTEIN, D. A. Instructional demand in a behavior avoidance test for claustrophobic fears. *Journal of Abnormal Psychology*, 1972, 80, 206-210.

MILLS, H. L., AGRAS, W. S., BARLOW, D. H., & MILLS, J. R. Compulsive rituals treated by response prevention. *Archives of General Psychiatry*, 1973, 28, 524-529.

MISCHEL, W. *Personality and Assessment.* New York: Wiley, 1968.

MISCHEL, W. Continuity and change in personality. *American Psychologist*, 1969, 24, 1012-1018.

MISCHEL, W. Direct versus indirect personality assessment: Evidence and implications. *Journal of Consulting and Clinical Psychology*, 1972, 38, 319-324.

MISCHEL, W. Toward a cognitive social learning reconceptualization of personality. *Psychological Review*, 1973, 80, 252-283.

MOOS, R. H. Assessment and impact of social climate. In P. McReynolds (Ed.), *Advances in Psychological assessment* (Vol. 3). San Francisco: Jossey-Bass, 1975.

MOUSTAKAS, C. E., SIGEL, I. E., & SCHALOCK, H. D. An objective method for the measurement and analysis of child-adult interaction. *Child Development*, 1956, 27, 109-134.

MURRAY, H. A. *Explorations in Personality.* New York: Oxford University Press, 1938.

NEDELSKY, L. Absolute grading standards for objective tests. *Educational and Psychological Measurement*, 1954, 14, 3-19.

NELSON, C. M., & McREYNOLDS, W. T. Self-recording and control of behavior: A reply to Simkins. *Behavior Therapy*, 1971, 2, 594-597.

NELSON, R. O., & HAY, L. R. Temporal stability coefficients: Relevant for behavioral assessment? Paper presented at the meeting of the American Psychological Association, Washington, D.C., September, 1976.

NELSON, R. O., HAY, L. R., HAY, W. M., & CARSTENS, C. B. The reactivity and reliability of teachers' self-monitoring of positive and negative classroom verbalizations. In press.

NELSON, R. O., HAY, L. R., & KOSLOW-GREEN, L. Cautions in the use of classroom self-monitoring with young children. Unpublished manuscript, University of North Carolina: Greensboro, 1976.

NELSON, R. O., KAPUST, J. A., & DORSEY, B. L. Differential behavioral change produced by instructions and by self-monitoring. Unpublished manuscript, University of North Carolina: Greensboro, 1976.

NELSON, R. O., LIPINSKI, D. P., & BLACK, J. L. The effects of expectancy on the reactivity of self-recording. *Behavior Therapy*, 1975, 6, 337-349.

NELSON, R. O., LIPINSKI, D. P., & BLACK, J. L. The reactivity of adult retardates' self-monitoring: A comparison among behaviors of different valences, and a comparison with token reinforcement. *Psychological Record,* 1976, 26, 189-201 (a).

NELSON, R. O., LIPINSKI, D. P., & BLACK, J. L. The relative reactivity of external observations and self-monitoring. *Behavior Therapy,* 1976, 1, 314-321 (b).

NELSON, R. O., LIPINSKI, D. P., & BOYKIN, R. A. The effects of self-recorders' training and the obtrusiveness of the self-recording device on the accuracy and reactivity of self-monitoring. Unpublished manuscript, University of North Carolina: Greensboro, 1976.

NELSON, R. O., RUDIN,-HAY, L., & HAY, W. M. Comments on Cone's "The relevance of reliability and validity for behavioral assessmen." *Behavior Therapy,* 1977.

NUSSBAUM, K., WITTIG, B. A., HANLIN, T. E., & KURLAND, A. A. Intravenous nialamide in the treatment of depressed female patients. *Comprehensive Psychiatry,* 1963, 4, 105-116.

OBER, D. C. Modification of smoking behavior. *Journal of Consulting and Clinical Psychology,* 1968, 32, 543-549.

O'BRIEN, F., & AZRIN, N. H. Behavior engineering: Control of posture of informational feedback. *Journal of Applied Behavior Analysis,* 1970, 3, 235-241.

OFFICE OF STRATEGIC SERVICES STAFF. *Assessment of Men.* New York: Rinehart & Co., 1948.

O'LEARY, K. D., KAUFMAN, K. F., KASS, R. E., & DRABMAN, R. S. The effects of loud and soft reprimands on the behavior of disruptive students. *Exceptional Children,* 1970, 37, 145-155.

O'LEARY, K. D., & KENT, R. Behavior modification for social action: Research tactics and problems. In L. A. Hamerlynck, L. C. Handy, and E. J. Mash (Eds.), *Behavior Change: Methodology, Concepts, and Practice.* Champaign, Ill.: Research Press, 1973.

O'LEARY, K. D., KENT, R. N., & KANTOWITZ, J. Shaping data collection congruent with experimental hypotheses. *Journal of Applied Behavior Analysis,* 1975, 8, 48-51.

O'LEARY, K. D., & WILSON, G. T. *Behavior Therapy: Application and Outcome.* Englewood Cliffs, N.J.: Prentice-Hall, 1975.

ORNE, M. T. Demand characteristics and the concept of quasi-controls. In R. Rosenthal, & R. Rosnow (Eds.), *Artifact in Behavioral Research.* New York: Academic Press, 1969.

ORNE, M. T. From the subject's point of view, when is behavior private and when is it public: Problems of inference. *Journal of Consulting and Clinical Psychology,* 1970, 35, 143-147.

PACOE, L. V., HIMMELHOCH, J. M., HERSEN, H., & GUYETT, I. Pharmacologic and behavioral approaches to the treatment of unipolar (non-psychotic) depression: A needed integration. Unpublished manuscript, University of Pittsburgh, 1975.

PALMER, J., & McGUIRE, F. L. The use of unobtrusive measures in mental health research. *Journal of Consulting and Clinical Psychology,* 1973, 40, 431-436.

PARTEN, M. B. Social participation among pre-school children. *The Journal of Abnormal and Social Psychology,* 1932, 27, 243-269.

PATTERSON, G. R. Interventions for boys with conduct problems: Multiple settings, treatments, and criteria. *Journal of Consulting and Clinical Psychology,* 1974, 42, 471-481.

PATTERSON, G. R., & GULLION, M. E. *Living with Children: New Methods for Parents and Teachers* (revised edition). Champaign, Ill.: Research Press, 1968.

PATTERSON, G. R., & HARRIS, A. Some methodological considerations for observation procedures. Paper presented at the meeting of the American Psychological Association, San Francisco, September 1968.

PATTERSON, G. R., RAY, R. S., SHAW, D. A., & COBB, J. A. *Manual for Coding of Family Interaction.* Available from: ASIS National Auxiliary Publications Service, c/o CMM Information Sciences, Inc., 909 Third Ave., New York, N.Y. 10022. Document #01234, 6th revision, 1969.

PAUL, G. L. Behavior modification research: Design and tactics. In C. M. Franks, *Behavior Therapy: Appraisal and Status.* New York: McGraw-Hill, 1969.

PAUL, G. L., TOBIAS, L. L., & HOLLEY, B. L. Maintenance psychotropic drugs in the presence of active treatment programs: A "triple blind" withdrawal study with long-term mental patients. *Archives of General Psychiatry*, 1972, 27, 106-115.

PAYNE, S. L. Interviewer memory faults. *Public Opinion Quarterly*, 1949, 13, 684-685.

PERVIN, L. A. *Personality: Theory, Assessment and Research.* New York: Wiley, 1970.

PETERSON, D. R. *The Clinical Study of Social Behavior.* New York: Appleton-Century-Crofts, 1968.

PETERSON, G. L., HOUSE, A. E., & ALFORD, H. F. Self-monitoring: Accuracy and reactivity in a patient's recording of three clinically targeted behaviors. Paper presented at the meeting of the Southeastern Psychological Association, Atlanta, March 1975.

PHILLIPS, E. L., PHILLIPS, E. A., FIXSEN, D. L., & WOLF, M. M. Achievement Place: The modification of the behaviors of pre-delinquent boys within a token economy. *Journal of Applied Behavior Analysis*, 1971, 4, 45-59.

PLATT, J. R. Strong inference. *Science*, 1964, 146, 347-353.

POLYA, G. *How to Solve It.* Princeton, N.J.: Princeton University Press, 1948.

POMERANZ, D. M., & GOLDFRIED, M. R. An intake report outline for behavior modification. *Psychological Reports*, 1970, 26, 447-450.

POPE, B., NUDLER, S., VONKORFF, M. R., & McGHEC, J. P. The experienced professional interviewer versus the complete novice. *Journal of Consulting and Clinical Psychology*, 1974, 42, 680-690.

POPE, B., & SIEGMAN, A. W. Relationship and verbal behavior in the initial interview. In A. Siegman, & B. Pope (Eds.), *Studies in Dyadic Communication.* New York: Pergamon Press, 1972.

POPHAM, W. J., & HUSEK, T. R. Implications of criterion-referenced measurement. *Journal of Educational Measurement*, 1969, 6, 1-9.

POTTER, J. C., & RAE, G. *Informal Reading Diagnosis: A Practical Guide for the Classroom Teacher.* Englewood Cliffs, N.J.: Prentice-Hall, 1973.

POWELL, J., MARTINDALE, A., & KULP, S. An evaluation of time-sample measures of behavior. *Journal of Applied Behavior Analysis*, 1975, 8, 463-469.

PURCELL, K., & BRADY, K. Adaptation to the invasion of privacy: Monitoring behavior with a miniature radio transmitter. *Merrill-Palmer Quarterly*, 1966, 12, 242-254.

QUINN, J. T., HARBISON, J. J. M., & McALLISTER, H. An attempt to shape human penile responses. *Behaviour Research and Therapy*, 1970, 8, 213-216.

QUINSEY, V. L., STEINMAN, C. M., BERGERSEN, S. G., & HOLMES, T. F. Penile circumference, skin conductance and ranking responses of child molesters and "normals" to sexual and nonsexual visual stimuli. *Behavior Therapy*, 1975, 6, 213-219.

RABIN, A. I. Projective methods: An historical introduction. In A. I. Rabin (Ed.), *Projective Techniques in Personality Assessment.* New York: Springer Publishing Co., 1968.

RACHLIN, H. Self-control. *Behaviorism*, 1974, 2, 94-107.

RACHMAN, S., & HODGSON, R. Synchrony and de-synchrony in fear and avoidance. *Behaviour Research and Therapy*, 1974, 12, 311-318.

RASHOTTE, M. E., KATZ, H. N., GRIFFIN, R. W., & WRIGHT, A. C. Vocalizations of White Carneaux pigeons during experiments on schedule-induced aggression. *Journal of the Experimental Analysis of Behavior*, 1975, 23, 285-294.

RATHUS, S. A. A 30-item schedule for assessing assertive behavior. *Behavior Therapy*, 1973, 4, 398-406.

REHM, L. P., & MARSTON, A. R. Reduction of social anxiety through modification of self-reinforcement. *Journal of Consulting and Clinical Psychology*, 1968, 32, 565-574.

REID, J. B. Reliability assessment of observation data: A possible methodological problem. *Child Development*, 1970, 41, 1143-1150.

REID, J. B., SKINDRUD, K. D., TAPLIN, P. S., & JONES, R. R. The role of complexity in the collection and evaluation of observation data. Paper presented at the meeting of the American Psychological Association, Montreal, Quebec, Canada, August 1973.

REPP, A. C., DEITZ, D. D., BOLES, S. M., DEITZ, S. M., & REPP, C. F. Differences among common methods for calculating interobserver agreement in applied behavioral studies. Paper presented at the meeting of SEPA, Hollywood, Florida, May, 1974.

REPP, A. C., ROBERTS, D. M., SLACK, D. J., REPP, C. F., & BERKLER, M. S. A comparison of frequency, interval, and time-sampling methods for data collection. *Journal of Applied Behavior Analysis*, 1976, 9, 501-508.

RESNICK, L. B., WANG, M. C., & KAPLAN, J. Task analysis in curriculum design: A hierarchically sequenced introductory mathematics curriculum. *Journal of Applied Behavior Analysis*, 1973, 6, 679-709.

RICHARDS, C. S. Behavior modification of studying through study skills advisement and self-control procedures. *Journal of Counseling Psychology*, 1975, 22, 431-436.

RICHARDS, C. S., McREYNOLDS, W. T., HOLT, S., & SEXTON, T. The effects of information feedback and self-administered consequences on self-monitoring study behavior. Unpublished manuscript, University of Missouri, 1975.

RICHARDS, T. W., & IRWIN, O. C. The use of the clinical method in experimental studies of behavior. *The Journal of Abnormal and Social Psychology*, 1936, 30, 455-461.

RISLEY, T. R. Behavior modification: An experimental-therapeutic endeavor. In L. A. Hamerlynck, P. O. Davidson, & L. E. Acker (Eds.), *Behavior Modification and Ideal Mental Health Services*. Calgary, Alberta: University of Calgary Press, 1970.

RISLEY, T. R., & HART, B. Developing correspondence between the non-verbal and verbal behavior of school children. *Journal of Applied Behavior Analysis*, 1968, 1, 267-281.

ROMANCZYK, R. G. Self-monitoring in the treatment of obesity: Parameters of reactivity. *Behavior Therapy*, 1974, 5, 531-540.

ROMANCZYK, R. G., KENT, R. N., DIAMENT, C., & O'LEARY, K. D. Measuring the reliability of observational data: A reactive process. *Journal of Applied Behavior Analysis*, 1973, 6, 175-186.

ROMANCZYK, R. G., TRACEY, D. A., WILSON, G. T., & THORPE, G. L. Behavioral techniques in the treatment of obesity: A comparative analysis. *Behaviour Research and Therapy*, 1973, 11, 629-640.

ROSEN, R. C. Suppression of penile tumescence by instrumental conditioning. *Psychosomatic Medicine*, 1973, 35, 509-514.

ROSENHAN, D. L. On being sane in insane places. *Science*, 1973, 179, 250-258.

ROSENTHAL, R. Interpersonal expectations effects of the experimenter's hypothesis. In R. Rosenthal, & R. Rosnow (Eds.), *Artifacts in Behavioral Research*. New York: Academic Press, 1969.

ROTTER, J. B. Generalized expectancies for internal versus external control of reinforcement. *Psychological Monographs*, 1966, 80, (1, Whole No. 609).

ROTTER, J. B., & WICKERS, D. D. The consistency and generality of ratings of "social aggressiveness" made from observation of role playing situations. *Journal of Consulting Psychology*, 1948, 12, 234-239.

ROUDABUSH, G. E., & GREEN, D. R. Aspects of a methodology for creating criterion-referenced tests. Paper presented at the annual meeting of the National Council on Measurement in Education, Chicago, April 1972.

ROZENSKY, R. H. The effect of timing of self-monitoring behavior on reducing cigarette consumption. *Journal of Behavior Therapy and Experimental Psychiatry,* 1974, *5,* 301-303.

RUBIN, S. E., LAWLIS, G. F., TASTO, D. L., & NAMENEH, T. Factor analysis of the 122-item fear survey schedule. *Behaviour Research and Therapy,* 1969, 7, 381-386.

RUTNER, I. T. The modification of smoking behavior through techniques of self-control. Unpublished master's thesis, Wichita State University, 1967.

RUTNER, I. T., & BUGLE, C. An experimental procedure for the modification of psychotic behavior. *Journal of Consulting and Clinical Psychology,* 1969, 33, 651-653.

SAMPH, T. The role of the observer and his effects on teacher classroom behavior. *Occasional Papers,* 1969, 2, Oakland Schools, Pontiac, Michigan.

SANFORD, D. A. Patterns of sexual arousal in heterosexual males. *The Journal of Sex Research,* 1974, 10, 150-155.

SANTOGROSSI, D. A. Self-reinforcement and external monitoring of performance on an academic task. Paper presented at the 5th Annual Conference on Applied Behavior Analysis in Education, Kansas City, Ks., October, 1974.

SARASON, I. G., Empirical findings and theoretical problems in the use of anxiety scales. *Psychological Bulletin,* 1960, 57, 405-415.

SCHACHTER, S. The interaction of cognitive and physiological determinants of emotional state. In L. Berkowitz (Ed.), *Advances in Experimental Social Psychology,* Vol. 1. New York: Academic Press, 1964.

SCHROEDER, H., & CRAINE, L. Relationships among measures of fear and anxiety for snake phobics. *Journal of Consulting and Clinical Psychology,* 1976, 36, 443.

SCHULMAN, R. E., SHOEMAKER, D. J., & MOELIS, I. Laboratory measurement of parental behavior. *Journal of Consulting Psychology,* 1962, 26, 109-114.

SCHULTZE, J. H., & LUTHE, W. *Autogenic Training: A Psychophysiologic Approach in Psychotherapy.* New York: Grune & Stratton, 1959.

SCHWARTZ, G. E. Biofeedback and physiological patterning in human emotion and consciousness. In J. Beatty and H. Legewie (Eds.), *Biofeedback and Behavior,* proceedings of the NATO Symposium on Biofeedback and behavior, Munich, July 1976. New York: Plenum Press, 1977.

SCHWARTZ, R. M., & GOTTMAN, J. M. Towards a task analysis of assertive behavior. *Journal of Consulting and Clinical Psychology,* 1976, 44, 910-920.

SCHWARZ, M. L., & HAWKINS, R. P. Application of delayed reinforcement procedures to the behavior of an elementary school child. *Journal of Applied Behavior Analysis,* 1970, 3, 85-96.

SCHWITZGEBEL, R. K., & KOLB, D. A. *Changing Human Behavior: Principles of Planned Intervention.* New York: McGraw-Hill, 1974.

SCOTT, P. M., BURTON, R. V., & YARROW, N. R. Social reinforcement under natural conditions. *Child Development,* 1967, 38, 53-63.

SCOTT, W. A., & JOHNSON, R. C. Comparative validities of direct and indirect personality tests. *Journal of Consulting and Clinical Psychology,* 1972, 38, 301-318.

SELEKMAN, W., & MEEHAN, E. An objective technique for recording shock-induced aggression in unrestrained pairs of rats. *Journal of the Experimental Analysis of Behavior,* 1974, 21, 177-182.

SERBER, M. Videotape feedback in the treatment of couples with sexual dysfunction. *Archives of Sexual Behavior,* 1974, 3, 377-380.

SEYMOUR, F. W., & STOKES, T. F. Self-recording in training girls to increase work and evoke staff praise in an institution for offenders. *Journal of Applied Behavior Analysis,* 1976, 9, 41-54.

SHANNON, C., & WEAVER, W. *The Mathematical Theory of Communication.* Urbana, Ill.: University of Illinois Press, 1949.

SHAW, D. L., PETERSON, G. L., & CONE, J. D. Aides' reports of behavior modification training: Experimental analysis of their validity. Paper presented at the meeting of the Southeastern Psychological Association, Hollywood, Fl., May, 1974.

SHELDON, W. H. Constitutional factors in personality. In J. McV. Hunt (Ed.), *Personality and the Behavior Disorders.* New York: Ronald Press, 1944, 526-549.

SHERMAN, M., TRIEF, P., & SPRAFKIN, R. Impression management in the psychiatric interview: Quality, style, and individual differences. *Journal of Consulting and Clinical Psychology,* 1975, 43, 867-871.

SHULLER, D. Y., & McNAMARA, J. R. Expectancy factors in behavioral observation. *Behavior Therapy,* 1976, 7, 519-527.

SIECK, W. A., & McFALL, R. M. Some determinants of self-monitoring effects. *Journal of Consulting and Clinical Psychology,* 1976, 44, 958-965.

SIEGMAN, A. W. Do noncontingent interviewer mm-hmms facilitate interviewee productivity? *Journal of Consulting and Clinical Psychology,* 1976, 44, 171-182.

SIMKINS, L. A rejoinder to Nelson and McReynolds on the self-recording of behavior. *Behavior Therapy,* 1971, 2, 598-601.

SIMPSON, R. H. The specific meanings of certain terms indicating different degrees of frequency. *Quarterly Journal of Speech,* 1944, 30, 328-330.

SINTCHAK, G., & GEER, J. H.: A vaginal plethysmograph system. *Psychophysiology,* 1975, 12, 113-115.

SIROTA, A. D., & MAHONEY, M. J. Relaxing on cue: The self-regulation of asthma. *Journal of Behavior Therapy and Experimental Psychiatry,* 1974, 5, 65-66.

SKINDRUD, K. *An Evaluation of Observer Bias in Experimental Field Studies of Social Interaction.* Unpublished doctoral dissertation, University of Oregon, 1972.

SKINDRUD, K. Field evaluation of observer bias under overt and covert monitoring. In L. A. Hamerlynck, L. C. Handy, & E. J. Mash (Eds.), *Behavior Change: Methodology, Concepts, and Practice.* Champaign, Ill.: Research Press, 1973.

SKINNER, B. F. Are theories of learning necessary? *Psychological Review,* 1950, 57, 193-216.

SKINNER, B. F. The experimental analysis of behavior. *American Scientist,* 1957, 45, 343-371.

SKINNER, B. F. What is the experimental analysis of behavior? *Journal of the Experimental Analysis of Behavior,* 1966, 9, 213-218.

SLACK, W. V., & VAN CURA, L. J. Patient reaction to computer-based medical interviewing. *Computers and Biomedical Research,* 1968, 1, 527-531.

SLOANE, R. B., STAPLES, F. R., CRISTOL, A. H., YORKSTON, N. J., & WHIPPLE, K. *Psychotherapy Versus Behavior Therapy.* Cambridge: Harvard University Press, 1975.

SLOANE, R. B., STAPLES, F. R., CRISTOL, A. H., YORKSTON, N. J., & WHIPPLE, K. Patient characteristics and outcomes in psychotherapy and behavior therapy. *Journal of Consulting and Clinical Psychology,* 1976, 44, 330-339.

SOBELL, L. C., & SOBELL, M. B. A self-feedback technique to monitor drinking behavior in alcoholics. *Behaviour Research and Therapy,* 1973, 11, 237-238.

SPIELBERGER, C. D. Anxiety as an emotional state. In C. D. Spielberger (Ed.), *Anxiety: Current Trends in Theory and Research.* New York: John Wiley & Sons, 1972.

SPIELBERGER, C. D., GORSUCH, R. L., & LUSHENE, R. E. *Manual for the State-Trait Anxiety Inventory.* Palo Alto, Ca.: Counseling Psychologist Press, 1970.

SPITZER, R. L., ENDICOTT, J., FLEISS, J. L., & COHEN, J. The psychiatric status schedule. *Archives of General Psychiatry,* 1970, 23, 41-55.

SPOSITO, V. A., & SMITH, W. A. A sufficient condition for L_1 estimation. Unpublished manuscript, Iowa State University, 1974.

STAATS, A. W. *Social Behaviorism*. Homewood, Ill.: Dorsey Press, 1975.

STAPLES, F. R., SLOANE, R. B., WHIPPLE, K., CRISTOL, A. H., & YORKSTON, N. Process and outcome in psychotherapy and behavior therapy. *Journal of Consulting and Clinical Psychology*, 1976, 44, 340-350.

STIERS, M., & SILVERBERG, A. Lever-contact response in rats: Automaintenance with and without a negative response-reinforcer dependency. *Journal of the Experimental Analysis of Behavior*, 1974, 22, 497-506.

STORROW, H. A. *Introduction to Scientific Psychiatry: A Behavioral Approach to Diagnosis and Treatment*. New York: Appleton-Century-Crofts, 1967.

STUART, R. B. *Trick or Treatment*. Champaign, Ill.: Research Press, 1970.

SUINN, R. M. The relationship between fears and anxiety: A further study. *Behaviour Research and Therapy*, 1969, 7, 317-318.

SUNDBERG, N. D., & TYLER, L. E. *Clinical Psychology*. New York: Appleton-Century-Crofts, 1962.

SWAMINATHAN, H., HAMBLETON, R. K., & ALGINA, J. A Bayesian decision-theoretic procedure for use with criterion-referenced tests. *Journal of Educational Measurement*, 1975, 12, 87-98.

TAPLIN, P. S., & REID, J. B. Effects of instructional set and experimenter influence on observer reliability. *Child Development*, 1973, 44, 547-554.

TAYLOR, J. A. A personality scale of manifest anxiety. *Journal of Abnormal Psychology*, 1953, 48, 285-270.

TENNET, G., BANCROFT, J., & CASS, G. The control of deviant sexual behavior by drugs: A double-blind controlled study of benperidol, chlorpromazine, and placebo. *Archives of Sexual Behavior*, 1973, 3, 261-271.

THOMAS, D. R. Preliminary findings on self-monitoring for modifying teaching behaviors. In E. A. Ramp, & B. L. Hopkins (Eds.), *A New Direction for Education, Behavior Analysis. 1971*. Lawrence, Ks.: University of Kansas, 1971.

THOMAS, D. S., LOOMIS, A. M., & ARRINGTON, R. E. *Observational Studies of Social Behavior*, Vol. 1. Yale University: Institute of Human Relations, 1933.

THOMAS, E. J. Bias and therapist influence in behavioral assessment. *Journal of Behavior Therapy and Experimental Psychiatry*, 1973, 4, 107-111.

THOMAS, E. J., ABRAMS, K. S., & JOHNSON, J. B. Self-monitoring and reciprocal inhibition in the modification of multiple tics of Gilles de la Tourette's syndrome. *Journal of Behavior Therapy and Experimental Psychiatry*, 1971, 2, 159-171.

THOMSON, C., HOLMBERG, M., & BAER, D. A brief report on a comparison of time-sampling procedures. *Journal of Applied Behavior Analysis*, 1974, 7, 623-626.

THORESEN, C. E., & MAHONEY, M. J. *Behavior Self-Control*. New York: Holt, Rinehart, & Winston, 1974.

TOKARZ, T., & LAWRENCE, P. S. An analysis of temporal and stimulus factors in the treatment of insomnia. Paper presented at the meeting of the Association for Advancement of Behavior Therapy, Chicago, November 1974.

TURKEWITZ, H., O'LEARY, K. D., & IRONSMITH, M. Generalization and maintenance of appropriate behavior through self-control. *Journal of Consulting and Clinical Psychology*, 1975, 43, 577-583.

TWENTYMAN, C. T., & McFALL, R. M. Behavioral training of social skills in shy males. *Journal of Consulting and Clinical Psychology*, 1975, 43, 384-495.

ULRICH, R. E., STACHNIK, T. J., & STAINTON, W. R. Student acceptance of generalized personality interpretations. *Psychological Reports*, 1963, 13, 831-834.

VARGAS, J. M., & ADESSO, V. J. A comparison of aversion therapies for nail-biting behavior. *Behavior Therapy*, 1976, 7, 322-329.

WAHLER, R. G., & CORMIER, W. H. The ecological interview: A first step in outpatient child behavior therapy. *Journal of Behavior Therapy and Experimental Psychiatry*, 1970, 1, 279-289.

WAHLER, R. G., & LESKE, G. Accurate and inaccurate observer summary reports. *Journal of Nervous and Mental Disease*, 1973, 156, 386-394.

WALK, R. D. Self-ratings of fear evoking situation. *Journal of Abnormal and Social Psychology*, 1976, 22, 171-178.

WALKER, H., & BUCKLEY, N. K. The use of positive reinforcement in conditioning attending behavior. *Journal of Applied Behavior Analysis*, 1968, 1, 245-250.

WALLACE, J. An abilities conception of personality: Some implications for personality measurement. *American Psychologist*, 1966, 21, 132-138.

WALLACE, J. What units shall we employ? Allport's question revisited. *Journal of Consulting Psychology*, 1967, 31, 56-64.

WATSON, D., & FRIEND, R. Measurement of social-evaluative anxiety. *Journal of Consulting and Clinical Psychology*, 1969, 33, 448-457.

WATSON, D. L., & THARP, R. G. *Self-directed Behavior: Self-modification for Personal Adjustment.* Monterey, Ca.: Brooks/Cole, 1972.

WEBB, E. J., CAMPBELL, D. T., SCHWARTZ, R. D., & SECHREST, L. *Unobtrusive Measures: Non-reactive Research in the Social Sciences.* Chicago: Rand McNally, 1966.

Webster's Seventh New Collegiate Dictionary. Springfield, Ma.: G. & C. Merriam, 1970.

WEICK, K. E. Systematic observational methods. In G. Lindzey and E. Aronson (Eds.), *The Handbook of Social Psychology*, 1968, 2, 357-451.

WERRY, J. S., & QUAY, H. C. Observing the classroom behavior of elementary school children. *Exceptional Children*, 1969, 35, 461-470.

WHITE, G. D. Effects of observer presence on family interaction. Paper presented at the meeting of the Western Psychological Association, Anaheim, April 1973.

WHITE, O. R. *Glossary of Behavioral Terminology.* Champaign, Ill.: Research Press, 1971 (a).

WHITE, O. R. A brief outline of the "corrected median slope" method of trend estimation. University of Oregon, Regional Center for Handicapped Children, Working Paper No. 2, 1971 (b).

WHITE, O. R. A pragmatic approach to the description of progress in the single case. Unpublished doctoral dissertation, Department of Special Education, University of Oregon, 1971 (c).

WHITE, O. R. *Working Paper No. 15. The Prediction of Human Performances in the Single Case: An Examination of Four Techniques.* Eugene, Oregon: Regional Resource Center for Handicapped Children, 1972 (a).

WHITE, O. R. *A Manual for the Calculation and Use of the Median Slope—A Method for Progress Estimation and Prediction in the Single Case.* University of Oregon, Regional Resource Center for Handicapped Children, Working Paper No. 16, 1972 (b).

WHITE, O. R. *The "Split-middle": A "Quickie" Method of Trend Estimation* (third revision). Working paper available through the Experimental Education Unit, University of Washington, 1974.

WHITE, O. R., & HARING, N. G. *Exceptional Teaching: A Multimedia Training Program.* Columbus, O.: Charles E. Merrill, 1976.

WHITE, O. R., & LIBERTY, K. A. Behavioral assessment and precise educational measurement. In N. G. Haring and R. Schiefelbusch (Eds.), *Teaching Special Children.* New York: McGraw-Hill, 1976.

WIGGINS, J. S. *Personality and Prediction: Principles of Personality Assessment.* Reading, Ma.: Addison-Wesley, 1973.

WILDMAN, B. G., ERICKSON, M. T., & KENT, R. N. The effect of two training procedures on observer agreement and variability of behavior ratings. *Child Development*, 1975, 46, 520-524.

WILLIAMS, J. G., BARLOW, D. H., & AGRAS, W. S. Behavioral measurement of severe depression. *Archives of General Psychiatry*, 1972, 27, 330-333.

WINTRE, M. G., & WEBSTER, C. D. A brief report on using a traditional social behavior scale with disturbed children. *Journal of Applied Behavior Analysis*, 1974, 7, 345-348.

WOLF, M. M. Social validity: The case for subjective measurement; or How applied behavior analysis is finding its heart. Invited address to Division of the Experimental Analysis of Behavior, presented at the meeting of the American Psychological Association, Washington, D.C., September 1976.

WOLPE, J. *The Practice of Behavior Therapy*. New York: Pergamon, 1973.

WOLPE, J., & LANG, P. J. A fear survey schedule for use in behavior therapy. *Behaviour Research and Therapy*, 1964, 2, 27-30.

WOLPE, J., & LAZARUS, A. A. *Behavior Therapy Techniques: A Guide to the Treatment of Neuroses*. Oxford: Pergamon, 1966.

WRIGHT, A. A., & NEVIN, J. A. *Journal of the Experimental Analysis of Behavior*, 1974, 21, 373-380.

YATES, A. J. *Theory and Practice in Behavior Therapy*. New York: John Wiley, 1975.

YELTON, A. R., WILDMAN, B. G., & ERICKSON, M. T. A probability-based formula for calculating interobserver agreement. *Journal of Applied Behavior Analysis*, 1977, 10, 127-131.

ZEGIOB, L. E., ARNOLD, S., & FOREHAND, R. An examination of observer effects in parent-child interactions. *Child Development*, 1975, 46, 509-512.

ZUCKERMAN, M. The development of an affect adjective checklist for the measurement of anxiety. *Journal of Consulting and Clinical Psychology*, 1960, 24, 457-462.

ZUCKERMAN, M. Physiological measures of sexual arousal in the human. *Psychological Bulletin*, 1971, 75, 297-329.

ZUNG, W. W. K. A self-rating depression scale. *Archives of General Psychiatry*, 1965, 12, 63-70.

ZUNG, W. W. K., RICHARDS, C. B., & SHORT, M. J. Self-rating depression scale in an out-patient clinic. *Archives of General Psychiatry*, 1965, 13, 508-515.

Subject Index

Rev. before a page number stands for reviewed, indicating that detailed information is provided on a checklist.

Author Index

"n" indicates a footnote or a reference.